Revise
AS & A2

Sociology

Contents

Specification lists

Unit	Specification topic	Chapter reference
Unit 1: SCLY 1	*Culture and Identity* *Families and Households* *Wealth, Poverty and Welfare*	2 1
Unit 2: SCLY 2	*Education with Research Methods* *Health with Research Methods*	3, 5 4, 5

Examination analysis

Unit 1: SCLY 1

Candidates choose one topic from three and answer one question. Each question consists of two pieces of source material focused on an aspect of the topic. The question is organised into five parts. Parts (a), (b) and (c) will follow either a 2, 4, 6 mark format or a 4, 4, 4 mark format. Parts (d) and (e) are each worth 24 marks and require candidates to use both the sources and their own knowledge to answer a general question. **1 hr   40% of AS**

Unit 2: SCLY 2

Candidates choose one topic (Education or Health) and answer one question on the chosen topic, one question on sociological research methods in context and one question on research methods.

The question on the chosen topic involves reading source material. The question is divided into four parts. Part (a) is worth 2 marks and part (b) is worth 6 marks. Part (c) is worth 12 marks and mainly tests candidates' knowledge and understanding of an aspect of the topic. Part (d) is worth 20 marks and asks candidates to evaluate a particular sociological argument or debate. Candidates are advised to spend 50 minutes on this question.

The question on Sociological Research Methods in Context is worth 20 marks and involves the candidates reading source material on the relationship between the topic (Education or Health) and Sociological Methods. Candidates have to choose one research method from a choice of two, and must use both the Source and their own knowledge to assess the strengths and limitations of that method with regard to either an Education or Health context. Candidates are advised to spend 30 minutes on this question.

The question on research methods is divided into four parts. Parts (a), (b) and (c) are worth 2, 4 and 4 marks respectively. Part (d), which is worth 20 marks, might ask candidates to examine the problems associated with a particular research method or the factors influencing the selection of research methods. Candidates are advised to spend 40 minutes on this question. **2 hr   60% of AS**

Unit	Specification topic	Chapter reference
Unit 3: SCLY 3	*Beliefs in Society* *Global Development* *Mass Media* *Power and Politics*	6 7
Unit 4: SCLY 4	*Crime and Deviance with Theory and Methods* *Stratification and Differentiation with Theory and Methods*	5, 8, 10 5, 9, 10

Examination analysis

Unit 3: SCLY 3

Candidates choose one topic from four and answer one compulsory question and one question from a choice of two. The compulsory question includes source material and is likely to be divided into two parts worth 9 marks and 18 marks respectively. Candidates are expected to use both the source material and their own knowledge to answer these questions.

The second question, which is worth 33 marks, comprises two essay titles. Candidates are expected to choose one of these titles and to evaluate general arguments and debates related to the topic. **1 hr 30 min   20% of A Level**

Unit 4: SCLY 4

Candidates choose one topic from two and answer one question on the chosen topic, one question on sociological research methods in context and one question on theory and methods.

The question on the chosen topic includes source material and is divided into two parts worth 12 and 21 marks respectively. Candidates are advised to spend 45 minutes on this section.

The question on sociological research methods in context is likely to be divided into two parts worth 9 and 15 marks respectively or three parts worth 3, 6 and 15 marks respectively. The part of this question that is worth 15 marks requires candidates to read source material and to apply their knowledge and understanding of sociological research methods to the study of a particular issue stated in the question. Candidates are advised to spend 30 minutes on this section.

The question on theory and methods is an essay question worth 33 marks focused on a general argument or debate related to sociological theories and/or sociological research methods. Candidates are advised to spend 45 minutes on this section. **2 hr   30% of A Level**

January 2012 will see a change in the mark distribution for this paper. The 12 mark question will become a 21 mark question, whilst the 9 mark sociological research methods in context question will no longer be set.

OCR AS

Unit	Specification topic	Chapter reference
Unit 1: Unit G671 Exploring socialisation, culture and identity	• *Formation of culture* • *Process of socialisation* • *Role of socialisation in the creation of identities* • *Exploring the research process* • *Exploring the use of quantitative data-collection methods and analysis in the context of research* • *Exploring the use of qualitative data-collection methods and analysis in the context of research* • *Exploring the use of mixed methods in the context of research*	2 2 2 5 5 5 5
Unit 2: Unit G672 Topics in socialisation, culture and identity	• *Sociology of the family* • *Sociology of health* • *Sociology of religion* • *Sociology of youth*	1 4 6

Examination analysis

Unit 1: G671: Exploring socialisation, culture and identity
The examination consists of **four compulsory** questions based on **one** piece of pre-released data, which is focused on sociological research related to the core AS themes of socialisation, culture and identity. The data includes details of the research process and/or the methods used.
The pre-released data consists of approximately **two** sides of A4 and is sent to centres before the examination date.
1 hr 30 min   **50% of AS**

Unit 2: G672: Topics in socialisation, culture and identity
This question paper has four sections, based on the four topic areas. Each section/topic area has two questions in it. Candidates are required to answer **any two** questions from any of the four sections.
1 hr 30 min   **50% of AS**

OCR A2

Unit	Specification topic	Chapter reference
Unit 3: Unit G673 Power and control	• *Sociology of crime and deviance* • *Sociology of education* • *Sociology of the mass media* • *Sociology of power and politics*	8 3 7
Unit 4: Unit G674 Exploring social inequality and difference	• *Social inequality and difference* • *Exploring sociological research on social inequality and difference*	9 5, 10

Examination analysis

Unit 3: G673: Power and control
This question paper has four sections, one for each of the four topics. Each section contains three essay questions. Candidates are required to answer **a total of two** essay questions from one or more of the four sections.
1 hr 30 min   **25% of A2**

Unit 4: G674: Exploring social inequality and difference
This question paper includes source material based on a piece of research on social inequality and difference upon which the examination is based. Questions (1) and (2) are compulsory. Additionally, candidates choose to answer **either** questions 3(a) and 3(b) **or** 4(a) and 4(b).
2 hr   **25% of A2**

AS/A2 Level Sociology courses

AS and A2

All A Level qualifications comprise two units of AS assessment and two units of A2 assessment. This offers Sociology students the opportunity to complete a freestanding AS course or to develop ideas, themes and concepts into a full A Level course via the more demanding and challenging A2 course.

How will you be tested?

Assessment units

For AS Sociology, you will be tested by two assessment units. For the full A Level, you will take a further two units.

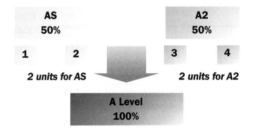

Each unit can normally be taken in either January or June. Alternatively, you can study the whole course before taking any of the unit tests. There is a lot of flexibility about when exams can be taken and the diagram below shows just some of the ways that the assessment units may be taken for AS and A2 Level Sociology.

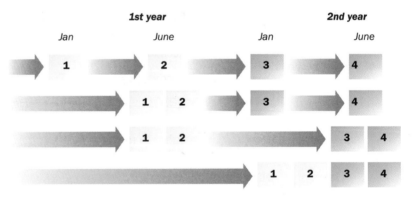

Remember that the combinations shown here might not be the route chosen by your school or college to go through the examination. There are other possible combinations.

If you are disappointed with a unit or module result, you can re-sit each module taken and most exam boards will offer papers in both January and June. The higher mark always counts.

A2 and synoptic assessment

After having studied AS Sociology, hopefully you will want to continue studying Sociology to A2 Level. For this you will need to take two further units of Sociology. Similar assessment arrangements apply except that some units draw together different parts of the course in a 'synoptic' assessment (see page 7).

Key skills

AS and A2 Sociology specifications identify opportunities for the development of the Key Skills of Communication, Information Technology, Working with Others, Improving Own Learning and Performance, and Problem Solving.

What skills will I need?

For AS and A2 Sociology, you will be tested by **assessment objectives**: these are the skills and abilities that you should have acquired by studying the course. The assessment objectives for Sociology are shown below.

Knowledge and understanding

This skill focuses on your knowledge and understanding of the theories, methods, concepts and various forms of evidence and of the links between them. For example, you will be expected in both AS and A2 Sociology to particularly demonstrate knowledge and understanding of the relationship between research methods, theory and specific sociological problems and topics. Knowledge and understanding also involves communicating in a clear and effective manner.

Analysis, evaluation and application

Analysis refers to the ability to interpret and apply evidence in the context of the question. You are expected to demonstrate the ability to distinguish between facts, opinions and value judgements and to be able to select a range of relevant concepts, theories and studies, as well as interpret different types of data. You will need to be able to use evidence to support and sustain arguments and conclusions. Moreover, you need to demonstrate a critical awareness in terms of identifying the strengths and weaknesses inherent in particular debates, arguments and studies. You are also required to demonstrate at A2 a wider range and greater depth of knowledge and understanding than at AS.

Synoptic assessment

Synoptic assessment in GCE Sociology is assessed in the A2 units. This requires you to demonstrate some holistic understanding of the subject. This means that you will be expected to link areas of content to each other. Some questions at A2 will expect you to draw together and synthesise the knowledge, understanding and skills learned in different parts of the course. In Unit 4, there are questions that require candidates to devise hypotheses and solutions, etc. to problems that go beyond the knowledge, skills and understanding studied within the unit. These questions aim to stretch and challenge you and offer you the opportunity to achieve an A* grade.

What grade do you want?

Your final grade depends on the extent to which you meet the assessment objectives. To gain the best possible mark you will have to work hard throughout the course and be highly motivated.

To achieve a grade A or A* you will need to:
- show relevant, accurate and detailed sociological knowledge
- demonstrate understanding of key concepts such as reliability and validity
- demonstrate understanding of the relationship between sociological theory and method
- show critical understanding of the use of source material
- be able to logically organise an argument and communicate it effectively.

AS/A2 Level Sociology examinations

AS and A2

All Sociology A Level courses are in two parts, with two separate units or modules in each part. Students first study the AS (Advanced Subsidiary) course. Some will then go on to study the second part of the A Level course, called A2. Advanced Subsidiary is assessed at the standard expected halfway through an A Level course: i.e. between GCSE and Advanced GCE. This means that AS and A2 courses are designed so that the level of difficulty steadily increases. AS Sociology requires no prior learning or achievement at GCSE whilst A2 naturally follows on from AS.

AQA AS assessment

Unit 1: SCLY 1

This examination paper is divided into three sections. You must choose one section only and answer all parts of the question from that section. You must not answer questions from more than one section.

Each section's questions are preceded by two items of stimulus material which you must read through carefully. These are most likely to be textual although there is the possibility that one of the items might be in the form of graphs, charts etc.

Question (a) may be worth 2 or 4 marks. If it is worth 2 marks, it will ask you to explain the meaning of a particular sociological concept. If it is worth 4 marks, it will ask you to explain or identify differences between two sociological concepts. Question (b) is usually worth 4 marks and may ask you to suggest two ways in which a sociological problem or trend shows itself or alternatively, two reasons why it might have come about. Question (c) might be worth 4 or 6 marks, and is likely to ask you to suggest two or three reasons why a sociological problem or process has occurred. Alternatively, it may ask you to identify two differences between two sociological problems or processes. Questions (d) and (e) are essay questions and therefore you should write in continuous prose. Question (d) is worth 24 marks. It may ask you to examine:

- a particular sociological explanation for a social trend, or
- the effect of a particular social process on the culture or the family or on poverty, welfare or wealth, or
- the effect of a particular social process or problem on a specific group.

Question (e) is also worth 24 marks. It will specifically ask you to use data, probably from the second Item, in your answer as well as the material you have revised. It is therefore important not to ignore this instruction otherwise you will not be able to gain full marks. This question will ask you to assess a particular sociological argument or explanation mentioned in the Item. You will be expected to outline and describe what is meant by that argument and to identify the strengths and weaknesses of it.

The SCLY 1 paper only lasts one hour. It is important to divide up your time accordingly. You should aim to spend about 10 minutes on questions (a) to (c) and 25 minutes on each of the essays.

Unit 2: SCLY 2

This paper is divided into two sections – Education and Health. You must choose one section and answer all the questions in that section. You must not answer questions from more than one section. Each section is divided into three parts.

Part 1: Questions on Education or Health
The first part comprises an Item of stimulus material on some aspect of the topic and four questions focused on the Sociology of Education or Health. You are advised to spend 50 minutes altogether answering these questions.

The first question (a) is worth 2 marks and will ask you to explain the meaning of a sociological term or concept. The second question (b) is worth 6 marks and will ask you to suggest three ways, reasons, examples, etc. relating to some aspect of the topic. The third question (c) is worth 12 marks and will ask you to write a mini-essay outlining the ways a particular sociological problem or process may show itself or describing a particular sociological theory or explanation. The fourth question (d) in this section is an essay title worth 20 marks which will ask you to use material in the Item and your revision knowledge to 'assess' a particular sociological claim or explanation. Your answer must be in continuous prose. Remember that if you ignore the instruction to use the Item you will not be able to gain full marks.

Part 2: Questions on Sociological Methods in Context

The next question requires you to apply your knowledge and understanding of sociological research methods to the study of education or health. You are advised to spend approximately 30 minutes on this question. It contains an Item of stimulus material focused on research carried out into Education or Health. The question, which is worth 20 marks, will ask you to use information from the Item as well as your revision knowledge to 'assess the strengths and limitations' of a particular research method when studying a specific aspect of Education or Health. The question will give you a choice between two research methods – you need to organise your answer (which must be written in continuous prose) around one of these methods.

Part 3: Questions on Sociological Research Methods

The final set of questions is exclusively focused on research methods. You are advised to spend 40 minutes on this part of the exam paper. Question (a), which is worth 2 marks, will ask you to explain or define a methodological concept. Questions (b) and (c) are worth 4 marks each and will ask you to identify or suggest two advantages, problems, techniques, etc. related to some aspect of research methods. Finally, question (d) is an essay question, worth 20 marks, which should be written in continuous prose. This may, for example, ask you to examine the problems that are associated with a particular research method or approach. This question is synoptic meaning that examples and illustrations can be drawn from any topic on the specification.

AQA A2 assessment

Unit 3: SCLY 3

This paper, which is one hour thirty minutes long, is divided into four sections. You must choose one section and answer all parts of the question from that section. You must not answer questions from more than one section.

Each section is divided into two parts. The first part contains an Item of stimulus material on some aspect of the topic which is followed by either a question worth 9 marks or two questions worth 3 marks and 6 marks respectively, as well as an essay question worth 18 marks. You should aim to spend 10 minutes on the first questions and 25 minutes on the 18 mark essay question.

The first questions will ask you to 'identify and briefly explain' three reasons, problems, ways etc. related to the material in the Item. The essay question will ask you specifically to use the material in the Item, along with your revision knowledge, to 'assess' a sociological view or the reasons why a social process has occurred. Your answer to this question should be in continuous prose. Remember that if you ignore the instruction to use the Item you will not be able to gain full marks.

The second part of the section offers you a choice of two essay questions each worth 33 marks. You must only do one of these essays and your answer should be in continuous prose. You should aim to spend about 55 minutes on this. The questions tend to be framed in a particular way. They may ask you to 'assess' a particular sociological argument or theory. Alternatively, a quotation may be followed by the question 'to what extent do sociological arguments and evidence support this view?'

Unit 4: SCLY 4

This paper, which is two hours long, is divided into two sections. You must choose one section and answer all

questions from that section. You must not answer questions from more than one section.

Each section is divided into three parts. The first part contains an Item of stimulus material on some aspect of the topic which is followed by two essay questions. The first question is worth 12 marks and will ask you to 'examine' some aspect of the material included in the Item. (The marks for this question will be increased to 21 marks for the January 2012 exam and thereafter). Your answer to this question should be in continuous prose. The second question is worth 21 marks and will ask you to 'assess' a sociological argument relating to the topic. Again, your answer should be in continuous prose. It is recommended that you spend about 45 minutes on this part.

The second part focuses on research methods in the context of the topic. The first question in this part will either be worth 9 marks or sub-divided into two questions worth 3 marks and 6 marks. The question will ask you to 'identify and briefly explain' three problems, reasons, etc. relating to the use of research methods to investigate the topic. (However, please note that this question will not appear after June 2011 and the 9 marks are being added to the first question in each section). The second question in this part of the section (worth 15 marks) involves reading an Item of stimulus material and answering an essay question which will ask you to use material from the Item as well as your revision knowledge to 'assess the strengths and limitations' of a particular research method to investigate some aspect of the topic. This question therefore requires you to apply your knowledge and understanding of sociological research methods to the study of the topic in the section. If you don't do this and fail to use the material in the Item, you cannot gain full marks. Your answer should be in continuous prose. It is recommended that you spend about 30 minutes on this part.

The final part of each section is composed of one essay question worth 33 marks. This may ask you to 'assess' a sociological argument, theory methods and evidence or provide you with a quotation and ask 'to what extent do sociological arguments and evidence support this view?'. Your answer should be in continuous prose. It is recommended that you spend about 45 minutes on this part.

OCR AS assessment

Unit 1: G671 Exploring socialisation, culture and identity

This paper, which lasts one hour and thirty minutes, is preceded by pre-release material which focuses on how a piece of research related to socialisation, culture and identity has been designed and organised. This material is normally sent out to centres at least a month before the exam.

The paper is composed of four questions. Question (1), which is worth 8 marks, will ask you to define a sociological concept relevant to socialisation, culture and identity. You will be expected to use examples to illustrate your answer. Question (2) is worth 16 marks and will ask you to 'outline and explain' two things e.g. two ways in which an agency or agencies of socialisation might affect some aspect of culture or identity. Question (3) is worth 24 marks and will ask you to 'explain and briefly evaluate' some aspect of socialisation, culture and identity. Question (4) is worth 52 marks. You will be instructed to use the pre-release material and your revision knowledge to 'explain and evaluate' the research methods used in the study which is the focus of the pre-release material.

Unit 2: G672 Topics in socialisation, culture and identity

This paper, which lasts one hour thirty minutes, contains eight questions, two per optional topic. You are expected to answer two questions. These may be from the same option or you may choose one question from two different options.

Each question is divided into two parts. The first part is worth 17 marks and will ask you to 'identify and explain' two reasons, ways, characteristics, features, difficulties, etc. of social processes relating to the specific topic. The second part of each question is worth 33 marks and will ask you to 'outline and evaluate' a sociological view, explanation or model.

OCR A2 assessment

Unit 3: G673 Power and control

This paper, which lasts one hour thirty minutes, contains twelve essay questions, three per optional topic. You have to answer any two of the twelve questions. Each question is worth 50 marks and will ask you to 'outline and assess' views, explanations, policies, etc. relating to the options.

Unit 4: G674 Exploring social inequality and difference

This paper, which lasts two hours, includes a piece of source material relating to research carried out into some aspect of social inequality and difference. You will be expected to use that source material and your revision knowledge to answer questions 1 and 2. Question 1 which is worth 15 marks will ask you to 'outline and explain' why a particular research method (usually mentioned in the source material) might be used in sociological research. Question 2 which is worth 25 marks will ask you to 'outline and assess' a view relating to whether a particular research method might be useful for researching some aspect of social inequality and difference.

The paper also contains two two-part questions worth 20 marks and 40 marks respectively. You will be expected to choose one of these questions. The first part of the question will ask you to 'outline the evidence' for a particular type of inequality or disadvantage. The second part of the question will ask you to 'outline and assess' a particular sociological explanation or theory related to social inequality and difference.

Exam technique

AS and on to A2

AS Sociology requires no prior learning or achievement at GCSE although it is useful to have a grade 'C' in GCSE English Language because of the emphasis on essay writing. It is, of course, necessary to have studied Sociology to AS Level in order to move onto A2! A2 builds on AS by drawing on more sophisticated content and evidence. It develops a more complex understanding of sociological concepts and the ability to produce more analytical responses and more substantial judgments. To get the most out of A2 Sociology you will need a critical enquiring mind and an ability to communicate ideas effectively.

It is important to remember that Sociology is not a subject that can be learnt from a single text. This Study Guide will provide you with the essential knowledge and ideas you need to understand the topics you study, but you will need to build on this by incorporating the wider reading suggested by your teacher.

What examiners are looking for

The most common types of question are those which require an analysis of **cause** and **consequence**, and those which require an **assessment** or **judgment**. Examiners are not looking for a pre-determined 'correct' answer but they expect you to address the question set and use your knowledge to support your argument. They indicate the type of answer they expect by command or trigger words in the questions:

- **State, define, what is meant by?** – Normally require a short concise answer although you may also be asked to illustrate by providing an example.
- **Explain, discuss** – Require you to outline or describe a theory or explanation or social phenomenon, and normally involve making reference to a set of ideas or both sides of a debate.

- **Identify, suggest, illustrate** – Normally require you to apply your knowledge to a particular sociological problem, phenomena or approach, e.g. suggest three reasons why a particular social problem has occurred or identify two characteristics of something.
- **Examine, assess, evaluate** – Require you to make a judgment. The examiners expect you to set out the main arguments on opposite sides and then balance them in your conclusion. For example, you might assess the success of a theory by explaining its strengths and then its weaknesses. Your judgment should be based on evidence.

Some dos and don'ts

- **Do read the set of instructions at the start of the exam paper** – You do not want to answer too many questions or not enough or from the wrong sections.
- **Do spend 5 minutes reading through the Items and the questions** – It is especially important to read through all the questions before attempting any of them.
- **Do answer the question** – Read questions carefully. Command words indicate the type of answer expected and the rest of the question specifies the issue to be addressed.
- **Do be sure to refer to source material if the question requires it** – You will lose marks if you ignore this. You will also lose marks if you answer entirely from the sources when a question asks you to use your own knowledge as well as the sources.
- **Do spend some time planning your answers** – This is especially important for questions requiring extended writing. It will ensure that your argument is coherent and that you avoid omissions.

- **Do pay attention to correct spelling, grammar and punctuation** – Quality of written communication is taken into account in all assessment units.
- **Do write legibly** – An examiner cannot give marks if the answer cannot be read.
- **Don't produce undirected narrative** – Most questions require you to use your knowledge to follow the instructions given in the command words of the question.
- **Don't introduce irrelevant material** – You will get no credit for it. A common fault is an 'all I know' response.
- **Don't mistake your own opinion for Sociology** – Always back up what you say with sociological evidence.Set what you say in a sociological context by referring to relevant sociological concepts and theory.
- **Don't waste time on lengthy introductions** – The ideal introduction sets outs briefly the line of argument you intend to pursue.

1 The family

The following topics are covered in this chapter:

- **The family and social structure**
- **Changing patterns in family life**
- **Demography and family**
- **Family diversity**
- **Gender roles and family life**
- **Childhood**

1.1 The family and social structure

LEARNING SUMMARY

After studying this section, you should be able to understand:

- key concepts such as nuclear families, extended families and households
- how social change, especially economic change, has impacted upon the family
- the functions of the family from a functionalist, Marxist and feminist perspective

Defining key terms of family structures

AQA **SCLY 1**   OCR **G672**

Some of the common terms used by sociologists to describe family structures include:

- **Kinship** – a concept that refers to family connections between people based on blood, marriage or adoption. It refers to relatives, both in the past and in the present, whether close or distant and whether contact is frequent, infrequent or even non–existent.
- **Household** – any person, or persons, who live under the same roof. These may be family members, but they may also be unrelated, e.g. a group of students sharing a house are a household.
- **Nuclear family** – the most basic family type which is experienced by the majority of people in Britain. This contains just two generations, i.e. an adult heterosexual couple (usually husband and wife) and their dependent children who live in the same household.
- **Extended families** – those family types in which the basic nuclear structure has been enlarged to include grandparents, uncles, cousins, etc. and who either live in the same household or in close proximity, e.g. in the same neighbourhood, or keep in close frequent contact, e.g. contact may be on a daily basis.

The functionalist view of the family

The functionalist approach argues that all social institutions (such as families and the education system) are functional or beneficial because they perform key functions for individuals and for society.

Murdock (1949) studied over 250 societies around the world and argued that the nuclear family was universal throughout the world. He claimed that it had the following features.

- It is small and compact in structure, composed of a mother, father and usually two or three children who are biologically related.

- It is a type of household in that its members normally share common residence.
- It is based on heterosexual romantic love reinforced by marriage and fidelity.
- Marriage is based on a natural, or biological, sexual division of labour in that women are mainly responsible for nurturing children, whilst men are responsible for the economic maintenance of the household by performing the role of breadwinner.
- The immediate family comes first and all other obligations and relationships come second. Kinship, therefore, is all important.
- It is assumed, almost without question, that the family is a positive and beneficial institution in which family members receive nurturing, unconditional love and care.

KEY POINT

The influence of these traditional beliefs about family life has been immense. They constitute a powerful conservative 'ideology' (i.e. dominant set of ideas) about what families should look like and how family members should behave, e.g. the following beliefs are very influential today in Britain.

- That women have maternal instincts and that the main responsibility for parenting lies with the mother.
- That cohabitation does not have the same value as marriage.
- That lone parents are not as effective as two parents.
- That homosexuals should not have the same fertility or parenting rights as heterosexuals.

Murdock claimed that this nuclear family performs four basic functions in all societies, which benefit both society and the individual.

- **Reproductive or procreative** – this is essential for the survival of society. Without reproduction, society would cease to exist.
- **Sexual** – marital sex creates a powerful emotional bond between a couple, encourages fidelity and therefore commits the individual to family life. Sex within marriage contributes to social order and stability, because marital fidelity sets the moral rules for general sexual behaviour.
- **Economic** – parents provide the economic things that are vital for sustaining life in children, such as shelter, food and protection, e.g. they take economic responsibility for the **welfare** of their children by becoming productive workers and bringing home an income.
- **Educational** – learning social values and norms via **primary socialisation** is necessary in order that culture be handed down from one generation to another.

> The family links to the key themes of socialisation and culture.

Criticism of Murdock

The main criticism of Murdock is that his definition of family life is very much a product of time and place (1940s USA) and consequently is **ethnocentric**, i.e. it is based on the view that Western, and especially American, culture produces the 'best' cultural institutions and that other cultural family types are somehow inferior.

Interpretivist sociologists argue that Murdock fails to acknowledge that families are the product of culture rather than biology, and that, consequently, family relationships and roles will take different forms even within the same society.

Murdock's model is value-laden and not objective, because it is clearly saying there are 'right' and 'wrong' ways to organise family life. It is also very dated and fails to take account of modern social processes such as the increased availability of career choices for women, the decline in male employment opportunities, the importance of the contraceptive pill, the relaxation in social and religious attitudes and the increasing recognition, from the 1970s onwards, that family life does not always benefit all family members.

However, despite his tendency to make moral judgements about heterosexuality and marriage, Murdock is largely correct in his view that the family is the fundamental building block of societies. Most members of society see kinship ties as the most important aspect of their obligations to others, whilst socialisation into the values, norms and morals of society, which is responsible for producing the next generation of citizens, mainly occurs within family contexts.

The family and industrialisation

Functionalists such as **Parsons** (1956) suggest that the modern nuclear family has evolved to meet the changing economic needs of industrial society. Parsons argued that the most common family type in pre-industrial society was the **extended family** and that this extended unit was 'multifunctional'. It was responsible for a number of functions, such as the economic function of production, which involved producing its own food, clothing, housing, education, health care and welfare.

Parsons argued that the Industrial Revolution brought about three fundamental changes in family structure and functions.
- Early industry's demand for a **geographically mobile** workforce to work in the factories, opening in urban areas, saw the nuclear unit breaking away from the extended unit.
- **Structural differentiation** was also brought about by industrialisation.
- Specialised agencies developed, which gradually took over many of the family's functions. In particular, factories took over the economic, or production function, and family members became wage earners as work and home became separate places for the first time. The State eventually took over the functions of education, health and welfare.

> **KEY POINT**
>
> Parsons argued that the modern family is left with two basic and irreducible functions.
> - The primary **socialisation** of children – Parsons saw nuclear families as 'personality factories', turning out young citizens committed to the rules, norms and beliefs that make value consensus and, therefore, social order possible.
> - The **stabilisation** of adult personality – the married couple provide emotional support to each other to counter the stress of everyday life. This idea is sometimes called the 'warm bath' theory because Parsons claimed that family life, by providing a warm, loving and stable environment, relaxes individuals and prevents the stress of the outside world overwhelming its members.

The 'nuclear unit' provides husband and wife with very clear **social roles**. The male is the 'instrumental leader' and is responsible for the economic maintenance of the family group. The female is the 'expressive leader' who is primarily responsible for the socialisation of children and emotional maintenance.

Parsons concludes that the nuclear family is **functional** (beneficial) to society. Moreover, it is beneficial for the individuals because it provides a stable environment for spouses and children to construct loving relationships.

However, **Fletcher** argues that the family has not experienced structural differentiation to the degree that Parsons claims. Fletcher argues that the family is still heavily involved in the functions of education, health and welfare. The State has not taken over these functions. Instead, the State and the family work hand-in-hand with each other. Moreover, Fletcher claims that the family is now responsible for the major economic function of consumption – most advertising of consumer goods is aimed at persuading families to spend their income so that the economy is stimulated.

> This is sometimes called the 'internal critique' because these sociologists agree with Parsons that the nuclear family is the ideal type of family for industrial societies.

The British functionalists **Willmott and Young** (1973) took issue with Parsons over the speed of change. Their empirical research, conducted in a working class area (Bethnal Green) in the 1950s, showed that classic extended families still existed in large numbers even at this advanced stage of industrialisation. Willmott and Young argue that this unit only went into decline in the 1960s. There were three broad reasons for this.

- State council housing and slum clearance led to extended working class communities being re-housed in new towns and council estates. Most new housing was geared to nuclear families.
- The **Welfare State** – opportunities created by the expansion of secondary education, and full employment in the 1950s, undermined the need for a mutual support system.
- Consumerism became the dominant ideology in the 1960s, especially as home technology, e.g. television, developed. This made the home a more attractive place.

> **KEY POINT**
>
> Willmott and Young argued that such developments encouraged the evolution of the **symmetrical family**, i.e. a home-centred, privatised nuclear unit. They claimed that this would become the dominant family type by the 1990s. In this sense they agreed with Parsons.

The historical critique of Parsons

Historians, such as **Anderson** (1971) and **Laslett** (1977), suggest that Parsons failed to acknowledge that industrialisation may follow different patterns in different industrial societies, e.g. modern Japan still retains a commitment to the extended family form.

Laslett's survey of English parish records reveals that most pre-industrial families were nuclear and not extended, as Parsons claimed. Laslett argues that this was due to late marriage, early death and the practice of sending children away to become servants or apprentices.

Anderson's research, using data from the 1851 census, found that the extended family was fairly common in industrial Preston. A mutual support system evolved, in reaction to the extreme poverty of the period, to share scarce housing and high rents and to pool low wages.

The Marxist theory of the family

Zaretsky is critical of Parsons, because he believes that instead of benefitting society by promoting consensus and stability, the nuclear family actually benefits the ruling capitalist class at the expense of other social classes. He argues that the family is an ideological agent of the ruling class because:

- It socialises children, especially working class children, into **capitalist ideology**, i.e. it is within the family that children learn obedience and respect to those in authority, that inequalities in power are 'natural' and that the capitalist organisation of society is 'normal' and unchangeable. They grow up into conformist adult workers who rarely challenge exploitation and inequality.
- The family also acts as a psychological comforting device for the worker against the hardships of the workplace in which problems such as low pay, exploitation or fear of losing one's job can be forgotten for a while.
- As the major agency of **consumption** the family is constantly encouraged by ideological agencies, such as the mass media, to invest in what **Marcuse** calls '**false needs**', i.e. consumer goods bought to be conspicuously consumed and which quickly become obsolete (such as designer goods). This ensures that the capitalist class continues to make vast profits.

The Marxist-feminist critique of Parsons

> **KEY POINT**
>
> Marxist-feminists suggest that the nuclear family meets the needs of capitalism for the reproduction and maintenance of class and patriarchal inequality. It benefits the powerful at the expense of the working class and women.

The Marxist-feminist **Benston** (1972) argues that the nuclear family provides the basic commodity required by capitalism, i.e. labour power, by:

- reproducing and rearing the future workforce at little cost to the capitalist class
- maintaining the present workforce's physical and emotional fitness through the wife's domestic labour.

Benston argues that capitalism essentially gets two labour powers (that of the husband and wife) for one wage. The nuclear family acts as a stabilising force in capitalist societies because workers find it difficult to withdraw their labour power if they have families to support. **Ansley** (1976) suggests that men may attempt to make up for the lack of power and control in the workplace by exerting control within the family through domestic violence.

The liberal feminist theory of the family

Liberal feminists suggest that in the family boys and girls learn, via **gender role socialisation**, that they occupy positions of power and subordination respectively. Boys learn that they are more likely to be the breadwinners, heads of the household and decision-makers, whilst girls learn that they are expected to subordinate their lives to the family.

Liberal feminists also believe that the legal and political barriers which have traditionally prevented women from achieving equality in the family and workplace are gradually being overcome, e,g. women have benefitted from changes in divorce laws, rape in marriage is now a crime and the authorities now take domestic violence more seriously than in the past. Women enjoy property rights and inheritance on an equal basis to men and they now enjoy improved maternity rights and pensions.

Liberal feminists consider that **progress** has been made over time in the relations between men and women and, consequently, family roles and relationships have become more **egalitarian**.

- The increasing importance of the service economy has been accompanied by a **feminisation** of the British workforce as most of the new service jobs available have been taken up by women. This has led to women acquiring more economic power.
- There has been a radical **cultural change** in women's attitudes which Wilkinson calls a **genderquake**. Wilkinson notes, that compared to previous generations, women today see education and careers as having more importance than settling down to marriage and children.
- Men may be taking a more active and, consequently, a more egalitarian role within families. There is evidence that fathers are more involved with their children.

However, these changes do not mean that liberal feminists are fully happy about the degree of change. There is still a long way to go, especially in the mass media's **representation** of women. There is also some evidence that equality in marriage may be exaggerated and that domestic violence is still a significant problem today. However, liberal feminists believe that gentle persuasion and consciousness raising will convince men that social change aimed at dismantling patriarchy will work for the benefit of all society.

The radical feminist critique

> Patriarchy is an extremely important concept which is frequently focused on by examiners. Know it well! Be able to evaluate the concept.

Radical feminists, such as **Millett** (1970), see modern societies and families as characterised by **patriarchy** – a system of subordination and domination in which men exercise power over women and children.

Millett argues that men originally acquired power over women because of biological factors (i.e. women who were frequently pregnant could not make the same contribution to society as men), but suggests that modern technology, e.g. the pill and modern machinery, has largely rendered this legitimation of male power redundant. However, patriarchy remains in place because of ideology. Both men and women are socialised into a set of ideas which confirm male power through **gender role socialisation** as children. Moreover, this patriarchal ideology stresses the primacy of the mother–housewife role for women and the breadwinner role for men. This ensures men's domination of the labour market. Finally, Millett sees the family as legitimating violence against women.

However, some argue that this model is dated as it is unable to consider recent trends, such as the feminisation of the workforce and women's use of divorce laws. **Hakim** (1995) argues that this model fails to consider that females might be exercising rational choices in choosing to become mothers and to adopt a domestic, rather than an occupational role.

The interpretivist critique

Parsons has been accused of painting an **over-socialised** view of children by interpretivist sociologists, who suggest that socialisation is a two-way interaction that can involve children changing and/or socialising their parents' behaviour, e.g. through **pester power**. It is also argued that the media is now a stronger socialising agency than the family because of the amount of time children spend watching TV, surfing the Internet or playing computer games.

The post-modern critique

Post-modernists suggest that a number of social changes are undermining the traditional nuclear family and, therefore, the effectiveness of how such a family functions for the good of society.

- Women now have many more choices available to them compared with previous generations. They are less likely to view romantic love, and therefore marriage, as their primary goal.
- Pre-marital sex and serial monogamy have become more socially acceptable.
- Some women are voluntarily choosing childlessness, whilst developments in reproductive technology mean that traditional heterosexual assumptions are undermined, as lesbians and single women use that technology to have children.
- The variety of career opportunities for women, and male unemployment, mean that females are now increasingly likely to be the economic providers for their families.
- Children are often fashion accessories, which convey status on their parents.
- Children are now less likely to be shaped by family socialisation, because many young people today grow up either outside of nuclear family life or they spend more time with professional childminders than with their parents.

PROGRESS CHECK

1. In what way does Laslett disagree with Parsons?
2. In what ways do Anderson and Willmott and Young disagree with Parsons?
3. What functions does the family retain according to Parsons?
4. Who benefits from the family according to Benston and Ansley?
5. What do feminist sociologists mean by 'patriarchy'?
6. Who benefits from the way families are organised, according to Millett?

Answers: 1. Parsons says it was nuclear; Laslett says it was extended. 2. Parsons says it became nuclear; Anderson says it was extended. Willmott and Young agree with Anderson, but argue it became nuclear during the late twentieth century. 3. Primary socialisation of children and stabilisation of adult personality. 4. The capitalist ruling class. 5. Patriarchy is both a gender and an age relationship based on male authority and dominance. 6. Men.

1.2 Changing patterns in family life

LEARNING SUMMARY

After studying this section, you should be able to understand:

- the recent changes in British family life relating to marriage, cohabitation and marital breakdown
- the arguments for and against the New Right view that the nuclear family is in decline as a result of these changes

Marriage

AQA **SCLY 1**   OCR **G672**

The New Right approach can be seen as a more recent re-working of the earlier functionalist approach to the family.

Some members of the **New Right** subscribe to the view that marriage, and therefore nuclear family life, is under attack and in decline. The New Right argue that marriage is becoming less popular, as shown by the fact that marriage rates have declined in Britain. In 2005, only 244 710 couples got married, compared with 480 000 in 1972. Moreover, the male marriage rate declined from 36.3% in 1994 to 27.8% in 2004, whilst the female rate declined from 30.6% to 24.6%.

However, the majority of people in Britain marry. Surveys indicate that most people still see marriage as a desirable objective in their lives. The number of re-marriages (i.e. in which one or both partners have been divorced) has increased as a percentage of all marriages from 15% in 1971 to 40% in 2006. These people are committed to the institution of marriage, despite their previous negative experience(s) of it.

Chester (1985) argues that society is not witnessing a mass rejection of marriage, instead, he suggests, people are delaying marriage. In other words, people are marrying later in life, probably after a period of cohabitation, for economic reasons. In 2005, seven in ten families were still headed by a married couple.

Cohabitation

Cohabitation is seen by the New Right as threatening the sanctity of marriage. It is suggested that this type of arrangement is too casual and does not involve the same sort of commitment and loyalty that marriage does. Moreover, New Right thinkers believe that children born outside of marriage are a sign of moral decline. In 2007 the Office for National Statistics (ONS) suggested that cohabiting couples are the fastest growing family type in Britain. Around 2.2 million families are cohabiting couples, with or without children. About 30% of births are now to cohabiting rather than married couples.

However, studies by sociologists such as **Burgoyne** (1982) suggest that in most cases cohabitation is a temporary phase. Most of those who cohabit eventually marry. Social attitudes tend to support marriage rather than cohabitation. Reasons for cohabitation may be pragmatic. The cost of marriage is high which may deter people, especially in areas hardest hit by unemployment.

Moreover, about three-quarters of births outside marriage are registered by both parents. This indicates that these births are occurring within stable relationships. **Fletcher** (1988) argues that cohabitation and births outside marriage conceal what are in fact rather conventional nuclear families based on stable relationships – even though they are not legitimised by marriage.

Cohabitation is not exclusive to heterosexual couples. Since the 1970s society has seen the emergence of lesbian and gay cohabitation, following the decriminalisation of homosexuality. **Plummer** (1995) notes that between 40% and 60% of gay men are cohabiting in relationships of over one year duration.

Marital breakdown

Marital breakdown is viewed by the New Right as a profound social problem with serious costs to society and individuals. There are three types of marital breakdown.

- **Divorce** refers to the legal termination of a marriage. This option is not always available in some societies.
- **Separation** refers to the physical separation of the spouses in that they are not living under the same roof.
- **Empty shell marriage** refers to a husband and wife who live together, and remain legally married, but who experience no intimate or emotional relationship, e.g. remaining together for the 'sake of the children'. It is difficult to measure how many marriages are in this state.

Divorce

There has been a steady rise in the divorce rate in Britain throughout the twentieth century. In 1961, two married couples per 1000 were divorced in England and Wales. By 1991, this had risen to 13. **Chandler** (1993) argues that if present trends continue, about 40% of current marriages will end in divorce. Explanations for the increasing divorce rate are as follows.

- **Changes in legislation** – changes in divorce law have generally made it easier and cheaper to get divorced. Before 1857, divorce was rare because it was expensive and required a private Act of Parliament. Four pieces of legislation can be identified as profoundly influencing the divorce statistics.
  - The **Matrimonial Causes Act** (1857) made divorce easier although it was still not affordable for most social groups. It also introduced the concept of 'marital crime', i.e. divorce was granted if offences such as cruelty or desertion were proved.
  - The **Legal Aid and Advice Act** (1949) gave financial assistance to the less well-off to help with divorce costs.
  - The **Divorce Reform Act** (1969) became law in 1971. This has been the most profound change. Marital partners now only have to demonstrate 'irretrievable breakdown of marriage' by separating for two years. 'Quickie' divorces could still be obtained by proving marital offences. A major rise in divorce followed the implementation of this act.
  - The **Matrimonial and Family Proceedings Act** (1984) reduced the period when couples could start to petition for divorce from three years to one year.

These changes in legislation resulted in a dramatic rise in the divorce rate especially in 1971 and in 1984–5. However, legislation is not the sole cause of higher divorce rates. Legal changes reflect changing attitudes in society.

- **Fletcher** sees higher divorce rates as evidence that marriage is increasingly valued. Couples are no longer prepared to put up with empty shell marriages. They want partners who can offer friendship, emotional fulfilment and sexual compatibility.

Bear in mind that a same sex couple can now register as civil partners and thereby have their relationship legally recognised. You will find more information on civil partnerships in section 1.4.

Be aware of any proposed changes to the divorce laws.

- In the 1960s most divorce petitions were initiated by men. However, in the 1990s 75% of divorce petitions were taken out by women. **Thornes and Collard's** (1979) survey of married couples discovered that women expect more from marriage than men and consequently tend to be less satisfied with their marriages.
- An important influence on women's attitudes has probably been the improvement in women's employment opportunities. In 1994 58% of the workforce was female. Women no longer have to stay unhappily married because they are not financially dependent upon their husband. However, the influence of this factor should not be exaggerated. Women's average earnings are still only 75% of men's. Women's economic independence is restricted because they are often employed in part-time and low-paid work.
- **Hart** (1976) argues that many women experience a 'dual burden'. They work, but are still primarily responsible for the bulk of housework and child-care. Failure by men to re-distribute power in the home may lead to divorce.
- There has been a general liberalisation of attitudes in society. Divorce no longer carries stigma. Some sociologists such as **Wilson** (1988) see such change in social attitudes as due to **secularisation**, i.e. a general decline in religious practices and thinking.
- Marriage, despite its popularity, receives little support from the State. Little public money is spent keeping marriages together, despite the emotional and economic costs of divorce.

Even members of the Royal Family have experienced divorce.

> **KEY POINT**
>
> Current trends indicate that four out of ten contemporary marriages will eventually end in divorce. **Monogamy**, i.e. one partner for life, may eventually be replaced by **serial monogamy**, i.e. people may have a series of relationships which result in cohabitation and/or marriage. However, most people spend their lives in a family environment and place a high value on it. **Abbott and Wallace** (1990) argue that the statistics indicate family stability, e.g. six out of ten couples who got married in the 1990s will stay together until one of them dies.

Post-modernist views on divorce

The post-modernist approach provides an alternative interpretation of divorce.

Beck and Beck-Gernsheim (1995) argue that rising divorce rates are the product of a rapidly changing world in which the traditional rules with regard to love, romance and relationships no longer apply. In particular, they point out that the post-modern world is characterised by individualisation, choice and conflict.

- **Individualisation** – people are under less pressure to conform to the traditional goals set by extended families, religions or cultures and have become more individualistic, selfish, etc.
- **Choice** – cultural and economic changes mean that people have a greater range of choices available in terms of lifestyles and living arrangements.
- **Conflict** – there is a potential clash between what people want as individuals (i.e. selfishness) and what they expect from others in a relationship like a marriage (i.e. selflessness).

Beck and Beck-Gernsheim argue that these three features have undermined relationships and marriages between men and women as demonstrated by rising divorce rates. However, this does not mean marriage is dying out. They point out that people still seek love and marriage because they believe that these compensate for the impersonal and uncertain nature of the modern world.

PROGRESS CHECK

1. Does the New Right approach have more in common with the functionalist or the feminist approach?
2. Which approach views the increase in cohabitation and divorce in negative terms?
3. Give one reason why some people may cohabit rather than get married.
4. What does the term 'divorce' refer to?
5. According to Beck and Beck-Gernsheim, what three features characterise the postmodern world?

Answers: 1. The functionalist approach. 2. The New Right approach. 3. The financial costs of getting married may deter some people. 4. The legal termination of a marriage. 5. Individualisation, choice and conflict.

1.3 Demography and the family

LEARNING SUMMARY

After studying this section, you should be able to understand:

- how demographic trends, such as birth rates and death rates, have led to an ageing population
- how birth rates and death rates have affected family size and organisation

The population of Britain

AQA **SCLY 1**   OCR **G672**

The study of **demography** is focused on how the number of births and deaths, and the number of people entering and leaving the country (migration), affect the size, sex and age structure of the population.

The population of Britain grew steadily between 1971 and 2003 to reach 61.2 million people in 2009. Population projections suggest that it will reach 65 million in 2023 and 67 million by 2031. The rate of population change over time depends upon five demographic factors.

- The **birth rate** – this refers to the number of live births per 1000 of the population over a year.
- The **fertility rate** – this refers to the number of live births per 1000 women aged 15–44 over one year.
- The **death rate** – this refers to the number of deaths per 1000 of the population over the course of a year.
- **International migration** – this refers to the movement of people from one country to another. **Immigration** refers to people entering a country and **emigration** refers to people leaving a country. Statistics on net migration provide information on the number of emigrants in proportion to the number of immigrants.

Changes in the birth rate

Only 716 000 children were born in Britain in 2004. This is 34% fewer births than in 1901 and 21% fewer than 1971. However, the birth rate has fluctuated throughout the last 100 years.

There was a fall in births during the First World War, followed by a post-war 'baby-boom', with births peaking at 1.1 million in 1920. The number of births then fell and remained low during the inter-war period. Births increased again after the Second World War with another 'baby-boom'. There was also an increase in births in the late 1980s and early 1990s. This was the result of the larger cohort of women born in the 1960s entering their childbearing years.

Since 2001, the birth rate has steadily risen. In 2007, the ONS announced that the 2006 birth rate was the highest for 26 years. However, the number of births in the twenty-first century is lower than the number of births in 1901.

- There was a major decline in the **infant mortality rate**, (i.e. the number of children dying at birth or in their first year of life per 1000 births per year) at the end of the nineteenth century which continued into the twentieth century. This was because of improvements in sanitation, water supplies and nutrition, rather than medical progress. The decline in child mortality rates meant that parents no longer needed to have lots of children to ensure that a few survived.
- As standards of living increased and childhood came to be seen as a special period in our lives, having children became an expensive business and, consequently, parents chose to limit the size of their families.
- Contraceptive technology in the form of the pill became widely available from the 1960s onwards.
- Attitudes towards women's roles dramatically changed during the course of the twentieth century and this had a profound effect upon women's attitudes towards family life, having children, education and careers. In particular, it resulted in a decline in fertility as women chose to have fewer children and some chose not to have children at all.

Changes in the fertility rate

The fertility rate generally refers to the number of children that women of childbearing age have in any one year. Fertility rates have generally declined over the past 100 years, e.g. in 1900 there were 115 live births per 1000 women aged 15–44, compared with only 57 in 1999 and 54.5 in 2001.

The **Total Fertility Rate (TFR)** refers to the number of children that are born to an average woman during her childbearing life. In 2004, Britain had a TFR of 1.77 children per woman, but recent ONS data suggests that the first baby-boom of the twenty-first century may be on its way because the fertility rate rose to 1.87 in 2006. Fertility rates have fallen for several reasons.

- Women are delaying having families and are having children at an older age than they were 30 years ago. The number of children born to women aged 40 and over has doubled in the last 20 years.
- Delay is possible because of reliable birth control.
- Women's attitudes towards settling down and having children underwent a profound change as they took advantage of greater opportunities in education and employment from the 1980s onwards.

The very recent rise in fertility has been credited to the increase in the number of immigrants who tend to have larger families, e.g. in 2005, 146 944 children were born to mothers who did not come from Britain. In 1998 the total was 86 345. Babies born to mothers from overseas accounted for 21.9% of all births in 2005, up from 20.8% in 2004.

The effect of changing birth and fertility rates on family size and organisation

- The decline in the number of children being born has led to a decline in family kinship networks, because it means people have fewer aunts, uncles, cousins, etc., to fall back on in times of need.
- There are more nuclear families with one child.
- There has been a decline in the number of full-time mothers and a rise in the number of children looked after by other relatives, especially grand parents, child-minders and nurseries.
- There has been a trend towards voluntary childlessness. In 2000, one in five women aged 40 had not had children compared with one in ten in 1980 and this figure is expected to rise to one in four by 2018.

The death rate and life expectancy

As the population of Britain has increased, **life expectancy** has increased and **death rates** have fallen. Between 1971 and 2004, the death rate for all males fell by 21%, while the death rate for all females fell by 9%.

In 1851, life expectancy at birth in England and Wales was 40 years for males and 44 years for females. Just 150 years later, in modern-day industrialised Britain, life expectancy has nearly doubled from Victorian levels. Children born in 2004 will, on average, live for 78 years. This increase in life expectancy is the result of:
- improved public health (sanitation and hygiene)
- improved medical technology and practice (drugs such as vaccines and antibiotics)
- rising living standards (which have improved nutritional intake and housing quality)
- better care and welfare facilities (which have been mainly provided by the State).

However, life expectancy is not uniform across the country. There is some evidence that life expectancy differs according to region, e.g. male life expectancy in 2002 was 76.2 years in England, but 73.5 in Scotland. There is evidence that life expectancy also depends on **social class** and **ethnicity**. Those in middle class jobs tend to live longer than those in manual jobs and the unemployed, whilst some ethnic minorities have lower life expectancy than White people.

The ageing population
The decline in the death rate, especially the **infant mortality rate**, and the increase in life expectancy, has led to an ageing of the British population. There are increasing numbers of people aged 65 and over and decreasing numbers of children under 16. Between 1971 and 2004, the number of young people aged under 16 declined by 18%, whilst the number of people aged over 65 increased by 29%. There are a number of consequences of an ageing population for families and households.

- There has been an increase in the number of **one-person households** over state pension age as a proportion of all households. In 2005, 14% of all households were of this type.
- Women aged 65 and over were more likely to live alone than men because of their longer **life expectancy** and because they tend to marry men older than themselves. In 2005, 59% of women aged 75 and over were living alone.
- Evidence from sociological studies such as **Finch and Mason, O'Brien and Jones et al.** and **Foster**, suggest that the elderly have regular contact with extended kin. Many elderly relatives use new technology such as e-mail to keep in contact with their extended kin.
- There are signs that the ageing population might lead to a growth in children caring for elderly parents, who do not have the economic resources to go into private residential care homes, by taking them into the family home or building granny flats.
- However, caring for the elderly might have three negative effects. Firstly, it may increase the **domestic burden** on women who take most responsibility for caring in families. Secondly, it may result in **financial hardship** for the family because one partner may have to give up work in order to care full-time for elderly relatives. Thirdly, there may be **emotional strain** and **over-crowding** if an elderly and physically dependent relative moves in, which causes conflict between couples and between parents and children.
- **Brannen** (2003) notes the increase in the number of **four-generational families** which include great-grandparents and great-grandchildren. Many of these multi-generational families are long and thin in shape and are typically described as **beanpole families**. They have fewer ties within a generation because of high divorce rates, falling fertility and smaller family size. They have more ties between the generations because of increased life expectancy. Brannen argues that the grandparent generation is more healthy and active compared with the past. People in this generation, particularly grandmothers, are increasingly looking after both their grandchildren and their own elderly parents, e.g. 20% of people in their fifties and sixties currently care for their parent(s), while 10% care for both an elderly person and a grandchild.
- Studies suggest that there may be more qualitative and enriching contact between grandparents and their grandchildren. This may result in more positive experiences of socialisation as grandparents pass on life lessons.

Migration

The population of Britain is also influenced by patterns of international migration and the net balance of immigration (people entering the country) and emigration (people leaving the country). In the period 1900–40 there was a net loss in the British population as people emigrated to Canada, New Zealand and Australia. The 1950s–60s saw a net gain as thousands of immigrants arrived from India, Pakistan and the Caribbean to meet a shortage of labour caused by the Second World War. The 1980s onwards saw a net gain in population as White immigrants from Eastern Europe, Australia and USA entered the country.

The effects of migration on family life

- Only 39% of British born African-Caribbeans under the age of 60 are married compared with 60% of Whites.
- Over 50% of African-Caribbean families are single-parent families.

- African-Caribbean mothers often choose to live independently from the fathers of their children, e.g. 66% of 20-year-old African-Caribbean mothers remain single compared with 11% of their peers. At 30 years, 60% of African-Caribbean men are unattached compared with 45% of Whites.
- Most Asian families are nuclear, although 33% of Asian families are vertically extended, (i.e. they include grandparents) or horizontally extended (they include brothers and their wives, e.g. Sikhs).
- Marriage is mainly arranged and negotiated with children in Asian families, although forced marriage is largely a thing of the past.
- Attitudes towards women tend to be very traditional in many Muslim families. Few Muslim mothers work outside the family. However, Hindus tend to encourage their young women to gain qualifications and to pursue careers.
- Parent–children relationships are based on stronger notions of respect, duty, and honour than are traditionally found in the White western community.
- Asian families tend to feel a strong sense of duty to help extended kin, especially those still living in their country of origin.
- There are at least 200 000 mixed-race marriages a year in Britain, mainly between Whites and African-Caribbeans. The Policy Studies Institute estimates half of Black men and one-third of Black women in relationships had a White partner.
- One in ten children live in a mixed-race family. Young people are six times more likely than adults to be from a mixed-race background.

PROGRESS CHECK

1. Identify three factors that can affect population size.
2. Which term refers to the number of live births per 1000 of the population per year?
3. What does the term 'international migration' refer to?
4. What does the infant mortality rate measure?
5. On average, do women or men in Britain have longer life expectancy?
6. Which sociologist has studied the recent increase in the number of multigenerational families?
7. Identify one way in which elderly people may keep in regular contact with their extended kin.

Answers: 1. The birth rate, the death rate, international migration (immigration and emigration). 2. The birth rate. 3. The movement of population from one country to another. 4. The number of infant deaths (before the age of one) per 1000 live births per year. 5. Women. 6. Brannen. 7. Possible answers include: e-mail, telephone.

1.4 Family diversity

LEARNING SUMMARY	**After studying this section, you should be able to understand:** - the diversity of family and household structures in Britain - New Right views on family diversity and the criticisms of these views

The diversity of family life

AQA **SCLY 1**   OCR **G672**

Sociologists, such as the **Rapoports**, argue that Britain is no longer dominated by one family type. They argue that we should be celebrating **family diversity** – there now exists a greater choice and variety than ever before in terms of family lifestyles.

Bear in mind that the reconstituted family is also referred to as a 'blended family' or as a 'step family'.

- The Rapoports note diversity in family structure. Family life in Britain is made up of the conventional nuclear family, cohabiting couples with children, the single-parent family and the **reconstituted family**. The reconstituted family is often made up of divorced or widowed people who have re-married and their children from the previous marriage. Such families are on the increase because of divorce, e.g. one in 15 families are step-families; one in 12 children were living in them in 1991. Reconstituted families, and especially children within them, are likely to have close ties with the families of previous partners. Children may be pulled in two directions and have tense relationships with their step-parents. These families may be further complicated if the parents decide to have children of their own. Family life, therefore, may be experienced quite differently from that experienced in a conventional nuclear family unit.

- Moreover, the study *Villains* by **Foster** (1991), of an East End London community, indicated that the lives of working class people, and its younger generation in the 1980s, were still dominated by the values and traditions of extended kin such as parents and grandparents who tended to live nearby. **Brannen** suggests the beanpole family is increasing in importance.

- The Rapoports note that families are households, but households are not necessarily families (though some will evolve into families or may have evolved out of them), e.g. 'married couple only' households. There is also evidence that single-person households are increasing and accounted for about 30% of all households in 2010. Surveys suggest that an increasing number of young, professional women are electing to live alone.

- There are distinct differences in the lifestyles of families with different **ethnic origins** and religious beliefs. Britain is now a **multicultural society** in that about 11% of the population is from an ethnic minority background. Asian family life is diverse and depends on a wide range of factors such as religion, presence of extended kin and cultural beliefs. We have seen a great deal of **inter-marriage** between Whites, African-Caribbeans and Chinese, which has resulted in a dramatic increase in **mixed-race children**.

- Diversity also exists in **patterns of kinship**. Some modern nuclear families are 'privatised' and 'relatively isolated' from kin. However, most are part of a 'modified extended family' set-up where nuclear family members still feel obliged to kin and offer emotional and material support in times of crisis. Studies also suggest that extended ties are important to the upper class in their attempt to maintain wealth and privilege.

- The number of **same-sex couples** who are cohabiting is increasing and it has become a trend for such couples to have families through **adoption, artificial insemination** and **surrogacy**. In 1999, the law lords ruled that homosexual couples can be legally defined as a family and the government has now introduced **same-sex civil partnerships** (a type of marriage) which means that same-sex partners have similar rights to heterosexual married couples, with regard to inheritance (e.g. of property and pensions) and next of kin status.

- **Eversley** and **Bonnerjea** note geographical variations in family life, e.g. that seaside areas have large concentrations of elderly couples and single-person households, whilst inner-city areas see large numbers of single-parent families, reconstituted families and ethnic minority families. Traditional working class areas see more extended families, whilst the affluent south-east sees a greater proportion of nuclear families.

- Diversity can be seen in the internal division of labour within families. The Rapoports argue that most nuclear families in Britain are now **dual-career** families. Some women will have responsibility for the bulk of child-care and housework. Others may have negotiated a greater, perhaps even equal, input from men in the domestic sphere. The media are fond of announcing the appearance of the so-called **New Man**. Others may have found husbands who are happy to reverse traditional roles and become **house-husbands**.

The Rapoports conclude that a fundamental change is taking place in British family life. However, **Chester** suggests that the Rapoports have exaggerated the degree of diversity in British society and argues that the basic features of family life have remained largely unchanged for the majority of the population since the 1950s.

The New Right perspective on family diversity

AQA **SCLY1**   OCR **G672**

New Right sociologists argue that nuclear family life is under threat. The nuclear family is said to be under attack and in decline because of the following trends which have been linked to state **social policies** rooted in the 1960s and 1970s.

- The impact of **feminism** on the home. It is argued that this has led to the introduction of **equal opportunities** and **equal pay legislation** which have distracted women from their 'natural' careers as mothers. The New Right claims that there have been few tax or benefit policies aimed at encouraging mothers to stay at home with their children. The New Right argue that feminism has led to gender confusion about family roles and a corresponding rise in divorce and the number of single-parent families.
- It is also suggested that working mothers are responsible for **social problems**, such as juvenile delinquency and anti-social behaviour, because children no longer experience long-term nurturing and socialisation from their mothers who are out at work. The New Right therefore claim that generations of children have been psychologically 'damaged' by maternal deprivation.
- The New Right claims that **sexual permissiveness** and **promiscuity** is on the increase and the cause of a moral decay in society. New Right writers argue that government social policy has actually encouraged this decline in morality by decriminalising homosexuality and abortion, making the contraceptive pill freely available on the National Health Service (NHS), making divorce easier through the **Divorce Reform Act** (1969) and by not doing enough to promote marriage over cohabitation.

New Right sociologists have suggested that social policy in Britain has resulted in the decline of the nuclear family and that this has created a range of social problems, such as unemployment, educational underachievement, rising crime rates and anti-social behaviour.

Criticism of the New Right perspective on family diversity

KEY POINT

The Rapoports are very critical of the New Right's insistence that there only exists one **ideal** family type. They note that in 1994 only 20% of nuclear families contained a division of labour, in which the father was the sole breadwinner and the mother was exclusively the home-maker/child-carer. The Rapoports argue that family life in Britain is characterised by a range of family types which reflect the plurality of British society.

Critics of the New Right suggest that the ideology of the traditional nuclear family has had some very significant influences on government thinking.

This material is relevant to social policy issues.

Bear in mind that social policies change over time as incoming governments introduce new policies or modify existing ones. It is important to keep up-to-date with key policy change by reading the quality press.

- Tax and welfare policies have generally favoured and encouraged the heterosexual married couple rather than cohabiting couples, single parents and same-sex couples. **Allan** (1985) goes so far as to suggest that these policies have actively discouraged cohabitation and single-parent families.
- Social policies such as the payment of **child benefit** to the mother, and the lack of free universal nursery care, has reinforced the idea that women should take prime responsibility for children.
- Expectant mothers receive **paid maternity leave** for six months and unpaid leave for twelve months. In contrast, fathers only receive two weeks paid paternity leave.
- The **Community Care Act** (1990) encourages families and voluntary agencies to have a greater involvement in the care of the elderly and sick. This has placed an increased burden on women who are often the ones who take on responsibility for the sick, the elderly and disabled relatives who would once have been given free residential care. Less state assistance is given to elderly people who live with their relatives.
- School hours and school holidays may make it difficult for women to find compatible employment outside the home.
- The best and most desirable council and private housing is designed for two-parent families.

The Labour government of 1997–2010 recognised that there are few families in the twenty-first century which have exclusively a male breadwinner. Most families rely on two incomes and most women work (albeit often part-time). **Lewis** notes that Labour:

- invested in subsidies for nursery child-care
- lengthened maternity care from 14 weeks to nine months
- almost doubled maternity pay
- introduced the right for parents of young children to ask for **flexible working patterns** from their employers.

However, this explicit family policy has attracted New Right criticism that Labour had constructed a **nanny state** which over-interferes in personal living arrangements. Feminists too were critical of Labour social policy which they felt emphasised motherhood, rather than fatherhood or parenting in general.

Many prominent feminists, such as **de Beauvoir** (1953) and **Greer** (1971), have claimed that nuclear family ideology is merely **patriarchal ideology** – a set of ideas deliberately encouraged by men because it ensures their dominance in the fields of work, economics and politics. Family ideology is used to tie women to men, marriage and children and consequently females do not enjoy the same opportunities as men.

Barrett and McIntosh (1982) argue that familial ideology is anti-social because it dismisses alternative family types as irrelevant, inferior and deviant, e.g. as a result of the emphasis on the nuclear family ideal and the view that families need fathers, single-parent families are seen as the cause of social problems, such as rising crime rates and disrespect for authority.

Single-parent families

The fastest growing type of 'new' family is the one-parent or single-parent family. The number of single-parent families with dependent children has tripled from 2% of British households in 1961 to 7% in 2005. There are now approximately 1.75 million single-parent families in Britain, making up about 23% of all families. A third of all British Black families are headed by a never married woman. Recent projections estimate that one in three families (36%) may be single-parent by the year 2016. The great majority of single-parent families are headed by women (91%). There are a variety of reasons why single-parent families come about.

- Divorce and/or separation – 53% of lone mothers are divorced.
- Death of a husband, wife or partner – 6% of lone mothers are widowed.
- Unplanned pregnancy that may be the result of a casual relationship. The media tends to focus on the number of teenage pregnancies, although only 5% of lone parents are teenagers. However, one-third of lone mothers have never been married; 80% are under thirty years of age.

> Note that the New Right's focus on teenage pregnancies is exaggerated although Britain has a worse problem than most other Western societies.

> **KEY POINT**
>
> New Right thinkers such as **Murray** (1990) have suggested that single parents are at the heart of a so-called **underclass** or 'new rabble' that has appeared in the inner-cities. This group is allegedly socialising its children into a **dependency culture** based around voluntary unemployment, claiming benefits and crime. The New Right are also concerned about the high economic costs of single-parent families in regard to welfare payments and alleged social security fraud. This led to the setting up of the Child Support Agency (CSA) and the pursuit of absent fathers for maintenance.

However, New Right attitudes towards single-parent families have been heavily criticised by feminist and critical thinkers.

- **Chester** argues that the ideology of **familism**, which stresses the nuclear family ideal, has led to the negative labelling of single-parent families by social agencies such as teachers, social workers, housing departments, the police and the courts.
- Labelling may result in a self-fulfilling prophecy, e.g. housing officers may allocate single-parent families to problem housing estates because of negative stereotypes. Consequently, their children may come into contact with deviant behaviour and are more likely to be stopped by the police.
- Marxists suggest that single parents, especially teenage mothers, have been scapegoated by regular **moral panics** about social problems which are caused by structural factors such as unemployment, poverty, racism and the decline of the inner-city.
- Critical sociologists point out that there is little material incentive to become a single parent. The social and economic situation of many single-parent families is extremely disadvantageous, e.g. 17% of those officially classed as poor are single parents.
- Single parenthood may be a realistic strategy in areas characterised by poverty and high unemployment. Fathers may be deemed unnecessary by some young women because they cannot provide financial support. Moreover, single parenthood may be an escape from domestic violence.
- **Cashmore** (1985) and **Phoenix** (1993) argue that it is often preferable for a child to live with one caring parent than with parents who are in conflict with each other and who may scapegoat the child.

- Most single mothers eventually marry or re-marry. Single-parent families are likely to evolve into reconstituted families.

1.5 Gender roles and family life

<table>
<tr><td>**LEARNING SUMMARY**</td><td>**After studying this section, you should be able to understand:**

• the arguments for and against the view that modern marriage is egalitarian in terms of the distribution of child-care, housework and decision-making
• how family life might be a negative experience for some of its members</td></tr>
</table>

Conjugal roles: the division of labour in marriage

AQA **SCLY 1**   OCR **G672**

Functionalist sociologists such as **Parsons**, **Fletcher** and, especially, **Willmott and Young** suggest that industrialisation has led to an increase in **egalitarian marriage**, i.e. that the relationship between the spouses has become more equal in terms of participation in housework, child-care and decision-making.

KEY POINT

Willmott and Young in their study *The Symmetrical Family* (1973) claimed that the extended family was characterised by **segregated conjugal roles**, i.e. husbands went out to work whilst wives were exclusively responsible for housework and child-care. Moreover, husbands and wives spent leisure time apart. Willmott and Young argued that the extended family has been replaced by a privatised nuclear family characterised by **symmetry**. Modern marriage is characterised by **joint conjugal roles** meaning that women are now going out to work and men are doing a fairer share of domestic tasks. Moreover, couples were now more likely to share both leisure time and decision-making. Willmott and Young concluded that egalitarian marriage was the norm in the symmetrical nuclear family of the 1970s.

The major challenge to the concept of symmetry has come mainly, but not exclusively, from **feminist sociologists**. Several broad areas of critique can be discerned in the sociological literature.

- **Oakley** (1974) is critical of the **methodological shortcomings** of the Willmott and Young study. She suggests that their empirical evidence is unconvincing because it was based on only one question. Moreover, their study excluded younger married women who are more likely to have young children who tend to be more time-consuming.

- A range of surveys appeared in the 1980s and 1990s which demonstrated continuing inequalities in the distribution of housework and child-care between husbands and wives.

> **KEY POINT**
>
> - **Elston's** (1980) survey of over 400 couples, in which both partners were doctors, found that 80% of female doctors reported that they took time off work to look after their sick children, compared with only 2% of male doctors. Elston concluded that only a minority of professional couples in her study genuinely shared housework and child care. **Drew et al.** (1998) confirm these trends in the mid 1990s.
> - **Pahl** (1984) conducted a survey of 750 couples and discovered that unemployed men did more around the home, but wives, when they were in work, were still expected to be responsible for the bulk of housework.
> - The **Time Use Survey of 2005** carried out by **Lader et al.** (2006) found that women in paid work spent 21 hours a week on average on housework, compared with only 12 hours spent by men on the same. Overall, this survey found that 92% of women do some housework per day, compared with only 77% of men. In 2005, women still spent more time than men cooking, washing up, cleaning, tidying, washing clothes and shopping. DIY and gardening tasks were still male dominated.
> - **Gershuny** (1994) and **Sullivan** (2000) both suggest a trend towards equality in the share of domestic work because of the increase in the number of women working full-time. Gershuny's data suggests that the longer the wife had been in paid work, the more housework her husband was likely to do.
> - **Crompton** (1997) argues that as women's earning power increases relative to men's, so men do more housework. However, so long as earnings remain unequal so too will the division of labour in the home.

- Data from the **British Household Panel Survey** (2001) suggests that whatever the work–domestic set-up, women do more in the home than men. For example, when both spouses work full-time, and even when the man is unemployed and his wife works, women put more hours into domestic labour than men. This is known as the **dual burden or shift** – women are still expected to be mainly responsible for the bulk of domestic tasks, despite holding down full-time jobs. **Bittman and Pixley** (1997) suggest that this inequality is a major cause of divorce today.
- **Edgell** (1980) focused on the distribution of **power** within marriages. Edgell discovered that wives deferred to their husbands in decision-making about important issues such as buying a new house or moving job. Similarly, **Gershuny's** (1996) survey of young married couples with children concludes that the decision to have children, although jointly reached, dramatically changes the life of the mother rather than the father – especially in regard to career advancement.
- Women are also responsible for the emotional well-being of their partners and children. **Duncombe and Marsden** (1995) found that women are expected not only to do a double shift of both housework and paid work, but also to work a triple shift that includes soothing the emotions of partners and children. This

emotion work often leads to the neglect of women's psychological well-being and can have negative consequences for their mental and physical health.

- **Bernard's** study of marriage (1982) found that the men in her study were more satisfied with their marriage than their wives, many of whom expressed emotional loneliness. Moreover, these men had no inkling that their wives were unhappy.
- **Barrett** argues that patriarchal ideology expects women to take only jobs which are compatible with family commitments. Women are often made to feel guilty about working because they subscribe to the idea that it somehow damages their children.
- In the early 1990s, many sociologists concluded that the role of fathers was changing, e.g. men in the 1990s were more likely to attend the birth of their babies than men in the 1960s and they were more likely to play a greater role in child-care than their own fathers. **Burghes** (1997) found that fathers were taking an increasingly active role in the emotional development of their children, whilst **Beck** (1992) notes that fathers increasingly look to their children to give them a sense of identity and purpose.
- However, it is important not to exaggerate men's role in child-care. Child-care is still overwhelmingly the responsibility of mothers, rather than jointly shared with fathers. **Gray** found that many fathers would like to spend more time with their children, but are prevented by long work hours from spending quality time with their children.

Modern marriages, therefore, do not appear to be as equal as functionalists suggest. Furthermore, although this inequality may be partly responsible for the rise in divorce, many women often accept this inequality without question because they too have been socialised by patriarchal ideology into seeing such inequality as natural and normal.

The dark side of family life

AQA **SCLY 1**   OCR **G672**

Many commentators argue that the rosy picture of nuclear family life transmitted by functionalism and the New Right obscures the contradictions that permeate family life in reality.

- If we examine criminal statistics, a very negative picture of family life emerges. Most recorded murders, assaults and child abuse – both sexual or otherwise – take place within the **family unit**. Three-quarters of all violence is domestic (and these are only the reported cases). On average, one child a week in Britain dies at the hands of its parents, usually its father or step-father. Despite the problems in measuring the extent of **child abuse**, most experts agree that it is a major social problem today.
- The radical psychiatrists **Laing** (1970) and **Cooper** (1972) argue that the family 'terrorises' children by destroying their free will, imagination and creativity. Both suggest that the family is responsible for turning imaginative children into conformist automata. Laing suggests that schizophrenia is caused by experiences within the family. He argues that family relationships are potentially destructive because the intensity of nuclear family life means that we worry about how much we are loved by other family members, particularly our parents. Laing argues that as a result of these anxieties, family members become like gangsters, offering each other mutual protection and love to be used against other family members. Consequently, we become mutually suspicious of each other's motives and this becomes the basis of mental breakdown and family arguments and feuds which can last for years.

Domestic violence

The official statistics tell us that violence by men against their female partners accounts for one-third of all reported violence. **Stanko's** (2000) survey found that one incident of domestic violence is reported by women to the police every minute in Britain. **Mirlees-Black and Byron** (1999), using data from the **British Crime Survey**, found that women were more likely to suffer domestic violence than men – 70% of reported domestic violence is violence by men against their female partners. **Nazroo's** research indicates that wives often live in fear of men's potential domestic violence or threats, whilst husbands rarely feel frightened or intimidated by their wives' potential for violence. There are a number of explanations for domestic violence.

- **Gender role socialisation** – feminist sociologists note that boys are socialised into 'masculine' values which revolve around risk-taking behaviour, toughness, aggression and proving oneself. Violence for some men may be a product of such socialisation.

- **A crisis in masculinity** – some men may experience a 'crisis of masculinity', as working women and unemployment have challenged men's status as head of the household and breadwinner. Some men, therefore, may use violence to re-assert their masculinity and status within the family unit.

- **Alienation and powerlessness at work** – Marxist-feminists suggest that capitalism has stripped male workers of dignity, power and control at work. Marxist feminists, such as **Ansley** and **Feeley**, argue that men's frustration and alienation within capitalism is absorbed by the wife in the form of domestic violence. The powerlessness that men experience at work can be partly compensated for by asserting power and authority in the home.

- **A patriarchal society and police force** – feminist sociologists point out that patriarchal society has until fairly recently condoned male violence in the home. **Dobash and Dobash** argue that both the State and the criminal justice system have failed to take the problem seriously in the past, e.g. the police traditionally regarded it as a 'domestic' or private affair between husband and wife and were extremely reluctant to prosecute husbands.

- **Familial ideology** – the mother-housewife role carries with it certain cultural expectations which are largely defined by men. If a woman fails to fulfil these expectations punishment in the form of domestic violence may be forthcoming. Research indicates that men's view that women have failed to be 'good' partners or mothers is often used to justify attacks or threats. However, even women are influenced by this ideology – many of them blame themselves for their partner's violence.

PROGRESS CHECK

1. What do sociologists mean by the term 'symmetrical family'?
2. On what grounds did Oakley criticise Willmott and Young's study?
3. According to Dunscombe and Marsden, what does women's triple shift include?
4. What do the views of Leach, Laing and Cooper have in common?
5. Which approaches tend to overlook the 'dark side' of nuclear family life?

Answers: 1. A nuclear unit in which husband and wife increasingly share child-care, housework, decision making and leisure time. 2. On methodological grounds. 3. Housework, paid work and emotion work. 4. They are all extremely critical of family life. 5. The functionalist and New Right approaches.

1.6 Childhood

LEARNING SUMMARY

After studying this section, you should be able to understand:

- how the experience of childhood today is a fairly recent social construct
- the evidence that suggests that modern societies, such as Britain, are child-centred societies

Childhood as a social construct

AQA **SCLY 1**   OCR **G672**

Cunningham (2006) argues that the nineteenth century saw the **social construction** of childhood by adults. Childhood was seen to have three major characteristics.

- It was the opposite of adulthood – children were seen to be in need of protection, to have the right not to work and to be dependent on adults.
- The world of the adult and the world of the child were to be kept separate – the home and the school were regarded as the ideal places for children and they were often banned from adult spaces such as workplaces.
- Children were seen to have the right to 'happiness'.

Child-centred society

The emergence of a **child-centred society** in twentieth century Britain was the result of a number of related developments.

- Improved living standards in terms of wages, housing, sanitation, nutrition, hygiene and improvements in maternal health care led to a major decline in the infant mortality rate. People no longer needed to have lots of children in order to ensure that a few survived.
- As society became more affluent, so children were needed less as economic assets and raising children became more expensive. Parents therefore chose to have fewer children.
- The increased availability and efficiency of **contraception** allowed people to choose to have fewer children.
- Cultural expectations about childhood changed as the media defined childhood and adolescence as separate categories from adulthood. Parents came to see childhood as a special time in terms of love, socialisation and protection.
- The State became more involved in the supervision, socialisation and protection of children. The State supervises the socialisation of children through **compulsory education** which lasts 11 years. The role of social services and social workers is to police those families in which children are thought to be at risk. The government also takes some **economic responsibility** by paying child benefit to parents.
- The **Children Act** (2004) has produced the influential policy **Every Child Matters** which focuses on the well-being of children and young people from birth to age 19. This stresses 'better outcomes' for children, such as 'being healthy, staying safe', and 'achieving economic well-being' at the centre of all government policies. Increasingly, children have come to be seen by the State as individuals with rights.

The social construction of childhood is also illustrated by interpretivist sociologists who point out that the experience of childhood is shaped by the fact that the relationship between parents and children is a two-way process in which the latter can, and do, influence the nature and quality of family life. Research by **Morrow** (1998) found that children did not want to make decisions for themselves, but they did want a say in what happened to them.

The social construction of childhood argument also points out that childhood is not a fixed, universal experience. Rather, it is a relative experience dependent upon a number of social factors. This relativity of childhood experience can be illustrated in a number of ways.

- In many less developed nations, the experience of childhood is extremely different from that in the industrialised world. Many children in such countries are constantly at risk of early death because of **poverty** and lack of basic health care, clean water and sanitation. They are unlikely to have access to education and may find themselves occupying adult roles as workers or soldiers.

- Experience of childhood may differ across **ethnic** and **religious** groups, e.g. there is evidence that children in Muslim, Hindu and Sikh families generally feel a stronger sense of obligation and duty to their parents than White western children. Inter-generational conflict is therefore less likely or is more likely to be hidden.

- Experiences of childhood in Britain may vary according to social class. Upper-class children may find that they spend most of their formative years in boarding schools, whilst working-class childhood may be made more difficult by the experience of poverty.

- Experiences of childhood may differ according to gender role socialisation, e.g. there is some evidence that girls are subjected to stricter **social controls** from parents, compared with boys, when they reach adolescence.

- Some children's experiences of childhood may be damaging. Different types of child abuse have been re-discovered in recent years, such as neglect and physical, sexual and emotional abuse. Up to 30 000 children are on child protection registers, because they are at risk of abuse from family members.

However, New Right thinkers believe that children have been given too many rights in recent years and that it is wrong that parents are increasingly criticised and even punished for using sanctions such as smacking children. New Right thinkers believe that childhood is under threat because the period of innocent childhood has been shortened and because children have been exposed too soon to the adult world. This has occurred for a number of reasons.

- **Postman** (1982) sees childhood as under threat because television exposes them too soon to the adult world. **Palmer** agrees and claims that parents are too happy to use television, electronic games and junk food to keep children quiet and that parents are either too busy or too distracted by consumerism to give children a traditional childhood and family life.

- **Pugh** (2002) suggests that parental spending on children is 'consumption as compensation' – parents who are '**cash-rich but time-poor**' alleviate their guilt about not spending time with their children by buying them whatever consumer goods they want.

- Some sociologists are alarmed by the fact that children are being targeted by advertisers as consumers. They note that children aged 7–11 are worth about £20 million a year as consumers and consequently advertisers have encouraged children to use 'pester power' to train, or manipulate, their parents to spend money on them in return for love and status.

- **Phillips** believes that the media and the **peer group** have become more influential than parents and sees the media in the form of magazines aimed at young girls, pop music videos and television as a particular problem, because they encourage young girls to envisage themselves as sexual beings at a much younger age. These trends mean that the period of childhood has been shortened – it is no longer a sacred and innocent period lasting up to 13 or 14 years. Phillips argues that the increase in social problems such as suicide, eating disorders, self-harm, depression and drug/alcohol abuse among children is a direct result of these processes.

PROGRESS CHECK

1. What do sociologists mean by the 'social construction' of childhood?
2. Identify three social factors that influence how children experience childhood in Britain today.
3. According to New Right thinkers, why is childhood under threat?
4. Identify one way in which children might exercise power over their parents.

Answers: 1. Childhood is seen as a social invention rather than as a fixed experience for all children. 2. Three from: social class, gender, ethnicity, religion. 3. The period of innocent childhood has been shortened and children are now exposed to the adult world (e.g. via the media and advertisers) when they are too young. 4. Through pester power.

Exam practice questions

These are typical OCR questions. The AS Unit G672 requires you to answer any two questions from a choice of eight. Each question consists of two parts. You will have one hour and thirty minutes to answer your two chosen questions. Remember to allocate some of this time to planning your responses and reading through them at the end.

Remember to check how many marks are available for each sub-question and to allocate your time accordingly.

It is recommended that you spend 45 minutes on each of these questions; 15 minutes on part (a) and 30 minutes for part (b).

1. (a) Identify and explain two key features of the reconstituted family. **(17 marks)**

   (b) Outline and evaluate New Right views on the diversity of the family in contemporary Britain. **(33 marks)**

2. (a) Identify and explain two reasons for the ageing of the population in Britain. **(17 marks)**

   (b) Outline and evaluate the view that lone-parent families are dysfunctional. **(33 marks)**

Sample questions and model answers

A typical AQA question. You will have one hour to answer this style of question. Remember to allocate some of this time to studying the Items, planning your response and reading through it at the end.

Note how brief this response is. You should not over-respond to 2-mark questions in terms of time spent or length.

Other possible answers include:
- **Through its role in stabilising adult personalities.**
- **Through its reproductive role/role in the procreation process.**
- **By setting moral rules for adult sexual behaviour.**

Three clear reasons are provided. Other possible answers include:
- **Marriage is increasingly valued and therefore couples are no longer prepared to tolerate 'empty shell marriages'.**
- **As a result of the secularisation process, the religious barrier to divorce has become weaker.**

Remember to check how many marks are available for each question and to allocate your time accordingly.

Item A

According to Jon Bernardes, there are powerful lobbies in Britain which support and revere the ideal of the nuclear family. This ideal stresses a very traditional model composed of a married heterosexual couple with children and based on a sexual division of domestic labour.

Commentators such as John Patten, the former Secretary of State for Education, have complained about the 'terrible moral and social time bomb' caused by the State backing marriage less and less and the liberal laws which have allegedly resulted in dramatic increases in divorce. Consequently people are less committed to marriage and family life.

Item B

In sociology, there are different theoretical approaches to the study of families and households. Some approaches, such as the functionalist approach, view the family in positive terms as playing an essential role by performing key functions for society and for individuals. However, other perspectives are critical of the family and its role in society. The radical feminist approach, for example, sees the family as helping to maintain the system of patriarchy.

(a) Explain what is meant by 'patriarchy'. **(2 marks)**

The term 'patriarchy' refers to a system of male power and dominance over women, e.g. in the fields of politics, work and education.

(b) Suggest two ways in which the family can be seen as performing key functions for society. **(4 marks)**

One way is through its role in the primary socialisation of children so that they learn the norms and values of society. Another way is through its economic role, whereby parents take economic responsibility for their children by providing things that are vital for sustaining life, e.g. food and shelter.

(c) Suggest three reasons for the general increase in the divorce rate since the 1960s. **(6 marks)**

One reason is changing social attitudes to divorce which, in general, has become more socially acceptable and less stigmatised. A second reason is the changing social and economic position of women who are now less likely to be economically dependent on their husband and therefore less likely to be tied into an unhappy marriage. Finally, changes in legislation (e.g. the 1969 Divorce Reform Act) mean that it is now easier, quicker and cheaper to get divorced.

(d) Examine the ways in which feminist sociologists have contributed to our understanding of the family. **(24 marks)**

Feminist approaches in sociology focus on gender and how gender impacts on the lives of women and men. Such approaches are critical of the family and while radical feminists focus on the role of families in reproducing patriarchy, Marxist feminists focus on the role of families in reproducing capitalism.

One way in which feminists have contributed is by challenging the methodology or findings of more 'male stream' studies of the domestic division of labour. Ann Oakley, for example, criticised Willmott and Young's work on the symmetrical family because their findings did 'not justify their conclusions. A range of feminist studies have appeared in the last thirty years which demonstrate continuing inequalities in the distribution of housework and child-care within both working class and middle class families.

Another way in which feminists have contributed is by challenging the earlier functionalist approach's optimistic emphasis on the positive aspects of nuclear family life. Feminist research has highlighted domestic violence experienced by many women and children and men's power in decision-making, e.g. determining how household income should be spent. It has also shown how families actively contribute to the construction of gender through primary socialisation.

Feminist writers have been criticised for focusing on the negative side of family life, e.g. research indicates that many women enjoy occupying traditional roles. Hakim argues that women make rational choices to occupy these roles. However, feminism has made a major contribution to family sociology because it has shown how some features of family life can reflect power inequalities between men and women. It has also drawn attention to the need to get more men involved in family life and argued convincingly for changes such as paternity rights to take the strain off women. It has also raised consciousness regarding social problems such as domestic violence and child poverty and therefore has contributed to social policy and social change.

(e) Using material from Item A and elsewhere, assess the view that 'people are less committed to marriage and family life' (A) than they were 30 years ago. **(24 marks)**

Marriage and family life have undergone significant changes over the last 30 years. Increases in divorce, cohabitation and births outside marriage have resulted in greater family diversity, e.g. more lone-parent and reconstituted families. Sociologists disagree, however, on how to interpret these changes.

The New Right approach argues that the nuclear family is the ideal family type, but that nuclear family life is under threat because of these changes. Family values are declining, marriage is less popular and this has put the family in crisis. Writers such as Charles Murray would agree with the views of Patten in Item A, arguing that an underclass has emerged in Britain whose members are not committed to family values. New Right approaches are critical of government policies such as the liberalisation of divorce laws which, in their view, threaten marriage and family life.

Many sociologists such as Bernardes in Item A are critical of the New Right approach which reveres the ideal of the nuclear family. The Rapoports emphasise the diversity of family life in contemporary Britain. Others challenge the idea that people are less committed to marriage given that most people in Britain see marriage as desirable and actually get married. Chester argues that people are delaying rather than rejecting marriage. Similarly, cohabitation often takes place before marriage rather than being an alternative to marriage.

Post-modernists argue that the post-modern world is characterised by individualisation, conflict and greater choice in terms of lifestyles and living arrangements. Beck and Beck-Gernsheim argue that these three features have undermined marriage as illustrated by the rise in divorce. However, this does not mean that marriage is dying out because people seek marriage and love in order to compensate for the impersonality and uncertainty of the modern world.

In conclusion, sociologists agree that society and family life are changing. However, the different perspectives interpret such changes differently. While the New Right would agree that people are now less committed to marriage and family life, and that this is a problem for society, other sociologists would challenge this assertion.

2 Socialisation, culture and identity

The following topics are covered in this chapter:

- **Defining culture**
- **The process of socialisation**
- **Theories of self and identity**
- **Culture, socialisation and the formation of identity**
- **Leisure, consumption and identity**

2.1 Defining culture

LEARNING SUMMARY

After studying this section, you should be able to understand:

- the concept of culture and aspects such as sub-culture and diversity
- the role of values, norms, roles and status in the formation of culture
- different types of culture such as mass culture, high culture, popular culture and global culture

Culture and identity

AQA **SCLY 1**   OCR **G671**

> Socialisation, culture and identity are key themes in sociology.

Culture is generally defined as **the way of life of a society** – what **Kluckhohn** calls a 'design for living'. **Marshall** (1998) suggests that culture is socially transmitted rather than biologically transmitted in social science. By culture, he means the shared values, norms and beliefs of a society, as well as the shared meanings and symbols (such as language) which people use to make sense of their world.

> Know your concepts well.

KEY POINT

Values are defined as widely accepted beliefs that something is worthwhile and desirable, e.g. a high value is placed on human life. **Norms** are essentially values put into practice – they are the specific rules of behaviour relative to particular social situations, e.g. people generally wear black at funerals in Britain. Turning up in a pink tuxedo would be regarded as norm-breaking behaviour, i.e. as **deviant**. There are norms governing all aspects of human behaviour from going to the toilet to boiling an egg!

All members of society are accorded a social position by culture, i.e. **statuses**. Generally, sociologists distinguish between **ascribed statuses** and **achieved statuses**. The former are fixed at birth usually by inheritance or biology, e.g. in some societies, females do not enjoy the same rights and are treated as second class citizens, regardless of their ability. Achieved statuses are statuses over which individuals have control – in Western societies, status is achieved through education, jobs and even marriage.

Society expects those of a certain status to behave in particular ways. A set of norms is imposed on a status, collectively known as a **role**, e.g. doctors are expected by patients to maintain confidentiality and to behave professionally.

> This is often referred to as the nature/nurture debate.

Sociobiologists argue that human behaviour is largely the product of **nature**. However, sociologists generally agree that human behaviour is not instinctive like that of animals or birds. If human behaviour is influenced by biology at all, it is only at the level of physiological need, i.e. we must sleep, eat, defecate, etc. However, even these biological influences are shaped by **culture**, e.g. cultural values and norms usually determine what is eaten (e.g. insects are not popular foodstuffs in Britain), how we eat (e.g. table manners) and toilet behaviour. Human cultures are enormously diverse. Values, norms, statuses and roles differ from society to society. Sociologists believe that it is important not to see culture as absolute, fixed and universal.

Different types of culture

AQA **SCLY 1**   OCR **G671**

High culture is a set of values and activities which is mainly followed by the powerful and wealthy elite. It has a number of characteristics.

- It is seen as 'superior' to popular culture in terms of its content which is expressive-arts based, e.g. classic literature, poetry, classical music, opera, ballet and art.
- It is claimed that a particular type of education and taste is required to truly appreciate its merits.
- It is seen as more special and worthy because it represents a nation's cultural heritage.
- It is often sponsored by government because it is seen to be central to the intellectual and creative development of its citizens.

Popular, or **mass**, **culture** refers to a set of entertainment activities that all members of society have access to via television, cinema, pop music, popular literature, newspapers, magazines and so on. It too has a number of common characteristics.

- It is manufactured by media conglomerates for profit.
- It is seen as a form of 'low culture' in that it is seen as having little artistic merit or worth compared with high culture.
- It is within reach of ordinary people and forms an important part of their leisure activities.
- It has made a major contribution to how people shape their identities in modern societies, in that it has made people more aware of the variety of choices available to them.

Marxist sociologists believe that popular culture is an **ideological** tool of the ruling class which aims to keep the working class from thinking critically about their exploited and unequal position in society. Popular culture allegedly focuses people's minds on celebrities and materialism and undermines the capacity of the working class to think for themselves.

Other sociologists suggest that popular culture corrupts young people by providing them with deviant **role models**. **Hutton** (2010) suggests that popular culture undermines ambition because it suggests that hard work and education are less important than celebrity.

An important aspect of popular culture is **consumer culture**. Shopping has become a major leisure pastime because of:

- the development of out-of-town super-shopping centres and hyper-markets
- internet shopping
- the easy availability of credit cards between 1995 and 2009
- the emphasis on the **conspicuous consumption** of designer goods.

As recently as 1980, British culture was mainly **localised** in character, in that most of the goods consumed were produced, or manufactured, within British borders. However, it can be argued that Britain is now part of a **global culture**, in that consumption of food, drink, manufactured goods and popular culture is increasingly influenced and shaped by the growth in global media and advertising. **Post-modernists** believe that global culture is a positive development because society now has access to more choice and diversity in constructing our sense of personal identity.

Sub-cultures and cultural diversity

AQA **SCLY 1**   OCR **G671**

Many Western societies are now characterised by **cultural diversity** because of another aspect of **globalisation** – the mass migration of people around the world. Culturally diverse societies contain **sub-cultures**.

Sub-cultures are social groups that have features which set them apart from the mass of society. The most obvious example of sub-cultures are ethnic minority or religious groups that wish to retain their own values, norms, beliefs, customs and lifestyles, although sociologists have also observed sub-cultures based on social class and age.

However, most sub-cultures are usually committed to the wider social system in that they share many of the cultural values of the majority and conform to most social norms and rules such as the law. About 11% of British society is now composed of ethnic minority groups and consequently Britain is now commonly referred to as a **multicultural society**.

> **PROGRESS CHECK**
>
> 1. What is culture?
> 2. What is an ascribed status?
>
> Answers: 1. The way of life of a particular society. 2. A social position that is fixed at birth.

2.2 The process of socialisation

LEARNING SUMMARY

After studying this section, you should be able to understand:

- the difference between primary and secondary forms of socialisation
- the role of different agencies of socialisation
- how theories, such as functionalism and Marxism, view the socialisation process

Primary and secondary socialisation

AQA **SCLY 1**   OCR **G671**

Societies operate effectively because members of society learn culture which needs to be transmitted generation by generation to ensure that it is shared. Shared culture allows society's members to communicate and co-operate. The process of learning culture is known as **socialisation** – a process that involves internalising the norms and values of a culture so that ways of thinking, behaving and seeing things are taken for granted.

> **KEY POINT**
>
> The family, specifically the parents, is central to **primary socialisation**, which is the first stage in a lifelong process. Children learn language and basic norms and values. These can be taught formally, but they are more likely to be picked up informally by **imitating parents**. Parents may use **sanctions** to reinforce approved behaviour and punish unacceptable behaviour. Such processes help children learn about their role in the family and in society.

This links to material on families in Chapter 1.

For most children, the family is the key **primary agency of socialisation**. **Baumeister** (1986) notes that family socialisation provides children with a sense of **identity** in that they learn to be part of a family and have pride in a family name. Family socialisation also leads to conformity, control and the eventual production of law-abiding citizens.

- Many children successfully learn their family identity and social roles through imitative play, i.e. by copying the behaviour of role models such as their parents.
- Socialisation teaches children 'civilised' norms such as politeness and table manners.
- Socialisation involves children learning to conform to cultural expectations about feminine and masculine gender roles.
- Parents use disciplinary sanctions to reinforce and reward socially approved behaviour and to punish deviant behaviour.
- Such sanctions help children to learn the difference between 'right' and 'wrong', and to respect laws and rules by encouraging the development of a conscience in children so that the potential for deviance is deterred by feelings of 'guilt'.

Socialisation is successful when the child realises that the costs in terms of parental punishment outweigh the benefits of deviant actions and so they exercise self-control.

Functionalists, such as **Parsons**, see primary socialisation as a process essential to **value consensus** and **social integration**, and consequently, to **social order**. Parsons described the family as a 'personality factory' – the function of the parents is to mould the child's personality in the image of society. Socialisation fills the child with cultural values and norms in such a way that it assumes these values are its own values, therefore, feels a strong sense of belonging to society.

On the other hand, **Marxists** like Zaretsky suggest that the cultural values into which parents socialise their children are the product of ruling class ideology and are intended to make sure that children turn into conformist and passive citizens that never challenge the inequality and exploitation that underpins the organisation of capitalist society.

A range of other institutions participate in the socialisation of children – these are **secondary agencies of socialisation**. For example, schools, religion and the mass media all play a role in teaching society's members how to behave in particular formal contexts.

Education

Functionalist sociologists believe that education is an important agency of socialisation because it teaches children that society is more important than the individual. It does this in a number of ways.

- **Durkheim** believed that education links the individual child to wider culture and society by teaching him or her knowledge that celebrates the achievements of that culture or society, for example the teaching of history, religion or literature may encourage nationalist pride and a sense of belonging.
- Parsons believed that education teaches children that they need to look beyond their families and to be willing to play a positive role in society as citizens and workers. Consequently, children are socialised into universal values such as achievement and individualism by schools. They are socialised into competing with others for qualifications and jobs and into accepting that they should be objectively judged, evaluated and sifted on the basis of examinations so that only the most intelligent and talented are selected for the most important jobs.

Marxism sees education as an agency of secondary socialisation in a more critical light. **Althusser** suggests that education is an ideological state apparatus that aims to socialise children into a **hidden curriculum** – a capitalist **ideology** that encourages **conformity** and an uncritical acceptance of inequality.

The hidden curriculum encourages working class children to:

- Uncritically accept conditions of existence, such as inequalities of power and wealth, hierarchy, etc. as 'normal' and 'natural' so that these are never challenged.
- See educational failure as deserved because it stems from their own individual lack of effort, intelligence, etc. However, Marxists argue that schools are **bourgeois institutions** run by agents of capitalism – the role of the hidden curriculum is to **alienate** the children of the working class so that they leave education with few qualifications thus fulfilling capitalism's need for a manual labour force.

Religion

The functionalist Durkheim saw the major function of religion as socializing society's members into 'moral codes' which regulate our social behaviour with regard to crime, sexual behaviour and obligation to others. Religion socialises people into greater moral communities such as Christians, Muslims, etc. which also encourages belonging and identity.

By socialising people into moral codes, religion operates as an informal mechanism of social control.

Marxists, on the other hand, describe religion as an ideological apparatus that serves to reflect ruling-class ideas and interests. According to Marxists, religion socialises poorer sections of society into believing that their socio-economic conditions are a product of their own sin, wickedness, etc, that poverty and inequality are God-given, and unchangeable, and that if they put up with suffering in the here and now they will be rewarded in some afterlife. Marxists argue that such religious beliefs deter revolutionary actions.

The mass media

Some sociologists claim that the mass media constitute the most important secondary agency of socialisation today. The media often provide young people with role models and designs for living, i.e. images and ideas that they use to fashion their identities. However, functionalists and New Right thinkers are critical of the role of the media as the following examples illustrate.

- **Postman** sees mass media as responsible for cutting short children's childhoods by exposing them too soon to sex and violence.
- **Palmer** (2007) argues that modern parents are too willing to substitute mass media for quality parenting and this is responsible for the rise in anti-social behavior amongst the young.

Marxists are critical of the socialisation functions of the mass media because they believe it to be responsible for the emergence of popular or mass culture which:

- encourages consumerism and materialism, therefore, distracting poorer sections of society from questioning inequality
- has led to a decline in serious and critical media in favour of dumbed down mindless celebrity entertainment which discourages people from thinking for themselves.

> This links to material on childhood in Chapter 1.

The peer group

The **peer group** refers to people of similar status who come into regular contact with each other and exert influence on each other. They can be friendship networks, school sub-cultures and occupational sub-cultures, i.e. workmates.

Peer groups have a particularly strong influence over adolescent behaviour and attitudes and this **peer pressure** is often the cause of tension between teenage children and their parents. Some teenagers may feel that they have to engage in 'deviant' behaviour, such as drug taking, delinquency and sex, in order to be accepted by their peers. Friendship networks may also put considerable pressure on teenagers to conform by using negative sanctions, such as gossip and bullying.

> Look out for links between this material and any concepts and theories that you have studied elsewhere.

Occupational peer groups

The experience of the workplace teaches:

- skills
- work discipline
- the informal rules that underpin work
- professional ethics
- a sense of community.

Criticisms of the concept of socialisation

Socialisation is not always a straightforward and positive process because:
- not all adults acquire the skills needed to nurture children – poor socialisation often results in neglect or child abuse
- childhood socialisation is not as effective today, as it was in the past, because there are too many agencies of socialisation competing with the family
- interpretivist sociologists point out that socialisation is a two-way process and that parenting itself is a learning process.

2.3 Theories of self and identity

LEARNING SUMMARY

After studying this section, you should be able to understand:

- the concepts of self and identity and how they relate to society and culture
- the different theoretical conceptions (such as functionalist and Marxist) of self and how they relate to culture

Social identity

AQA **SCLY 1**   OCR **G671**

> Be able to distinguish between different aspects of identity.

Social identity refers to the personality characteristics that particular cultures associate with certain social roles, e.g. in our culture, mothers are supposed to be loving, nurturing and selfless. Women who are mothers will attempt to live up to this description and, consequently, will acquire that social identity. As children grow up, they too acquire a range of social identities, e.g. brother, sister, best friend, student. Interaction with others makes clear to them what our culture expects of these roles in terms of obligations, duties and behaviour.

Personal identity refers to those **markers of individuality** (**Fulcher and Scott**) which identify people as distinct from others, e.g. personal name, nickname, signature, photograph, address, national insurance number.

Self refers to an individual's subjective sense of his or her own identity. It is partly the product of what others expect from a person's social identity, e.g. a mother may see herself as a good mother because she achieves society's standards in that respect. However, self is also the product of how the individual interprets their own experience, e.g. some women may, in their own mind, have serious misgivings about whether they live up to society's expectations of mothers. The self, then, is the connection between social norms and the individual's interpretation of those norms.

Functionalism, self and identity

AQA **SCLY 1**   OCR **G671**

Functionalism is a **structuralist** theory, i.e. it sees the individual as less important than the social structure of society because the individual is viewed as the **product of society**.

Functionalists believe that society exists externally to the individual, e.g. people are born into society and play a role in it. Their deaths do not mean the end of society, which continues long after they are gone. Functionalists suggest that the social institutions that make up society are 'social facts' which exert a profound influence over human behaviour. Functionalists do not believe that people choose their own identities; rather these are imposed on us by the social institutions to which we belong which produce a **value** or **moral consensus** which provides guidelines for behaviour and therefore **social order** in society. For example, this consensus shapes our socialisation, through the family, education, religion and media into key values such as the importance of nuclear family life, achievement respect for authority.

Critique of functionalism

Functionalism is criticised on the grounds that it:
- presents 'an over-socialised' picture of human beings – it fails to acknowledge that culture is the product of human action and thought
- presents socialisation as a positive process that never fails – if this were the case, crime, child abuse, etc. would not be the social problems they are
- ignores the fact that power is unequally distributed in society – some groups have more wealth and power than others and can impose their norms and values on less powerful groups.

Marxism, self and identity

AQA **SCLY 1**   OCR **G671**

Althusser rejects the functionalist view that social institutions promote a common culture and argues that cultural institutions, such as the family, education, mass media and religion, transmit **ruling class norms** as 'normal' and 'natural'. The role of such institutions therefore is **ideological** because their aim is to convince members of society that their socio-economic position is deserved. This encourages **conformity**.

> **KEY POINT**
>
> Marxists argue that culture is the **net sum** of ruling class values and norms. Moreover, because the relationship between social classes is primarily economic, **work** is the major source of identity in capitalist societies. Social identity is dependent upon a person's **class position** and people's identities are judged according to what work they do and how much they are paid. Some members of the working class thus develop a low-status identity, e.g. they may feel deprived in terms of education and income, bored by the dead-end job they do or powerless to change their situation.

Be able to contrast this theory with functionalism.

However, Marxists, like functionalists, neglect the view that people can choose how to behave. Marxists too rarely acknowledge the idea that people create culture.

Interpretivism, self and identity

AQA **SCLY 1**   OCR **G671**

Interpretivist theories focus on the interaction between the individual and society and suggest it is this interaction that creates culture and identity.

An important aspect of interpretivism is **labelling theory**. This argues that some identities are constructed by the negative reaction of others. Interpretivists are generally critical of functionalist and Marxist theories of identity, because they believe that they under-estimate the role of **human consciousness, interpretation and social interaction** in the construction of identity, culture and society. From an interpretivist perspective, the human self is not shaped by social structure or social laws, rather it is the product of **free will**, that is the conscious and deliberate choices made by people who make up social groups such as the family.

Mead argued that the self is made up of two parts; the '**I**' and the '**Me**'. The 'I' refers to the spontaneous, and often selfish, part of the self which is normally powered by impulsive desires. However, we rarely act upon such desires because we are socially controlled and censored by the 'Me' part of the self. The 'Me' is the ability to see ourselves through the eyes of others and to understand how our impulsive desires might harm others.

Mead argues that interaction with others in social groups, like the family which make up society, involves the self constantly applying **symbolic meanings** or interpretations to the behaviour of others and deciding how to respond. This comes fairly easy to us because primary socialisation involves learning '**role-taking**', i.e. putting ourselves in the place of others and seeing ourselves as others see us. We learn to do this mainly through imitative play.

Goffman takes this one stage further when he notes that social life is **dramaturgical** – it is like a play with thousands of scenes. However, everyone knows their roles and their lines. Social life involves people playing hundreds of roles and through interpretation and interaction skillfully **managing the impression** others have of them.

> Becker's work is also relevant to the study of crime and deviance.

Becker notes how the media and **agents of social control**, such as the police and courts, may apply deviant labels to individuals acting outside the 'norm'. Deviant labels have the power of a '**master status**', e.g. the master status of 'criminal' can override all other statuses such as father, son, etc. Becker argues that such deviant labels can radically alter social identity, for instance someone labelled as 'criminal' may be discriminated against and thus find it difficult to regain an 'acceptable' social identity, e.g. 'worker'. They may end up seeking others with similar identities and values and form sub-cultures.

Interpretivist theories have been criticised because they tend to be very vague about who is responsible for defining acceptable norms of behaviour and fail to explain who is responsible for making the rules that so-called deviant groups break. They fail to explore the origin of power, and neglect potential sources such as social class, gender and ethnicity, e.g. Marxists argue that the capitalist ruling class is responsible. In other words, interpretivist theories largely ignore the influence of social structures on human behaviour.

PROGRESS CHECK

1. What do structural theories believe about culture and identity?
2. What theory argues culture reflects value consensus?
3. What theory believes culture is ideological?

Answers: 1 That they are structured by factors beyond the control of the individual. Society is more important than the individual. 2 Functionalism. 3 Marxism.

2.4 Culture, socialisation and the formation of identity

LEARNING SUMMARY

After studying this section, you should be able to understand:

- how different social class categories interpret identity
- the relationship of identity to gender and to sexuality
- how ethnicity and nationality influence identity and particularly the emergence of hybridised identities
- the relationship between disability and identity
- how age identities, particularly those related to youth, middle-age and old age, are constructed

Class identity

AQA **SCLY 1**   OCR **G671**

Working class identity

Be able to illustrate how social class shaped working class leisure, family life, etc.

KEY POINT

Fulcher and Scott point out that until the late twentieth century, people's identities and interests were tied up with the type of work they did and the work-based communities they lived in. In particular, the working class had a strong sense of their social class position. Virtually all aspects of their lives including gender roles, family life, political affiliation and leisure were a product of their keen sense of working class identity.

Lockwood argues that the **traditional working class** which was mainly employed in factories, mines, iron and steel mills and in shipyards saw manual work as a source of respect and masculine dignity. They defined themselves through their manual work.

Moreover, the fact that such workers relied on each other led to a strong sense of working class identity and solidarity which was expressed in a number of ways in the **workplace**.

- Manual workers were very **politicised** in their view of employer–employee relationships which were often seen in terms of 'them' (the bosses) exploiting 'us' (the workers).
- Many workers believed in 'collectivism' – the idea that the group's, or community's, interests should come before those of the individual.
- Manual workers were more likely to believe in **socialist** values, i.e. that people should be treated equally and fairly. and that income and wealth should be used to make sure that all sections of society, especially the sick, elderly and poor were taken care of and not exploited by those more powerful than themselves.
- Manual workers were usually members of **trade unions** which sought to protect the economic and social interests of workers and which engaged in industrial action, e.g. strikes, to protect those interests.
- Manual workers tended to vote in the interests of their class identity – this meant identifying with the **Labour Party** which traditionally supported the interests of workers.

- Manual workers often took their loyalty and commitment to each other beyond the workplace and into leisure time by socialising with each other in working men's associations and clubs.
- The traditional working class tended to live in **close knit** communities very close to where they worked.

Another very important agency of socialisation for the traditional working class was the **extended family**. Sociological studies such as **Willmott and Young's** study of extended families in the East End of London, suggested that such families socialised their members into the following values and norms.

- A strong sense of **duty** and **obligation** to other family members expressed by seeing extended kin on a regular basis and the existence of a mutual support system, i.e. helping out with child-care services, finances and helping kin find work.
- **Segregated conjugal roles** in that a working class man's identity was closely wrapped up with providing for the family by being the breadwinner, whereas the women's identity was strongly shaped by her responsibility for child-care and housework.
- Education was not a priority because boys expected to follow their father into the factory or the mine, whilst girls expected to become wives and mothers.

However, this traditional working class identity started to go into decline in the 1960s because of the decline in heavy manual work and factory work – manual workers in these industries now only make up a fraction of the workforce. Later in the 1980s, with the **feminisation** of the economy, new jobs in factories and offices were mainly for women workers.

The 'new' working class

A **new working class** is thought to have appeared in the 1970s which largely replaced the traditional working class (although elements of the latter persist in some areas such as the North, South Wales and the East End of London). This new working class is thought to have the following characteristics.

- It works in the newer manufacturing industries which are often non-unionised and situated in the south of England.
- It is **instrumental** in that it sees work as means to an end, i.e. money and affluence, rather than as a source of identity or community. It therefore does not automatically identify with or see itself as working class.
- It has no developed sense of 'them' versus 'us'. It is not hostile to capitalism and it can see the benefits of capitalism in terms of improving its living standards. It is therefore not as politicised as the traditional working class.
- It is **individualistic** rather than collectivistic – such workers put self and immediate family before community and other workers.
- It does not automatically identify with Labour. Rather it votes for whichever party increases its standard of living.
- It is **privatised** – this type of worker is very focused on spending time and money in the home.

The underclass

Some sociologists have identified a third type of working class identity in the twenty-first century – the **underclass**. There are two broad sociological views of this underclass which is made up of those on the margins of society, i.e. the long-term unemployed and poor. This latter group may be made up of the low-paid, the elderly, the sick and disabled, single mothers, etc.

- Sociologists such as **Charlesworth** and **Jordan** argue that people are in poverty because of **structural influences** beyond their control such as globalisation or recession. Unemployment, and living on benefits, often results in loss of self-respect and dignity, feelings of shame, hopelessness and helplessness, as well as physical and mental problems with health.
- New Right sociologists, such as **Murray**, see membership of the underclass as a voluntary choice of those who are happy to be part of a culture of idleness and immorality, and dependent on welfare benefits and crime for their income.

The upper class

If we examine the **upper class** in Britain, we can see that they share a number of common characteristics.

- Most members of the upper class are usually extremely wealthy. In 2008, 42% of all financial **wealth** Britain was owned by 5% of the population; the top 1% owned 22% of total wealth. Most wealth in Britain is inherited, although about 30% is self-made.
- The upper class generally share a common background – it is mainly made up of a fairly small number of wealthy extended families often inter-connected by marriage. Parents strongly encourage their children to choose partners from other upper class families. This ensures that the upper class is a self-selecting and exclusive elite which is closed to outsiders. This process is known as **social closure**.
- Children are socialised by upper class families into a culture of privilege and social superiority through exposure to nannies, servants, rules of etiquette, etc. Families socialise children into high cultural pursuits, e.g. classical music, ballet or opera, as well as exclusive sports such as shooting, polo and show jumping.
- The upper class family socialises its children into a very distinct set of upper class values, such as respect for tradition, being conservative or anti-change, thinking that authority, hierarchy, inequality, etc. are good things, that good breeding (i.e. being born into particular families, going to the right schools and following etiquette) is the most important characteristic of a human being.
- The upper class share a common background in terms of education at public schools and Oxbridge. **Scott** argues that the main purpose of these schools is to mould the ideas and outlooks of their pupils so that they quickly realise their common upper class interests and see themselves as the future leadership of the country.
- The school peer group leads to 'old-boy' or 'old-school tie' networks which operate informally in adulthood to further contacts, careers and wealth.

There is little evidence that **upper class identity** has changed dramatically in the last 100 years. The evidence suggests that they have consolidated their position, both in terms of wealth and **political power**, as seen in the number of politicians in the 2010 Coalition government that come from privileged and wealthy upper class backgrounds.

The middle classes

The term 'middle classes' is used in a broad way to describe a range of non-manual workers that includes:

- a wealthy managerial and financial elite responsible for running the top companies and banks
- professionals such as surgeons, doctors, barristers, accountants, teachers
- middle managers
- the self-employed
- white-collar or office workers.

In terms of pay and status, these groups have little in common. However, there may be some shared values and norms especially amongst the less wealthy and lower status middle class groups such as:

- a focus on home ownership
- a suburban home-centred lifestyle
- a strong **meritocratic** belief in further and higher education
- the need to communicate social position to others through, e.g. moderate conspicuous consumption, such as having the 'right' type of car
- a concern about what other people think and a fear of acute social embarrassment.

Professionals

Savage notes that professionals see their **identity** as shaped by their job and consequently they value **cultural capital** assets, such as knowledge and qualifications. Furthermore, many professionals tend to subscribe to **altruistic** values – they often put service to society before financial rewards – but they expect to exercise **discretion** at work in return, i.e. to be able to make decisions without deferring to a higher authority.

Managers

Savage argues that middle managers, on the other hand, often lack qualifications – their position is usually the result of experience gained in a particular job. Savage found that this group defined its identity in terms of **standard of living** and leisure pursuits rather than the status of their jobs. However, they are less secure in their jobs compared with professionals and often encourage their children to go into higher education so that they train to be professionals.

The self-employed

Roberts argues that the self-employed tend to be more **individualistic** than the other middle class groups They believe that people should be independent and stand on their own feet rather than rely on the Welfare State. They also have great faith in hard work and discipline – they firmly believe that success in life is a result of effort and application rather than luck.

White-collar workers

Some sociologists, notably **Braverman**, have questioned the middle class status of white-collar workers, especially those who work in call-centres, whose pay and working conditions are not dissimilar from those who work in factories. However, surveys of clerical workers indicate that they still see themselves as middle class. They rarely mix with manual workers, and spend their leisure time and money in quite different ways.

Consumption

Consumption cleavage refers to the social and economic divisions created by the way goods and services are consumed.

Some sociologists in the 1990s argued that class has ceased to be a prime determinant of identity and that societies are now organised around **consumption** rather than production. They suggest that people now identify themselves in terms of what they **consume** rather than their social class position, e.g. **Saunders** (1990) argues that society is now characterised by a major **consumption cleavage** – a division between those who mainly rely on the market for work and those who rely mainly on the State, i.e. the underclass, which is workshy and welfare dependent.

Post-modernism

Post-modernists argue that identity in the twenty-first century has fragmented into numerous separate identities. Social identity is now more pluralistic, e.g. **Pakulski and Waters** (1996) argue that social class is no longer important as a source of identity, because people can now exercise more choice about what type of people they want to be. Gender, ethnicity, age, region and family role interact, and impact, with consumption and media images to construct post-modern culture and identity.

However, are post-modern ideas exaggerated? **Marshall's** research indicates that members of a range of classes are still aware of class differences and are happy to identify themselves using class categories. Marshall does concede that workers today are largely indifferent about capitalism and therefore less likely to subscribe to 'them versus us' attitudes. Finally, post-modernists conveniently ignore that for many, consumption depends on having a job and an income, e.g. poverty is going to inhibit any desire to pursue a post-modern lifestyle, i.e. consumption and social class are closely related.

Gender identity

Sociologists distinguish between 'sex' and 'gender'. **Sex** describes the biological differences between males and females, e.g. chromosomes, hormones and genitals. **Gender** refers to the cultural expectations attached to how males and females are supposed to behave.

> **KEY POINT**
>
> Sociologists argue that gender is socially constructed rather than biologically determined. In other words, **nurture** is more important than **nature**, e.g. feminist sociologists see gender as shaped by a social and cultural environment dominated by a **culture of patriarchy**. Gender expectations regarding masculine and feminine identities are transmitted to the next generation through **gender-role socialisation**.

Sociologists have noted the existence of a set of hegemonic, or culturally dominant, ideas or **stereotypes** about how masculine and feminine identities should be organised which have only been challenged in the last few decades.

- Families should be organised according to a 'natural' sexual division of labour in that men should be breadwinners, protectors and heads of households whilst women should primarily be mothers and housewives, i.e. the nurturers or emotional caretakers.

- Men have patriarchal power and consequently dominate decision-making, whilst women are subordinate and should defer to men.
- Men are active sexual predators. Women who behave in similar sexual ways to men are labelled as sexually deviant.
- Women are mainly judged in terms of their looks and bodies whereas men are judged on a greater range of criteria, e.g. intelligence and skills.
- The use of violence is a legitimate problem-solving device for males.
- Females are handicapped by their emotions whereas men are rational and objective in their outlook.

The family

From an early age, people are trained to conform to social expectations in regard to gender behaviour. Much of this training goes on in the family during primary socialisation, e.g. people use gender-oriented terms of endearment when talking to children, they dress boys and girls differently and sex-typed toys are given to children. **Oakley** (1981) identifies two processes central to the construction of gender identity.

- **Manipulation** – how parents encourage or discourage behaviour on the basis of appropriateness for the sex.
- **Canalisation** – how parents channel children's interests into toys and activities seen as normal for that sex.

These types of gender reinforcements are extremely powerful. Oakley notes that by the age of five, most children have acquired a clear gender identity. They know what gender they belong to and have a clear idea what constitutes appropriate behaviour for that gender.

Education

Other agencies of secondary socialisation also contributed to the construction of these traditional gender identities. Studies of education in the 1970s suggested that teachers and schools saw female education, especially in the sciences, as less important than male education. **Sharpe's** survey of working class girls in the early 1970s found that such experiences meant that female identity revolved around love, marriage, husbands, children, jobs and careers more or less in that order.

Gender identity and social change

Four major changes occurred in the late twentieth century which have challenged traditional notions of masculinity and femininity and led to new forms of gender identity.

- The primary and secondary sectors of the British economy went into decline because of global recession causing a massive rise in male unemployment. This undermined the traditional male identity which was mainly shaped by work and the breadwinner role. **Mac An Ghaill** argues that such changes in the economy have led to a **crisis in masculinity** and that this has made worse social problems such as domestic violence, boys' underachievement in education, and crime, anti-social behaviour and suicide amongst young men.
- As heavy industry and manufacturing declined, there was a rise in demand for tertiary or service sector jobs which are mainly focused on the consumption of services and information. The public sector (i.e. state-sector jobs in health,

education, etc.), the retail sector and the financial services sector recruited female workers in large numbers. This feminisation of the workforce meant that large numbers of women postponed having families in favour of having careers.

- There is some evidence that this feminisation of the economy and the positive female role models led to what **Wilkinson** calls a **gender quake** – a radical change in attitude towards feminine identity among more recent generations of girls. Sharpe's repeat of her 1970s survey in the mid 1990s suggests that girls' priorities have drastically changed and education, careers, and independence are now the defining features of young women's identity and self-esteem. This genderquake can particularly be seen in the British education system – girls now out-perform boys at every stage of education.

- **Post-modernists** argue that society today is characterised by greater choice and diversity because of globalisation and greater levels of consumption. They suggest that increasing economic independence for women means they are now viewed as significant consumers by the mass media and that consumption and leisure are now the most significant shapers of masculine and feminine identity. Such processes have supposedly led to the emergence of **girl power** and **ladettes** who are increasingly adopting male forms of behaviour, e.g. they drink and smoke heavily and they are sexually aggressive. Other commentators have noted the emergence of the male **metrosexual** who pays more attention to personal grooming and of a more caring and sensitive **new man** who is responsive to women's needs and emotions.

Critiques of changing gender identities

Delamont is sceptical of claims that feminine and masculine identities have radically changed. Delamont notes that the mother–housewife role is still regarded as the most important identity for women and this is reflected in the fact that women, rather than men, are expected to take extensive time out of employment to nurture and look after children. Most studies of family life show that equality in terms of the distribution of childcare tasks between the sexes is a myth.

This links to the debates on the domestic division of labour in Chapter 1.

Moreover, studies of mass media representations suggest that even in 2010 women are over-represented in domestic settings as housewives, mothers, consumers and sex objects. Women are rarely shown in high-status occupational roles and when they are, they are often portrayed as unfulfilled. Delamont argues that **patriarchy** is still deeply embedded in modern culture and suggests that consumption and choice are only **temporary phases** that young women go through before they settle down to the culturally expected paths of relationships and motherhood.

Sexual identity

AQA **SCLY 1**

In Britain, **heterosexual identity** has been traditionally defined as the dominant and ideal form of sexuality because of its links to reproduction. In contrast, homosexuality was seen in the early part of the twentieth century as a form of criminal and abnormal sexuality, and it was consequently punishable by law. However, by the 1990s, a distinct gay sub-culture and identity had emerged in British culture for several reasons.

This links to material in Chapter 1.

- Homosexual acts between consenting adults were gradually de-criminalised to the extent that homosexuals are now permitted to enter into a type of marriage – the **civil partnership**.

- Cultural attitudes towards homosexuality began to shift. The decision of people in the public eye to come out as homosexual probably made it more socially acceptable.
- Gay professionals have a great deal of spending power and the leisure industry targeted the **pink pound** from the 1980s onwards.
- Gay culture became **politicised** from the 1970s onwards as gay organisations, such as Stonewall, sought changes in the law so that homosexuals enjoyed the same rights as heterosexuals.
- In cities such as London, Brighton and Manchester, **Gay Pride** marches sought to increase the visibility and social acceptability of gay people.

However, it is important not to exaggerate the degree of change. Western societies like Britain are still characterised by a fierce **compulsory heterosexuality** which is mainly transmitted through the mass media, e.g. homosexuality is rarely portrayed as a normal or ideal condition and there is continuing evidence of **homophobia** in the world of business, sport and politics. Religious organisations too continue to criticise homosexuality as sinful, wicked and immoral. Homophobic attacks on gay people are still relatively common and suggest that this type of sexuality is not totally accepted by all sections of the community.

Ethnic identity

AQA **SCLY 1**   OCR **G671**

Sociologists note that significant numbers of people in Britain share an **ethnic minority identity**, i.e. they share sub-cultural characteristics that distinguish them from the majority White Anglo-Saxon culture. These characteristics may include:

- physical characteristics, e.g. skin colour
- geographical links and identification with a mother country
- a common history
- a common language used in the home other than English
- religious beliefs
- traditions and rituals passed down the generations
- experience of racism.

In Britain, ethnic minority identity is mainly associated with **ethnic sub-cultures** from the former British colonies on the Indian sub-continent, in the Caribbean and in Africa. However, this categorisation ignores significant White minority ethnic groups resident in Britain, such as Jews, gypsies and Irish people.

Asian identity

Ghumann's (1999) work on Asian sub-cultures and identities suggests that the following sub-cultural values are transmitted to British Asian children during primary socialisation in the family.

- Social conformity in terms of obedience, loyalty and respect, particularly to elders and the community around them.
- Duty and obligation to the extended family community.
- The maintenance of **family honour**.
- Deferring to parents with regard to decision-making whatever the age of the child, especially with regard to negotiated arranged marriages.
- **Bi-lingualism** – the mother tongue is seen as essential in maintaining links between the generations.

Religion has a very important influence as an agency of socialisation in shaping the identity of young Asians. **Modood** (1997) found that 67% of Pakistani Asians in Britain agreed that religion was very important to how they lived their lives, compared with only 5% of young Whites. Modood notes that religion permeates Muslim identity in Britain to the extent that it influences:

- dress codes, e.g. the burqa, niqab and hijab
- diet, e.g. only halal meat may be eaten
- education, e.g. an increasing number of children are attending Muslim schools
- an adherence to religious codes as an ethical way of life, e.g. regularly attending the mosque, praying
- political consciousness, e.g. many young Muslims may identify with other Muslims world wide, especially those seen as oppressed in places such as Palestine, Iraq and Afghanistan rather than with their fellow Britons
- male–female relations, e.g. women may be seen as primarily suited to domestic rather than public roles
- family lifestyles, e.g. marriage to non-Muslims is rare, divorce is seen as bringing disgrace.

African-Caribbean identity

With regard to African-Caribbean identity, Modood (1997) found that some African-Caribbean youth celebrated their skin colour as an expression of Black pride and power in reaction to their experience of racial prejudice and discrimination from White society.

On the other hand, **Sewell** (1996) sees six factors as important in shaping the identity of young African–Caribbean males in inner-city areas.

1. The lack of a positive **father-figure** role model in their lives. Many African-Caribbean males come from single-parent families headed by females who lose control of their male teenage children.
2. A negative experience of **education** which probably resulted in under-achievement in terms of qualifications and/or exclusion.
3. A negative experience of life on the streets in terms of regular and negative contact with the police with regards to **stop and search**.
4. A perception that society is **racist** in that it discriminates against them, which is reinforced by their experience of unemployment.
5. A celebrity driven consumerist culture which implies that **materialism** in the form of designer goods is all important and consequently possession of such goods is crucial in gaining respect from their peers.
6. A peer group pressure in the form of gang membership which stresses the use of violence to 'prove' one's masculinity and to gain respect.

Hybrid ethnic identities

Some sociologists note that ethnic identities are evolving and modern **hybrid forms** are now developing among Britain's younger ethnic minority citizens.

Recently, sociologists have observed that **inter-marriage**, especially between Whites and African-Caribbeans, has increased considerably. As a result, mixed-race children now outnumber children born to African-Caribbean couples. **Tizard and Phoenix** (1993) found that mixed-race children experienced racism from both White and Black populations.

Johal (1998) focused on second- and third-generation British-Asians and found that some have a **dual**, or **hybrid identity**, in that they inherit an Asian identity and adopt a British one. This results in Asian youth adopting aspects of White British culture in order to enhance their interaction with their White peers and teachers, but emphasising their cultural difference when it is necessary, e.g. through their dress or social behavior such as not drinking alcohol. They may talk to each other in a combination of English and their home language, as well as constructing an identity using aspects of British, Asian and global culture relating to fashion, music and food.

National identity

AQA **SCLY 1**

National identity is the sense of purpose that results from a feeling of belonging to a larger community in the form of a nation.

According to **Guibernau and Goldblatt**, British national identity has been gradually created over the past 300 years by eight key influences.

1. **The political and legal system** – before 1707, England and Scotland were separate nations with completely different identities. The countries of Wales and Ireland were separate entities until they were conquered and colonised by the English.
2. **Geography** – the fact that Britain is an island has resulted in its people seeing Europe as a distinct and separate entity. Few British people consequently identify with Europe or see themselves as European.
3. **Language** – the global use of English as the language of business, entertainment, the Internet, etc. has contributed our keen sense of British cultural identity.
4. **Religion** – although Britain is increasingly becoming secular, religion still plays a central role, e.g. 'God Save The Queen' is the national anthem.
5. **War** – the British have been remarkably successful at waging war over the past 300 years and this has contributed to the feeling that there are uniquely British values such as fair play, self-sacrifice and putting up with exceptional hardship.
6. **The British Empire** – Britain's success as an imperial power in the eighteenth and nineteenth centuries brought both economic success and a sense of pride and achievement in what was perceived as British superiority over other cultures.
7. **Monarchy** – the Royal Family, and particularly the Queen, are potent symbols of British identity today.
8. **Symbols** – particular symbols and places such as the Union Jack, drinking tea, red buses, Buckingham Palace and Big Ben are specifically associated with British identity in both the eyes of the British people and foreigners.

Schudsen (1994) points out that the British people are socialised into a British identity in several ways.

- **Education** – the teaching of history, English literature and religion in British schools promotes national identity.
- **The mass media** – newspapers and television promote British identity in a number of ways. The media report on the royal and state occasions that underpin the British way of life, e.g. the Cenotaph ceremony on Remembrance Sunday, the State Opening of Parliament, royal weddings and funerals, and the Queen's televised Christmas speech. The media report the activities of

the Royal Family in considerable detail. The media also play a key role in reinforcing our sense of national identity by talking up British achievement. In times of war, the media focus on 'our boys', while sporting events such as the Olympic Games are reported almost as quasi-wars against other nations.

- **The political and legal systems** – aim to protect the legal and human rights of those who have British nationality, e.g. possession of a British passport means that the British State will assist a citizen who gets into trouble in another country.
- **Families** – generally tend to promote a British identity by teaching children British values and norms, language, diet, traditions and rituals. We usually take all these things for granted and their **Britishness** is not clear to us until we travel abroad and experience foreign values, norms and traditions.

Sociologists, such as **Waters** (1995), suggest that British identity may be under threat in the twenty-first century for a number of reasons.

- Many citizens of Britain, defined as British in the law, identify with **nations within the nation**, i.e. they see themselves primarily as English, Scottish, Welsh or Irish.
- Celtic identity, especially Welsh and Scottish identity, has always been a powerful source of competing national identity to Britishness, e.g. the majority of Welsh language speakers see themselves as Welsh, rather than British. Welsh identity is expressed through the Welsh education system which stresses the teaching of Welsh history and literature, and a specifically Welsh mass media encompassing newspapers, television, radio and rock music. Similar institutions exist in Scotland celebrating Scottish culture. Furthermore, a great deal of political power has been devolved to the Welsh Assembly and Scottish Parliament.
- Research by **Curtice and Heath** (2000) suggests that about six million adults in England identify themselves as 'English' rather than 'British'. About one-third of this group, known as **Little Englanders**, admit to being racially prejudiced, to being against **multiculturalism** and to being anti-Europe.
- Many British subjects may see their national identity as primarily tied up with their country or region of origin and so see themselves as African-Caribbean, Punjabi, Bengali, Pakistani, etc. Others may subscribe first and foremost to identities deriving from their religious affiliations, such as Muslim or Jewish. **Modood** (2005) found that Asians and African-Caribbeans did not feel comfortable with a 'British' identity, because they felt that the majority of White people did not accept them as British because of their colour and cultural background.
- **Globalisation** may be undermining British identity because transnational companies (TNCs) and international financial markets, rather than specifically British companies and products, increasingly dominate world trade. Global, especially American, culture is dominating the British high street through companies such as McDonald's and Starbucks. There are fears that the entertainment or popular culture to which young people subscribe, e.g. in terms of film, music, television and social networking sites is less and less British and more and more a single commercialised global culture.

Some post-modern sociologists claim to have observed new **hybrid types** of British identity slowly emerging which are shaped by an interaction between British traditions and global influences. They suggest that a number of factors have resulted in greater opportunities and choices being available to people which have influenced how people see their national identities.

- The **mass media** has become globalised in that events from across the world are now often reported as they happen. The British people through satellite television and the Internet are now exposed to a greater range of cultural and religious influences than ever before.
- Cheap air travel and the consequent greater number of British people travelling abroad have broadened our **cultural experiences**.
- **Multiculturalism** has led to new home-based experiences in terms of the food and drink choices available in shops, restaurants and takeaways. It is also normal for young White people to be exposed to multicultural and global influences through their everyday contact with their ethnic minority peers in schools and colleges. As a result, they tend to be more receptive than their older relatives to these new experiences. Such globalised experiences mean that 'British' identity is probably in a state of flux today.

Disability

AQA **SCLY 1**

Most sociologists distinguish between **impairment** – an abnormal functioning of the body – and **disability** – a person's inability to fully participate in everyday activities that others take for granted. There are two broad sociological approaches to disability; the biomedical and social constructionist approaches.

The **biomedical approach** sees the identity of disabled people as a product of their physical or mental condition. It sees disability as:
- a personal tragedy which deserves both the pity and charity of the able-bodied
- a condition of dependence where it is assumed that disabled people cannot function effectively without the assistance of able-bodied people.

However, the **social constructionist approach** suggests that whilst impairment is a problem, disability is mainly caused by social reaction – stereotypical and negative **social attitudes** held by the able-bodied about disability. As **Oliver** argues, the physically and mentally impaired are disabled by society. It is this **social disability** that shapes the disabled identity in modern societies because prejudices about disability lead to forms of **discrimination** and **exclusion** which make it impossible for disabled people to follow 'normal' lifestyles.

Moreover, **Shakespeare** points out that society seems to have adopted a relativist approach to disability in that some types of impairment, e.g. short-sightedness and old age are socially judged to be less deviant or abnormal than others such as being confined to a wheelchair. Consequently, society has produced a social and physical environment in which people who use wheelchairs are more likely to be judged as disabled than those who are short-sighted.

The negative social reaction to disability has a number of possible origins.
- **Finkelstein** (1980) has suggested that our negative cultural attitudes towards disabled people stem from capitalism's need for a healthy and fit workforce that could be exploited in order to generate profits and wealth for the capitalist class. Ruling class ideology emphasised the dignity of work as a source of identity, status and power. Consequently, those who did not fit the definition of 'healthy' and 'fit', i.e. disabled people, were soon labelled as a social problem, as an economic burden and as inferior in terms of their contribution to society.
- **Longmore** found that disabled people were generally negatively represented in films and television drama as evil or maladjusted inhuman monsters who are both dangerous and deviant. When disabled people are portrayed as

courageous, the able-bodied are encouraged to see their condition as tragic. Charity and pity are seen as the 'normal' responses to their condition. The disabled identity is nearly always presented as a problem by the mass media. Disabled people are rarely portrayed as individuals or as personalities who just happen to also have a physical impairment. The emphasis on performing family roles to the best of our abilities may result in people fearing disability because they believe that they would not be able to provide for their families.

- The family socialisation process involves learning to avoid certain types of behavior because of the **social embarrassment** that might result. This creates the potential for ignorance about disability as the able-bodied become uncomfortable in the company of people with disabilities and, in their social embarrassment fail to ask how disabled people interpret the world around them.

Discrimination towards people with disabilities can take several forms.

- The **physical environment** may prove an obstacle to their ability to take part in everyday activities, e.g. wheelchair users may not be able to access buildings, toilets, shops and public transport.
- People with disabilities may be rendered invisible as they are **segregated** from able-bodied people in terms of education, sport, etc.
- Employers may not treat applications for jobs from disabled people seriously.
- Social workers and other professionals may discourage disabled people from long-term relationships with other disabled people. They may discourage disabled people from having sex and having children because they believe that they are not responsible enough to cope. Disabled women have been sterilised against their will in the past and have had their children taken into care.
- Disabled people are often treated in **patronising** ways by other people in social situations, e.g. a person in a wheelchair may be ignored altogether because it is assumed that they are incapable of normal interaction.

Watson argues that the disabled identity can be undermined by such prejudices and discriminatory practices. Disabled people may respond to the constant assumption that they are helpless and dependent by developing low social esteem and worth. They learn that they should be helpless because this is what the experts expect. This **learned helplessness** becomes the dominant aspect of the disabled person's identity and the master status of **dependency** shapes all interaction between the disabled person and others. All other aspects of that disabled person's identity and personality are subordinated to the notion that they are incapable of leading independent lives.

However, there are signs that some disabled people are resisting prejudices and stereotypes. Disabled campaigners now openly promote independence, choice and autonomy for disabled people. There are also signs that prejudice, discrimination and the physical environment are being addressed by the able-bodied.

Age identity

AQA **SCLY 1**   OCR **G671**

It is a fact that Britain segregates its members by age – how young or how old people are has a significant influence on their identity. Although biology is important in this process, sociologists suggest age identities are **socially constructed**. They are the product of social factors such as attitudes, e.g. in both pre-industrial societies and modern societies, young people go through the biological experiences of puberty and adolescence. However, teenagers are not recognised as a distinct category in pre-industrial societies because as soon as a child enters puberty, he or she is defined as an adult with adult responsibilities.

Bradley notes that in modern societies, such as Britain, five ages, or generational, identities can be identified.

> Remember that the participation age has been raised and all teenagers will remain in education or training until the age of 17 from 2013 and 18 from 2015.

1. **Children** – childhood is regarded as an innocent period in which children are vulnerable and in need of protection and care. **The State** supports parents in this respect by regulating the quality of parenting and prosecuting those guilty of neglect or abuse. The State also defines what social behaviour is culturally expected from children through its insistence on compulsory education between the ages of 5 and 16 and by defining when children become responsible for criminal offences.

2. **Youth** – in Britain youth is generally regarded as covering the teenage years and 18 years is the age at which the State confers legal adulthood via being able to vote, to marry or leave home without parental consent and to sit on a jury.

Many sociologists have noted that family tensions are often experienced as young people strive for more independence and responsibility as adults, but are still dependent on their parents for their economic maintenance usually because they are still in full-time education. Sociologists have suggested that the emergence of **deviant youth cultures**, from the 1950s onwards, is the means by which young people cope with the anxieties and tensions created by the transition from childhood to adulthood.

Functionalists, such as **Eisenstadt**, argued that youth cultures are functional, or beneficial, to society because they help teenagers cope with the **status contradictions** and **powerlessness** that they experience within the family and wider society. Getting together with their peers and celebrating aspects of teenage identity, such as fashion or music, help negotiate the difficult path between childhood and adulthood and help to gradually introduce teenagers to their adult responsibilities.

Marxist sociologists, on the other hand, have focused on working class deviant youth sub-cultures such as teddy boys (1950s), mods and rockers (1960s), skinheads (1970s), punks (late 1970s) and ravers (1980s/1990s). Marxists suggest that these can be seen as a form of **ideological resistance** to the dominant adult value system shaped by middle class and capitalist values. They argue that youth sub-cultural styles use **symbolism** through dress and music to shock and resist an oppressive capitalist system.

> Cohen's work is also relevant to the study of the mass media and crime and deviance.

Other sociological studies of the mass media have focused on how youth is demonised by the mass media. **Cohen** argues that the media often defines youth as a social problem and creates **moral panics,** or social anxiety, about the behaviour of young people and that this results in teenagers being labelled as **folk devils**, i.e. as dysfunctional, deviant and in need of social control.

However, studies of young people suggest that the alleged generation gap implied by moral panics is exaggerated. Very few young people have got involved with deviant youth sub-cultures. Most young people are generally conformist – they get on well with their parents and place a high value on traditional goals such as getting married, having children and buying a house.

3. **Young adulthood** – young adulthood refers to the period between leaving the parental home and middle-age. **Pilcher** suggests that adult identity revolves

around living with a sexual partner, having children, having a job and maintaining a home. **Hockey and James** (1993) see it as bound up with having freedom and independence from parents, having control over material resources and having responsibilities.

4. **Middle-age** – there are physical indicators of middle-age, e.g. greying hair, the appearance of the 'middle-aged spread' and the menopause in women, as well as social indicators, e.g. children leaving home to go to university or having more money for leisure pursuits. There may even be emotional or psychological indicators, i.e. the mid-life crisis.

5. **Old age** – this period officially and legally begins at 65 years in Britain, when people are expected to retire from paid work and state pensions are paid. Evidence suggests that in contrast to pre-industrial societies, the elderly in Britain are not accorded a great deal of respect or status, because work is the major source of status in industrial societies. Loss of work due to retirement can result in a significant decline in self-esteem, social contacts with others and income, as well as a consequent rise in loneliness, poverty, depression and poor health in general.

> Changes to the state pension age were announced in 2010. It is important to keep abreast of such changes, e.g. by reading a quality newspaper.

Ageism

There is significant evidence that the elderly suffer from **ageism** – the offensive and negative exercise of prejudice and discrimination based on the view that the greater one's age, the lesser one's ability and reasoning. Such ageism takes a number of forms.

- It is often **institutionalised** in the practice of government and other organisations, e.g. the elderly may be excluded from work and jury service or denied particular types of medical help.

- **Arber and Ginn** (1993) suggest that ageism against the elderly is reinforced and perpetuated by employment practices such as redundancy, unemployment and retirement.

- **Bradley** (1996) notes that old people are often seen by employers as less suitable for employment because they are assumed to be physically slow, lacking in dynamism and not very adaptable to change.

> Rather than lumping all 'old people' together, some commentators distinguish between the 'young old' (65–75) and the 'old old' (late 70s plus).

- It is often expressed through the **stereotypical prejudices** that underpin everyday interaction, especially derogatory name calling which stereotypes and marginalises old people as inferior.

- Mass media representations, especially in advertising, reinforce the view that the appearance of youth is central to looking good and that ageing should be resisted at all costs. **Sontag** (1978) suggests that there is a double standard of ageing especially in television, whereby women are required to be youthful throughout their media careers, but men are not.

PROGRESS CHECK

1. What has allegedly replaced social class as a major source of identity?
2. What is meant by the 'crisis in masculinity'?
3. What are hybrid identities?
4. What is globalisation?
5. How does the social constructionist approach view disability?

Answers: 1. Consumption. 2. The idea that young men's traditional sense of masculine identity is under threat from changes in the nature of work and relationships. 3. New identities that draw on two or more different cultures. 4. The process by which national boundaries are becoming less important and inter-connections between societies are increasing as the same consumer goods, brands and economic interests spread across the globe. 5. As caused by social reaction.

2.5 Leisure, consumption and identity

LEARNING SUMMARY

After studying this section, you should be able to understand:

- the relationship between leisure, consumption and identity
- how age, social class, gender and ethnicity influence the relationship between leisure choices and identity

Defining leisure

AQA **SCLY 1**

Leisure generally means the time in which individuals are free from other social obligations, especially work. **Fulcher and Scott** suggest that it is normally a time of freedom, individual choice, self-expression and creativity. However, it is not a straightforward phenomenon to define.

Parker (1971) points out that work and leisure are only two categories of 'life space'. There are also 'intermediate categories' such as eating, sleeping and attending to hygiene, which are physiological needs.

Thompson (1967) suggests that industrialisation is responsible for the division of time into work and leisure. Parker argues that the major influence on leisure is work and notes that there are three types of relationship between work and leisure.

- The **extension pattern** where work spills over into leisure time. People who fit this pattern generally enjoy their work. They enjoy the creative aspect of work and are generally workaholics.
- The **neutrality pattern** where family life and leisure become the major life interests because work is regarded as generally unfulfilling and even alienating.
- The **opposition (segmentalist) pattern** where leisure compensates for the hazards and physical demands of dangerous jobs, e.g. people may compensate for the stresses of a dangerous job by drinking heavily.

However, Parker is criticised for ignoring other factors which impact on leisure, e.g. the influence of **social class** and the availability of material resources such as income and wealth. He fails to examine the impact of poverty on people's leisure choices. He also neglects the leisure patterns of women, i.e. he fails to examine the impact of housework and motherhood on women's experience of leisure.

Marxist theories of leisure

AQA **SCLY 1**

Sociologists who adopt a Neo-Marxist approach draw on the theories and concepts of Karl Marx (1818–83), but apply these to contemporary capitalist societies.

The **Neo-Marxists**, **Clarke and Critcher** (1985), suggest that leisure is shaped and constrained by **capitalism**. They argue that there are three important influences on leisure.

- The State plays a central role in **regulating leisure activities** through the law and policing of public space such as streets and parks. The State also promotes and subsidises bourgeois leisure activities, e.g. high culture such as opera, theatre and ballet because they are seen as more 'civilised' and worthy than working class activities such as sport.
- Leisure has been transformed by capitalism into a **commodity** and consumers of leisure are exploited in a similar way to workers, e.g. working

class pubs have been commercialised by big business in the form of brewers. Capitalist leisure industries have created false leisure needs using intensive media and advertising campaigns.

- The **material conditions** of the working class prevent them from making real leisure choices. They may lack the material resources to join health clubs, play golf and visit the ballet.

Feminist theories of leisure

AQA **SCLY 1**

McIntosh (1987) argues that most theories of leisure neglect the influence of **gender** and argues that men and women take part in very different types of leisure activity, probably as a result of **gender role socialisation** and **patriarchal** influences, e.g. some sports do not welcome the participation of females. Consequently, men and women have different leisure interests, e.g. shopping is a leisure activity associated with females.

Women tend to have less access to leisure activities than men – probably because men have more time and financial resources for leisure. Most time outside paid work for women with children is not leisure time, but dominated by domestic responsibilities. These often blur the distinction between work and leisure for women. **Green, Hebron and Woodward** (1987) suggest that women's leisure is constrained by patriarchal influences outside the home too, e.g. fear of attack narrows leisure options in the public sphere for women.

Post-modern theories of leisure

AQA **SCLY 1**

Post-modern theories of leisure focus on the **consumption** patterns of individuals. They suggest that the individual has many more leisure choices because of new technologies, especially in the field of media. This is reinforced by the **globalisation of culture** via the new technologies of digital and satellite television and the Internet. Leisure experience is no longer tied to a particular time or place. People now use leisure time and activities to construct unique lifestyles and social identities for themselves. They are no longer constrained by social class, gender and ethnicity.

Bocock (2004) argues that the expansion of media outlets in recent years, and especially the Internet, has resulted in more choices being available with regard to how we use leisure to construct identity. Popular media culture is used more extensively by individuals today to help shape their identity. Global media has brought people into contact with a greater range of cultures and as a result people 'pick and mix' from local and global influences to create their own unique and individualised identity.

Post-modernists also suggest that shopping has become a major leisure activity in recent years because there has been a globalisation of consumption. Global advertising and production of designer goods and logos have become the norm. Post-modernists believe that shopping is now also part of how people construct their identity. It is about buying into a particular lifestyle. Particular goods have symbolic significance in that the label or brand has become more important than the product itself. This is known as **conspicuous consumption**.

The post-modern argument is mainly centred on young people because they are the main target of most advertising campaigns. This is because they have fewer financial commitments than other age groups in terms of mortgages and children, and therefore, have more money to spend on leisure.

Criticism of post-modernist theories of leisure

Critics of post-modernism, such as **Scraton and Braham** (1995), note that class, gender and ethnicity are still very influential in how people experience leisure.

- For many women, leisure is influenced by the fact that they have less disposable income than men and that their domestic responsibilities mean that leisure time is not clearly defined.
- Social class also constrains, e.g. access to post-modern forms of leisure is heavily dependent on a relatively high income. The post-modernist view that consumption shapes identities only applies to those with the money to consume. This obviously depends on occupation and social class position.
- Ethnicity, too, may constrain leisure choices and identity, e.g. high unemployment, poverty in inner-city areas and racism can negatively affect ethnic minority leisure choices. Leisure choices may also be shaped by cultural and religious traditions. Some Asian women may be restricted in their choice of leisure activities because they are restricted to the home. Young British born ethnic minorities may be taking part in **hybridised leisure activities** that are less constrained by their parental cultures although these may bring them into conflict with their parents.

Exam practice questions

Question 1 is a typical AQA question on Culture and Identity.

1 Read Items A and B and then answer parts (a)–(e).

Item A

Feminist sociologists focus on social inequalities based on gender. They distinguish between sex and gender and examine the ways in which gender is socially constructed, e.g. they explore how agencies of socialisation such as families, the mass media and the education system, contribute to the process of gender socialisation.

Item B

Social class has long been seen as the main source of social identity for most people in Britain. Working class culture, in particular, was located within localised occupational communities. On the whole, working class culture was characterised by a shared view of the world and a common set of norms and values. Individuals gained their sense of identity from belonging to such communities.

However, more recently, post-modernist theories have suggested that social class is no longer significant as a source of identity because individuals can now exercise more choice about the type of person they want to be.

(a) Explain what is meant by 'norms'. (Item B)	**(2 marks)**
(b) Explain the difference between sex and gender. (Item A)	**(4 marks)**
(c) Suggest three ways in which young people may be influenced by peer groups.	**(6 marks)**
(d) Examine the contribution of functionalism to the sociological understanding of the process of primary socialisation.	**(24 marks)**
(e) Using material from Item B and elsewhere, assess the view that social class is no longer significant as a source of identity.	**(24 marks)**

Questions 2 and 3 are typical OCR questions.

2 Define the concept of ethnicity. Illustrate your answer with examples.	**(8 marks)**
3 Outline and explain how any two agencies of socialisation transmit values and norms.	**(16 marks)**

3 Education

The following topics are covered in this chapter:

- Educational social policy
- The role and purpose of education
- Differential educational achievement

3.1 Educational social policy

LEARNING SUMMARY

After studying this section, you should be able to understand:

- the structure and organisation of the education system including different types of school
- the significance of educational policies, especially those focused on selection, comprehensive education, equality of opportunity, vocational education and training, marketisation and parentocracy

Educational social policy: 1944–79

AQA **SCLY 2**   OCR **G673**

> **KEY POINT**
>
> The period 1944–79 was predominantly a **social democratic** era concerned with providing **equal opportunities** for groups such as the working class, females and ethnic minorities.

Remember that OCR unit G673 is synoptic. When revising this topic, think about the links with other topics and with concepts such as power, control and inequality.

The **Education Act** (1944) aimed to abolish class-based inequalities within education by making secondary education **free for all**. The basic principle underpinning the Act was **equality of opportunity for all**. All children would take an IQ test at 11 (**the 11+**) in order to allocate them to a school suited to their abilities. The Act aimed to provide three types of secondary school (the **tripartite system**): the grammar school for the academic (20% of pupils); the secondary technical for the practical (5%); the secondary modern for everyone else. All schools were supposed to have similar standards of provision, i.e. **parity of esteem**.

Criticisms of the tripartite system

Some felt that the 11+ tests were not a reliable measurement of intelligence. They were accused of being **culturally biased** against working class children because of the number of working class children disproportionately selected for the secondary moderns. Moreover, working class self-esteem was damaged by the poor image of the secondary moderns. Employers, parents and children generally viewed these schools as inferior to grammar schools. Pupils were seen as 'succeeding' if they went to the grammar schools and 'failing' if they went to the secondary moderns. Many middle class children who failed the 11+ were sent to schools within the private sector.

By the mid 1950s it was generally felt that this social policy had failed in its aims. Educational attainment was overwhelmingly class-based as most working class children left school at 15 and entered work, whilst middle class children continued into further and higher education.

Comprehensive schools are secondary schools. The education system is structured into five stages:
1. Early years education.
2. Primary education.
3. Secondary education.
4. Further education (FE).
5. Higher education (HE).

Comprehensive schools

> **KEY POINT**
>
> In 1965 as an attempt to apply the principle of equality of opportunity for all, the Labour Government abolished the tripartite system (although some Conservative councils resisted and 130 grammar schools continue to this day). The **comprehensive system** was introduced, based on the principle that there should be one type of school which should educate all children, regardless of social background and ability, under one roof. The general aims of such a system are to promote equal opportunities, social justice and greater tolerance of others.

Arguments in support of comprehensive education suggest that:

- Comprehensives often exist alongside both grammar schools and private schools which 'cream-off' the most able pupils. Despite this, educational standards in the form of exam results have actually improved since the 1960s according to data from the National Children's Bureau.
- There is no evidence that high-ability children are held back by comprehensives. On average, they make about the same amount of progress in reading and maths as grammar school pupils with the same IQ.
- Lower ability children do better in comprehensives than they did in secondary moderns. Furthermore, **McPherson and Williams'** data suggests that the achievement of working class children rose faster than any other social group between 1976 and 1984.

Arguments against comprehensive education suggest that:

- Class differences have largely remained unchanged. **Heath** (1982) concludes that comprehensive reorganisation has had little effect on the social class inequalities that existed before 1965. Exam results have got better, but the **gap** between top and bottom has more or less stayed the same. However, is it fair to expect schools to compensate for inequalities which are caused by the organisation of society?
- Many comprehensives **stream** their pupils. Evidence indicates that streaming results in social-class segregation. Working class pupils are disproportionately found in lower streams and thus may be labelled as failures. Streaming is criticised as a form of social selection – the tripartite system under one roof.
- Comprehensives recruit on the basis of **catchment areas**. This has often led to **intakes** being 'single-class' rather than socially mixed. Schools in more affluent areas with mainly middle class intakes tend to do better than schools in depressed inner-city areas with largely working class intakes.
- Inner-city comprehensives have attracted a great deal of negative publicity for declining standards in terms of exam league table positions, truancy, failed inspections, discipline problems, large class sizes, etc.

Educational social policy 1979–97

AQA **SCLY 2**   OCR **G673**

> **KEY POINT**
>
> The period 1979–97 was mainly concerned with linking education to the demands of the **free-market economy**. Aspects of the education system such as the curriculum, qualifications and teaching were reorganised by Conservative governments in an attempt to raise standards and produce a more flexible workforce.

Economic recession and rising unemployment, especially amongst youth, led to a fundamental change in educational social policy in the 1970s. Some politicians, especially the Labour Prime Minister James Callaghan, and Margaret Thatcher (who became Conservative Prime Minister in 1979), suggested that poor education was a major cause of Britain's industrial decline.

During 1979–97 Conservative governments made radical changes to the organisation of schooling in order to fulfil three aims. In brief, these were to:
(i)   increase employability
(ii) raise standards
(iii) create an education market.

(i) Policies to increase employability

The New Right claimed that the British workforce lacked technical skills needed by industry and that schooling should be more relevant to work thereby producing the skills required by industry to make Britain more competitive in the global marketplace. A number of training and education schemes were developed which became collectively known as the 'new vocationalism'. These aimed to make young people more **employable** by giving them work experience.

These schemes included college and school-based courses such as:
- **National Vocational Qualifications (NVQ):** job-specific qualifications studied part-time or on day-release in colleges whilst employed.
- **General National Vocational Qualifications (GNVQ):** studied in school as an alternative to academic courses. They include qualifications in Health and Social Care, Leisure and Tourism, Business, etc.

Moreover, **Youth Training** expanded in the 1980s. After 1987, young people could be denied state benefits if they refused to take part in this scheme.

Criticisms of the 'new vocationalism'
Marxists are particularly critical of the **new vocationalism** and especially Youth Training.
- **Cohen** argued that the real function of YTS was to cultivate in young people conformist attitudes, work discipline and the acceptance of a future of low-paid and unskilled work with frequent bouts of unemployment and job changes.
- **Green's** research indicated that most schemes resulted in low-ability trainees getting low paid jobs which were relatively unskilled and insecure.
- Vocational schemes help to legitimise class divisions because they encourage the idea that the working class are trained whilst the middle class are educated. In this sense, they operate as a form of selection.
- **Feminist** sociologists note that vocational training has done little to break down the gender stereotyping found in the economy. **Buswell** argues that such schemes actually reinforce such stereotyping by encouraging girls to go into retail work.

(ii) Policies to raise standards

To take more centralised control of the curriculum and teaching methods in order to raise standards and increase efficiency. The **1988 Education Reform Act** was the most important piece of educational policy since 1944 and focused on centralising state regulation of education in six ways.

SATs tests have been heavily criticised. Consequently, testing at 7, 11 and 14 has now been abolished in Wales.

- A **national curriculum** was introduced based around three core and seven foundation subjects for pupils aged 5–16. This policy shifted power over teaching and content from teachers and examination boards to the government.
- **National tests (SATs)** at 7, 11 and 14 were introduced. The results of these (along with other criteria such as GCSE, A Level and truancy statistics) are published annually as part of **league tables** that aim to compare the performance of schools.
- Responsibility for managing school budgets was largely removed from local authority control and given to head teachers. This was known as **local management of schools (LMS)**.
- Comprehensive schools were allowed to **opt out** and become **grant-maintained schools** (GM schools) on the basis of a majority parental vote. The head teachers of such schools were given complete control over the school budget and how their schools were organised and run.
- **City Technology Colleges** (CTCs), specialising in the arts, maths, science and technology, were set up in inner-city areas. These were independent of local authorities and supposed to be financed by private industry.
- A new system of school and college inspection was introduced, i.e. OFSTED to make sure that they met certain standards.

(iii) To subject education to marketisation

The marketisation of education refers to the policy of bringing market forces (such as choice and competition) into education.

Conservative governments encouraged diversity through specialisation, by providing greater diversity and particularly a wider **choice** for parents, e.g. by 1996 there were 15 CTCs and over 180 language or technology colleges. **Selection** too was encouraged in a number of ways. The 130 grammar schools continued undisturbed alongside the comprehensive system and a **private sector**. GM schools were allowed to introduce parental interviews and tests in order to select their intakes.

Parentocracy refers to the rise of parent power in schools.

Parental power, or **parentocracy**, was encouraged in that parents were given the right to send their children to the school of their choice – 'open enrolment'. Schools now had to **compete** for students and league tables and school prospectuses were published to assist **parental choice**.

The critique of marketisation

Whitty (1998) claims that **marketisation** has contributed to the worsening of class differences in education. He focuses on three aspects.

1. League tables have led to the high-ranking schools becoming more selective and consequently their intakes have become more middle class. The number of pupils claiming free school meals in such schools is very low. By contrast, those schools ranked low in the league tables are unable to select – they have no choice but to accept less able working class pupils. This is **self-fulfilling** in terms of exam results and makes it very unlikely that such schools can climb the league tables and become more attractive to middle class parents.
2. Schools are allocated funds according to how many pupils they attract. Popular schools therefore get more money and can afford quality resources and teaching staff. Unpopular schools attract less funding and therefore have less money to spend on resources such as books and teaching staff.
3. Marketisation creates the myth that all parents have the same choices and that the British education system is a true parentocracy. However, working class and ethnic minority parents (especially of low-ability or special needs children) do not have the same choices in terms of which school to send their

children because of the selective practices used by some schools. In addition to this, middle class parents have the knowledge and confidence (i.e. **cultural capital**) as well as the **economic** capital to get their children into the schools of their choice. Furthermore, if they are unhappy with the state system, they can often afford to send their children to fee charging schools in the private education sector.

Educational social policy 1997–2010

AQA **SCLY 2**   OCR **G673**

In 1997 New Labour were elected and, generally speaking, their educational policy retained the New Right emphasis on selection, standards, choice and diversity. For example:

- Grant–maintained schools were renamed **foundation schools**. They no longer received grants from central government but they still retained special status and therefore had a great deal of autonomy in how they recruited and selected pupils.
- Labour inherited nearly 200 **specialist schools** from the Conservatives. Labour encouraged more schools to specialise in particular subjects and consequently 2500 have re-invented themselves as 'colleges' specialising in art, business, maths and computing, languages, music, science, sport, etc. Specialist schools can raise money from business sponsors and select up to 10% of their pupils who show ability in the specialist subject.
- **Grammar schools** continue to exist and select on the basis of the 11+ exam.
- Labour made no attempt to abolish or reform **private education**.
- In an attempt to apply tighter control over quality and standards, some schools were publicly identified as underachieving ('naming and shaming') in regard to poor exam results, high rates of truancy and exclusion and discipline problems.

> Grammar schools are selective. Other types of school include faith schools, private schools and special schools.

However, New Labour's educational policy is distinctive in some respects from previous Conservative governments – leading some commentators to describe it as a 'third way'. In particular, Labour's educational policy was based on the concept of **social inclusion**, which argued that education, especially at the further and higher levels, has traditionally excluded certain disadvantaged groups, e.g. the unemployed, single mothers, the elderly. Labour therefore argued that choice and diversity in education should be accessible to all social groups – this was known as **widening social participation**. The following educational social policies were introduced with this in mind.

- The **New Deal for Young People** aimed to improve educational and training opportunities for the long-term unemployed and single mothers by giving them financial assistance and personal advisors to attend further education for 12 months and work for six months. However, refusal to take part resulted in loss of benefits.
- The Labour government set a target of 50% of young people to be in higher education by 2010. This was partly going to be done via widening social participation – encouraging bright working class and ethnic minority students to go into higher education by providing them with financial support.
- At the further education level, widening social participation in higher education was encouraged by the **Aim Higher** programme which aimed to raise the aspirations of pupils, particularly those from ethnic minority backgrounds and by the introduction of the Education Maintenance Allowance (EMA).

> Try to keep up-to-date with current educational policies, e.g. in 2010 the coalition government announced plans to withdraw the EMA.

- Excellence in Cities was a £350 million programme which led to the creation of 'education action zones' in six major cities in which extra help was given to underachievers in schools. In particular, Academies were to be built in partnership with businesses in deprived areas to replace failing comprehensive schools which would attract the best heads and teachers.
- Sure Start – in some deprived areas, free nursery education became available along with children's centres to compensate for disadvantages such as poverty.

PROGRESS CHECK

1. What does the term 'marketisation of education' refer to?
2. What is the goal of 'widening participation' policies?

Answers: 1. The policy of bringing market forces into education e.g. by increasing parental choice and competition between schools. 2. To increase the participation of under-represented groups (such as working class, minority ethnic and mature students) in higher education and ensure equality of opportunity for all.

3.2 The role and purpose of education

LEARNING SUMMARY

After studying this section, you should be able to understand:

- different sociological explanations of the role of education
- how to define and illustrate the concept of 'the hidden curriculum'
- the relationship between education, training and the economy
- the concept of 'meritocracy'.

The functions of education

AQA **SCLY 2**   OCR **G673**

KEY POINT

Most sociologists agree that formal education systems are essential because children and adolescents need to be taught the knowledge and skills required to function effectively as workers and citizens. From Key Stage 1 to university, children and young adults experience a teaching and learning process focused on the acquisition of knowledge and the testing through examinations of the ability to understand and apply that knowledge. However, this process is not the sole purpose of education. Most sociologists agree that there also exists a **hidden curriculum** which involves children and adolescents learning (often without realisation) a range of values, norms, rules and unwritten assumptions that result in social conformity and generally obedient citizenship.

The 'hidden curriculum' refers to the things that are learnt in school (such as valuing punctuality or obedience) that are not formally taught as part of the official, or National Curriculum.

Both **functionalist** and Marxist sociologists agree that education (and consequently, the hidden curriculum) in modern societies such as Britain has three broad functions as described below. Functionalists generally see these functions as benefitting society as a whole. However, Marxists see these functions as benefitting only the wealthy and powerful, i.e. the capitalist bourgeoisie and suggest that such functions actually have a damaging effect on the working class.

In brief, the following three functions relate to:

(i) secondary socialisation
(ii) the economic role
(iii) selection and allocation.

(i) Education as a secondary agent of socialisation

You can link this to material in Chapter 2 on socialisation.

Functionalists see education as an essential agency of **secondary socialisation** whose function is to transmit common values to the next generation – a process crucial to the maintenance of **value consensus** and therefore **social order** in society.

Parsons argued that schools act as a bridge between the family and wider society. In families, children learn that their status and relationships with others are shaped by '**particularistic**' standards, i.e. they are loved regardless of ability. However, functionalists point out that if society is to operate effectively, members of society need to learn '**universalistic**' values and standards, i.e. that they will be judged by the same criteria as everyone else. Therefore, the role of education is to promote **universal values** such as achievement, individualism, competition and particularly equality of opportunity, i.e. the idea that everybody has an equal chance of getting on.

Durkheim too argued that education is a crucial agency of socialisation because it is central to the **reproduction of culture** and therefore **society**. He argued that the teaching of subjects like English, history and religious education is central to **social solidarity** because it enables children to feel a sense of pride and belonging to society. Moreover, he believed that education could promote social solidarity by promoting moral responsibility towards others, citizenship, tolerance and diversity.

However, Marxists such as **Althusser**, argue that education is an **ideological state apparatus** (like religion and the mass media) whose main function is to maintain, legitimate and reproduce (generation by generation) ruling class ideology as well as social class inequalities in wealth and power.

Althusser believed that the hidden curriculum was central to this ideological process which aimed to:
- promote ruling-class values as common values
- justify, or legitimate, class inequality as 'normal' and even 'natural' by encouraging those who under-achieved in the education system (who were mainly from working class backgrounds) to believe that failure and the resulting inequality they experienced were the product of individual shortcomings and therefore deserved and accepted without challenge.

Althusser identified two ways in which the hidden curriculum promotes capitalist values as common values, as well as convincing the working class that the capitalist system is fair and natural.
- Through the **knowledge** which is taught in schools Althusser argued that students rarely come into contact with ways of thinking that are critical and which challenge inequality. In particular, Marxist thinkers have criticised the national curriculum because potentially critical subjects such as economics, politics and sociology were deliberately excluded from it for ideological reasons.
- Through the ways that schools, teaching and learning are internally **organised** Althusser argued that the everyday rules and routines of schools transmit very different messages to middle class and working class pupils about the purpose of school. Formal and informal rules in schools serve to train children to accept without question authority, hierarchy, inequality and the idea that failure is self inflicted, whilst the way in which teaching and learning is organised rarely invites pupils and students to challenge or criticise dominant definitions and perceptions of knowledge. Furthermore, devices such as streaming and examinations serve to convince working class pupils (who tend to be disproportionately allocated to lower streams or sets or to

under–perform in exams compared with their middle class peers) that their knowledge and experiences are irrelevant and to accept failure as their fault.

Consequently, Marxists see the main purpose of education as the reproduction of a capitalist system underpinned by extreme inequalities in wealth and power. Moreover, the way the educational system is organised handicaps working class pupils, therefore producing a ready-made manual and factory workforce. However, this workforce passively accepts its subordinate social and economic position and inequality in general, because it has been socialised by the educational system into believing that its educational failure is deserved.

(ii) Teaching the academic and vocational skills required by a developing economy

Functionalists claim that there is a strong relationship between education and the **economy**. As the economy becomes more complex, it requires new skills and greater technical expertise and education must provide a labour force to meet these needs. The workforce therefore needs skills beyond literacy and numeracy. Consequently, a range of occupational qualifications exist, particularly at further and higher educational levels ranging from vocational certificates and apprenticeships to professional training.

However, New Right politicians in the late 1970s were convinced that education had failed to fulfil this role convincingly. In response to these fears, the Conservative Government developed a range of educational courses known collectively as the **new vocationalism** (see page 69) which aimed to make young people more employable by increasing their skill levels and making them more aware of the world of work.

However, Marxists have criticised the idea that education is about transmitting skills. **Bowles and Gintis** suggest instead that the purpose of education is to make sure that workers are equipped with the 'right' attitudes towards work, i.e. that they are docile and conformist and prepared to accept low levels of skills, satisfaction and pay without complaint.

Bowles and Gintis focus on the hidden curriculum of schools and note that what goes on in schools 'corresponds' with what goes on in factories. For example:

- The hierarchical relationship between teachers and pupils is very similar to the relationships between employers and workers. The latter group in both cases rarely challenges the authority of the former.
- The experience of school is thought of as boring and routine which is very similar to the experience of factory workers engaged in assembly-line production.
- At school, learning for its own sake is rarely encouraged. Pupils are encouraged to work for external rewards such as grades and qualifications. Similarly, few workers derive satisfaction from their work. Instead they work for external rewards, i.e. wages, promotion.
- At school, pupils are rewarded through streaming, qualifications and entry into higher education for having greater abilities than others. Promotion through the ranks at work operates in a similar way.

Moreover, Bowles and Gintis note that success is not only related to ability. They also suggest that success is related to conformity. Those pupils who are willing to fit in and conform, who express the 'correct' attitudes and who do not challenge the system are more likely to succeed than intelligent students who 'rock the boat'. Bowles and Gintis suggest that this is why middle class pupils do better in the long-term than their working class peers regardless of ability.

However, Bowles and Gintis have been criticised because:
- They may have over-stated the relationship between education and the economy, e.g. much of the knowledge taught at school is simply not relevant for the jobs most people end up in. Moreover, the existence of social problems in schools such as indiscipline, truancy, exclusion, etc. and industrial action at work suggests that neither pupils nor workers are as docile as Marxists believe they are.
- Employers are very critical of the low level of employability of both school leavers and graduates which contradicts the notion of correspondence between education and work.

(iii) Allocating people to their most appropriate occupational role

KEY POINT

The functionalists **Davis and Moore** argue that the role of education is to **select** and **allocate** people to occupations which best suit their abilities. Educational mechanisms such as grades, examinations, references and qualifications are used to sift and sort individuals into hierarchical layers based on intelligence and ability. In this sense, functionalists regard society as a **meritocracy** underpinned by equality of opportunity in which people are rewarded for intelligence, ability and effort.

In a meritocracy, social position is based on individual talent and ability rather than on social background or origins. In other words, status is achieved rather than ascribed.

Both the most talented and the least talented will end up in jobs in which they will make efficient contributions to the smooth running of society. In this sense, inequality is functional and necessary. However, Marxists, and other critical thinkers, reject the view that the educational system is meritocratic for three broad reasons.

1. They argue that as long as **private education** continues to exist society can never be meritocratic, because expensive public schools symbolise class inequality.
2. Some argue that the British educational system is composed of a hierarchy of educational institutions based on types of selection rather than equality of opportunity, e.g. in the secondary sector, both grammar schools and foundation schools practise overt selection whilst **selection by mortgage** is becoming a norm in the comprehensive sector, i.e. only the middle class can afford to buy homes in the catchment areas of high-achieving schools. The focus on parental choice and league tables has created an incentive for schools to be more selective in their intake and exclude children likely to perform badly. As money and resources follow pupils, schools in deprived inner-city areas find it difficult to attract pupils and resources. They consequently 'sink' to the bottom of league tables, which undermines staff and pupil morale and makes it difficult to escape from the spiral of failure and potential closure.
3. The concept of meritocracy is undermined by the disproportionate inequalities in achievement experienced by groups such as the working class and particular ethnic minorities in the British education system.

Similarities between functionalism and Marxism

It is important to appreciate that whilst they have fundamental differences, the functionalist and Marxist approaches also have broad similarities.

Despite their differences, functionalist and Marxist accounts of education do share three broad similarities.

KEY POINT

1. They are both **structuralist theories** in that they see the way societies are structurally organised and particularly the social institutions that make up societies as more important than individuals.

2. They do not pay much attention to **classroom interaction** or how both teachers and pupils interpret what goes on in schools.

3. **Willis** provides a major critique of both perspectives by pointing out that both theories are **over-deterministic**, i.e. both see pupils as passive products of the educational system. Functionalists see pupils as being turned into model citizens whilst Marxists argue that working class children are turned into conformist workers. Both theories fail to take into account the power of pupils to **resist** these processes. In Willis' study, *Learning to Labour,* the children took little notice of the hidden curriculum – they substituted their own definitions of what school was about, based upon 'having a laff'. The children in his study were quite happy to take factory jobs because their working class culture valued factory work. Taking such jobs was seen as success rather than failure.

PROGRESS CHECK

1. Identify three roles or functions of education systems.
2. Identify two ways in which schools act as agencies of secondary socialisation.
3. Define the concept 'hidden curriculum'.
4. What does the term 'new vocationalism' refer to?
5. What does the functionalist approach mean when it describes the education system as meritocratic?
6. Identify two criticisms that apply to both the functionalist and the Marxist approaches.

Answers: 1. Secondary socialisation; the economic role – meeting the needs of the economy; selection and allocation of people to jobs. 2. Any two from: schools socialise pupils into accepting key social values such as achievement, competition and individualism; they encourage social integration through the teaching of subjects such as English, History, Citizenship and R.E.; they encourage conformity through the hidden curriculum. 3. This refers to the cultural values and attitudes (such as obedience to authority, conformity, respect) that are transmitted outside the formal curriculum e.g. through the organisation of the school. 4. A number of vocational education and training schemes that aimed to increase young people's employability by providing work experience. 5. That intelligence and individual effort are the main criteria for success within education. 6. Such criticisms include: they both ignore classroom interaction; they ignore how teachers and students themselves interpret their situation; they are over-deterministic; they ignore pupil resistance

3.3 Differential educational achievement

LEARNING SUMMARY

After studying this section, you should be able to understand:

- patterns of achievement and underachievement according to social class, gender and ethnicity
- the differences in achievement with reference to a range of sociological theories focused on the home, relationships and processes within schools such as teacher–pupil interaction, pupil subcultures and the hidden curriculum and the economic system.

Class, educational achievement and under-achievement

AQA **SCLY 2**   OCR **G673**

At all stages of education, students from working class backgrounds tend to achieve less than their middle class counterparts. Even when the former have the same level of intelligence as the latter, they:

- are less likely to be found in nursery schools or pre-school play groups
- are more likely to start school unable to read
- are more likely to fall behind in reading, writing and maths skills
- are more likely to be placed in lower sets or streams
- are more likely to get fewer GCSEs or low grades
- are more likely to leave school at the age of 16
- are less likely to go on into the sixth form and then on to university.

> **KEY POINT**
>
> There are essentially six broad explanations of educational under–achievement which can be applied to social class inequalities in education.
> 1. Intelligence.
> 2. Cultural deprivation.
> 3. Material deprivation.
> 4. Interaction and labelling in the classroom.
> 5. The role of educational social policies.
> 6. Marxism – the needs of the capitalist economic system.

Intelligence

This approach focuses on individuals and tends to blame the victims.

Some New Right sociologists, e.g. **Saunders**, argue that working class people have less innate, or inherited, intelligence as shown by IQ tests than middle class people. However, it is impossible to separate genetic influences from environmental influences such as poverty, quality of school, etc.

IQ tests may be culture-biased because they measure what middle class academics regard as intelligence. Experts now agree that different types of intelligence exist in addition to that tested by exams. Performance in IQ tests and examinations may simply measure length of time spent in education.

Cultural deprivation

This approach blames the victims and their culture.

> **KEY POINT**
>
> This collection of sociological explanations blames working class **home culture** for the failure of working class children to achieve. It suggests that the reason working class children under-achieve compared to their middle class counterparts is because their home culture is inadequate or deprived, especially in terms of parental attitudes, child–rearing practices and language development.

- **Douglas** argued that working class parents are less interested in their children's education. He measured **parental interest** by counting the number of times parents visited schools for parents' evenings, etc. Consequently he suggests that middle class parenting is more geared to stimulating interest in education than working class parenting.

- The **Newsons** argued that middle class parents are more child-centred than working class parents and this is reflected in greater cultural investment in nursery education, private schooling, educational toys and games and other educational resources such as computers and revision aids.
- **Bernstein** suggested working class children suffer from **linguistic deprivation**. He argued that middle class parents socialise their children into **elaborated codes** of speech which mean that middle class children generally understand the detailed and complex language used by textbooks, examinations and teachers in the classroom. However, working class parents allegedly transmit an inferior **restricted code** of speech and vocabulary to their children which means that they fail to understand teacher explanations and consequently do badly in examinations.

Cultural deprivation theory influenced educational policy in the 1960s and led to the founding of six Educational Priority Areas made up of deprived inner-city areas. Extra money was spent on primary schools in these communities. This type of scheme was known as positive discrimination or **compensatory education** because it aimed to discriminate positively in favour of the working class and compensate for the above 'deficiencies' in their culture. However, there are criticisms of cultural deprivation theory.

- It is methodologically suspect – is counting the number of times a parent visits a school a reliable indicator of parental interest? The fact that working class parents make fewer visits to school may have more to do with the nature of their jobs, e.g. they work longer hours or are more likely to be working shifts.
- It is **ethnocentric** – it dismisses working class culture as irrelevant and defines it as less valuable than middle class culture.
- **Bernstein** offered little evidence that different classes used different language codes. In contrast, **Labov's** research in the USA concluded that the working class 'street language' is capable of transmitting ideas as complex as any of those transmitted by middle class speech patterns.
- It fails to take account of **material deprivation**. Factors such as poverty may be more important than attitudes in explaining the failure of working class children to stay on in post-16 education.
- Cultural deprivationists tend to over-generalise about the behaviour and values of both the working class and middle class. They fail to recognise that there is a diversity of sub-cultural values and lifestyles within these broad social groupings.
- **Keddie** argues that cultural deprivation theory distracts attention away from the deficiencies of schools themselves.

Material deprivation

> This approach focuses on social factors rather than individual factors.

Smith and Noble (1995) listed three broad 'barriers to learning' that result from **poverty** and **low income**.

1. Low income may mean some children lack access to learning support resources such as computers and access to the internet, revision materials, extra tuition, their own room, etc.
2. There is some evidence that affluent parents can afford to buy homes in the catchment areas of schools that perform well (thus further driving up house prices). This 'selection by mortgage' further increases the inequalities in achievement between schools in suburban areas which tend to be dominated by middle class children and those in inner-city areas which tend to be dominated by working class children (measured by eligibility for free school meals).

3. Some children may be bullied, isolated and stigmatised if parents cannot afford elements of schooling such as uniform, school trips and school dinners that other families and pupils take for granted.

A number of studies of students, in both further and higher education, support the idea that material deprivation is a major obstacle in the educational achievement of bright working class teenagers.

- **Connor and Dewson** (2001) found that bright children from poor families lowered their educational and career aspirations and often failed to apply to university because they did not want to put their parents under economic pressure.
- **Payne's** (2001) survey of A-level students found that middle class parents had the economic resources to push children of moderate intelligence higher than bright working class children by paying for re-sits, hiring private tutors, etc.
- **Forsyth and Furlong** (2000) found that many working class A-level students were put off higher education by the cost and the prospect of debt. They also found that working class students were more likely to be juggling academic commitments with part–time work and this often impacted negatively on their ability to attend lectures and fulfil assignments. Working class students were more likely to drop-out of university because of economic pressures.
- In 2010 about 7% of pupils in England and Wales were educated privately in about 1200 fee paying schools. Critics of private education suggest that they make a significant contribution to the growing class divide in education. Privately educated pupils achieved a disproportionate number of A* grades at A-level in 2010 compared with their state-educated peers. Moreover, the **Sutton Trust** (2010) reports that private school pupils with the same A-level grades as state school pupils are 25 times more likely to be given a university place. In recent years, over 40% of undergraduates at Oxbridge had attended public schools such as Eton and Harrow. Fees at the top private schools average £28 000 per year. The average annual wage in Britain is £24 000.

> From 2011, EMA closed to new applicants in England. Look out for information on funds now available to support learners to continue in education and training.

The Education Maintenance Allowance (EMA) for further education students is a type of compensatory educational policy that acknowledges that differences in material wealth can profoundly influence educational achievement. The EMA is available to those students from low-income families and aims to provide economic assistance for travel, equipment, etc.

Interaction and labelling in the classroom

> This approach focuses on school-based factors.

KEY POINT

Interactionism, or labelling theory, focuses exclusively on **in-school** factors such as relationships and processes and specifically the classroom interaction that goes on between teachers and pupils. It argues that teachers judge or label pupils on the basis of factors such as social class, gender, race, behaviour, attitude and appearance rather than on ability and intelligence.

With regard to social class inequalities, interactionist studies suggest that some middle class teachers all too often attach negative labels about educational potential to working class pupils based on stereotypical and critical assumptions about working class families and homes, council estates, broken homes, etc.

Consequently, such teachers see middle class pupils as closest to their evaluation of the 'ideal pupil' label in terms of performance, conduct, attitude and appearance, whilst working–class pupils are seen as furthest from it. Studies by **Becker and Rist** confirm that ideal pupils tend to be those middle class pupils who have generally met all the requirements of conformity that the hidden curriculum demands.

Interactionists argue that the labels applied by teachers to pupils during classroom interaction shape the nature and quality of the relationship between pupil and teacher. The teacher, consciously or unconsciously, communicates the positive or negative label to the pupil via facial expression, tone of voice, encouragement, comments about work, use of praise and discipline, etc. Pupils react either positively or negatively to teacher judgements and there is a **self-fulfilling prophecy** effect, i.e. the pupil internalises the teacher label and eventually conforms to the teacher prediction (i.e. prophecy).

> Interactionist studies explore areas such as teacher-pupil interaction in classrooms and processes within schools such as labelling.

Rosenthal and Jacobson (1968) carried out a social experiment to test the notion of the self–fulfilling prophecy. They randomly selected 20% of the new intake of an elementary school in the USA and told the teachers that these children were likely to develop better than the rest, despite the fact that this was untrue. However, when they tested the children one year later, they found that their sample had made significantly more progress than the other pupils. Despite lack of observational data, Rosenthal and Jacobson concluded that the teachers had somehow communicated positive labels to these pupils during classroom interaction and the pupils had responded by fulfilling the prophecy.

> Rosenthal and Jacobson's study has been criticised on ethical grounds, e.g. it involved deceiving the teachers.

Teacher labelling often leads to selective practices in schools such as **setting** or **streaming**. There is evidence that teachers expect less of those in bottom streams and this undermines the quality of their teaching.

- **Campbell** (2001) found that setting and streaming by ability benefits those in the top groups only. However, the overall effect for those in lower sets was to make worse their attainment. This is because pupils in bottom sets are often taught by the youngest and least experienced teachers with the highest rates of staff turnover. Moreover, there is less interaction between pupils and teachers in lower sets compared with higher sets.

- **Stephen and Cape** (2003) on the basis of a small scale, but in-depth, study of 27 children transferring from nursery to primary school found that setting at the age of 5 or 6 years can damage the self–esteem and motivation of young children.

- **Ball** (2003) argues that those in the bottom streams experience lower self-esteem because they are both depressed and humiliated by the experience. They are more likely to be alienated from school, apathetic about education and consequently disaffected and disruptive. **Box** notes that they often socially react to their perceived inferior status by truanting or by forming delinquent or **anti-school subcultures** which award status to their members on the basis of anti-school activity, for example by being disruptive. Pupils in the bottom sets are also more likely to be suspended or excluded from schooling.

> You can link this to material in Chapter 2 on peer groups.

However, **interactionist** studies of teacher labelling have both strengths and weaknesses.

- On a positive note, interactionism has drawn our attention to how schools, teachers and children interact and how **classroom processes** can affect educational outcomes.

- Interactionism tends to ignore social influences external to the classroom, e.g. Marxists point out that schools are shaped by social-class inequalities in income, wealth and political power rooted in the organisation of wider capitalist society.

- The **interpretivist Marxist Willis** argues that this theory underestimates working class culture. Working class children do not fail because they are labelled by teachers. Many of them reject qualifications because they do not see them as relevant to the type of factory jobs they want to do. Their behaviour is a result of a conscious choice to reject schooling rather than a reaction to teacher labelling (which they resist). The children in Willis' study took little notice of teacher labelling because they refuse to recognise the legitimacy of education, schools and teachers.
- Interactionism fails to recognise the external constraints and pressures put on teachers which lead to processes such as labelling and setting, for example educational policies which demand constant testing and evaluation of pupils, funding policies which may result in larger class sizes, etc.
- **Woods** notes that many pupils adopt 'work avoidance strategies' without attracting negative teacher judgements.
- There is little empirical evidence in support of the self-fulfilling prophecy. Rosenthal and Jacobson's experiment did not observe teacher-pupil interaction.

The role of educational social policies

> **KEY POINT**
>
> Some commentators argue that social class inequalities have been worsened by educational social policy, particularly those aimed at the **marketisation** of education that appeared after 1988. Marketisation introduced exam league tables and competition between schools for pupils.

This approach focuses on government policies.

Educational experts argue that these processes have led to three consequences that have increased class differences in education.

1. **The educational triage effect**: **Gillborn and Youdell** (2001) examined two secondary schools in London and argued that the publication of league tables has created an 'A-to-C economy', meaning that schools only focus their energy and resources on those pupils who have the potential to achieve 5 grade Cs at GCSE. Pupils are subjected to a form of '**triage**' (or sorting) where schools categorise or label them into three groups:
   - those who will pass
   - borderline grade C–D pupils who are targeted for extra help
   - those labelled as 'hopeless cases' (which disproportionately contain large numbers of working class and ethnic minority pupils) who are placed in the bottom streams and largely written-off by the school.

2. **Screening**: popular schools that attract a large number of applicants can screen pupils and weed out the potentially less-able, the socially and economically disadvantaged and those with special needs. Less popular schools have to take such pupils and generally this lack of choice serves to worsen their league table position. Popular schools can also use school-home contracts to ensure that certain quality standards are consistently maintained which may put off less advantaged parents in their demands.

3. **The return to traditionalism**: studies suggest that foundation schools and city technology schools are adopting elitist and traditionalist marketing in order to sell themselves as superior to the run-of-the-mill comprehensive schools. Their specialism in particular subjects has operated to increase their snob

appeal to middle class parents. Some have even adopted the traditional language and paraphernalia of the grammar schools to distinguish themselves from comprehensives.

Marxism

Marxists point out that working class failure is pre-determined by the needs of the capitalist economic system.

This is a structuralist approach in that it focuses on the structure of society rather than on individuals.

1. The capitalist infrastructure requires a compliant manual labour force. The labour-power of the working class produces the **surplus value** which is the main source of profit and therefore the wealth of those who own the means of production – the **bourgeoisie**. A sudden rise in educational achievement amongst working class children would threaten the supply of that workforce.

2. Capitalism is characterised by great inequalities in wealth, income and political power. The educational success of the working class potentially threatens the ruling class' monopoly of wealth and power. Consequently, Marxists argue that the hidden curriculum, and teacher labelling, function to ensure working class under-achievement, by socialising them into a culture of failure so that they are resigned to taking up the relatively unrewarding and routine jobs provided by the factory system.

3. Education functions to ensure that ruling class culture is accepted by all members of society, therefore, reducing any future challenge to the bourgeoisie's monopoly of wealth and power. **Bourdieu** argues schools are ideological agencies working on behalf of the ruling class. The capitalist class is able to determine what is defined as knowledge and culture. As a result, the children of the dominant classes come to school with **cultural capital** – their values, experiences, language skills, and ways of behaving are seen to fit the culture of the school and they are consequently rewarded with teacher attention, selection into the top sets and streams and educational success. On the other hand, working class children find that their cultural experiences, values, ways of speaking and behaving, etc. are not defined as important, and consequently they are more likely to be negatively labelled, placed into bottom sets and streams, disproportionately punished for their behaviour, etc. They may be excluded from school or truant because they cannot identify with the content of schooling. They are therefore more likely to under-achieve. Bourdieu suggests that the working class experience of schooling is a form of 'symbolic violence'.

A number of studies, most notably, **Ball** (1994), **Sullivan** (2001) and **Power** (2003) have attempted to quantify Bourdieu's concept of cultural capital with regard to middle class parents and children.

- Ball found that middle class parents were able to use their knowledge of the educational system, their confidence as professional people and their contacts to ensure that their children were allocated the school of their choice.

- Sullivan found that pupils who read more widely and watched 'sophisticated' television programmes such as arts, science and current affairs documentaries were more likely to perform well at school. Sullivan's questionnaire survey suggested that these children were overwhelmingly middle class.

- Power notes that an important aspect of cultural capital is the fact than many middle class parents judge themselves and others on the 'conspicuous academic achievement' of their children, e.g. middle class parents may encourage their child to go to a 'traditional' university rather than a 'new' university because the latter is seen by their middle class peers as 'inferior'.

However, critics of cultural capital point out that working class pupils may choose to negotiate their way through the education system or even reject education altogether. The work of Willis, for example, suggests that educational 'failure' may be partly the product of some working class pupils resisting dominant definitions of what constitutes 'success' and 'failure'.

Ethnicity and educational achievement

AQA **SCLY 2**   OCR **G673**

Patterns of underachievement

Britain is a **multicultural society** made up of dozens of ethnic groups. However, it is not simply the case that all members of ethnic minority groups under-perform and under-achieve in the education system, e.g. the following patterns can be consistently seen in the British educational system.

- Children from Chinese, Indian and White middle class backgrounds perform best at all levels of the educational system.
- African-Caribbean and mixed-race males are less likely than any other group to achieve 5 or more GCSEs A*–C.
- African-Caribbean and mixed-race females do significantly better than working-class White pupils.
- Pakistani and Bangladeshi children, especially males, do relatively poorly at school compared with White pupils although the statistical evidence suggests that they are more likely than working class white pupils to go on into further and higher education.
- A disproportionate number of African-Caribbean males are excluded from school. Nationally, African-Caribbean children are 3.4 times more likely to be excluded from school than white children. Asian pupils, on the other hand, are less likely to be excluded compared with white children.

> **KEY POINT**
>
> Some sociologists suggest that we can only truly understand the relationship between ethnicity and educational inequality by examining the complex **interplay** between ethnicity, social class and gender. A number of sociological theories have evolved to explain ethnic inequality in educational attainment:
> - cultural deprivation
> - material deprivation
> - in-school factors
> - institutional racism
> - Marxist interpretivism.

Cultural deprivation

> This approach can be seen as blaming the victims and their culture.

Generally, explanations influenced by **cultural deprivation** suggest that educational success and failure is shaped by aspects of ethnic minority culture, especially family and home background. A number of themes can be observed.

- It is argued that there is a strong emphasis on self-improvement in Indian and Chinese culture. **Strand** (2007) notes that Indian parents have high aspirations for their children and encourage their children to be ambitious by providing them with the resources required for educational success, as well as closely monitoring their children's whereabouts and academic progress.
- Some New Right sociologists, such as **Murray**, suggest that male African-Caribbean underachievement and exclusion is caused by the lack of male

This links to material in Chapter 1 on families.

parental role models in this community. As many as 57% of African-Caribbean families are single-parent families and consequently many Black and mixed-race children in inner city areas are brought up by single mothers who often lose control of their male children when they become teenagers. It is argued that the Black street culture in inner city areas which stresses gang loyalty, hyper-masculinity and material rewards gained from crime becomes more attractive than educational success.

● Some critics claim that religion is an influential factor in encouraging both success and failure. It is argued that the Muslim faith encourages parents to invest more in a son's education and that the traditional roles expected of females are likely to de-motivate Muslim females in the long-term.

However, evidence from **Strand** also contradicts the idea that African-Caribbeans are less motivated by education. His study indicated that African-Caribbean pupils and their parents had high educational aspirations and positive attitudes towards schooling. Moreover, most African-Caribbean children live in nuclear families. **Driver and Ballard** (1981) and **Bhattu** (1999) too found that Asian parents had positive attitudes towards education irrespective of class or ethnic background.

Some sociologists have suggested that **mainstream culture** rather than home culture may be responsible for the underachievement of some ethnic minority groups. Some ethnic minority children may internalise negative self-images and develop low self-esteem because of their everyday experiences of **racial prejudice** and **discrimination**. This may undermine their confidence in the classroom.

Material deprivation

This approach focuses on social rather than individual factors.

The influence of **material deprivation** (e.g. poverty) on ethnic minority educational achievement is neglected by cultural deprivation theory.

Indian-heritage pupils' success in education may partly stem from the fact that Indian parents are often found in white-collar, managerial and professional occupations and consequently may enjoy some of the advantages of middle class privilege.

On the other hand, it is a fact that African-Caribbeans, Pakistanis and Bangladeshis are more likely than the white population to be part of the working class and therefore economically disadvantaged, e.g. they are more likely to occupy poor housing, to earn low incomes, to be unemployed or be in insecure jobs. The Child Poverty Action Group estimates that 73% of Pakistani and Bangladeshi households in Britain live on or below the official poverty line whilst Strand notes that in 2006, 58.5% of Bangladeshi children, 38.2% of Pakistani children and 26.2% of African-Caribbean children were entitled to free school meals compared with only 12.8% of white children.

Furthermore, African-Caribbean single-parent families are also more likely to experience low income and it may be that single-parents suffer more stress, especially if they combine paid work with childcare, and have less time and fewer resources to spend on their child's education.

All of these material disadvantages act as obstacles to educational success. The attitudes of ethnic minority groups towards education therefore cannot be examined in isolation from their material environment – they may be the product of it.

However, despite the importance of economic factors, **Drew and Baker** (1990) suggest that African-Caribbean achievement cannot be wholly explained by material deprivation. The evidence suggests that African-Caribbean educational performance lags behind other ethnic groups even when controlled for social class. **Gender** too may be exerting some influence. A number of studies suggest that African-Caribbean girls perform better at all levels than African-Caribbean boys. Strand suggests that girls are less affected by living in a single-parent family because a strong independent mother is a positive motivating experience.

In-school factors

This approach focuses on school-based factors rather than home-based factors.

Interactionists have examined and observed **classroom interaction** between a predominantly white teaching profession and pupils from ethnic minority backgrounds. Some sociologists have argued that teachers have low and/or negative expectations about ethnic minority pupils and attach negative labels to members of such groups. For example:

- **Brittan** (1976) suggests that the ideal pupil stereotype subscribed to by many teachers is white.
- **Brah and Minhas** (1985) noted that teachers stereotyped Asian females as passive and docile in ways which led them to be overlooked or under-estimated in the classroom.
- **Wright** (1987) found that African-Caribbean boys were more likely to be blamed by teachers for classroom disruption and consequently harshly disciplined compared with white or Asian children. Classroom interaction between black youth and white teachers was often characterised by conflict and confrontation.
- **Gillborn's** (1990) case study of a comprehensive school revealed that many teachers felt that the way African-Caribbean boys dressed or talked challenged their authority. Teachers, especially female teachers, often misinterpreted the dress and speech of African-Caribbean boys as disrespectful and consequently disproportionately punished the boys with detentions.
- **Connolly** (1998) found that teachers may channel African-Caribbeans away from academic interests by labelling them as more interested in sports, music and dance and encouraging their interests in this direction. He also found that Asian boys were less likely than African-Caribbean boys to be labelled deviant. Teachers generally had high **expectations** about the academic potential of Asian boys and consequently they were often praised and encouraged.
- **Gillborn and Mirza** (2000) note how black students are treated more harshly than their white peers and how teachers have lower expectations about the motivation, ability and achievement of black pupils.

Interactionists have suggested that this classroom labelling of ethnic minority pupils has several consequences.

- It may produce a **self-fulfilling prophecy** as some ethnic minority pupils internalise the low expectations that teachers have of them. This may result in exclusion as such pupils become disaffected by the treatment meted out to them.
- This disaffection might take the form of deviant **anti-school** and delinquent **racially-exclusive subcultures**. **Troyna** (1978) noted the emergence of African-Caribbean anti-school subcultures in London schools based on distinct styles of dress, musical taste and linguistic styles (for example the adoption of Rasta slang). Such subcultures awarded status on the basis of opposition and resistance towards the school and teachers and were likely to bring them further into conflict with authority.

- **Sewell** (2010) suggests that a negative experience of education especially when combined with poor job prospects and perceived police harassment has produced a street gang culture organised around opposition to education, respect based on a distorted view of masculinity and a casual attitude towards violence. Consequently, Sewell argues that educational failure is often a badge worn with pride. Young Black males who do achieve academically are often marked out for bullying.
- Ethnic minority pupils may find themselves allocated to bottom bands, sets or streams on the basis of teacher stereotypes rather than intelligence or ability. **Gillborn** (2002) notes that ethnic minority children in bottom sets are often taught a restricted curriculum and entered for exams that did not allow them to gain the highest grades no matter how well they do.

However, the **Runnymede Trust** is critical of labelling theory and suggests that race cannot be divorced from social class. It notes that between 1988 and 1997, the largest educational inequality was to be found between children from managerial and professional families and those from unskilled and manual families, regardless of ethnicity. Similarly, the **End Child Poverty** charity (2003) found that children from more affluent ethnic minority families were three times more likely than their poorer classmates to gain five good GCSEs.

Institutional Racism

A number of studies conducted in the 1980s suggested that the education system itself might be **institutionally racist**, i.e. that policies and classroom practices may be discriminating in hidden ways against pupils from ethnic minority backgrounds. For example, the **Swann Report** (1986) argued that the curriculum in many schools is **ethnocentric** – knowledge, teaching methods and modes of assessment are biased in favour of a 'white, Christian, English vision of things'. **Gillborn and Mirza** (2000) too argue that institutional racism is embedded in the hidden curriculum of the British education system in the following ways.

- An ethnocentric curriculum, particularly in history, literature and science over-focuses on white British culture and rarely acknowledges the multicultural character of British society.
- Textbooks and other resources overwhelmingly focus on the achievements of white people in literature, poetry, history, etc. and ignore the cultural and historical contributions of ethnic minority people. **Tikly** (2006) found in his survey of black children in 30 comprehensive schools that they were frustrated with the near-invisibility of black role models in the curriculum and the focus on slavery in black history weeks.
- There is a lack of ethnic minority role models in both teaching and management which might act as positive and empathetic motivators for black children.
- There is some evidence that school governing bodies give low priority to racial issues and fail to deal satisfactorily with pupil racism which some commentators argue is on the increase.

However, it is unlikely that institutional racism is solely to blame for the educational underachievement of ethnic minority groups, e.g. it does not explain why such processes seem to have little effect on the excellent achievement levels of Indian or Chinese pupils or why Asians have such high staying on rates.

Marxist interpretivism

Pryce (1979) observed African-Caribbean boys who had left school with few, or no, qualifications in their natural environment of St. Pauls in Bristol and concluded that they had made **rational choices** with regard to their education. He argued that many young African-Caribbeans are aware of racial discrimination, prejudice and inequality in Britain and interpret schools as white agencies which reproduce and justify such processes. Consequently, many black boys choose not to cooperate with the value system of the school and teachers. Rather, they often choose to actively **resist** schooling and take up 'deviant' careers in petty crime because they see this as the only way in a racist society to achieve economic success. From this perspective, Pryce suggests that black boys are not passive victims of institutional racism or teacher labelling – they are able to resist these processes and substitute their own set of values and goals based on street experience.

Gender and educational achievement

AQA **SCLY 2**   OCR **G673**

Patterns of achievement

> **KEY POINT**
>
> Until the late 1980s, the major concern in educational sociology was with the perceived underachievement of girls. They were less likely than boys to pursue further or higher education. However, in the early 1990s, girls began to outperform boys at most levels of the education system as indicated below.

- **Atkinson and Wilson's** (2003) study of 500 000 children shows that, despite boys outperforming girls in mathematics and science in early schooling, by the age of 16, girls achieved better results in both subjects.
- Generally, girls outperform males at GCSE and A-level in terms of both number of qualifications and grades achieved.
- In 2000, the number of women gaining first class honours degrees outnumbered males for the first time.

Wilkinson suggests that young women have experienced a **genderquake** in terms of profound changes in attitude and expectation compared with earlier generations of women. In particular, many women today see education and career as having a greater priority than marriage and family, e.g. in a 1976 survey **Sharpe** discovered that girls' priorities were love, marriage, husbands, children, jobs and careers, more or less in that order. When the research was repeated in 1994, she found that the priorities had changed to job, career and being able to support themselves.

This links to material on gender identity in Chapter 2.

A range of influences have raised the expectations, aspirations and achievement levels of young females in the last twenty years.

- Since the late 1970s, there have been more **job opportunities** for women, especially in the service sector of the economy, e.g. in the public sector, such as the civil service, education and health, as well as in finance, retail and personal services. The majority of new jobs in this sector were taken up by women. Women therefore have more choice available to them.
- Many girls had mothers in paid full-time or part-time employment – these **role models** showed that females could successfully pursue careers.

- The **women's movement** was successful in spreading and popularising the idea that women could enjoy the same economic, legal, sexual and social opportunities as men.
- Schools adopted **equal opportunities policies** and practices from the 1980s onwards, which resulted in the monitoring of teaching strategies and resources for sex-bias in order to ensure more girl-friendly schooling. Teachers were strongly encouraged to be more sensitive to the educational needs of females.
- Changes in the organisation of education may have benefited girls – the national curriculum's emphasis on science meant that girls cannot avoid doing some hard science. The introduction of coursework too may have suited girls more than boys. There is mounting evidence that girls work harder, are more conscientious and are better motivated than boys. Girls put more effort into their work and spend more time on coursework and homework. They take more care with presentation, are better organised and consequently meet deadlines better than boys do.

Recent changes to the assessment patterns at both GCSE and A-level have involved a reduction in the amount of coursework on some courses and a removal of the coursework component in others.

However, female underachievement is still a problem.

- Working class girls still disproportionately underachieve, e.g. one-third of the 40 000 pupils who leave school at 16 years with no qualifications are female and the majority are from materially deprived socio-economic backgrounds. This has prompted some sociologists to suggest that social class is more influential than gender as a factor in shaping failure.
- **Subject choices** and particularly A-level and higher education entry are still gender-stereotyped. Males still dominate the hard sciences whilst females are disproportionately found in the humanities subjects, languages and English.
- **Kelly** (1987) notes that science is packaged and presented in a very masculine way in both education and society and this may be putting females off choosing both degree courses and careers in scientific fields.
- **Colley** (1998) argues that cultural beliefs about femininity and masculinity, family pressures and peer pressure are combining to divert females away from higher education courses perceived to be masculine such as mathematics, physics and information technology.
- Employment barriers may prevent females from choosing particular higher education courses and therefore careers. Females can see that males continue to dominate the top positions within particular sectors (i.e. **vertical segregation**) and that many sectors of employment are seen by society as either male or female jobs (i.e. **horizontal segregation**). Females may consequently choose to enter traditional feminine sectors of employment.

Male underachievement

The end of the 1990s saw a **moral panic** about boys' underachievement. By the age of 16, nearly 40% of boys have dropped out of education with few or no qualifications. **Epstein *et al.*** (1999) note that boys' underachievement only became a problem in the 1990s because the factory jobs they previously went into experienced serious decline. Mass unemployment of males meant that these boys had the potential to be a serious threat in terms of social disorder.

A number of explanations have been offered for the underachievement of boys.

- Interactionists argue that teachers see females as their **ideal pupils** and consequently develop **lower expectations** about the ability of boys and are more likely to label them as lazy, untidy or disruptive. This may have a self-fulfilling effect. **Browne and Mitsos** (1998) suggest boys lose valuable learning time by messing about, getting sent out of the room and by being excluded. Boys account for 90% of those permanently excluded from school. **Warrington and Younger** (2002) found that some teachers still treat boys and girls unequally – girls tend to obtain more constructive help with their work whereas boys are subjected to putdowns and reprimands more frequently than girls.

> This links to material in Chapter 2 on gender identity.

- **Mac An Ghaill** (1996) argues that changes in the economy, especially the decline of factory labour and the rise in male unemployment may have undermined boys' motivation and ambition, i.e. they may feel that qualifications are a waste of time because there are only limited job opportunities. He suggests that boys are experiencing a **crisis of masculinity** which means that they feel unsure about their role in the light of these economic changes. Young working class men are no longer sure of their place in society especially as young women compete with them for jobs and careers. It is suggested that working class male adolescents conclude that education and qualifications are irrelevant because they can see that the jobs they will end up doing are unskilled or semi-skilled at best.

- Such boys are likely to look for alternative sources of status and means of expressing their masculinity. These are likely to be found in **delinquent anti-school subcultures** in which they gain street credibility for being **anti-intellectual** or anti-school. Schoolwork is seen as 'uncool' and reading, in particular, is regarded as boring, 'sissy', feminine and to be avoided at all costs. This may explain why boys lack the application for coursework skills. **Willis** points out that such anti-intellectualism is rigorously policed by the subculture. Boys who follow an intellectual path are likely to be labelled by their peers as feminine or as teachers' pets and consequently bullied.

> Rather than seeing gender, ethnicity and social class as completely separate social categories, think about the ways in which they may interact.

Gender is regarded by feminist sociologists as a key factor explaining underachievement. However, **Warrington and Younger** suggest that it is only the fifth most important determinant of a child's educational performance, coming way below prior attainment, social class, ethnicity and quality of school.

PROGRESS CHECK

1. How does Saunders explain the underachievement of working class pupils?
2. Identify three home-based factors that cultural deprivation theory focuses on.
3. On what grounds does Keddie criticise cultural deprivation theory?
4. Members of which minority ethnic groups tend to perform well within education?
5. Members of which minority ethnic group experience the highest rate of exclusion from school?
6. Which theory can be described by the phrase 'what teachers believe, their students will achieve'?
7. According to Colley, which three factors divert females from HE courses that are perceived as masculine?

Answers: 1. In individual/genetic terms - their lack of inherited intelligence. 2. Parental interest in education, child-rearing practices and language use. 3. It distracts attention away from any school-based issues/deficiencies. 4. Pupils of Indian and Chinese heritage. 5. Pupils of African-Caribbean heritage. 6. Labelling theory. 7. Cultural beliefs about gender, family pressures and peer pressure.

Exam practice questions

Questions 1–4 are typical AQA questions. During the exam, remember to spend some time studying the Item, planning your responses and checking them at the end. If you choose the Education option on the AQA SCLY2 paper, remember that the Methods in Context question will focus on the application of sociological research methods to the study of education.

Questions 5 and 6 are typical OCR questions. During the exam, remember to allocate some time to reading the questions, planning your answers and checking them at the end.
Try to get plenty of practice at writing essays under timed conditions. This will help you to develop your time management skills.

Read through Item A and then answer questions 1–4 that follow.

Item A

Marxists argue that the education system serves to reproduce – generation by generation – class inequalities in wealth and power. Through the hidden curriculum, schools transmit values that benefit the ruling class. Working class pupils learn to accept social inequalities, e.g. devices such as streaming and examinations serve to convince working class pupils to accept failure as their own fault.

However, Paul Willis found that the working-class boys in his study rejected the school's definition of success and failure. They constructed a counter-school culture based around 'having a laugh'. These boys resisted the authority of their teachers and the school rules.

1. Explain what is meant by the term 'meritocracy'. **(2 marks)**

2. Suggest three reasons for the improvement in girls' educational attainment since the 1980s. **(6 marks)**

3. Outline some of the ways in which school processes may lead to the educational underachievement of some minority ethnic pupils. **(12 marks)**

4. Using material from Item A and elsewhere, assess the claim that 'the education system serves to reproduce – generation by generation – class inequalities in wealth and power' (Item A). **(20 marks)**

5. Outline and assess educational policies designed to increase equality of opportunity since 1988. **(50 marks)**

6. Outline and assess the view that it is school-based factors which are most significant in explaining the educational underachievement of working class boys. **(50 marks)**

4 Health

The following topics are covered in this chapter:

- The social construction of health and illness
- The social construction of disability and mental illness
- Health inequalities
- The role of health professionals

4.1 The social construction of health and illness

LEARNING SUMMARY

After studying this section, you should be able to understand:

- key concepts and definitions relating to the biomedical approach to health and illness
- the view that health and illness are socially constructed.

Defining health and illness

AQA **SCLY 2**   OCR **G672**

> **KEY POINT**
>
> Sociologists define **illness** as the **subjective** experience of feeling unwell, i.e. how people feel or experience symptoms which undermine their well-being. **Disease** is defined more **objectively** in that it is the recognition of a physical or mental abnormality such as a virus, cancer, high blood pressure. It is normally identified after the patient's symptoms have been subjected to a rigorous medical examination by qualified doctors.

Blaxter notes that it is possible to have an illness without a disease and a disease without an illness, e.g. women in early pregnancy often experience illness in the form of nausea or morning sickness, whilst people who are HIV positive often lead normal lives without any overt symptoms of disease. **Dubos** (1987) defines **health** as the absence of disease, or disability, which allows people to function effectively. The **World Health Organization** (WHO) defines health as a state of complete physical, social and mental well-being.

Health is usually measured by examining **morbidity** and **mortality** statistics. The **morbidity rate** refers to the amount of illness in society. This is normally officially measured in two ways; by counting the number of visits to general practitioners (GPs) and the numbers of admissions to hospital. The **mortality rate** refers to the death rate – the number of people who die in any given year per 100 000 of the population. Often mortality rates are used in conjunction with statistics relating to life expectancy, e.g. societies may be viewed as unhealthy if they have high infant mortality rates or if large numbers of people die pre-retirement age.

This links with material in Chapter 1.

The biomedical model of health

The model subscribed to by health professionals.

Hart notes that an approach to health, known as the **bio medical** model, became influential in the late nineteenth century and became dominant with the setting up of the National Health Service (NHS) in 1946. This model claims that the good health and long life expectancy generally enjoyed today is the result of practices introduced by this approach. Hart identifies six important components that make up this biomedical approach.

1. It concentrates on **scientifically** cataloguing and tackling the **physical symptoms** of both physical and mental illness such as germs, disease, viruses and malfunctioning organs.
2. Doctors are the only **medical experts** worth listening to because they are extensively trained and consequently are the only people who have the necessary skills to identify symptoms of illness.
3. Medical care should be **allopathic**, or cure-orientated, and focus on treatments such as surgery and drugs.
4. Illness is a **temporary** affair. Germs are identified and driven off by medical expertise.
5. The **individual** is the site of the disease. The causes of disease are rarely located in the environment that the individual occupies.
6. Treatment too is best located in a medical environment, i.e. in a hospital rather than in the environment where the symptoms may have arisen.

> **KEY POINT**
>
> At its simplest, the biomedical model presents the human body as a type of machine – parts can go wrong and need repairing. Over time, the body 'wears out' just as a machine does and eventually it stops working altogether.

The **strength** of the biomedical approach to health, illness and disease is that scientific solutions to health problems have been very successful in increasing life expectancy, curing disease and reducing death rates.

The social model: health and illness as socially constructed

AQA **SCLY 2**   OCR **G672**

The **social model** of health and illness developed as a sociological critique of the biomedical model. This view, which is put forward by **interpretivist** sociologists, points out that illness, disease and health are not the objective facts that the biomedical model suggests they are. Rather they argue that the process of becoming ill is **socially constructed**, e.g. there are a number of social stages which people must go through before they are officially defined as being ill. These are:

- **Recognition** – people need to recognise that the symptoms that they are experiencing are signs of illness. However, this is not straightforward because people may not recognise, or may choose to ignore, symptoms of illness.
- **Definition** – people need to define their symptoms as serious enough to see a doctor.
- **Action** – the act of consulting a doctor is also a **social process** which may be dependent on a range of social factors such as the nature of the illness, how the doctor interacts with his or her patients or how social class, gender and ethnicity shape the perception doctors and patients have of each other.

Interpretations of illness and health are influenced by **cultural relativity**. There is some evidence that subcultural differences exist in the interpretation of illness. **Krause** (1989) found that Hindu and Sikh Punjabis living in Bedford suffered an illness called 'sinking heart' characterised by physical chest pain which was brought on by public shame. No such illness is known to exist among other sub-cultures in Britain.

Evidence suggests that how ordinary people define health and illness (i.e. lay definitions) within the same culture also influences interpretations as the following examples show.

- **Age differences** – the elderly do not share the same interpretations of health and illness as the young. Being elderly seems to involve the acceptance of greater levels of physical discomfort as a natural part of the ageing process. Young people are more willing to see health as tied to exercise, diet and physical fitness, whereas the elderly define health as the ability to cope with everyday tasks.
- **Gender differences** – there are differing masculine and feminine approaches to health and illness. Evidence suggests women are more aware of their bodies than men because of factors such as menstruation and pregnancy. It has been suggested that men interpret illness as weakness and consequently are less likely to consult with doctors.
- **Social class differences** – **Blaxter's** research suggests working class people are far more tolerant of illness, pain and discomfort than middle class people.

The social construction of illness can also be illustrated using **historical** and **international** examples. Up to the eighteenth century, medical science was in its infancy and interpretations of health and illness were dominated by **religious** explanations. The Church blamed the plague (or Black Death) on God punishing mankind for wickedness whilst mental illness was often viewed as demonic possession. Similar ways of thinking can be seen in many pre-industrial societies which blame magic or witchcraft for illness and disease.

> **KEY POINT**
>
> **Gomm** notes that definitions of health and illness are not fixed or universal. Rather, they are subjected to constant change as powerful groups use medicine to control the behaviour of less powerful groups, e.g. slaves who ran away from plantations in the eighteenth century were defined as mentally ill, whilst many heterosexuals defined homosexuality as a mental illness until the 1980s.

The critique of morbidity statistics

Sociologists who focus on the social construction argument suggest that the morbidity or illness statistics cannot be trusted as a **valid measurement** of illness in society. These statistics are collected by the NHS by counting the number of visits to GPs. However, the social constructionist argument notes that very few people who experience illness actually visit their GP. Most prefer to self-medicate or are cared for by family members. Some sociologists claim that the official morbidity statistics only account for 6% of illness because there is a 'clinical iceberg' of illness that never comes to the attention of the NHS (and therefore the biomedical approach).

Link to research methods. Think about how this will affect the validity of official statistics on morbidity.

The role of public health

> **KEY POINT**
>
> The medical historian **McKeown** (1979) argued that the biomedical model exaggerates its role in the improvement of the nation's health and life expectancy.

McKeown pointed out that health levels as measured by increases in life expectancy and decreases in child mortality had dramatically improved before the development of modern biomedical techniques such as vaccination. He argues that nineteenth century **public health** measures, such as the introduction of clean piped water and sanitation to homes, as well as improvements in **nutrition** and **diet** are mainly responsible for the good health enjoyed by the majority of society today.

This links to material on life expectancy in Chapter 1.

Iatrogenesis

'Iatrogenic' means caused by medical examination or treatment.

Illich was a major critic of the biomedical model of medicine because he believed GPs and the NHS are responsible for a great deal of the illness that exists today in Western societies. Illich identifies four 'harms' or types of 'iatrogenesis' created by modern medicine.

Watch out for media reports on issues such as 'superbugs' in hospitals.

- **Clinical iatrogenesis** – this is direct harm that is caused by medical intervention such as clinical errors in diagnosis and during operations or treatment, e.g. it is estimated that about 7% of all hospital patients are injured by medical personnel during the course of operations and about 2% of patients die from errors committed by doctors during surgery. Furthermore, thousands of patients die from highly virulent and antibiotic–resistant superbugs picked up whilst in hospital. Prescribed drugs also have unpleasant and sometimes addictive and fatal side-effects. Illich estimated that there are approximately 225 000 deaths per year in the USA from iatrogenesis which makes it the third leading cause of death in the USA, after heart disease and cancer.
- **Social iatrogenesis** – this refers to the increasing influence that medical professionals, especially mental health professionals, are having over all aspects of social life. **Gomm** notes that alcoholism, obesity, learning difficulties, children's behaviour and sexual problems have all come to be defined as medical problems, specifically mental health problems, in recent years. As a result, in Britain, the total number of consultant psychiatrists and clinical psychology staff (such as counsellors) has risen considerably in recent years, whilst the number of prescriptions written for anti-depressants rose from 9 million to 21 million during the 1990s.
- **The Sisyphus Syndrome** – Illich noted that modern health care can keep more people alive for longer periods, but at what cost to people's quality of life? Old age often results in degenerative and chronic diseases, such as Alzheimer's disease, which can seriously reduce the capacity of people to enjoy life and which often requires even more expensive health care.
- **Cultural iatrogenesis** – Illich argued that modern industrial societies are over-dependent on the medical profession. Society requires a pill for every ache, every sad mood, every stomach upset, etc.

Post-modernism

Post-modern sociologists such as **Giddens** (1991) argue that in late modernity, the body and health have become important 'sites' for making statements about oneself. Giddens argues that in contemporary society, **identity** is something that people 'work at' – young people, in particular, construct an image which they present to others as their real 'selves'. Giddens calls this **reflexive mobilisation**.

This links to material in Chapter 2 on identity.

Shilling (2003), building on Giddens' ideas, notes that identity is increasingly focused on the 'healthy or fit body'. He argues that people often physically alter their bodies in order to express their individuality. In post-modern societies, there are considerably more choices in the ways in which people might do this. For example:

- going to the gym to exercise or 'work out' or even body-build
- following a specific diet, e.g. Atkins, being aware of calorie intake, or slimming
- having cosmetic surgery or botox injections
- tattooing or piercing the face or body
- using health supplements such as vitamin tablets
- using anti-ageing agents.

However, the pursuit of the body project in the desire to construct an identity can create health problems such as eating disorders like anorexia and bulimia.

Complementary or alternative medicine

Post-modernists also note that the dominance of the biomedical model has been challenged in recent years by the rise of **complementary** and **alternative types of medicine** such as homeopathy and acupuncture. These approaches tend to be 'holistic' – they see the causes of illness as located in a breakdown in the relationship between the body and the mind/spirit of the ill person.

Post-modernist sociologists, such as **Hardey** (1998), have argued that the popularity of complementary medicine is the result of the general public who no longer uncritically believe in the authority of biomedicine's scientific approach. People are increasingly aware that the biomedical model carries the sorts of unacceptable risks identified by Illich and consequently they are rejecting conventional medicine in favour of alternative therapies.

> **KEY POINT**
>
> Post-modernists note that choosing alternative medicine is also an **identity choice** that demonstrates both **individuality** and **free expression**.

> **PROGRESS CHECK**
>
> 1. What is biomedicine?
> 2. Explain what is mean by 'morbidity'.
> 3. According to McKeown, what factors are responsible for improving the nation's health?
>
> Answers: 1. An approach to health dominated by a medical elite which defines illness as being determined by biological or physical factors. 2. Morbidity refers to ill health resulting from disease. 3. Nineteenth century public health measures such as the introduction of clean water supplies and sanitation to homes plus improvements in diet and nutrition.

4.2 The social construction of disability and mental illness

> **LEARNING SUMMARY**
>
> **After studying this section, you should be able to understand:**
>
> - biomedical and social approaches to disability
> - biomedical and social approaches to mental illness with particular focus on structural and interactionist explanations
> - patterns in mental illness relating to social class, ethnicity and gender

Biomedical and social approaches to disability

AQA **SCLY 2**   OCR **G672**

Dominant definitions of disability are shaped by the **biomedical** model of disability which assumes that a physical or mental impairment such as the loss of a limb or a physically degenerative disease (such as multiple sclerosis) prevents some people from operating 'normally', i.e. from taking part in activities most people take for granted. The biomedical approach largely assumes that the disabled are mostly dependent upon the able-bodied and that the disabled are entitled to the pity and charity of the rest of society.

The social model of disability

This links to material in Chapter 2 on identity.

Interpretivist sociologists suggest that disability is a **socially constructed** concept rather than an objective reality. This can be illustrated in a number of ways.

- **Shakespeare** argues that there is no such thing as a 'normal body'. He argues instead that bodies should be viewed as part of a **continuum** with fit able-bodied people at one end of the continuum and the severely disabled, who are usually bedridden, at the other end. In between, there is a range of abilities and impairments which are interpreted in different ways by society.
- **Oliver** suggests that most members of the British population are impaired in some way, but they are rarely classified as 'disabled', e.g. not everyone can run, catch or throw a ball, but society does not label those who cannot do these things well as disabled. Society accepts these differences as part of the normal range of human abilities.
- There are **degrees of physical impairment** which attract different social responses. People who are short-sighted or who break a leg are not interpreted by society as disabled.

> **KEY POINT**
>
> The **social model** argues that prejudicial social attitudes and discriminatory practices develop about particular types of disability, which view the disability as **deviant** in that it is interpreted as a problem, as **abnormal** and as **inferior**.

Oliver argues it is the **social reaction** to disability that is responsible for handicapping the disabled rather than their biological bodies – people with disabilities are deliberately excluded from full participation in society by the stereotypical and negative attitudes held by able-bodied people. This can be illustrated in a number of ways.

This links to material in Chapter 2 on disability and discrimination.

- The **built environment** is often not suitable to the needs of people with disabilities, e.g. toilets, access to buildings and transport systems, although this is improving.
- Their activities and achievements, e.g. in sport, may not be regarded as having the same **status** as those of the able–bodied.
- Disabled people may find themselves **segregated** from able-bodied society, e.g. in special schools, which consequently makes it more difficult for them to be 'normal' and to integrate into society.

Bear in mind that people with disabilities are protected by laws against discrimination.

- Prejudice may be translated into **discrimination** in the field of employment as employers may be reluctant to take them on. Disabled people therefore may be more likely to be on welfare benefits and to experience poverty.
- **Longmore** (1987) suggests that disabled people tend to be **represented** on television and in films as evil, as monsters, as inhuman, as dependent on

others, as maladjusted, as the objects of pity or charity and as dangerous and deviant. **Cumberbatch and Negrine** (1992) argue media representations of the disabled rarely present them as a person but an individual who also happens to have a disability.

A Marxist interpretation of disability

Marxists, such as **Finkelstein** (1980), have suggested that negative cultural attitudes towards disabled people may be the product of capitalism's emphasis on work as a source of income, status and power. Capitalist society requires a healthy and fit workforce to generate profits for the capitalist class. In this context people with disabilities are viewed as a **burden** on society and defined as having an inferior status.

Interactionism

Interactionists, such as **Goffman,** suggest that the **negative labelling** or **stigma** that disabled people experience has several consequences.

- A disabled person is judged in terms of their disability rather than as a human being – other statuses such as son, daughter, brother, sister and professional, become less important than the **master status** of 'disabled'. The person who is unable to walk unaided is seen simply as 'wheelchair-bound' (not as an intelligent, articulate woman, for example).
- It is assumed by able-bodied people that the disabled person is **dependent** on the able-bodied and incapable of having normal social relations.
- Goffman points out that disabled individuals may come to accept and internalise this master status and see themselves solely in terms of their dependent status. A **self-fulfilling prophecy** comes about – they develop low self-esteem and learn to be helpless.

Critiques of the social model of disability

Critiques of the social model of disability argue that we cannot ignore the fact that physical and biological factors such as pain, mental impairment, and so on, *do* negatively impact on how disabled people experience social life and can make it unpleasant and difficult. The disabled identity is therefore probably made up of:
- coping with the limitations caused by the physical impairment of the body or mind
- the limitations of the social environment shaped by negative and stereotypical attitudes towards disability.

This links to material in Chapter 2 on disability. It is important to look out for links between different topics and units.

Biomedical and social approaches to mental illness

AQA **SCLY 2**   OCR **G672**

The biomedical approach

Biomedical accounts of mental illness are very influenced by the biomedical model of health. They see the causes of mental illness as situated in the **physical** or **biological body,** e.g. as a result of brain damage, tumours and lesions, genetic factors, chemical and hormonal influences or as the result of external factors that damage the biological development of the brain, e.g. poor diet or pollution.

The biomedical approach believes that symptoms can be scientifically diagnosed and categorised. Mental health practitioners, e.g. psychiatrists have therefore diagnosed problematic human behaviour into over 350 psychiatric categories or conditions, e.g. psychoses, neuroses, phobias, anxieties, depression. Consequently, they see treatment as **allopathic**, i.e. cure-orientated through the use of drugs, electric shock treatment and surgery. The biomedical model has sometimes recommended that sufferers from extreme mental health problems, such as psychoses that pose a threat to others, need to be isolated from wider society in secure mental health institutions.

Social constructionism

> **KEY POINT**
>
> The **social constructionist** perspective focuses on the relationship between **mental illness**, **power inequalities** and **social action**. The social constructionist approach believes that definitions of mental health and illness are problematic because they are socially constructed – they are a product of **social interactions** between different groups. Some of these groups have the power to define or label the behaviour of less powerful groups in society as a problem, i.e. as a product of mental illness.

In other words behaviour considered as 'mentally ill' has varied historically and cross-culturally.

The **social construction** argument points out that what is considered mentally or emotionally normal varies over time and from society to society, e.g. in the eighteenth and nineteenth centuries slaves who ran away from the plantations in the West Indies were thought to be suffering from 'drapetomania', a form of mental illness that caused slaves to flee from captivity. In the twentieth century, people who complained about the way that Soviet society was run (political dissidents) were defined as mentally ill and confined to psychiatric institutions.

The social construction argument also notes that behaviour which is defined as normal in some societies may be seen as evidence of madness in others, e.g. a person who says that they are possessed by the spirit of their ancestor would be labelled 'mad' in Britain, but this sort of statement would be regarded as normal and true in Native American and some West African religious cultures.

Labelling theory and mental health

> **KEY POINT**
>
> The most important part of the social constructionist argument is known as the **labelling theory**. This theory examines how the labelling of behaviour as 'mental illness' occurs in the first place and what effects it has on those who are so labelled.

Szasz (1973) argues that the label 'mental illness' is simply a convenient way to deal with behaviour that those in power find disruptive. Szasz is very critical of the way that American psychiatry has expanded its influence over the control of everyday behaviour. He notes that there are in reality very few psychological conditions or symptoms which can be diagnosed with reference to biological evidence. However, he argues that psychiatrists are too willing to medicalise social life and interpret behaviour which is normal natural or as symptomatic of mental health problems, e.g. Szasz suggests that being sad, shy or vain is a normal part of the human psyche. However, American psychiatrists have now categorised all these 'conditions' as clinical mental health disorders. Szasz also argues that such labels are confusing, e.g. the label of clinical depression may disguise the fact that someone is very miserable for good reason.

Another labelling theorist, **Scheff** (1966) argues that whether someone is labelled or not as 'mentally ill' is determined by the **benefits** that others might gain from that labelling. Scheff notes that people who are interpreted as a nuisance, or who prevent others from doing something they want to do, are far more likely to be defined as being mentally ill than those who pose no threat or inconvenience and who can safely be ignored. A good example of this is that many women in the early part of the twentieth century were forced into mental hospitals by their well-to-do families because they had caused **social embarrassment** to their parents and families by either getting pregnant outside of marriage or because they were seen to be behaving in a 'sexually promiscuous' way.

Institutionalisation and mental health

Goffman (1968) claims that there is great **stigma** attached to mental illness in Western society and so societal reaction to the label is likely to be negative. Labelling and the consequent treatment by mental health professionals can result in a deviant career, i.e. those labelled accept the definition of themselves as ill.

In his study, Rosenhan and a small group of other pseudo-patients faked the symptoms of schizophrenia by claiming to hear voices. Most were diagnosed as schizophrenic by staff and all were admitted to psychiatric hospitals. Once admitted, they behaved normally. However, none was detected as a fake and their behaviour (such as writing notes) was now interpreted as evidence of their mental illness.

Goffman is particularly critical of the role of psychiatric hospitals in this process. His observations of patients suggest that such institutions attempt to make patients conform to institutional labels by stripping them of their old identities – what he calls mortification of self. Institutional life involves learning to conform to the new role of 'mentally ill' as defined by psychiatric workers. **Rosenhan's** (1975) pseudo-patient experiment showed that staff rarely challenge the label of mentally ill and consequently all behaviour, however normal, is interpreted in the context of mental illness.

> **KEY POINT**
>
> Goffman notes that patients respond in a variety of ways to this labelling. Some will withdraw, i.e. become introverted while others will rebel, but be subjected to harsher treatment for their trouble. Some patients cooperate with staff, while others become dependent upon their labels, i.e. institutionalised. Others 'play it cool' and attempt to avoid trouble.

Goffman's **case study** was a useful insight into institutionalisation despite being too small to **generalise** from. However, he has been criticised by both Marxists and feminists for neglecting influences on mental illness such as poverty and patriarchy.

In a later experimental study by Rosenhan, staff in another psychiatric hospital were told that Rosenhan's experiment was being repeated in their institution. They were asked to work out which of their patients were undercover researchers who were just pretending to be ill. In this study, staff routinely judged people who were genuinely ill as merely pretending. It would seem, therefore, that even experts cannot decide who is actually mentally ill.

Another experiment by **Katz** seems to support Rosenhan's observations. He showed groups of British and American psychiatrists, films of interviews with patients and asked them to note down what they saw in the patients' behavior as symptoms of mental illness. They were then asked to make a diagnosis. Katz discovered that there were major disagreements in diagnosis between the two groups. The British saw less evidence of mental illness generally, e.g. one patient was diagnosed as 'schizophrenic' by one-third of the Americans, but by none of the British psychiatrists.

Criticisms of the labelling perspective

Gove (1982) argues that the arguments that mental illness is merely a label for behaviour which we don't like, or that the label worsens the chance of recovery, are wrong because the vast majority of people who receive treatment for mental illness actually have serious problems before they are treated. He argues that labelling theory provides no adequate explanation for why some people are mentally ill in the first place.

Structuralist perspectives on mental health

AQA **SCLY 2**   OCR **G672**

Structuralist perspectives on mental health accept the reality of mental illness and set out to discover what factors in the **organisation**, or **structure of society**, might cause the illness. This perspective has uncovered evidence of clear mental health differences between social groups.

Social class and mental illness

This highlights the links between health, illness and the theme of social inequality.

There is evidence of a very strong relationship between **poverty** and mental illness according to **Link** and **Phelan**. They found that children from the poorest backgrounds were three times more likely to have behaviour disorders than those whose parents were in professional occupations.

Wilkinson notes that the poor are more likely to live in urban areas with little sense of community. People are more likely to be mutually suspicious of each other because of high crime rates. Anti-social behaviour may mean that people are hostile towards others or frightened of coming into contact with others. The poor are also more likely to experience family breakdown. They are likely to be in debt too. Consequently, the poor experience more **stress** and therefore their potential for experiencing mental health problems such as depression is much greater than for other social groups.

Mental illness and ethnicity

Members of ethnic minorities have significantly different chances of mental illness compared with the majority White population. According to **Nazroo** (2001) people of South Asian origin (e.g. Indians, Pakistanis and Bangladeshis) have very low rates of mental illness, while those from African-Caribbean backgrounds are three times more likely to develop schizophrenia compared with the British population as a whole.

Virdee (1997) argues that ethnic minorities are more likely to experience stress because of the double disadvantage of **poverty** and **racism**. Ethnic minorities in Britain are more likely than other social groups to experience unemployment and low-pay which makes them more vulnerable to poverty. The everyday stress of racism, especially abusive language, racial harassment, fears of attack and police harassment also contributes to the potential for stress and mental health problems.

Labelling theorists note that people of African-Caribbean origin are far more likely to reach the mental health system via the courts and prisons because magistrates and judges are more likely to refer them for psychiatric reports compared with other social groups. They are much more likely to be referred by prisons if they do not cooperate with the authorities.

Mental illness and gender

A higher proportion of women than men experience mental health problems, e.g. women's rate of admission to psychiatric hospitals in England and Wales is about 30% above the rate for men. Women are at least three times more likely than men to be suffering from depression.

Brown et al. (1995), argue that women are more likely to lead stressful lives than men because they often combine careers and the responsibility for childcare. They are also more likely to experience poverty and poor housing conditions.

However, feminist labelling theorists such as **Chesler** (1972) argue that the behaviour of women is more likely to be defined as evidence of mental illness because the **diagnosis**, or **labeling**, is normally carried out by a male-dominated psychiatric profession which interprets women as more prone to mental illness. Consequently, any emotional behaviour in a male is likely to be labelled by such doctors as physical and as resulting from mental exhaustion and the patient is advised to rest. However, the same behaviour in a woman may be **labelled** as **hysterical** or as symptoms of a nervous breakdown. Consequently, the female patient may be advised to go on an anti-depressant drug regime.

PROGRESS CHECK

1. How was mental illness explained before the twentieth century?
2. What, according to Scheff and Szasz, is mental illness?

Answers: 1 As either demonic possession or moral weakness. 2 A label applied by society to people whose behaviour is regarded as different or threatening.

4.3 Health inequalities

LEARNING SUMMARY

After studying this section, you should be able to understand:

- patterns in the social distribution of health and illness in regard to social class, gender, ethnicity, region, age and globally
- different sociological explanations of health inequalities, particularly those relating to cultural, material and structural factors as well as provision of, and access to, healthcare

---

Social class and health inequalities

AQA **SCLY 2**   OCR **G672**

Patterns of inequality

> Social inequality is a key theme in sociology.

If health and illness were chance occurrences we could expect to see them randomly distributed across the population. However, we can see that some groups can expect an over-proportionate amount of death and illness.

The Registrar General's social class scale identified five social classes based on occupation. These were Class I (professional occupations such as architects), Class II (managerial and technical occupations such as teachers), Class III (N) (skilled non-manual occupations such as clerks), III M (Skilled manual occupations such as electricians), IV (partly skilled occupations such as caretakers) and Class V (unskilled occupations such as cleaners).

- Men in social class I can expect to live for almost eight and a half years longer than men from social class V, while women in social class I can expect to live four and a half years longer than their social class V peers.
- Death rates between social classes have actually worsened in the past forty years, e.g. in the 1970s, the death rate among men of working age was almost twice as high for those in class V compared with those in class I. By 2003, it was almost two and a half times as high.
- The working class experience worse infant mortality rates than the middle class, e.g. more than 3500 working class babies would survive per year if the working class infant mortality rate was reduced to middle class levels.
- The working class are more likely to die pre-retirement of cancer, stroke and heart disease than the middle class.

Explanations for differences in health between social classes

AQA **SCLY 2**   OCR **G672**

The artefact approach

An artefact is something that occurs as a result of an investigative procedure, e.g. **Illsley** (1986) believes that the link between the working class and poor health is not real, but a statistical illusion. Illsley points out that the number of people who can be defined as manual working class has declined so much over the last 30 years that any change in the behavior of this group is statistically meaningless.

However, **Acheson** (1998) showed that, even when the classes were regrouped to include classes IV and V together, significant differences between social classes remained, e.g. in the late 1970s, death rates were 53% higher among men in classes IV and V compared with those in classes I and II.

Social selection

The social selection approach claims that social class does not cause ill health, but that ill health may be a significant cause of social class, e.g. if a person is chronically ill or is disabled in some way, it is usually difficult for them to obtain a secure, well–paid job. The fit and healthy are more likely to be successful in life and upwardly mobile in terms of social class.

The problem with this approach is that studies of health differences indicate that poor health is a result of poverty rather than a cause of it.

Cultural deprivation theory

Note that this theory links to material in Chapter 3 on Education.

> **KEY POINT**
>
> Cultural deprivation theory argues that inequalities in health between the working class and middle class are the product of **culture**.

Working class culture is seen to be composed of values which are harmful to health. Working class people are seen as making harmful health choices in the following respects.
- **Diet:** Manual workers consume twice as much white bread as professionals, have higher sugar consumption, eat more pre-prepared meals and junk food and eat less fresh fruit and vegetables.

This approach can be seen as blaming the victims and their culture.

- **Cigarette smoking:** Manual workers are at least three times more likely to smoke than the middle classes.
- **Leisure and lifestyle:** Roberts argues that the working class indulge in less exercise and are more passive in terms of their leisure pursuits whereas in contrast middle class people take part in a wider range of sporting and health activities.
- **Alcohol:** The working class consume more alcohol than the middle class.

Cultural deprivation theorists have also suggested that the working class are less likely to take advantage of preventative health care, vaccination or ante-natal care. **Howlett and Ashley** suggest that the middle class have more knowledge of what constitutes good health than the working class. Consequently the middle class attempt to prevent health problems through exercise and diet.

However, critics of cultural deprivation theory argue that:
- smoking and drinking may be an attempt to relieve stress.
- the working class take-up of NHS facilities may have little to do with poor attitudes. Research by **Cartwright and O'Brien** suggests that working class patients feel intimidated by the middle class nature of health care. They found that doctors spend much more time with middle class patients than with working class patients and that they know far more about their middle class patients.

> **KEY POINT**
>
> Cultural values may be a realistic response to the poverty and material deprivation caused by unemployment and/or low wages. Cost may be the major reason why working class people do not subscribe to healthy diets, exercise and take-up of NHS facilities. They may be well aware of the benefits of these but unable to afford them.

Materialist explanations

Materialist sociologists are critical of the cultural deprivation approach because it fails to ask why these groups have poor diets and high alcohol and cigarette consumption. There may be reasons why people are 'forced' into an unhealthy lifestyle. In some cases, these choices may even be rational as the following examples illustrate.

- Research by **Dobson** (1994) found that in working class households, shopping for food was shaped by poverty which restricted choice to cheap brands. Mothers bought 'unhealthy' foods such as crisps and biscuits because they knew these would definitely be eaten by their children and they did not want to risk wasting money on foodstuffs their children might not eat. In the context of poverty, these decisions were **rational choices** made in difficult economic circumstances.
- **Blackburn** (1991) found that the poor were less likely to invest in healthy eating because of the high costs, e.g. organic vegetables and free range chickens and eggs tend to be a lot more expensive than processed foods.
- The **National Food Alliance** points to the existence of 'food deserts', that is inner-city areas where cheap nutritious foods are not available because of the absence of large supermarkets. People in deprived areas have to rely upon corner shops or smaller retail outlets that do not have the same economy of scale as the larger chains. These often have less choice of healthy foods and are more expensive.

- The **National Children's Homes** (1991) survey on nutrition and poverty found that one child in ten and one adult in five, especially mothers, skipped meals because of **cost**. Consequently, malnutrition is a problem among poorer social groups in Britain.
- There is some evidence too that **fast-food chains**, such as Burger King, McDonalds and KFC, target poorer areas with special offers.

> **KEY POINT**
>
> Materialist approaches stress that poverty is the key factor in understanding and explaining health inequalities. The poor have unique experiences and characteristics that lead to poor health and low life expectancy. They experience lower than average incomes and the worst housing conditions.

Regional inequalities

Shaw (1999) has drawn attention to how there appears to be some type of **relationship between health, poverty and region**. She compared one million people living in poor constituencies with the worst health records, with a million people living in more affluent areas with the best health records and she found that in the poorer areas:

- children under the age of 1 are twice as likely to die in their first year of life
- adults have a 70% greater chance of dying before the age of 65.

Many of the most poverty-stricken areas have **mortality rates** twice the national average, e.g. Glasgow Shettleston has a mortality rate of 234 compared with affluent Wokingham which has a mortality rate of 65. Shaw estimates that 71% of deaths in Glasgow Shettleston are premature and could have been avoided if the population had been lifted out of poverty.

Structuralist explanations

This approach focuses on social and economic inequalities inherent in capitalism.

Many of the above problems associated with poverty are blamed by **structuralist** sociologists, particularly **Marxist** sociologists, on the way British society is organised. In other words, the British economy is structured or organised along **capitalist** lines. Marxists suggest that this has a number of negative consequences for health.

- It has produced great **inequalities** in the distribution of wealth and income, e.g. Marxist sociologists note that poverty exists because **wealth** (the money found in shares, savings, land, property, artwork, jewellery, etc.) is concentrated in very few hands. In 2001, the wealthiest 1% of the population owned as much wealth as the poorest 50%.
- Employers have a vested interest in keeping wages at a low level in order to **maximise profits**. This may result in poverty. Two government sponsored reports, **The Black Report** (1980) and **The Health Divide** (1987) identify the chief causes of ill health amongst the working class as poverty. **Townsend and Phillimore** (1986), in a study of health in the North East, note the relationship between bad housing, poor diet, lack of play areas, overcrowding, poor education and exposure to infection. They conclude that the health gap is a consequence of the wealth gap.
- **Davey Smith** (1990) links mortality rates to position at work. He found that workers with little power or control over their work are likely to experience worse health than those with more responsibility. His research on civil

servants has shown that routine clerical workers are much more likely to die young than workers in higher grades. If the lowest and highest grades are compared, those in the lowest grades are actually three times more likely to die before reaching the age of 65.

- The health of manual workers is threatened by employer breaches of health and safety laws. On average, about 500 workers die at work every year. Furthermore, thousands are injured. Industrial diseases too contribute to the poor health of hundreds of thousands of working class people because of prolonged exposure to toxic substances whilst at work.

Psycho-social or neo-materialist explanations

Wilkinson (1996) argues that the greater the inequality in a society like in Britain, the less **social cohesion** or community it has and, therefore, the more insecurity, isolation and stress will be experienced by the most disadvantaged groups leading to greater levels of ill health.

Wilkinson suggests that **social inequality** leads to feelings of **resentment, insecurity and isolation** – all these are stress factors that can trigger off physical and mental ill health. Wilkinson notes too that the physical experience of living in poor communities can lead to increased anxiety and stress, e.g. low income can lead to worry about how bills are going to be paid and debt. Some residents may realistically fear being a victim of crime or anti-social behaviour.

> **KEY POINT**
>
> Unemployment could lead to shame, powerlessness, depression and suicidal tendencies. Wilkinson argues that these experiences lead to stress which can undermine our immune systems and our ability to fight off infection and disease.

Social administration theory – regional inequalities in access to health care

The main focus here is on the inadequacies of health policies.

Social administration theory argues that health inequalities are largely caused by inequalities in the distribution of NHS resources.

> **KEY POINT**
>
> **Hart** (1971) suggests that the allocation of NHS resources is so unequal that it conforms to an 'inverse care law' – a law which states that those whose need is less get more NHS funding and resources whilst those in greatest need get less. In general, in practice this means that working class areas have fewer GPs, dentists, hospitals and specialist units such as cancer screening than more affluent middle class areas.

There is some evidence that the inverse care law is underpinned by a **north–south divide**. Some experts have even described this unequal access to health services as a **postcode lottery**, e.g. an examination of NHS facilities reveals that the industrial areas of northern England, Scotland and Wales have:

- fewer and older hospitals
- fewer high status hospitals, i.e. foundation trust hospitals which are given higher levels of funding than other hospitals.

- fewer and less adequate specialised facilities, such as for cancer and kidney treatments
- fewer hospital beds per head of population
- fewer GP practices and therefore higher patient–doctor ratios – so there are fewer doctors for those most likely to get ill
- slower access to diagnostic tests, anti-cancer drugs and chemotherapy.

Gordon *et al*. (1999) argue that there is a large body of evidence to support what they describe as the **inverse prevention law** in front-line health care – those social groups who are in greatest need of preventative care are least likely to have access to preventative services such as health promotion, dental check-ups, immunisation, cancer screening and so on. They are, however, more likely to use accident and emergency services because conditions that have not been treated have become more serious and life-threatening. Consequently, these services are under greater strain.

However, in criticism of the social administration model, the healthiest part of Britain (East Anglia), has never received a fair share of funding, whilst Scotland has always received more funding than England and Wales.

The role of private health care

> **KEY POINT**
>
> Inequalities in access to health care exist between those who rely upon the NHS and those who use the **private sector**. Private health care is used by those who pay directly for medical services or who have private health insurance.

The middle classes are much more likely than the working class to have access to private medicine because they earn more whilst take-up of private medical insurance is far greater in the South than it is in the North. Furthermore, the vast majority of private hospitals are situated in London and the South East.

Private health care increases inequalities in morbidity and mortality by:
- allowing those who can pay to have treatment without waiting, whereas NHS patients have to join a waiting list
- giving private patients access to a range of medical services that may not be available on the NHS
- limiting the number of hours worked by some consultants (senior specialists) in the NHS, who prefer to earn more money in the private sector
- employing nurses and other specialists who have been trained by the NHS – thus contributing to the shortage of trained staff in NHS hospitals.

Gender and health inequalities

AQA **SCLY 2**   OCR **G672**

Patterns of inequality

A number of differences in mortality and morbidity can be identified between men and women.
- Women live longer than men in all social classes. Life expectancy at birth in Britain is 77 years for females, but 71 for males.

- Women experience more chronic sickness (i.e. long-standing illness, disability or infirmity) than men. Two-thirds of the four million disabled people in Britain are women.
- Women are more likely to suffer from emotional disturbance, depression and acute stress than men and are much more likely to be receiving drug treatment for such problems.
- Women see their doctor more frequently than men.

Explanations for gender inequalities

McFarlane suggests that the statistics are misleading. She notes that once visits to the GP in connection with contraception, menstruation, gynaecology and post-natal care are taken into consideration, the differences between males and females in terms of morbidity disappear.

However, it is still a fact that more women are treated for mental health problems and degenerative diseases. The latter is probably due to the fact that women are more likely than men to survive beyond retirement age.

Gender role socialisation

> This links to material on gender socialisation and identity in Chapters 1 and 2.

Gender role socialisation is seen by some liberal feminists as the reason for differences in mortality and morbidity.
- Men are socialised into being more **aggressive** and into taking more **risks**. This could account for the relatively high death rate for males aged 15–35. Many of these deaths result from acts of violence and motor accidents.
- It is more acceptable for men to smoke and drink alcohol, which may account for the higher rate of death from cancer and heart disease in the 45–55 age-group.

> Many sociologists argue that expectations surrounding gender are changing.

- Men are expected to be breadwinners in our culture. Therefore they are more likely to be victims of industrial accidents, disease and stress. They are more likely to suffer the stress of unemployment.

> **KEY POINT**
>
> **O'Brien et al.** (2005) found that the majority of men preferred to shrug off illness and to put off as long as possible seeking a consultation with a doctor. Masculine ideas of being able to cope in the face of adversity, being able to endure pain and suffering, and not appearing to be weak were cited by the men in their study for not going to the doctor.

- Women are socialised to express their feelings and to talk about their problems more than men. Women may therefore be more willing to admit to health problems and to see a doctor.

> This links to the domestic division of labour.

- Girls and women may be socialised into being more aware of health issues because of menstruation, contraception, pregnancy and childbirth. When they become mothers, they are expected to 'manage' family health matters because they are likely to be the main nurturers and carers of children, the disabled, the elderly, etc.

Feminist explanations

Feminist explanations tend to focus on the concept of **patriarchy**, i.e. male domination of social institutions such as the family and marriage.

This is relevant to material in Chapter 1.

Bernard takes the view that women may suffer more ill-health because of **marriage**. In her study, she found that married women were less healthy than single women and full-time housewives were less healthy than women who worked full-time. Furthermore, married men were healthier than single men. Bernard concludes that giving up work and becoming a full-time mother–housewife can lead to depression, insomnia and nervous anxiety. However, Bernard's measurement of women's health was measured by visits to the doctor which may be problematic.

Feminist sociologists suggest that the patriarchal social expectations which state that women should take primary responsibility for **child-care** and **domestic labour** can have a negative effect on women's health. Oakley found that housework is rarely experienced as fulfilling and the high rates of depression in women may be linked to the unpaid, repetitive, unrewarding, often isolating and low status nature of housework in a society where only paid employment is really respected.

Many women work a 'triple' shift comprising paid work, house, work and emotional work. In many cases, the stress of these responsibilities is increased by having to manage limited household budgets and by having little leisure time (compared with males) in order to relax.

Feminists argue that women's health is harmed by patriarchal assumptions that women should take the responsibility for **birth control**. They note that young women are at risk from the **clinical iatrogenesis**, especially the increased risk of cancer or heart conditions, associated with the contraceptive pill. Women's increased use of mental health services may mean that iatrogenesis is also brought about by addiction to anti-depressants and sleeping pills.

Busfield claims that one reason women appear to be more ill is because of patriarchal control over all aspects of health. She suggests that male doctors see themselves as the norm by which women should be judged. Busfield argues that this means that women's health is not taken seriously by the medical profession. This can be illustrated in a number of ways.

- Firstly, some women's health conditions, particularly pre-menstrual tension and post-natal depression have only been recently recognised as types of illness.

Another example of the labelling process.

- Secondly, the same symptoms in men and women may be **diagnosed** and **labelled quite differently**, e.g. anxiety and stress in a man may be diagnosed as symptoms of over-work and rest might be advised. Similar symptoms in a woman maybe viewed as a 'natural' aspect of women's 'weaker' character that can only be treated with drugs. Women are therefore more likely to be diagnosed as depressed or suffering from anxiety than men. They are also more likely to be treated in mental hospitals. This may have more to do with how male doctors interpret female symptoms than with objective scientific analysis.
- Thirdly, problems such as depression may be interpreted by male doctors as an inability to cope with children or with housework. In other words, doctors see the causes of women's ill-health in terms of individual emotional weakness rather than as resulting from the patriarchal problems they face in the family, e.g. inequality in the distribution of housework and childcare, the triple shift, domestic violence and in society, e.g. low pay, discrimination in the workplace, poverty.

In criticism of these feminist views, there is evidence that health services have greatly benefitted women. Women's life expectancy remains significantly higher than men's and the NHS has introduced very successful screening programmes for both breast and cervical cancer. Breast cancer attracts the most funds of all research into sex-specific cancers. However, prostate cancer which kills about 10 000 males a year (five times as many women who die from cervical cancer) and testicular cancer have no national screening programmes.

Ethnicity and health inequalities

AQA **SCLY 2**   OCR **G672**

Patterns of inequality

A number of patterns can be seen in regard to ethnicity and health in Britain.

- Most ethnic minority groups have higher mortality rates than the white population (although white people in poverty experience similar rates). In particular, infant mortality rates tend to be significantly higher than the white population.
- Life expectancy in ethnic minority populations is generally lower than the White majority population.
- People from African-Caribbean, Indian, Pakistani and Bangladeshi backgrounds are all more likely to suffer and die from tuberculosis, liver cancer or diabetes compared with the White population. However, apart from liver cancer, all ethnic minority groups have lower levels of death from cancer than the White population.
- Indians and Pakistanis are more likely to die from heart disease compared with other ethnic groups. African-Caribbeans have the lowest level of death from coronary heart disease compared with other ethnic groups.
- Africans and African-Caribbeans are more likely to suffer from strokes and high blood pressure than other ethnic groups.
- Indians and African-Caribbeans are more likely to experience mental illness, especially schizophrenia compared with other ethnic groups. Furthermore African-Caribbeans are five times more likely than other ethnic groups to be hospitalised for mental illness. On the other hand, Chinese people experience less mental illness than any other ethnic group.

Explanations for ethnic inequalities in health

AQA **SCLY 2**   OCR **G672**

Cultural deprivation theory

Culturalist explanations suggest that the culture of ethnic minorities is responsible for their poor mortality and morbidity rates. It is suggested that ethnic minorities choose to pursue particular courses of action that result in ill-health.

Blaming the victims.

- In particular, **diet** is blamed for the high rates of heart disease amongst Asians, e.g. ghee is a supposedly less healthy form of cooking fat. The high rate of diabetes among Asians is blamed on **high carbohydrate foods** which encourage obesity. It is argued that Asian foods also tend to **lack vitamin D** and that this may account for the higher level of rickets found among Asian children.
- **Levels of smoking** remain high among Asian and Black groups compared with whites.
- Evidence suggests Asian people are less likely to engage in **physical exercise and sport** compared with other ethnic groups.

- Asian women are less likely to visit **ante- and post-natal clinics** which may help explain higher levels of infant mortality.
- Many older Asian women **speak poor English** which may create difficulties in taking up **NHS preventative services** such as screening for breast and cervical cancer, or in obtaining treatment, advice and guidance from health workers.

> **KEY POINT**
>
> However, critics of the culturalist approach suggest it is not Asian culture that is responsible for their poor health, but the NHS response to ethnic minority cultures, e.g. despite big improvements, there is still a lack of information available in minority ethnic group languages as well as a lack of translation services.

Moreover, Asian women prefer to see female doctors, but there is a shortage of female GPs in those areas with the largest concentration of Asian households. Also, health professionals may fail to meet the health needs or react to the health concerns of ethnic minorities because they are not familiar enough with the religious, cultural and dietary practices of ethnic minority cultures.

Materialist explanations

Materialists are very critical of culturalists for failing to acknowledge that cultural practices are not voluntarily chosen – rather they are shaped by **economic and social circumstances** over which the individual has little or no control.

Sociologists such as **Dorling** and **Shaw** suggest that **poverty** is more likely to be experienced by ethnic minorities, e.g. 40% of ethnic minorities live in poverty compared with 20% of the White community. This figure increases to 69% for people of Pakistani and Bangladeshi origin. Ethnic minority poverty is caused by the fact that ethnic minorities are more likely to be found in **low-paid jobs** or to be **unemployed**. Ethnic minorities are more likely than whites to be over–concentrated in lower paid semi-skilled and unskilled work which often involves working night-shifts in hazardous and toxic work environments.

> **KEY POINT**
>
> Ethnic minorities experience high unemployment rates compared with White people, e.g. in 2008, 5% of Whites were unemployed compared with 14% of African-Caribbeans, 13% of Bangladeshis and 11% of Pakistanis.

This is relevant to the sociological study of education.

Poverty also leads to **housing inequalities** – 70% of ethnic minority people in Britain live in council housing in the 88 most economically and socially deprived local authority districts. Only 2% of whites live in poor, damp and overcrowded housing compared with 30% of Bangladeshis and 22% of Pakistanis. **Alcock** found that poor damp housing often leads to poor health in ethnic minority children, as well as time off school and fewer qualifications, leading to low-paid low-skilled jobs or unemployment.

Another major factor that increases the possibility of illness and early death is the **experience of racism**, e.g. racist name calling, racial attacks and racial harassment. All these experiences of abuse may increase fear, stress and anxiety – all of which may result in ill-health.

The Inverse Care Law

This approach focuses on the inadequacies of health policies.

Hart (see page 105) suggests that areas that need health care the most actually have less NHS funding and fewer specialist hospitals, consultants and general practitioners (GPs). This is especially true of those areas in which there are concentrations of ethnic minorities in the north of England or inner city areas of London.

Furthermore, it is argued that what NHS services do exist do not cater sufficiently for ethnic minority cultural and religious needs. The NHS has been criticised for being an '**ethnocentric**' or **institutionally racist** institution – it is mainly focused on the needs of the majority white population, rather than all social groups. Surveys indicate that Asians report higher levels of dissatisfaction with health care than white people.

It has been suggested that ethnic minority people may be put off seeking medical help because:
- women may not be guaranteed a female doctor
- the unique religious and dietary needs of ethnic minorities may not be recognised
- preventative publicity campaigns, e.g. anti-smoking and advice about diet are rarely aimed at ethnic minorities.

Social constructionist or interactionist theories

Some **Interactionist** accounts explore the treatment of African-Caribbeans with regard to mental health. **Nazroo** argues that African-Caribbeans, especially Rastafarians, are more likely than any other group to be diagnosed as 'mentally ill'. However, Nazroo argues this may not reflect real illness. Rather, he accuses White psychiatrists of wrongly interpreting and negatively labelling behaviour which is culturally or religiously 'different' as 'mental illness' or 'schizophrenia'.

Nazroo notes that many Rastafarians refuse to co-operate with the White authorities because they subscribe to the religious view that White society is 'evil' (Babylon) for enslaving Africans during the slave trade. Nazroo argues that the price they pay for this non-cooperation is being remanded to psychiatric units for reports. He argues that this is not a scientific diagnosis – rather it is a form of white **social control**.

Rosenhan's study illustrated this.

Once a person has been admitted to a psychiatric institution it can be quite difficult to get out because all behaviour is interpreted in the context of the 'mentally ill' label. There is some evidence too that continuing non-cooperation leads to greater controls over African-Caribbeans inside the system through the use of drugs and electric shock treatment.

Psycho-social explanations

Some studies have suggested that there exists a **health gradient**, in that at every level of the social hierarchy, there are health differences. Some writers, most notably **Wilkinson** suggest that those who are low in the socio-economic hierarchy such as ethnic minorities have less social control over their working and living conditions and consequently they experience greater stress and greater feelings of low self-esteem.

Wilkinson also argues that income inequality affects health because it undermines **social cohesion** (see pages 100 and 105). Ethnic minorities are more likely than most other groups to experience a lack of social cohesion. Wilkinson claims this triggers off psycho-social behaviour such as smoking and drinking, poor eating habits and inactivity. This combination of psycho-social and lifestyle factors, in turn, produces greater levels of depression, high blood pressure, increased susceptibility to infection and build–up of cholesterol, i.e. all factors that contribute to the lower life expectancy, high death rates and general ill-health of ethnic minority communities.

When discussing topics such as health and education, it is important to consider how social influences such as ethnicity, gender and social class intersect or inter-relate.

> **KEY POINT**
>
> It is important to note that race interacts with other important social factors especially social class and gender, e.g. some Asian groups (notably East African Asian), tend to occupy higher social-class positions than other Asian groups and consequently enjoy health levels similar to the white middle class. Ethnic-minority women may experience worse health than ethnic-minority men, according to **Blackburn** (1991).

Global or international inequalities in health

AQA **SCLY 2**

Patterns of inequality

> **KEY POINT**
>
> There are dramatic health differences between the richer and poorer countries of the world, e.g. the probability of premature adult death (i.e. before the age of 65) varies widely between (and within) different regions of the world.

- In some parts of sub-Saharan Africa premature adult death rates are nearly four times higher than those experienced in Western European countries.
- While life expectancy is generally increasing across the world, in Africa the reverse is true – adults in Africa today die at a younger age than they did in 1990.
- Half a million women die each year as a consequence of pregnancy and childbirth. Of these deaths, 99% are in the developing world, e.g. the maternal death rate in developing countries is 479 per 100 000 live births compared with 27 in developed countries.
- Infant mortality rates remain very high in developing countries compared with industrialised countries. The least developed countries such as Angola, Sierra Leone and Afghanistan had infant mortality rates on average 17 times higher than countries in the industrialised West.
- It is estimated that 30 000 children a day die of preventable diseases, especially communicable diseases caused by infected and polluted water supplies, particularly in sub-Saharan Africa. Thirteen million African children were killed by diarrhoea alone in the 1990s.

Explanations for international inequalities

AQA **SCLY 2**

Poverty

The main cause of the high rates of mortality and morbidity in the developing world is **poverty**. Poverty causes malnutrition and poor diet, and consequently decreases resistance to diseases such as measles, e.g. some 800 million children are estimated by the United Nations to be malnourished. Moreover, poverty means that developing societies lack the resources to invest in clean water and sanitation systems.

Health care systems

Poverty also means that many developing societies do not have the money to invest in **national health care systems**. Western-led public **health education** with regard to hygiene and clean water, the processing of food, medical advances in the eradication of diseases such as smallpox, and the control of disease such as measles and malaria have all contributed to a fall in the death rates of the developing world.

Moreover, Western-led educational health programmes aimed at women have also been successful in reducing infant mortality rates, e.g. Oxfam has observed that in Ghana, the children of educated mothers are twice as likely as children of uneducated mothers to survive to their first birthday.

Debt

> **KEY POINT**
>
> Many developing countries are heavily in debt to Western banks and as a result they cannot afford to invest in health care and education systems. There is evidence that the more a country pays to reduce its debt as a percentage of its earnings, the more likely its infant mortality rate will increase because it has less money to invest in essential medicines or the wages of doctors and nurses.

Another problem faced by the developing world is the high cost of manufactured pharmaceuticals and medical technology, which are mainly produced by Western-based multi-national companies and which developing societies often cannot afford. Western pharmaceutical companies have been accused of exploiting the African AIDS epidemic for profit, in that the prices they charge the developing world for the drugs is well in excess of their costs.

Western companies have also been accused of creating further health problems through irresponsible and aggressive advertising of unhealthy products such as baby milk powder, cigarettes and pesticides as well as the dumping of toxic materials in the developing world.

Health, happiness and well-being

Wilkinson (1996) compared health and economic data for 23 different countries and found very strong evidence that links the health of a population with the degree of economic inequality in a country. He found that Cuba has better standards of health than the USA, despite being much poorer. Wilkinson's conclusions were that societies with low levels of inequality had high levels of **social cohesion** – that is a sense of belonging and place in a society. This sense of belonging had the effect of increasing the sense of happiness and well-being, which in turn improved standards of health. On the other hand, a lack of social cohesion results in greater stress, anxiety, envy, anger and frustration and a rise in health problems (see also pages 105 and 111).

Age and health inequalities

AQA SCLY 2

Blaxter's national survey of health definitions found that young people tend to define health in terms of physical fitness, but gradually as people age, health comes to be defined in terms of being able or unable to cope with everyday tasks. She found examples of older people with serious arthritis who defined themselves as relatively healthy because they could still carry out routine activities.

Children and health inequalities

> This highlights the interaction of social class and ethnicity.

The evidence suggests that threats to health in childhood are influenced by both **social class** and **ethnic** background. For example:

- babies born to professional fathers have levels of infant mortality half that of babies born to unskilled manual fathers
- babies born into ethnic minority families have higher levels of infant mortality than children born into white families
- children from poorer backgrounds, whether white or ethnic minority, are five times more likely to die as a result of accidents than children from better off families.

The elderly and access to health care

> This links to material on the ageing population in Chapter 1.

In Britain 16% of the total population is now aged over 65 and it is estimated that 20% will be aged 65 and over by 2026. As medical knowledge improves, **life expectancy** will increase and more people will survive into old age. It is estimated that five million people will be aged over 80 years by 2030.

Expectations of health are also increasing – people want not just an old age, but a healthy old age. However, this is linked to social factors such as social class and ethnicity. In general, the healthiest older people are the White middle class, whilst the least healthy tend to be poorer people from minority ethnic backgrounds.

The elderly and the National Health Service

The elderly are the largest users of hospitals and community care within the NHS – this has a number of consequences.

- More money will have to be spent on long-term **health care**, e.g. the Joseph Rowntree Foundation suggests that NHS funding on long-term care for the elderly will need to rise from £13 billion in 2004 to £54 billion by 2051.
- The **private health care** sector will benefit from the ageing of the population with demand for nursing and residential care for the elderly expected to triple to 1.1 million places. The middle class elderly will benefit more from this provision than the working class or ethnic minority elderly because they can afford to buy such services.

However, **geriatric medicine** (the health care of the elderly) is seen by doctors and patients as having **low social prestige** and consequently both staffing and funding levels are very low. It does not get the allocation of staff expertise and other resources that are needed to give the best care to older people.

However, despite being the group most expected to have health needs, there is evidence that the elderly actually under-use the NHS. This is probably because:

- generational differences mean that the elderly are often unwilling to 'pester' or bother their GP when they are ill – older people see themselves as 'wasting the doctor's time'
- older people may put up with a lot more pain and discomfort than younger people
- the elderly tend to play down their illnesses and fail to seek treatment for what they dismiss as symptoms of old age
- the elderly are less willing to take up preventative measures to assist their health, e.g. despite high profile advertising, take-up of flu vaccinations among the elderly is very low although this varies by region.

The NHS and institutional ageism

Both Age Concern and Help the Aged (now Age UK) have accused the NHS of **institutional ageism**. A Help the Aged survey found that the elderly feel that:
- they have had second class treatment and care simply because of their age
- they are sometimes not referred to consultants or for surgery because of their age
- they face inappropriate comments about their age and patronising attitudes while in hospital
- they often lack transport in order to access health care services
- they are less able to access NHS specialised services leaving them in pain, housebound and at an increased risk of falls
- they receive little help with difficulties they may face in interpreting and understanding instructions on medications
- they receive poor advice from their GPs.

An Age Concern survey of the NHS's treatment of the elderly found **age discrimination** being routinely practised. For example:
- women aged over 65 are not invited for routine breast screenings despite the fact that almost two-thirds of deaths from the disease occur in this group
- a fifth of all heart units operate an age-related admissions policy, even though two-thirds of those treated for heart attacks are over 65
- many clinical trials investigating cancer exclude the elderly, despite a third of cancers occurring in the over 75 age group.

PROGRESS CHECK

1. What does cultural deprivation theory blame for inequalities in health?
2. What do material deprivationists blame for inequalities in health?
3. What is the 'inverse care law'?
4. What do Marxists claim is the major cause of ill health?
5. What female social role is blamed by Oakley, Bernard and Graham for the poor health of women?
6. What sociological explanation has been given for the large number of African-Caribbean people in the mental health system?

Answers: 1. The cultural habits of the poor. 2. Poverty. 3. Those whose need is less get more health resources, whilst those in greatest need get less. 4. Inequalities within capitalism. 5. The mother–housewife role. 6. Racist labelling, e.g. in the criminal justice system.

4.4 The role of health professionals

LEARNING SUMMARY	After studying this section, you should be able to understand: • different explanations of the role of medicine and health professions • differences between conventional medicine and complementary/alternative medicines

Functionalism

AQA **SCLY 2**   OCR **G672**

> Doctors as public servants.

For functionalist sociologists, medical professionals are seen as **selfless** and **altruistic** individuals working for the **good of the community**, often making great personal sacrifices. Functionalists argue that people who want to be doctors need to be of the highest intelligence and skill, undergo years of training and in their early careers earn very little. They therefore argue that high levels of reward later, are necessary to attract, retain and motivate the best people into the medical profession.

The sick role

Most functionalist sociologists argue that the medical profession is beneficial to society. The first functionalist to argue this was **Parsons** who saw doctors as central to the functioning of what he called **the sick role**. Parsons argued that too much sickness could be bad for society because it was a threat to **social order**. It could lead to the breakdown of the economy, especially the specialised **division of labour**, i.e. the way work is organised.

> **KEY POINT**
>
> Parsons argues that in order to manage sickness, modern industrial societies have created the sick role. This means that society has agreed that people need to conform to certain social characteristics in order to be officially and legitimately defined as 'sick', i.e. to be excused work by employers or teachers, to obtain a sick note, or to be officially recognised as disabled or chronically ill enough to receive welfare benefits.

The sick role involves certain rights, duties and obligations that 'sick' people need to adopt.
- They must see sickness as undesirable and want to get better.
- They must seek medical help and follow the advice of doctors, etc.
- They must be exempted from their normal activities such as work or school.

Parsons argued that the medical profession's main **function** was to promote the sick role to ensure that sickness does not threaten **social order**. Doctors therefore act as official **gatekeepers** to the sick role and consequently they have certain rights and responsibilities such as:
- the right to carry out an examination of the patient's physical condition and to ask personal questions about lifestyle
- authority over the patient (i.e. the patient must follow doctor's orders regardless of their status)
- autonomy in practice – other doctors and medical professionals must not interfere.

However, Parsons notes that doctors have obligations or responsibilities towards patients too including:

- the patient's needs must be put before the doctor's self-interest
- confidentiality, i.e. the Hippocratic Oath is central to the relationship between doctor and patient
- the doctor must use all possible medical expertise to restore health.

The professionalisation of medicine

Barber (1963) argued that the medical profession is very important for society because doctors deal with people when they are in particularly vulnerable positions. Consequently, the medical community has developed a number of professional traits to increase the trust people have in them.

- They have developed a theoretical and scientific base of knowledge that underpins medical practice.
- They are fully trained to the highest possible standards.
- Competence is tested by rigorous examination.
- There is a strict **code of ethics** to ensure that no patient is exploited.
- Medical practice is regulated and controlled by the General Medical Council (GMC) which has the power to punish and exclude doctors from the profession for misconduct (i.e. to strike them off the medical register so that they can no longer practise medicine anywhere in Britain).

Criticisms of functionalism

However, **Waitzkin** (1979) argues that for many years these professional characteristics and standards were mainly used as a **barrier** to prevent groups, other than upper, middle class White males, from entering the profession. It is only in the last 20 years that there has been significant recruitment of women and ethnic minorities into the medical profession. Some sociologists are critical of the role of the GMC which is supposed to supervise the profession. It is argued that this body usually whitewashes or ignores cases of incompetence. Final sanctions, such as striking a doctor off the medical register, are used only rarely and then more often for sexual misconduct than for gross incompetence.

Functionalists claim that people become doctors because they are public spirited. However, the existence of **private medicine** and the high financial rewards paid to plastic surgeons, e.g. to enhance feminine features suggests that some people are attracted to the medical profession for the money.

Illich suggests some doctors do more harm than good and that clinical iatrogenesis (i.e. mistakes made by doctors in surgery and diagnosis as well as the tendency to prescribe addictive drugs) is responsible for a high number of patient deaths and harms.

The Weberian approach

Weber argued that all occupational groups compete with each other for status and high rewards. He noticed that one way in which they did this was to organise themselves along professional lines, i.e. to form professional associations in order to bargain with employers and protect their financial interests.

Parry and Parry (1976) suggest that the **professionalisation** of medicine is merely an **occupational strategy** for controlling the labour market to the advantage of doctors. They note that in pursuit of greater financial rewards, doctors have deliberately acquired the following professional characteristics.

- They have gained **control** over the training and entry requirements necessary for membership. This means that they are able to control the numbers of people qualifying as doctors by constructing a series of specialist educational courses and qualifications. The number of new doctors is deliberately kept quite low in order to ensure scarcity and consequently this means they can demand or charge more for their services.
- All doctors have to belong to the **British Medical Association (BMA)**. This means that doctors can claim they are maintaining the highest public standards because they also claim the right to investigate and punish their own members. This makes it difficult for other groups such as the police or politicians to examine their activities.
- Doctors have managed to convince the government that only their members are **qualified** to carry out medical diagnosis and treatment. This monopoly is backed by law – it is a criminal offence to impersonate a doctor and to carry out medical diagnosis.
- The medical profession has attempted to **exclude any competition** to doctors' expertise and knowledge. Alternative medicines such as faith healing, homeopathy and aromatherapy. have been attacked and discredited by the medical profession who claim that only scientific medicine and surgery are effective.

> **KEY POINT**
>
> **Parry and Parry** argue that doctors are self-seeking individuals who adopt market strategies in order to maximise their earning power. In particular, controlling access to the profession and limiting the number of doctors being trained have been very effective occupational strategies which have resulted in doctors becoming very wealthy, privileged and secure. From a Weberian perspective, then, the medical profession is looking after its own interests as well as those of its patients.

Marxist approaches

> **KEY POINT**
>
> Marxists, such as **Navarro** (1977), argue that in capitalist societies such as Britain, a small ruling class exploits society for its own benefit. He argues that doctors are agents of this capitalist class and their high status and salaries are the rewards they receive from the capitalist ruling class for playing their part in maintaining economic inequality and exploitation.

Marxists argue that doctors are agents of the state who work on behalf of the capitalist class in a number of ways.

- Marxist writers on health, such as **Doyal** (1979) and **O'Connor** (1973), argue that doctors and the health service have a 'legitimation' role, in that they persuade the bulk of the population that capitalism 'cares' for them. In this role, it acts to limit class conflict and social unrest by creating a sense of harmony.
- **Doyal and Pennell** argue that doctors mislead the population as to the real cause of illness. The medical profession explains health and illness in terms of individuals' actions and genetics. Marxists claim that doctors very rarely

focus on the unequal and exploitative organisation of capitalism which result in poor working conditions, poverty, poor housing and inequalities in society, which are the underlying causes of ill health.

- Doctors ensure the health and fitness of the manual workforce so that capitalist production, exploitation and profit-making continue undisturbed.

However, critics point out that Marxism ignores the genuinely beneficial work that doctors do, and that to characterise their work as mainly focused on misleading and controlling the population is inaccurate. Doctors do mainly work in the context of individual problems but they also recognise and acknowledge stress in the workplace and the role of poverty.

Some Marxists, notably **McKinley** suggest that Navarro and Doyal and Pennell exaggerate the power of doctors. He argues that their professional freedom has been weakened by the state to the extent that they too are exploited by the capitalist bourgeoisie. McKinley argues that their role has been reduced to 'drug pushers' in that they prescribe drugs for all ills and so generate greater profits for the bourgeoisie who own and control the drug companies.

Post-modernist approaches

Post-modernists argue that the **professional power** of the medical profession has been challenged in recent years. Doctors are no longer seen as infallible and the concept of **iatrogenesis** has undermined the concept of medical professionalism. However, the biggest external challenge to the power of doctors has come from complementary or alternative medicines, which include homeopathy, herbal remedies, acupuncture and a range of other techniques.

> **KEY POINT**
>
> **Giddens** argues that in post-modern society, alternative medicine has benefitted from the fact that there is now a greater stress on **individual choice**.

Feminist approaches

Feminist sociologists, such as **Oakley** (1986) and **Witz** (1992), suggest that the professional activities of doctors contribute to the **social control** of women, both as patients and as medical practitioners. They point out that medicine has traditionally been a male occupation, with women excluded or marginalised into junior roles. This simply reinforces the subordinate position of women in society.

In recent years, feminist sociologists such as Oakley have complained that doctors have attempted to take control of areas of health such as **childbirth** that were previously dominated by female health workers such as midwives. **Graham** points out that men still dominate the top jobs in the NHS, i.e. consultants and surgeons. Women consultants are disproportionately represented in stereotypically feminine areas such as paediatrics.

However, in criticism of the feminist perspective, the traditional male-dominated medical profession's monopoly of healthcare has been strongly challenged over the last 20 years by an influx of ethnic minorities and women. There is also evidence that doctors are failing to meet men's health needs, for example prostate and testicular cancer prevention and screening programmes have not been given the same priority as breast or cervical cancer.

Exam practice questions

Questions 1–4 are typical AQA questions.

If you are following the AQA specification and choose the Health option, remember that the Methods in Context question will focus on the application of sociological research methods to the study of health.

Questions 5 and 6 are typical OCR questions.

When answering question 5(a) try to spend equal amounts of time on each of the two causes.

When answering questions that ask you to evaluate a particular view or claim, remember to include words or phrases such as 'however' and 'on the other hand'. By doing this, you will highlight the evaluative points that you are making.

It's important to manage your time effectively during the exam. Try to practise answering essay questions under timed conditions.

Read Item A and then answer questions 1–4 that follow.

Item A

The major causes of death in nineteenth century Britain were infectious diseases such as tuberculosis and smallpox. It is widely believed that biomedical advances were responsible for the increase in life expectancy.

However, McKeown (1979) has challenged this view. He shows that deaths from such diseases were long in decline before the introduction of effective medical treatments such as vaccinations. McKeown argues that people became more resistant to disease because of better nutrition, improved public-health conditions (such as the introduction of sewage disposal systems) and changes in personal behaviour such as better personal hygiene.

1 Explain what is meant by the term 'infant mortality'. **(2 marks)**

2 Suggest three ways in which people might work on their body. **(6 marks)**

3 Outline some of the reasons for ethnic inequalities in health. **(12 marks)**

4 Using material from Item A and elsewhere, assess the biomedical model of health and illness. **(20 marks)**

5 (a) Identify and explain two causes of class inequalities in health. **(17 marks)**

(b) Outline and evaluate the view that mental illness is socially defined. **(33 marks)**

6 (a) Identify and explain two ways in which women's social roles may affect their health. **(17 marks)**

(b) Outline and evaluate the view that increases in life expectancy over the last hundred years are linked primarily to medical advances. **(33 marks)**

Research methods

The following topics are covered in this chapter:

- Influences on the research process
- Primary research methods
- Secondary sources of data
- The use of multiple methods

5.1 Influences on the research process

LEARNING SUMMARY

After studying this section, you should be able to understand:

- the key concepts including reliability, validity, objectivity and representativeness
- key practical influences on the choice of topic and method
- the influence of ethics on the research process
- how the theories of positivism and interpretivism shape the research process

Key research concepts

AQA **SCLY 2** OCR **G671**
SCLY 4 **G674**

Primary data

Primary data is gathered 'first-hand' by the sociologist using a variety of methods, e.g. by asking people questions via questionnaires or interviews or by observing their behaviour, or by conducting experiments.

Secondary data

Secondary data is data which has been collected by other people and published or written down, e.g. education statistics relating to achievement and truancy are collected by the government and collated and published by civil servants at the Department for Education. Journalists may research health issues and publish their findings in the form of a newspaper or magazine article. Sociologists also draw on other studies carried out by their peers.

Quantitative data

Quantitative data collection methods include questionnaires, structured interviews and statistical data.

The form the data can take also differs. Some data appears in the form of numbers or statistics and is called **quantitative data**. It is normally displayed in various ways, such as tables, graphs, bar charts, pie charts, tally charts, columns of figures and lists of percentages. This type of data tends to be very factual.

Qualitative data

Qualitative data collection methods include unstructured interviews, observation and personal documents.

Other data takes a written form and provides a more personal account of the social world, e.g. it might be in the form of transcripts or summaries of interviews, selected quotations from conversations or descriptions of a place, a group or a situation or in the form of a diary entry. This type of data is known as **qualitative data**. It tends to be concerned with how people see or interpret the world around them, e.g. feelings, attitudes and experiences.

Reliability

A research method is said to have high **reliability** if another researcher is able to repeat the study exactly and obtain the same results. In sociological research, a questionnaire or structured interview might be said to be reliable if every respondent has understood the questions in the same way and their responses have been collected in exactly the same way. However, any method that involves a lone researcher in a situation that cannot be repeated, like observation, is always in danger of being criticised as unreliable.

Objectivity

Objectivity refers to the ability to be open-minded and free from personal or political bias. It is sometimes referred to as 'value-freedom'.

Validity

The data or evidence collected by a particular method has **validity** for sociologists if it accurately reflects the reality of those being studied, i.e. whether it is a true picture. Validity is difficult to achieve, particularly on sensitive or personal issues because people may not be entirely truthful in what they tell you or they may not even be aware of aspects of their behaviour. People may claim or believe that they eat a nutritious healthy diet or take lots of exercise but is this really the case? Teachers may believe they treat every pupil equally, but sociological observation may reveal this to be untrue. This may be further complicated by the fact that some people unconsciously change their behaviour when they know they are being observed.

Representativeness and generalisability

Representativeness refers to whether the group being studied is typical of the larger group to which the sociologist thinks they belong. It is not usually possible for a researcher to collect data from every person in the population they are studying for practical and financial reasons. The sociologist therefore has to select a **sample** of the research population which is representative of the wider population that the researcher is interested in.

A sample is a sub-group of the population that is selected for study.

It is important that the sample is representative because researchers usually want to **generalise** from the data collected, e.g. if the majority of a representative sample of working class people who filled in a questionnaire said they took very little exercise, it is probably safe to generalise that most working class people generally do not exercise very much.

> **KEY POINT**
>
> Generally, the larger the sample, the more representative it is likely to be. Consequently, a method such as the survey questionnaire which is normally aimed at large groups of people is potentially more representative than observation which is generally focused on much smaller social groups.

Practical factors influencing the choice of research topic and method

AQA **SCLY 2**	OCR **G671**
SCLY 4	**G674**

There are practical reasons why a particular research topic or research method might be chosen.

- **Funding** – research plans, i.e. what to research, how to research, the size of the research team, etc. are dependent on the funding available. Large-scale research projects are expensive: salaries, equipment, living expenses, travel, computer resources and secretarial help have to be paid for. Therefore, if funding is generous, the researcher might decide to employ and train a large interviewing team or carry out long-term participant observation (i.e. to live alongside or amongst a social group) that could last up to 2–3 years. However, if funding is low, a survey using postal questionnaires may be more practical in terms of costs than methods that involve the employment of several people.

- **Time** – if the sociologist has funding for 3–4 years, participant observation may be possible. However, most sociological research has a fairly restricted time-span (because of a shortage of funding) and therefore sociologists may adopt methods such as questionnaires and/or structured interviews that can be carried out quite quickly.

- **The subject matter** – research into trends may suit quantitative methods, e.g. the social survey questionnaire or structured interviews, whilst research into experiences, motives, etc. may suit qualitative research methods such as unstructured interviews. Some topics are more accessible than others – some people may feel comfortable discussing how their health is shaped by exercise or lack of exercise. However, sexual behaviour is a particularly difficult area for ordinary researchers because people may feel that questions on this subject are unnecessarily intrusive and embarrassing and refuse to cooperate. The nature of the subject matter is therefore very important in terms of what can be studied and how it is researched.

- **The research population** – powerful people, such as head teachers, doctors and consultants, can deny **access** to a researcher more easily than teachers or pupils or patients who may come from poorer social backgrounds. The research population may also not be accessible because it is regarded as deviant and may feel threatened. The research population may be geographically dispersed. If it is, a postal questionnaire may be necessary, especially if funding is limited.

The population is the group under study.

The influence of ethics on the research process

AQA **SCLY 2**	OCR **G671**
SCLY 4	**G674**

KEY POINT

Research can have a very powerful impact on people's lives. The researcher must always think very carefully about the impact of the research and how he/she ought to behave, so that no harm comes to the subject of the research or to society in general. In other words, **ethics** or **moral principles** must guide research. There is a growing awareness that the people on whom sociologists conduct their research have **rights** and that researchers have **responsibilities** and **obligations** to their research subjects.

Generally, it has been agreed by British sociologists that there are broad **ethical guidelines** which should underpin all sociological research.

- Research should be based on the freely given, **informed consent** of those being studied. People should know research is being carried out upon them

Some methods throw up more ethical issues than others, e.g. covert participation observation.

and how the results will be used so that they can make an intelligent choice as to whether they will take part. Informed consent means that deception should be avoided. Information should not be kept from research subjects nor should they be lied to. Covert participant observation is regarded as ethically problematic by some sociologists because it always involves deception. Informed consent is not always a straightforward matter, e.g. very young children or people with learning disabilities may not be able to fully understand what the researcher is doing.

- Research should not involve an intrusion on privacy, and research subjects should be allowed **anonymity** and **confidentiality** if they so wish. However, sociological research is by its very nature **intrusive** – sociologists are generally interested in what goes on in families, how people behave, what they think, etc. The problem of maintaining privacy can be addressed by keeping the identity of research participants secret. Confidentiality means that the information an individual gives to the researcher cannot be disclosed or traced back to that individual. Ethical researchers are usually careful to disguise the **identity** of individual participants when they write up their research. If people know they cannot be identified, they may be more willing to reveal all sorts of personal and private matters. In other words, confidentiality may increase the **validity** of the data collected.

- Most sociologists would agree that research participants should be protected from any sort of physical or emotional harm. Sociologists need to be aware that some people might face harmful **social consequences** as a result of the research being published, e.g. people's reputations may be damaged or they may be exposed to ridicule.

- Sociologists need to avoid being drawn into situations where they break the law and commit crimes or witness deviant acts.

Theoretical influences on the research process

AQA **SCLY 2** OCR **G671**
    SCLY 4   **G674**

Traditionally, a sociologist's choice of research method depended on whether they subscribed to a positivist or interpretivist view of society.

Positivism

> **KEY POINT**
>
> **Positivists** are very influenced by the **natural sciences**. Natural scientists, such as biologists, physicists and chemists, have shown that plants, animals and chemicals behave in very predictable ways because of the existence of **natural laws**, e.g. water obeys certain physical laws when it boils or freezes. Positivist sociologists have therefore adapted and applied these ideas to human behaviour. In other words, they argue that we should treat people as objects whose behaviour can be directly observed and counted in the same way as animals, the weather, chemical elements, etc.

Positivists see human or social behaviour as the product of the organisation of the society in which we live. The organisation of society is called the **social structure** and the sociologists who study the organisation of society are known as **structuralists**. Positivists argue that the social structure of a particular society produces **social facts** or **laws** over which we have no control or choice. These social laws **determine** our behaviour and future outcomes. In a sense, positivists see people as the puppets of society.

Positivists, therefore, argue that human behaviour is **patterned** because whole groups of people behave in very similar ways on the basis of social facts such as social class, value consensus and gender. Human behaviour, therefore, is very **predictable**, e.g. we can predict with some accuracy how a working class English White male is going to turn out in terms of education, e.g. what age he will leave school, what qualifications he will have, what sort of job he will get or what sort of wage he will earn.

What research methods do positivists prefer to use?

> **KEY POINT**
>
> Positivists believe that only **scientific methods** can provide the objective 'truth' or facts about the world. They therefore believe that sociology should be a scientific discipline based on the logic and methods of the natural sciences. The job of sociologists is to uncover the social laws that govern human behaviour.

When positivists collect information about the social world, they usually subscribe to a scientific model known as the **hypothetico-deductive** approach. This is the model that natural science employs in, e.g., **laboratory experiments**. It involves five stages.

- Stage 1 – phenomena are observed.
- Stage 2 – a testable **hypothesis** (or educated scientific guess) is constructed to explain the phenomena.
- Stage 3 – empirical data (factual evidence) is collected in a systematic way.
- Stage 4 – the data is interpreted and analysed to see whether it confirms or refutes the hypothesis.
- Stage 5 – if the hypothesis is confirmed time and time again, it becomes a **theory**. If the data refutes the hypothesis, the scientist should reject or revise it and begin the data-collection process again.

Empirical data is based on observation or experiment.

Positivists therefore believe that:
- sociologists should study only what they can **objectively** see, measure and count
- research methods should produce quantifiable or statistical data
- **reliability** is all important, i.e. another sociologist should be able to use the method to repeat the research and should get the same results
- **statistical relationships** (i.e. correlations) need to be established between various factors which if they are confirmed time after time can be classified as 'social laws' that can explain the causes of events in the social world.

Positivists consequently prefer sociological research methods that are likely to produce data in numerical form. Questionnaire surveys, structured interviews and some types of experiments do this – it is fairly easy to turn the data collected by these methods into statistics. Positivists are also keen to use some forms of **secondary data**, particularly official statistics, i.e. those collected by sources such as the government agencies.

Interpretivism

> **KEY POINT**
>
> **Interpretivist**, or **anti-positivist**, sociologists are sceptical about sociology's scientific status. They argue that human behaviour is not the result of external social laws. They argue that we are not the puppets of society – rather, human beings are the architects of society; without us, society would simply not exist. They also reject the view that human beings can be treated like objects in much the same way as things in the natural world. They note that chemicals, animals, etc. have no self-awareness or **consciousness** and do not act with purpose, i.e. they cannot choose to behave in particular ways.

Interpretivists point out that people are active, conscious beings who act with intention and purpose. They are not propelled against their will to take certain predetermined courses of action. Rather they make **choices** based upon **free will**.

Interpretivists argue that society is the net sum of people choosing to come together in social groups – this is known as **social interaction**. Interpretivists point out that when we interact, we are constantly **interpreting** (i.e. giving meaning to) our own behaviour and that of others, e.g. a family is not just a group of people with a biological relationship, but a group of people who interpret themselves as a family and interact accordingly.

Interpretivists, therefore, argue that in order to understand social behaviour (and therefore, society), it is essential to discover and understand the **meanings**, or **interpretations**, that underpin people's actions.

Interpretivist sociologists stress the concept of **validity** – seeing the world as it really is. They argue that we need to adopt sociological research methods that get inside people's heads in order to see the social world through the eyes of those being studied. They stress that sociologists need to adopt **ethnographic methods** which access the everyday world of those being studied so that the sociologist can achieve **verstehen**, i.e. an empathetic understanding of why people behave and think in the ways they do.

Ethnography involves the study of people in everyday settings.

Such sociologists prefer unstructured interviews which allow people to talk at length about how they feel, and participant observation, i.e. observing people's behaviour by joining in their activities because these methods produce **qualitative data**, i.e. concerned with motives, feelings, experiences, etc. that give us firsthand insight into how people interpret the world around them. Often the data collected is in the actual words of those being studied.

5.2 Primary research methods

LEARNING SUMMARY

After studying this section, you should be able to understand:

- the differences between primary research methods and secondary sources of evidence
- the strengths and weaknesses of experiments
- the advantages and disadvantages of quantitative research methods including the social survey questionnaire and structured interview
- the strengths and weaknesses of qualitative research methods including unstructured interviews and participant observation.

Primary methods of data collection

AQA **SCLY 2**   OCR **G671**
    SCLY 4   **G674**

KEY POINT

Primary data is that which is collected by sociologists themselves during their own research using research tools such as experiments, survey questionnaires, interviews and observation.

Primary data can take a **quantitative** or statistical form, e.g. charts, graphs, diagrams and tables. However, it can also be **qualitative**, e.g. in the form of extracts from the conversations of those being studied. Some researchers present their arguments virtually entirely in the words of their research subjects. Consequently, the data speaks for itself and readers are encouraged to make their own judgements.

Experiments

KEY POINT

Experiments are the main method used by natural scientists. **Experimentation** normally involves the testing of a hypothesis about the relationship between an independent variable (**cause**) and a dependent variable (**effect**). Experiments are usually set up so that the scientist controls the introduction of possible independent variables. In the natural sciences, such control is enhanced by use of a laboratory. Any change in the participant's behaviour should be the result of the change introduced by the experimenter.

> Experiments are used more by psychologists than sociologists.

Interpretivist sociologists note that the experimental method is rarely used in sociological research for both practical and ethical reasons.

- **Practical reasons** – sociologists can never be sure that behaviour is caused by the social phenomena they are interested in, e.g. people differ from the usual subject of experiments such as chemicals and natural phenomena in that they have consciousness and usually know that they are taking part in an experiment. Their performance may therefore be distorted by their desire to impress the experimenter. Moreover, only a limited number of 'normal' or 'natural' social conditions can be re-created in a laboratory context.
- **Ethical reasons** – some sociologists argue that it is morally wrong not to tell people they are part of an experiment or to expose them to adverse social conditions.

These difficulties have led to some sociologists adopting variations on the experimental method, e.g. the **comparative method** is an experimental method which uses the social world as the laboratory. The researcher, usually using official statistics, compares a before and after situation in a social group where a change has taken place with one where it has not.

Interpretivist sociologists have used the **field**, or social experiment which involves a qualitative examination of particular social contexts in order to explore the interpretations which underpin everyday interaction. For example, **Rosenthal** and **Jacobson** conducted a field experiment in a school to test the hypothesis that teachers' expectations influenced their pupils' academic achievements. However, these too involve some degree of manipulation. Positivists note that this type of experiment may suffer lower levels of reliability because the researcher cannot control all possible variables.

> The Hawthorne effect suggests that the group's behaviour will change if it is aware that it is the subject of research.

> This links to material in Chapter 3 on education. Bear in mind that Rosenthal and Jacobson's research was criticised on ethical grounds.

The social survey

AQA **SCLY 2** OCR **G671**
SCLY 4 **G674**

The social survey is the method most favoured by positivist sociologists. It normally involves the **random selection** of a sample which is representative of the population the sociologist is interested in studying. This sample may be sent standardised questionnaires through the post and/or may be asked to take part in structured interviews. The social survey normally generates large amounts of quantitative data in a relatively short period of time.

> Questionnaire surveys may also be delivered by e-mail.

Sampling

The selected sample must be **representative** of the population being studied because normally sociologists wish to generalise. It is important to find a **sampling frame** (a list of people who may potentially take part in a survey) which is representative of the population being studied. Sociologists prefer to use **random sampling methods** in order to minimise the possibility of **bias**. At its most basic, random sampling allows everyone the same chance of being selected. A number of sampling methods are available to sociologists.

> Examples include school registers, membership lists and the Royal Mail's list of postcode addresses.

- **Systematic sampling** – every nth person is chosen from a sampling frame, e.g. 50 people out of a group of 500 may be chosen by randomly selecting a number between 1 and 10, e.g. 6. Every tenth name beginning with the randomly selected number '6' is taken from the list, e.g. 6, 16, 26, 36, 46 ... up to 496. This process will generate fifty names for the sample.
- **Stratified sampling** – a random sample is taken from particular social categories, e.g. age, gender, race, which make up the population being studied.

- **Cluster or multi-stage sampling** – households may be randomly selected from a random sample of streets from a random selection of areas using a map.

Non-random sampling

Sometimes non-random sampling methods may be used although the samples are unlikely to be representative.

- **Quota sampling** is mainly used by market researchers in the street, e.g. they may be under instructions to stop and interview a quota of housewives aged between 25 and 40 years of age.
- **Snowball sampling** is mainly used when it is difficult to find a sample because the behaviour under study is seen as deviant by society, e.g. a researcher interested in heroin addiction may find an addict willing to introduce him or her to other addicts.

The strengths of social surveys

> **KEY POINT**
>
> Positivists approve of the social survey because it is regarded as **scientific** (variables are controlled via sampling and questionnaire design), **reliable** (standardised questionnaires can be replicated), **objective** (samples are randomly selected) and **quantifiable**. However, some social groups are difficult (and sometimes impossible) to survey, e.g. people who are homeless could not complete a postal questionnaire sent to a household.

Longitudinal surveys

Surveys which monitor a group over a period of years are called **longitudinal surveys**. They supply an in-depth picture of a group or social trends over time. Trust can be built up between a group and the researchers. This may generate more valid data and lessen the possibility of non-response. However, it can be difficult to find samples and research teams committed to long-term research. The sample may drop out, die or move away. This increases the chance of it being unrepresentative. If different researchers are used, it can be difficult to re-establish trust with a group. The sample may become too 'survey-friendly'. Respondents may consciously or unconsciously tell researchers what they think they want to hear.

Questionnaires

AQA **SCLY 2** OCR **G671**
    SCLY 4   **G674**

> **KEY POINT**
>
> Most social surveys use a **postal questionnaire**. The questions can be **closed**, meaning that respondents are normally given a fixed number of responses to tick. Some questionnaires use **open-ended questions**, especially attitude surveys. The postal questionnaire has particular advantages.
> - It is cheap – especially if the sample is large or geographically scattered.
> - It can use larger samples than any other method.
> - It is also reasonably quick in that the bulk of returned questionnaires are usually back within a month.
> - Questionnaires based on closed questions are user-friendly and easily quantified.

A pilot study can also highlight problems with the wording of questions and whether the questionnaire takes too long for respondents to complete.

Positivist sociologists are very keen on using questionnaires because they are thought to be scientific and high in reliability. It is argued that if a questionnaire is well-designed and questions are neutral and objective (i.e. not leading, loaded, etc.) another researcher using the same questionnaire should achieve similar results. It is also argued that a well-designed questionnaire should be high in validity if it has been pre-tested via a **pilot questionnaire**. This is a dress rehearsal which works out whether all people filling it in are interpreting the questions in the same way. This should increase validity because any difference in the answers should reflect differences in real life.

However, the questionnaire suffers from a number of potential problems.

- Many people cannot be bothered to reply to questionnaires. In other words, questionnaires, especially if postal, suffer from a **low response rate**. The returned questionnaires therefore may not be **representative** of the research population because there is always the possibility that those who replied may not hold typical views, whereas those who did not send back their questionnaire may have completely different views.

> **KEY POINT**
>
> Those who do return the questionnaires as part of a very low response may not be typical of the people the sociologist is interested in.

- It is difficult to motivate people to return postal questionnaires – stamped-addressed envelopes need to be provided as well as other incentives, e.g. people can be encouraged to return the questionnaire by making them eligible for entry in a free prize draw or for a free gift. This obviously drives costs up.
- It is difficult to go into any **depth** in a questionnaire because the questions need to be as clear and simple as possible. It is difficult to use open-ended questions because the questionnaires often do not include enough space for detailed opinions and attitudes and this type of data is also difficult to quantify or analyse. Questionnaires may therefore not be suitable for finding out why people behave the way they do, i.e. for uncovering motives. Real-life is often too complex to categorise in closed questions and pre-set responses.
- Respondents may **interpret** the question in a different way to that intended by the researcher, e.g. if the sociologist asks people about their experience of education, it is important that everybody filling in the questionnaire understands what is meant by 'education' in the same way, otherwise their responses may mean something totally different from what the researcher believes they mean. This undermines validity. The fact that the sociologist is not present when the postal questionnaire is filled in to clarify any misunderstandings or to make sure the correct person fills it in may mean misinterpretation of questions is more likely to occur, therefore, undermining validity.
- Questionnaires sometimes ask people to recall events. Memory can be problematic – people may exaggerate, under-estimate or telescope specific events in their lives and therefore provide the sociologist with invalid data.
- **Validity** is not guaranteed because people may **deceive** the researcher for a variety of reasons. Questionnaires are artificial devices which are not a normal part of everyday reality – people may therefore respond to them with suspicion, i.e. they may feel that any information they write on the questionnaire may be used against them in some way.

> **KEY POINT**
>
> People may simply not tell the truth or be partial with it because they feel threatened by the research or researchers, e.g. they may feel that the researcher may **socially disapprove** of certain aspects of their behaviour or because they feel that the researcher is prying into an aspect of their lives that they regard as sensitive and/or **private**. So, even if the questionnaire is completed, it may contain evasive, partial or false information. However, guarantees of anonymity and confidentiality can sometimes help minimise these problems and therefore increase the possibility of obtaining valid data.

- People like to **manage the impression** other people have of them and this can shape their responses to a questionnaire, e.g. people often respond negatively to questions asking about mental illness (whether they have experienced mental health problems or not) to give an impression of themselves as 'normal' citizens.

This is sometimes referred to as researcher imposition.

- All types of questionnaires that use closed questions with pre-set responses suffer from the **imposition problem** meaning that they measure what the sociologist thinks is important rather than what the person completing the questionnaire experiences. The sociologist, by including particular questions and responses, has already mapped out the experiences and interpretations of the respondents. Respondents completing questionnaires may be forced to tick boxes that only approximate to their experiences and views which will undermine the validity of the data. It may also frustrate respondents and result in non-response.

- There are always going to be some social groups who will never respond positively to a questionnaire because they are regarded by society as 'deviant' and consequently they associate such devices with authority. In order to research such groups, trust needs to be established. The nature of the questionnaire method is unlikely to achieve this. Moreover, it may seem obvious, but questionnaires can only be used with literate people and would not be effective in researching the relationship between illiteracy and poor health.

The structured interview

AQA **SCLY 2** OCR **G671**
　　SCLY 4 　　**G674**

> **KEY POINT**
>
> The structured or formal interview involves the researcher working through a questionnaire or interview schedule as part of a social survey. Like the postal questionnaire, all respondents are exposed to the same standardised set of questions.

Positivists like this type of interview because:
- it produces large amounts of factual and quantitative information very cheaply and quickly compared with the unstructured interview and observation
- an interviewer can explain the questionnaire, thus reducing the possibility of non-response, and ask for clarification of vague responses
- an interviewer can observe the social context in which answers are given, e.g. the facial expression, tone of voice, body language or status of the respondent.

Problems with structured interviews

- The structured interview has much the same problems as the questionnaire. Interviews are **artificial devices** which are not a normal part of everyday reality – people may therefore respond to them with suspicion, i.e. they may feel that any information they tell the interviewer may be used against them in some way and they may therefore fail to cooperate or complete. If they do complete the interview, there is always the possibility that it may contain evasive, partial or false information.
- Interviews that use closed questions with pre-set responses suffer from the 'imposition problem' meaning that they measure what the sociologist thinks is important rather than what the interviewee experiences. Consequently the sociologist may fail to ask the really important questions.

> **KEY POINT**
>
> Interviewees may be forced to choose answers that only **approximate** to their experiences and views which will undermine the validity of the data. Other respondents may get frustrated that their experiences or views are not reflected in the questions or pre-set responses and fail to complete the interview.

- Interviewing is not really suitable for studies that require extremely large samples that are geographically dispersed across the country. **Interview samples** are therefore less likely to be representative compared with postal questionnaire survey samples.
- Structured interviews, like questionnaires, may depend on asking people to recall events. Memory can be problematic – people may exaggerate, under-estimate or telescope specific events in their lives and therefore provide the sociologist with invalid data.
- There is often a gap between what people say they do and what they actually do because people do not care to reveal their prejudices or quite simply because they are not aware that they behave in certain ways.

The unstructured interview

AQA **SCLY 2** OCR **G671**
  SCLY 4 **G674**

> **KEY POINT**
>
> Interpretivists argue that research should focus on the respondent's view of the world through the use of unstructured interviews (sometimes known as 'guided conversations'). This method involves the interviewer informally asking open-ended questions about a topic and allowing the respondent to respond freely and in depth.

Interpretivists claim a number of strengths for this method.
- Trust and rapport can be developed, which may generate more qualitative information about the respondent's interpretation of the world.
- They are **flexible** because the conversation is not constrained by fixed standardised questions. This may generate more **valid** information (especially if the respondent can see their input is valued) and allows for probing of deeper meanings.
- They provide more opportunity for respondents to say what they want rather than what the interviewer expects.

Problems with unstructured interviews

KEY POINT

Positivist sociologists criticise unstructured interviews for being **unscientific** and that such interviews lack a number of characteristics which they see as essential in scientific research, such as reliability and objectivity.

- Such interviews are seen to **lack reliability** because everyone is different as it depends on the unique relationship established between the interviewer and interviewee. It cannot be replicated and checked by another sociologist.
- Such interviews are thought to **lack objectivity** as the researcher has got a personal relationship with the interviewee. Researchers might overly sympathise with the interviewee and the final data may not be balanced.
- The final research report cannot practically contain all the information gathered and often, the interviewer will select aspects of the interview transcript that fit the hypothesis. It is argued that such **selectivity** reflects the ideological biases of the researcher. What is left out of the final analysis may actually contradict their hypothesis, e.g. **Willis** used quotes from his interviews with working class males to illustrate how they opposed the school system, but there may have been lots of material in his interview transcripts that he selectively ignored which showed the boys conforming.
- Interviews are exceptionally **time consuming** to conduct and transcribe. Consequently, sociological research which uses unstructured interviews tends to use fewer participants than surveys. Positivists claim that interview participants tend to be **less representative** of the research population as a result. It is therefore **difficult to generalise** from them to similar populations in the wider community.
- The data from unstructured interviews is difficult to analyse because of the sheer volume of material in the respondent's own words. Positivists don't like this sort of data because it is not often quantified and it is difficult to turn into graphs or tables to compare or make links between variables, i.e. correlate.

This links with material on education in Chapter 3.

Interview bias or effect

Both structured and unstructured interviews share similar potential problems. The major problem is interview bias or effect. People may not act naturally in interviews because all interviews are **interaction situations** and may be adversely affected by social differences between the interviewer and interviewee, e.g. based on social class, gender, ethnicity and age. Bias may be caused by the interviewer's facial expression or tone of voice, leading the interviewee to a response that reflects the interviewer's own opinions. A **social desirability** effect may occur in that the interviewee may wish to please the interviewer.

Observation

AQA **SCLY 2** OCR **G671**
SCLY 4 **G674**

KEY POINT

Interviews only provide a snapshot of social life, whereas other methods, such as observation, may be better at capturing everyday life, by providing more of a moving picture.

Ethnographic studies describe the way of life of a group of people from their point of view and so appeal most to interpretivist sociologists. Observation is the main type of ethnographic approach. There are several types.

- **External observation** involves an observer objectively viewing a group, but not taking any part in their activities, e.g. classroom observation.
- **Non-participant covert observation** involves secretly observing a group, e.g. through a one-way mirror.
- **Overt participant observation** involves the sociologist joining the everyday routines of a group and observing action in its natural context. Those being observed have given their permission and are aware of the research aims.
- **Covert participant observation** involves the sociologist concealing their identity and totally immersing themselves in a group culture.

Participant observation

AQA **SCLY 2** OCR **G671**
    SCLY 4   **G674**

Participant observation is the most common type of observation and involves the sociologist immersing themselves in the lifestyle of the group they wish to study. In other words, these sociologists participate in the same activities of the group being researched and observe their everyday lives. **Goffman's** study of a mental health institution is a good example of this, although he took on the role of a physical education teacher rather than a patient.

> **KEY POINT**
>
> The aim of participant observation is to understand what is happening from the point of view of those involved, to 'get inside their heads' and to understand the **meaning** that they give to their situation. This research is **naturalistic**, i.e. it is done in the environment in which the respondents normally find themselves and is not based on the artificial situation created by an interview or questionnaire. This type of research may take many months and even years to complete.

Participant observation can either be:
- **overt**, i.e. the researcher joins in the activities of a group under study, but some or all of the group know his or her identity, or
- **covert**, i.e. the researcher conceals the fact that they are doing research – he or she pretends to be a member of the group. Goffman's research was of this type because patients, nurses and doctors thought he was a PE teacher.

The strengths of participant observation

- The researcher-observer sees things through the eyes and actions of the people in the group. The researcher is placed in exactly the same situation as the group under study, fully experiencing what is happening. Life is seen from the same perspective as the group.
- The **validity** of the data generated by observation is high for a number of reasons.
  - Firstly, a good researcher will focus on 'looking and listening' and going with the flow of social life once they have gained **entry** to the group. A skilled researcher will not try to force the pace or interfere with or disrupt 'normality'. Instead they will blend into the background until they have gained the **trust** of the group and their presence is taken for granted. A good deal of participant observation, therefore, involves 'hanging around' – much of the research is often informal, unstructured and unplanned.

- Secondly, what people say and what they actually do are sometimes very different. People lie, exaggerate, mislead, etc. in questionnaires and interviews. Often people are not aware that they are acting in the way they do. However, in observation studies, the sociologist can see what people really do and the truth is more likely to be recorded.
  - Thirdly, observation can be supplemented with asking questions although if the researcher is carrying out covert research, this might arouse suspicion and mistrust. Observers sometimes develop special relationships with **key people** within groups who can clarify the motives for particular types of behaviour.
- Observation can **generate new ideas and lead to new insights**, i.e. the sociologist might see things that inspire ideas that they would not have had if they had been using questionnaires and/or interviews. Looking back on his observation of a street corner gang in Boston, **Whyte** noted that by listening to group members he was able to find answers to questions that he wouldn't have thought to ask in an interview.
- What the researcher observes is **first hand** and not the product of what he, or she, thinks is important as is often the case with questionnaires and interviews. Questionnaires and interviews are **artificial situations** and often the sociologist has made up his or her mind as to what is important as symbolised by the standardised questions and pre-set answers. However, with observation, by watching and listening, a participant observer has the chance to discover the priorities and concerns, the meanings and definitions of the people being studied in their **everyday natural contexts**.
- Participant observation takes place over a long period of time and therefore allows an understanding of how **changes** in attitudes and behaviour take place over months and years. Other methods, such as questionnaires and interviews, only give a **snapshot picture**, i.e. an understanding of the moment the questionnaire was filled in or the day the interview was conducted.
- Observation may be the only practical method available to research hard-to-reach groups, such as criminal gangs, or religious sects who may be hostile to conventional society or engaged in illegal or deviant behaviour. However, observation of these groups is likely to be covert, unless you are sponsored by a trusted member of the group or you can offer the group some sort of service or role.

In some participant observation studies, the researcher is sponsored by a 'gatekeeper', i.e. a key figure from the group under study who controls access to the group.

The weaknesses of participant observation

- It can be very difficult to gain **entry** or access to a group and, even if this is achieved, it may be difficult to be **accepted** by them. Success at this stage is dependent on whether the observation is overt or covert. If overt, the sociologist may need to offer the group a service if he or she is to be accepted and trusted. If covert, the sociologist will need to share the social characteristics of the group being observed and will need to be a good actor.
- The biggest problem, especially with overt forms of participant observation, is **observer or researcher effect**. This means that the presence of the observer may result in the group acting less 'naturally' because they are aware that they are being observed. In **Whyte's** study, *Doc*, the leader of the gang said that he used to do things on instinct, but now thought about how he was going to justify his actions to Whyte. Some sociologists recommend a 'settling in' period where no notes are taken. The sociologists should begin the observation once they are satisfied that the group accepts their presence.

However, the overt observer can never be sure that their presence is not undermining validity. **Covert observation** is less likely to lead to this effect.

- Some observers can get too close or attached to the group they are observing and consequently their observations become biased. The observer becomes too sympathetic towards the group and 'goes native', i.e. the observer loses detachment and objectivity, and identifies too closely with the group. **Rock** suggests that if the group a sociologist is observing no longer surprises or shocks the observer, the researcher has lost their objectivity and the research should be brought to an end. Rock argues that a good observer will always be critical of the group they are studying.

- A major problem with covert observation is **ethics**. Some sociologists object to this method because it involves lying to people and misleading or manipulating them. People are unable to give their **consent** to having this type of research conducted on them. The sociologist may be forced to take part in criminal or immoral activities in order to either gain or retain the trust of the group or to protect their cover. It can also bring with it great dangers. The African-Caribbean sociologist, **Pryce**, who carried out a very successful participant observation of St. Pauls in Bristol, was actually murdered whilst attempting to carry out a different participant observation study of organised crime. Eventually, the researcher must **leave** the group – this too raises ethical issues, especially in regard to covert observation. Is it right to pretend to be someone else and use the friendships made in the group for research purposes? Could the published research get the group into trouble with the police? Is there any risk of harm, ridicule or reprisal to those identified by the researcher?

- There can be major **practical difficulties** with observation.
  - Firstly, these types of study generally take months, sometimes years, and require terrific dedication. They are consequently very expensive projects.
  - Secondly, **recording the observations** and conversations can be a problem in both overt and covert forms of observation. The researcher needs to write up conversations whilst they are still fresh in his or her mind, but constantly taking notes can be off-putting to those who are being observed. If the researcher is carrying out covert observation of a criminal or deviant group, writing information down or disappearing for periods to do so may arouse suspicion and put the researcher in danger. However, most researchers will keep a **research diary** documenting the everyday activities of the group and reflecting on problems that they might have experienced.

- Positivist sociologists generally disapprove of observation studies for a number of reasons.
  - Firstly, they question the **reliability** of both overt and covert participant observation, because there is no way of knowing whether the findings of the research are true or not, since it is impossible to repeat the research and verify the data. Often the success of the research is due to the personality of the sociologist and the unique relationships that they have established with members of the group. Another sociologist who attempted to replicate this may produce quite different results.
  - Secondly, positivists criticise observation studies for their lack of representativeness which makes it difficult to generalise to other people who belong to similar social groups. Often the type of groups studied are not very **representative** because they are either very **exotic** and therefore not typical of 'average' people, e.g. jazz musicians, or the number of

people observed is quite small. The observer cannot be everywhere observing large numbers of people. In view of these small numbers, it is not possible to generalise from the findings of participant observation.

However, interpretivists argue that these problems are made up for by the validity of the information produced.

PROGRESS CHECK

1. Cause and effect is the relationship between which two variables?
2. Why is it important to use random sampling methods?
3. What sampling method is best suited to the study of deviants?
4. Why is it important to get a good response rate to questionnaires?
5. What major problem is caused by the fact that interviews involve interaction?
6. What is ethnography?

Answers: 1. Independent (cause) and dependent (effect). 2. To minimise the possibility of bias and to obtain a representative sample from which generalisations can be made. 3. Snowball sampling. 4. In order that the sample be representative of the population that is being studied and to generalise. 5. Interview bias or effect. 6. The study of people in their everyday environments.

5.3 Secondary sources of data

LEARNING SUMMARY

After studying this section, you should be able to understand:

- the different secondary sources of data including official statistics, mass media reports and personal documents
- the strengths and limitations of different sources of secondary data and methods of research

Secondary research methods

AQA **SCLY 2**	OCR **G671**
SCLY 4	**G674**

KEY POINT

Secondary data is that produced by agencies or individuals other than the sociologist doing the research, e.g. a sociologist studying joy riding will try to read all other sociological literature on this topic. Secondary data is also produced by agencies such as the government, the mass media and private individuals.

Official statistics

Official statistics mainly refers to data already collected by governments, e.g. statistics relating to births, marriages, deaths, health, education, crime, the economy. Official statistics are seen as scientific because they are collected in a highly **standardised** way, e.g. some data has to be registered by law. Government surveys such as the **census**, the General Household Survey and the British Crime Survey are viewed as highly **reliable** and **objective** in their design and execution.

Strengths of official statistics

- Official statistics are extremely **easy** and **cheap** to access – they involve little effort on behalf of the sociologist.
- They are usually extremely **contemporary**, e.g. the 2010 education and health statistics were published in 2011.
- They are often gathered by surveys which involve **large representative samples** and their findings can usually be **generalised** to similar populations.
- Positivist sociologists see official statistics as 'hard' **reliable facts** because they have been collected in a standardised, systematic and scientific fashion, e.g. registration data on birth, marriage, divorce and death is highly reliable and valid because it is the outcome of long-standing and systematic procedures.
- **Statistical relationships** can be identified by comparing official statistics from regularly conducted surveys such as the **census**, e.g. by examining groups of statistics, sociologists might see a relationship between poverty and educational underachievement or high mortality rates.
- **Trends** over a period of time can easily be seen, e.g. an improvement in life expectancy for some social groups as they gradually give up smoking.

> The census is a national survey that is carried out every 10 years.

Weaknesses of official statistics

- Official statistics may not present a **complete picture**, e.g. illness statistics only cover reported illness to doctors and hospitals. Many people may be ill, but not attend a doctor's surgery or go to hospital.

> This links to material in Chapter 4.

KEY POINT

There is a 'clinical iceberg' of unreported self-medicated illness. Official statistics on illness, therefore, may not give us a valid picture of illness because illness which is self-medicated, or where the family looks after the patient, will not be included.

- Official statistics are open to **political abuse** – statistics can be manipulated or 'massaged' by governments for political advantage, e.g. governments frequently change the ways in which hospital waiting list statistics are defined and collected in order to give a positive impression of their health policies.
- Statistics are **socially constructed** – this means they don't just appear or happen. They are the end result of someone making a decision that a particular set of activities needs recording and that statistics need collecting. These decisions are sometimes selective and biased, e.g. health authorities might be happy to publish statistics relating to success in surgery, but reluctant to publicise statistics about hospital infections.
- Statistics tell us very little about the human stories or interpretations that underpin them, e.g. morbidity statistics tell us very little about the social experience of illness or what it feels like to be on a hospital waiting list for a life-saving operation.
- Official statistics may be based on **operational definitions** that sociologists would not agree with, e.g. the government objectively works out the amount of illness in a society by counting visits to doctors and hospitals, whereas sociologists may prefer to uncover the amount of illness by asking people about their subjective experiences of being well, or unwell, which may uncover a dark figure of unreported illness.

> This links to material in Chapter 4 on the social construction of official statistics of morbidity.

> Illustrate with reference to divorce statistics.

Mass media reports

AQA	**SCLY 2**	OCR	**G671**
	SCLY 4		**G673**
			G674

Content analysis

The content analysis method is seen by some as a secondary method, but in reality it involves working with media secondary data, but using it to generate **new knowledge**. It can therefore also be seen as a primary method that uses secondary data.

Content analysis involves the analysis of patterns or 'messages' in the mass media and can generate both quantitative and qualitative data. The sociologist can work with any form of media product, e.g. newspapers, magazines and television programmes. The aim of the research, generally, is to identify how particular social groups or social situations are portrayed in the product being analysed.

- The **quantitative** form of content analysis involves a **counting approach** and normally uses a **content analysis schedule** that records the patterns and frequency of certain images or themes, e.g. a study of a link between media and anorexia might involve the sociologist counting the numbers of times the images of ultra-thin models appear in magazines aimed at young females.
- The **qualitative** form of content analysis known as **semiology** involves **analysing language**, or **images**, to work out how they might symbolise a particular political or cultural position, e.g. a health promotion campaign might be analysed in terms of the photographs or language used to find out why particular ethnic minority groups have not changed their behaviour, such as the frequent use of images of white people may have convinced them that the campaign was not aimed at them.

Strengths of media content analysis

- Content analysis is **cheap**. All the sociologist needs to do is buy the magazines or newspapers or watch the television programmes.
- It allows the sociologist to compare depictions and representations over a period of time if a longitudinal version of content analysis is used, e.g. anti-smoking television advertisements could be analysed from different time periods to work out their effectiveness.

- Quantitative content analysis is regarded as **reliable** because other sociologists can cross-check the results by looking at the same media using the same categories.

Weaknesses of media content analysis

- It can be a very **time-consuming** method because media products would need to be checked over a fairly long period of time.
- It can often be a very **subjective** method, e.g. semiotics largely depends upon the interpretation of the researcher. Different researchers may interpret the same images in different ways.
- Sociologists who have used this method have been accused of **taking the meaning** of an image or set of words out of context.
- The use of content analysis of media products often assumes that these products have an **effect** upon their audience – this may not be the case. Media products may only tell us about the personal and political beliefs of those who produce media products, i.e. the prejudices of journalists and broadcasters.

Personal documents

| AQA | **SCLY 2** | OCR | **G671** |
| | **SCLY 4** | | **G674** |

Personal documents are usually diaries, letters and other expressive documents, e.g. long-term patients in hospitals might keep a diary of their daily life in the institution. These can provide a sociologist with a rich source of qualitative data, i.e. about experiences, feelings, attitudes, emotions or motives for behaviour.

Strengths of personal documents

- Personal documents are often used to **supplement** quantitative secondary data such as official statistics, e.g. a patient's diary or letters can be used alongside statistics about the treatment of mental health.
- Such documents can give a **rich, detailed and valid insight** into everyday health experiences and practices in their natural environment.
- They may also be used where no other source of data exists, e.g. sociologists might not be able to gain access to mental health institutions because the authorities might suspect that the sociologist intends to be critical. However, doctors, nurses and patients may be able to give the sociologist a valid insider story if they keep a diary or even write a novel about their experiences.
- They are often the only insight that sociologists have into the past.

Weaknesses of personal documents

- There is always the danger of personal documents being **biased** and therefore invalid, because the person doing the writing might want to justify their actions and may not present an objective view of the situation.
- This type of data may be **unreliable** because it cannot be checked for accuracy by the sociologist.
- This type of data may be **unrepresentative** and not typical – diaries, letters and novels tend to be mainly the product of middle class professionals, e.g. literary or political people.
- There may be doubts about the **authenticity** and therefore the validity of the document – letters and diaries can be forged.
- There is always the danger that the sociologist will **interpret** what the writer is saying in a different way to what the writer intended.

Public and historical documents

AQA **SCLY 2** OCR **G671**
   SCLY 4   **G674**

Public and historical documents are published documents such as government reports, reports of companies, reports from trade unions and so on. They can be **contemporary** or **historical** documents, such as historical records (e.g. parish records). The census which began in 1851 and past government White Papers are useful in terms of giving insight into public health in the nineteenth century, e.g. how the introduction of clean water supplies, sewage systems and better housing led to rises in life expectancy.

Strengths of public and historical documents

- Public and historical documents are often our only way of finding out how things were done in the past.
- Historical documents allow comparisons over time in order to identify trends in mortality, morbidity and health care.
- They can help show the effectiveness (or otherwise) of social policy measures, e.g. the impact of the introduction of the NHS can be examined by looking at documents relating to the 1940s and 1950s.

Weaknesses of public and historical documents

- There may be doubts about the **authenticity** of documents that undermine their validity, i.e. a document may not have been written by the person whom it is claimed wrote it.
- The **validity and objectivity** of documents may be questioned because they may have been written selectively, i.e. to justify a particular event, and consequently, they may only give a partial picture of the reality.
- Documents are not regarded as **reliable** by some sociologists because they cannot be checked in a firsthand way by sociologists.
- The content of the document may not be clear and consequently it may be open to **misinterpretation**.

KEY POINT

McKeown used historical documents to demonstrate the importance of public health in the nineteenth century in bringing down death rates, especially infant mortality rates.

PROGRESS CHECK

1. Why do divorce statistics only give sociologists a partial picture of marital breakdown?
2. Why are unemployment statistics problematic?
3. Why don't positivists like semiological analysis of media content?
4. Which sociological approach most favours the use of documents, diaries and letters?

Answers: 1. They don't include separations and empty shell marriages. 2. Because governments frequently change the rules as to which groups should be included. 3. It is not seen as an objective method because sociologists subjectively interpret content according to categories they have chosen. 4. Interpretivism.

5.4 The use of multiple methods

LEARNING SUMMARY	After studying this section, you should be able to understand:
	• the use of triangulation
	• the use of methodological pluralism

Multiple methods

AQA **SCLY 2**   OCR **G671**
        SCLY 4   **G674**

> **KEY POINT**
>
> The 1980s and 1990s saw sociologists take a pragmatic view when it came to the choice of methods. Many now use a combination of quantitative and qualitative methods. For these sociologists what works best is best and the principle of fitness for purpose guides their choice of methods. Consequently, what **Morgan** calls 'the theory war' may now be coming to an end.

Most sociologists use a **combination** of techniques and data. There are two common approaches to combining research methods, triangulation and methodological pluralism.

Triangulation

> Triangulation can be expensive. It can produce vast amounts of data which can be time-consuming to analyse.

Triangulation is the combining of research methods in order to **check** or **verify** the validity and reliability of research findings, e.g. a sociologist using observation to investigate doctor–patient relationships might check the validity (i.e. truth) of his or her findings by asking patients who were the subject of the research to fill in questionnaires to make sure that the sociologist fully understood what he or she was observing. Such sociologists might also carry out unstructured interviews with doctors to compare what the doctors thought was happening with the sociologist's interpretation of what was going on.

Methodological pluralism

Methodological pluralism is the combining of different research methods in order to **build up a fuller picture** of what is being studied, e.g. if a sociologist was investigating disability, a methodological pluralist approach might begin with an examination of secondary data about disability. The sociologist might examine Department of Health statistics to work out how many people in a particular region were disabled. They might look at local newspapers to see whether there were any reports about the disabled being discriminated against. The sociologist might then carry out a questionnaire survey of local people to find out what attitudes towards the disabled are like.

Unstructured interviews might be carried out with a range of disabled people to uncover how they feel about how they have been treated by the able-bodied. Finally, the sociologist may carry out an observational experiment by going out into the local community in a wheelchair or by pretending to be blind to investigate how people react to disability in a natural context.

Rich (2006) used a mixture of methods in her research into how women manage anorexia.

- She undertook semi-structured interviews with young women under the age of 16 who were experiencing anorexia and bulimia and who attended a special school for the treatment of eating disorders.
- She employed a researcher of slim build to stay at the centre and interact with the girls. This researcher observed and informally interviewed the girls in their natural environment.
- She used the internet to enter websites and chat-rooms that offered support networks to women with eating disorders and interviewed/discussed eating disorder issues with on-line users.
- She thoroughly reviewed all the secondary data into eating disorders, including reports of research carried out by other sociologists and psychologists.

PROGRESS CHECK

1. What is the name of the approach which uses two or more research methods in one study in order to check the validity and reliability of the research findings?
2. What is the name of the approach which uses a variety of different research methods in one study?

Answers: 1. Triangulation. 2. Methodological pluralism.

Exam practice questions

These questions are typical of the type of questions on research methods that you are likely to be asked on the AQA Unit 2 SCLY2 paper. You should aim to spend around 40 minutes in total on questions 1–4.

When answering these questions, you can draw on examples from the areas of sociology that you have studied.

In other words, question 4 is asking you to 'assess how far' and, in doing so, is testing your evaluation skills. When answering such questions, it is a good idea to include words or phrases such as 'however', 'on the other hand', 'critics argue that … ', 'other theoretical approaches disagree and instead suggest that…'. By doing this, you will highlight evaluative points.

1. Explain what is meant by the term 'ethnography'. **(2 marks)**

2. Suggest one advantage and one disadvantage of using closed questions in social surveys. **(4 marks)**

3. Suggest two ethical issues that researchers may have to address when carrying out sociological research. **(4 marks)**

4. Examine the extent to which theoretical considerations are the most important issue influencing choice of research methods. **(20 marks)**

6 Religion

The following topics are covered in this chapter:

- **Religious organisations and practices**
- **The role of religion in society and social change**
- **The significance of religion and religiosity in the contemporary world**
- **Religion and social position**
- **Theories of ideology, science and religion**

6.1 Religious organisations and practices

LEARNING SUMMARY

After studying this section, you should be able to understand:

- what is meant by religion and different types of religion
- the differences between types of religious institutions and organisations
- the reasons why specific types of religious organisations have developed
- specific types of religious and spiritual belief and practice and their relationship to particular religious organisations

Defining religion

AQA **SCLY 3**   OCR **G672**

> **KEY POINT**
>
> Sociologists generally see religions as **belief systems** – collections of knowledge, beliefs, attitudes and practices which aim to give meaning to human life and existence. Belief systems are usually **institutionalised** and they can be represented by organisations and administered by symbolic individuals.

> Remember that AQA Unit 3 (SCLY 3) is a synoptic unit.

> Religion is a key aspect of socialisation, culture and identity.

Religious belief systems once had a monopoly over 'truth' and knowledge, but the nineteenth century saw the emergence of **non-religious** belief systems such as **political** belief systems (e.g. Marxism/communism) and, in particular, **science** which challenged the dominance of religious knowledge with regard to the creation of the world, natural disasters, illness, etc.

Substantive definitions of religion

Substantive definitions of religion attempt to explain **what religion actually is**. A good example is provided by the functionalist thinker **Durkheim** (1915).

- Durkheim claimed that religion is a unified system of beliefs and practices related to the **sacred**. Durkheim defined sacred as those things which humans set apart as 'not-knowable' because they are assumed to be the work of a higher spiritual power, e.g. life after death, the meaning of life, the power of prayer and supernatural occurrences.
- Durkheim argued that these sacred beliefs underpin a single moral community which large numbers of people identify with and which provide guidelines for behaviour.

Robinson (1970) defines religious belief systems as a collection of beliefs relating to the existence of supernatural beings that have the ability to shape people's everyday actions.

However, some religious belief systems, notably Buddhism and some new age religions contain no references to the notion of higher spiritual powers or supernatural beings. The substantive approach is also undermined by the problem of what should be counted as 'religious' or 'spiritual', e.g. many religions are organised around concepts such as magic and energy. Some sociologists would argue that these do not count as 'religious'.

Functional definitions of religion

Functional definitions define religion in terms of its **uses** or **purposes**, both for individuals and societies. **Yinger** (1970) claims that the function of religion is to struggle with the ultimate problem of human life.

However, functional definitions are criticised for being too broad. Belief systems that are specifically anti-religious, such as Marxism, secularism or atheism, also function to give meaning to life for their followers. Using this definition, devotion to a football team or country could count as religious. Generally, functional definitions are too inclusive – it is too easy to qualify as a religion using this approach.

The functional definition is also criticised because it assumes that the functions of religion are generally the same in all societies. This may not be the case.

Polythetic definitions

Polythetic definitions define religion in terms of a list of possible characteristics.

Polythetic definitions define religion by creating an ideal type list of characteristics that make up a religion, but accepts that no one example will have them all, e.g. **Southwold** (1978) suggests the following.

- There is usually a **faith** in power outside ourselves, personified by a god-like being.
- There is usually a **theology** – a body of knowledge that sets out the beliefs which might be encapsulated in sacred books, e.g. the Qu'ran or the Bible.
- Theology and faith usually provide people with a 'universe of meaning', i.e. they assist people in making sense of the world, purpose, death, etc.
- It provides an **ethical** or **moral code** that is supposed to underpin all behaviour and decision-making.
- There are usually sanctions in the form of rewards and punishments, e.g. those who violate the religious code may be **punished** by other followers of the religion or be subjected to supernatural sanctions, such as the Christian faith which believes that sinners go to Hell.
- There is often a promise of **salvation** from the ordinary world, e.g. heaven.
- Belief and dependency are often expressed in **religious rituals** or **rites of passage** in which the sacred or holy is worshipped and asked for direction, forgiveness, blessing, etc.
- Those united in belief and faith usually form a **single moral community**, e.g. Christians or Muslims.

However, the polythetic approach can be criticised because it is not clear how many of these factors need to be shared for something to be considered a religion and the decision about what to include on the list is itself a matter of **value judgement**.

Types of religion

AQA **SCLY 3**   OCR **G672**

We can categorise religions broadly into three main types.

- Totemism
- Animism
- Theism

Totemism

Totemism religions are normally associated with small-scale tribal societies and cultures. Totems are animals or plants that are believed to possess supernatural powers of some kind. Religious rituals and ceremonies are usually organised around a particular totem, i.e. the plant or animal may be carved in wood or stone which is then regarded and treated as a sacred (i.e. very special) object which becomes central to religious activities.

Animism

Animism religions are also associated with small-scale tribal societies and cultures.

Animism religions believe in ghosts or spirits, which may be forces for good or evil. These spirits are regarded as having a huge influence on human behaviour causing illness, accidents and deaths.

Theism

Theistic religions centre around a belief in a sacred higher power which has the power of control over human behaviour. This power is the source of moral codes and attracts great reverence from its followers. Theistic religions come in two types.

- **Monotheistic religion** – these religions believe in one divine power or god. These include the major world religions such as Christianity and Islam.
- **Polytheistic religion** – these religions normally believe in a number of gods. Hinduism is a good example.

Types of religious organisation

AQA **SCLY 3**   OCR **G672**

There are four ideal types of religious organisation:

- church
- denomination
- sect
- cult.

Ideal types are models put together by sociologists to help them analyse concepts. Sociologists recognise that, in practice, things are often not so clear cut.

The church

Weber and Troeltsch (1931) identified six social characteristics which make churches distinct from other forms of religious organisation.

- **Large membership** – 25 million people identified with the Church of England in 2006, whilst five million identified themselves as Roman Catholic.
- **Inclusiveness** – people are born into churches. Only a minority choose to join or are converted.
- **Bureaucratic** – churches are generally large organisations employing thousands of people. Consequently, they tend to be bureaucratic and hierarchical, e.g. the Church of England is led by the Archbishop of Canterbury and employs thousands of bureaucrats and secretaries like any other business.

- **Professional clergy** – churches employ professional clergy who are trained and who receive a salary, pension, etc.
- **Acceptance of wider society** – churches generally support the State and the way society is currently organised, e.g. Church of England bishops sit in the House of Lords.
- **A monopoly of the truth** – churches claim to have the correct theology compared with other religious and non-religious belief systems, e.g. Anglicans will claim their version of Christianity is more valid than that of Roman Catholics and vice versa.

The denomination

For example, Methodism.

Sociologists suggest that denominations generally share the following ideal type characteristics.

- **A large, inclusive membership** – religions, such as the Methodists and Baptists, have a significant number of followers, e.g. 1.3 million people identified themselves as Methodist in 2006. People are usually born into a denomination because their parents practise the religion and generally they identify with that religion for most of their life.
- **A paid bureaucracy** – this administers the everyday affairs of the religion.
- **A professional clergy** – pastors are employed full-time and part-time although a significant number are lay-clergy, i.e. they lead a congregation whilst holding down a full-time conventional job.
- **An acceptance of wider society** – the views of denominational members, such as Methodists, do not usually conflict with wider social or cultural beliefs and values, nor do they reject conventional mainstream ideas and beliefs.
- **Acceptance of religious diversity** – they are happy to co-exist alongside other religions.
- **No monopoly of the truth** – they do not usually claim to be the only 'true' religion.
- **A high level of commitment is not expected** – members are not expected to be evangelical, i.e. to convert others.

The sect

In many ways, sects are the opposite to churches as can be seen in the following list of ideal type characteristics.

- **A charismatic leader/founder** – **Weber** argues that all sects are originally based on personal charisma, that is, on a leader who has special qualities, which followers see as inspirational. One example is Sun Myung Moon who leads the Unification Church (actually a sect!) and claims he is the true Son of God and offers an alternative to mainstream Christianity.
- **A small membership** – sects are usually small in terms of the numbers involved, although some sects which have been around for over 100 years have a fairly large worldwide memberships, e.g. the Jehovah's Witnesses and Christian Scientists.
- **An exclusive membership** – membership is exclusive; sect members claim that only they know the truth and that they are the chosen ones. This knowledge shapes their interaction with the rest of society.
- **Opposition to wider society** – sects are much more likely than churches to reject what the wider society has to say and to be hostile to that wider society, e.g. the Amish, who formed small communities in the USA reject

almost all of modern technology, such as cars, zips and radios. Some sects engage in behaviour that wider society does not like and consequently society may take steps to control that behaviour or suppress the sect altogether, e.g. the US authorities attempted to investigate Jim Jones' People's Temple and David Koresh's Branch Davidians which triggered violent responses.

- **Total commitment** – members are often asked to give their total commitment to the sect and this may include giving up their income, property and contact with friends and kin for the benefit of the sect. Some sects insist that members give up their names. These may be replaced with a name allocated to them by the sect. Such sects are often accused of **brainwashing** by the relatives of those who converted to the sect cause.

- **No professional clergy or bureaucracy** – being small, sects are rarely bureaucratic and rarely have a professional clergy, separate from the ordinary members.

Types of sect

Wilson argued that sects develop and change – they are not static entities, but are diverse and complex. Sects are attempts by people to construct their own mini-societies with values and norms that fit their ideologies and which are usually in opposition to those of wider, secular society. Wilson identified a number of different types of sect.

- **Introversionist** sects believe that 'God calls us to abandon the world'. They suggest that the chosen people must cut themselves off from the secular world and follow a spiritual way of life, e.g. the Amish.

- **Reformist** sects believe that their role is to gradually change the world for the better using spiritual means and good deeds. The **Quakers**, established in 1652, are a good example. They often used their wealth to provide good facilities, e.g. homes for their factory workers.

- **Conversionist** sects are evangelical sects whose members crusade to save souls who are in danger of eternal damnation. They hold meetings and constantly seek to convert new supporters, e.g. Jehovah's Witnesses, Seventh Day Adventists, the Moonies and Mormons.

Wilson is aware that the categories he suggested can never describe every sect with precision.

The cult

In media discussions of religious movements, the cult is often mistaken for a sect and presented as a problem, e.g. sects such as the Branch Davidians and the People's Temple are often mistakenly described as cults. However, as we shall see, most religious organisations defined as cults by sociologists are not a problem to society. Sociologists believe that cults have the following characteristics.

- They often offer a service based around some sort of supernatural or mystical ideas, e.g. New Age, rather than an exclusive set of religious beliefs or doctrine that must be rigidly followed. This service usually costs money.

- Those who use the services of cults are **clients** or **customers** rather than followers or converts. Cults tend to offer services to individuals.

- Being a member of a 'special selected' group is not that important. People may have relatively little involvement with any organisation once they have learnt the rudiments of the beliefs around which the cult is based. Membership, or involvement, is therefore informal and loosely knit.

- Cults often tolerate other beliefs and, because their own beliefs are often so vague, they often have no conception of heresy.
- Cults are often **world affirming** – they see their purpose as enhancing or improving people's everyday lives, whether at home, leisure or at work. In this sense, they offer practical advice, services and goods which aim to do this, e.g. yoga, aromatherapy, reflexology, astrology, feng shui and pilates.
- Cults are often short-lived – they may come and go with fashion and trends, e.g. the Jewish cult of Kabbalah was popular because of Madonna's involvement.

New Age religions

The term **New Age** has been applied to a range of ideas which became popular from the 1980s onwards. In many cases these beliefs were not closely attached to particular organisations. Instead, New Age ideas were spread through films, shops, seminars, meetings, music and television.

Examples of New Age interests include meditation, psychotherapy, alternative medicine, paganism, yoga, feng shui and astrology. Many of the organisations connected to the New Age are essentially **client cults**. A number of connected themes underpin the beliefs and practices of such cults.

- The New Age is generally opposed to the traditional scientific ways of doing things because they see scientists as too closed-minded. **Heelas** claims some people have lost faith in science and are looking to more ancient and spiritual ideas in order to discover a more authentic self.
- The New Age is fundamentally **green**. However, it is different to mainstream views on the environment because it claims the planet is a living organism and that all aspects of the environment are connected, e.g. many followers of New Age religions believe in vegetarianism because they believe that it is immoral to kill living things.
- New Age cults stress the **self** and the **spirit**. Heelas calls these groups self-religions because they talk about human potential for self-improvement. Salvation or spiritual fulfilment comes from discovering and perfecting yourself.

Explanations for the rise in New Age religions

Bruce suggests New Age cults have become popular for several reasons.
- A university educated middle class has increasingly taken an interest in spirituality and human potential. **Bird** (1999) notes that cults may appeal to the affluent middle classes because:
  - they provide a spiritual component in an increasingly rationalised world and they therefore offer the possibility of achieving mystical goals
  - they provide techniques and knowledge which allow people to work on themselves to bring about personal and spiritual growth
  - they provide techniques and knowledge to help people become wealthy, powerful and successful.
- Traditional religion has gone into decline. People have lost faith in conventional religions. The decline of mainstream religion leaves New Age cults as the only spiritual solution to the problems created by modernity.
- Consumer culture encourages people to try to become the perfect person – this creates a potential **climate of discontent** as people fail to achieve the perfection portrayed by advertisers.

New religious movements

AQA **SCLY 3**   OCR **G672**

> **KEY POINT**
>
> **New religious movements (NRMs)** are defined by **Wallis** as those sects, cults (i.e. many of these are organised around New Age beliefs and practices) and evangelical Christian movements that have emerged mainly since the Second World War, or which came to prominence in Western societies in the late 1960s and 1970s.

Wallis divided NRMs into three main categories:
- world-rejecting groups
- world-accommodating groups
- world-affirming groups.

World-rejecting groups

World-rejecting groups are sects which have a very **definite and clear conception of God**, e.g. the Unification Church, known as the 'Moonies', pray in a conventional way to a Heavenly Father. However, the theologies and ideologies of world-rejecting NRMs are unusual because they are usually highly critical of the outside world, and consequently they actively seek radical change because they claim to have the only access to the truth about the world. The Moonies, for example, seek to unify all world religions.

Society generally regards such world-rejecting groups as **deviant** because they believe that in order to achieve salvation, their members should cut themselves off from their conventional lives and adopt the communal lifestyle of the sect. These sects therefore act as **total institutions** controlling all aspects of their members' lives. Some of the demands on followers have led to the suicide of the group, e.g. a number of sects, such as The People's Temple and Heaven's Gate, have committed **mass suicide** on the instructions of their leaders. As a result, sects often develop a reputation for brainwashing their members, because families and friends find it hard to understand the change that has taken place in a member.

World-rejecting NRMs vary enormously in size, e.g. the Moonies have an international following, while other groups are often small and locally based.

World-accommodating groups

World-accommodating groups have generally broken away from mainstream religions. They are usually **fundamentalist** and **evangelical** in character, e.g. 'born again' Christian movements such as Elim Pentecostal and the Alpha course fit this description, as well as Subud which is an Islamic sect and Kabbalah, a Jewish sect.

These groups are primarily concerned with religious rather than worldly questions and consequently aim to restore spiritual purity to religious worship, rather than change the world, e.g. Pentecostalists argue that the belief in the Holy Spirit has been lost in other Christian religions. They believe that the Holy Spirit speaks through them, i.e. the gift of 'speaking in tongues'.

Wallis suggests that this type of NRM is more similar to a **denomination** than a sect or cult because it generally subscribes to a respectable and socially acceptable set of religious beliefs. Furthermore, they are tolerant of other religions. Most of their members live conventional and respectable lives outside their religious activities, i.e., they generally conform to social rules and are not regarded with suspicion or seen as deviant.

World-affirming groups

World-affirming groups lack many of the features normally thought to be central to a religion, e.g. they often lack a physical church where they meet and have no rituals of worship, theology or ethics. However, they are religions because they offer access to spiritual fulfilment. Sociologically they are **cults**.

> **KEY POINT**
>
> World-affirming groups are happy with the world as it is. They generally tend to help individuals unlock their potential so that they can make the most of their abilities and potential at work and in relationships. Salvation is seen as a personal achievement and as a solution to personal problems such as unhappiness, suffering or disability.

World-affirming groups aim to seek as many clients as possible because they offer a commercial service, i.e. they involve the payment of fees. Consequently, their clientele tend to be affluent middle class professionals. Followers therefore carry on their normal lives except when undergoing training. Wallis argues that world-affirming NRMs often have a rapid turnover in membership and are relatively undemanding on their followers.

> **KEY POINT**
>
> Wallis realises that no religious group will conform exactly to the three categories he outlines and suggests that NRMs may combine elements of each type to some extent.

Explanations for the emergence of NRMs

There are essentially three broad reasons why people join sects or cults, i.e. new religious movements. These are linked to disillusionment, deprivation and social change.

Disillusionment with traditional religions

World-affirming NRMs, and some world-rejecting NRMs, may reflect disillusionment with the established churches. **Nelson** argues that the young, in particular, may be turned-off by the overly bureaucratic and formal nature of the traditional churches. Religious worship in these churches is interpreted as too routinised and consequently as having little to do with God or spirituality.

However, Nelson argues that a **religious revival** is underway in evangelical circles. These world-accommodating NRMs organised around fundamentalist and evangelist forms of Christianity, such as Elim Pentecostals and Baptists, offer a more spontaneous and joyful version of religion which is less reliant on ritual and consequently more attractive to the young. These world-accommodating movements therefore may be the product of a search for more genuine and creative ways of satisfying spiritual needs.

Deprivation

Some sociologists, notably **Glock and Stark**, have suggested that various types of **deprivation** may result in people seeking compensation and solace in sect membership.

- **Economic deprivation** – there is evidence that world-rejecting NRMs, or sects, are more likely to emerge amongst those at the bottom of the socio-economic hierarchy, i.e. amongst the poor. Sects often offer the poor what **Weber** called a **theodicy of disprivilege**, i.e. a set of religious ideas which explains and justifies why they are in that position. This may give members a feeling of superiority by telling them they have been chosen by God. This may compensate them for their low economic and social standing, e.g. the **Rastafarian** sect may perform this function for some young African-Caribbeans in Britain. Their membership may symbolise a protest against White society and racial discrimination which denies them social and economic status. It is argued that sect membership is symbolic of opposition to a White dominated society which confers second class citizenship upon them.

- **Social or status deprivation** – some sects, such as the Jehovah's Witnesses, recruit from the skilled working class and white collar sectors of employment. People may join these sects because they experience a lack of power, status and satisfaction in their work. The evangelical goals set by some NRMs, such as the Pentecostals, the Jehovah's Witnesses and Mormons, may therefore compensate for boring dead-end jobs.

- **Organismic deprivation** – those who suffer from physical, mental and addiction problems may turn to sects in the hope of being healed or as an alternative to drugs, alcohol and gambling. Evangelical sects may stress faith-healing powers whilst sects such as scientology stress that people can achieve levels of personal fulfilment that will improve their lives.

- **Ethical deprivation** – some people may feel that the world is in moral decline and retreat into fundamentalist sects that feel threatened by liberal values and progress. Others argue that modern technology is dangerous and is the work of the devil, and should be rejected, e.g. the Amish and the Plymouth Brethren. Some people may be concerned about damage to the environment, cruelty to animals and turn to cults that stress the positive relationship between people and nature.

- **Psychic deprivation** – some people may reject the dominant value system of individualism and consumerism. They may not lack material wealth, but they may feel spiritually deprived in a world they see as too materialistic, lonely and impersonal. Sects and cults based around Eastern, especially Hindu and Buddhist mystical ideas have proved especially popular with the middle classes, e.g. Hare Krishna, TM, the Divine Light Mission.

Social change

> **KEY POINT**
>
> NRMs may be the product of **social change**. Such change may create the conditions for various types of deprivation, especially economic and ethical.

There are four important periods of social change which may have led to increases in NRM recruitment.

(1) The movement from non-industrial to industrial society

Durkheim argued that the popularity of religious sects in Britain and USA in the late eighteenth and early nineteenth centuries was a reaction to anxieties created by **industrialisation** and **urbanisation**. This created great social disruption, undermined value consensus and produced **anomie** – feelings of moral confusion, lack of integration, uncertainty about the future, etc. Such feelings led to the appearance of the nineteenth century religious sects such as Methodism (this began as a sect and later developed into a denomination), and the American sects such as the Mormons, Jehovah's Witnesses and Christian Scientists.

In a situation of change and uncertainty, therefore, sects may offer the warmth and support of a strong community. They provide meaning, explanations and most importantly, they re-equip members with clear goals, purpose and moral certainty (in other words, the traditional values that industrialisation was destroying).

(2) The 1960s and 1970s

These two decades were particularly fertile for recruitment into sects and cults. **Wallis** suggested that NRMs were the specific product of social changes occurring in this period.

- The growth of **higher education** and the gradual lengthening of time spent in education which extended the period of transition from child/youth to adult responsibilities. This gave young people more time, freedom and knowledge than previous generations to think about their role in the world and may have encouraged experimentation with different belief systems.
- Middle class youth also rejected the **utilitarian individualism** of their parents' generation which was focused on making the most of modern technology in terms of consumerism, materialism and making money.
- Wallis argues that many young people at the end of the 1960s were suffering from a 'crisis of meaning' – middle class youth were suffering from **ethical** and **psychic deprivation**.

Wallis suggests that NRMs appealed to young people because they opposed the individualistic adult world. Their emphasis on cutting themselves off from the world to set up communal living arrangements proved a strong selling point. Young people attracted to these ideas were successfully targeted by sects such as the Children of God, the Jesus People, the Moonies and the People's Temple which stressed hippy-type values. Other NRMs based themselves on Eastern mysticism (many of them were actually led by gurus from the Indian sub-continent). These were seen as attractive because their emphasis on inner experience, harmony and close relationships with others was seen as uncontaminated by the dominant parent culture. However, high patterns of drop-out from NRMs suggest that the need they fulfil may be temporary.

(3) The millennium – 2000

Fears and uncertainties about what the millennium would bring sparked off another period of sect recruitment in the 1990s. A number of sects appeared which suggested that the world was on the verge of destruction, that Jesus, aliens, etc. were about to reveal themselves and that technology in the form of computers was about to send the world into chaos.

(4) The movement to post-modern society

> **KEY POINT**
>
> In the twenty-first century, post-modernists argue that people have become disillusioned with the old **meta-narratives** of science, politics and religion. Moreover, people's **identities** are no longer shaped by structural forces such as social class. Instead, people construct their identities from a range of choices. Religion is now one **lifestyle choice** that people opt to buy into alongside other lifestyle choices such as fashion or music.

Meta-narratives are broad theories or grand explanations for how societies and the world operate.

Lyon argues that people choose religious beliefs and practices to meet their individual needs from the vast range available. This involves people in a process of **spiritual shopping** trying out the various alternatives until they find a belief system that makes sense to them. People therefore no longer have to sign up to the religious tradition into which they were born – they **pick and mix** aspects of different faiths in the 'spiritual supermarket' to suit their tastes until something more trendy or attractive comes along.

This links to material on identity in Chapter 2.

The future of new religious movements

Denomination or death

Niebuhr argues that sects are short-lived and are unlikely to survive beyond a single generation. He argues that they are likely to change their characteristics, compromise and become denominations or they are likely to die out and disappear altogether.

- Sect membership is based upon voluntary adult commitment in that members choose to dedicate themselves to the organisation. However, the children of the first generation cannot sustain the enthusiasm and commitment of the first generation.
- Sects that rely upon a charismatic leader will disappear when the leader dies.
- Alternatively, the nature of the leadership would change when the charismatic leader dies. A bureaucratic structure of a denomination with a hierarchy of paid officials is likely to emerge.
- The ideology of some sects contains the seeds of their own destruction because sects encourage their members to work hard and save their money. As a result the membership is likely to become **upwardly socially mobile** and they may no longer wish to belong to a religious group which catered for marginal members. The sect would have to adapt or die.

Wallis argues that world-rejecting groups often soften their opposition to society and become more world accommodating or denominational. This is because some charismatic leaders may have difficulty maintaining personal control. If the organisation is successful, a 'routinisation of charisma' may take place and a more bureaucratic organisation may evolve as the organisation's officials take over the day-to-day control of the NRM.

Wallis also recognises that sects can disappear because they may destroy themselves via mass suicide, e.g. Jim Jones' People's Temple, or because society regards them as so threatening that society represses, or destroys them, as was the case with David Koresh's Branch Davidians.

Wallis notes that world-affirming groups are vulnerable to market forces in that their clients may decide to buy their spiritual products elsewhere. However, Wallis argues that world-affirming groups are more adaptable than the other types of NRMs. They are more likely than other NRMs to attract a new clientele because they are more flexible in their beliefs and practices and can change relatively easily as they seek to survive and prosper. **Dianetics** is a good example of this – founded in the 1950s this cult declined in the 1960s, but re-invented itself as **Scientology** in the 1970s.

Wallis says little about how world-accommodating groups develop, but these seem to be the most stable of the NRMs.

PROGRESS CHECK

1. What is meant by a 'substantive' definition of religion?
2. What is meant by a 'functional' definition of religion?
3. What is the difference between a monotheistic religion and a polytheistic religion?
4. Identify three types of NRM.

Answers: 1. One that defines religion in terms of what religion actually is (i.e. its substance). For example, a substantive definition might define religion as a set of beliefs and practices related to the sacred. 2. One that defines religion in terms of its uses or purposes (i.e. its functions) for both individuals and society. 3. A monotheistic religion believes in one divine power or God (e.g. Islam) and a polytheistic religion believes in the existence of a number of Gods (e.g. Hinduism). 4. World-rejecting, world-accommodating and world-affirming NRMs.

6.2 The role of religion in society and social change

LEARNING SUMMARY

After studying this section, you should be able to understand:

- functionalist theories on the role of religion in society
- Marxist accounts of the role of religion in society
- Weber's explanation of the role of religion in society
- post-modern views

Functionalist theories of the role of religion

AQA **SCLY 3** OCR **G672**

Sociologists are interested in the relationship between religion and social change. Some approaches see religion as change inhibiting or as a conservative force in society. Others see religion as promoting social change.

Durkheim has presented the most influential interpretation of religion from a functionalist perspective. He argued that the fact that thousands of religions actually exist suggests that god and the supernatural have no foundation in reality. He believed that religion was a set of myths and imaginary forces constructed by human beings which functioned to bring about **social order** in societies.

Durkheim argued that all societies divide the world into two categories: the 'sacred' (spiritual) and the 'profane' (everyday ordinary things). Durkheim suggests that sacred things are symbols – they represent something. He argues that to understand the role of religion in society, the relationship between sacred symbols and what they represent must be established.

Totemism

Durkheim examined **totemism** – the religion of various groups of Australian aborigines to develop his argument. He noted that aboriginal society was divided into a number of clans. Each clan had a totem, i.e. a symbolic animal or a plant, which was also the emblem or symbol of the clan and which distinguished each clan from the other.

The totem was a sacred object because the animal or plant that it represented was thought to have divine properties. It was the outward form of 'God' and it brought the clan together in **collective rituals** and worship to affirm their common membership of the clan or community.

Durkheim argued that the totem represented both god and society. It stands for the values of the sacred as well as the community and consequently, he concluded that god and society are one and the same thing.

KEY POINT

Durkheim is suggesting that in worshipping god what people are really doing is worshipping society. Society is the real object of religious veneration.

Western religions and society

Like the totem in aboriginal society, Durkheim sees modern sacred objects, such as the cross, as representing both religion and western society. Durkheim sees religion as the expression of the **collective conscience** or value consensus over the individual. The act of group worship through religious ceremony brings members of society together and creates group identity and solidarity, i.e. a feeling of belonging to the same moral community. The worship of god therefore in Western societies is actually the recognition that society is more important than the individual.

Religion as a secondary agent of socialisation

> **KEY POINT**
>
> Durkheim believed that religion is a **secondary agent of socialisation** whose major function is to **socialise** society's members into **value consensus** (i.e. common agreement about values and ways of behaving).

Religion inhibits change and performs positive functions in society. It does this by:

- investing particular values with a sacred quality – certain values are set apart by religion and infused with religious symbolism and special significance. These values become 'moral codes' – beliefs which society agrees to revere and socialise children into. Consequently such 'mores' socially control our behaviour in regard to crime, sexual behaviour and obligation to others, and reinforce **social order**.
- encouraging collective worship – people come together with other like-minded people and feel a sense of belonging to the same group or society, i.e. **social solidarity**. In other words, being a Christian, Muslim, Hindu, Jew, Jehovah's Witness, etc. gives people a sense of community and encourages them to identify with others like themselves.

> This links to material in Chapter 2 on socialisation.

Bronislaw Malinowski

Malinowski saw religion as functioning to appease the stress and anxieties created by **life crises** such as birth, puberty, marriage and death. These events have the potential to undermine people's commitment to wider society and therefore threaten social order. Malinowski points out that most societies have evolved **religious rites of passage ceremonies** such as christenings, weddings and funerals, in order to minimise this potential social disruption, e.g. the death of a loved one can cause the bereaved to feel helpless and alone, unable to cope with life. The funeral ceremony allows people to adjust to their new situation. The group mourning also re-affirms the fact that the group outlives the passing of particular individuals and is there to support its members.

Malinowski's anthropological study of the **Trobriand Islanders** discovered that they took part in religious services before they fished in the open sea because it was dangerous and the religious ceremonies committed them to the protection of their gods. As a result, if the fishermen died at sea, this event was interpreted by the rest of the islanders as the will of the gods. This reduced the potential of grief to disrupt the smooth running of society and therefore reduced the potential for **social disorder**.

Talcott Parsons

The American functionalist **Parsons** suggested that religion performed three major functions.

- Religion provides guidelines for human action against which people's behaviour can be judged as moral or immoral. Religious beliefs therefore form the basis of **social control** and punishment in most societies.
- Religion provides the means of adjusting to events such as death which are out of the control of humanity.
- Religion gives meaning to life by applying meaning to events which people think ought not to happen such as sudden death, suffering or evil, e.g.

suffering tests a person's faith, punishes them for their sins and gives dignity to those who struggle on in the face of adversity.

> **KEY POINT**
>
> Functionalist sociologists generally argue that the role of religion is to **socialise** members of society into collective sacred values and to promote **social solidarity**. In this sense, religion aims to preserve the traditional and the status quo rather than promote social change. Most functionalists generally agree that religion is a beneficial **conservative force** because it maintains **consensus** and consequently **social order**.

Religion is seen as encouraging social stability and inhibiting social change.

The critique of the functionalist theory of religion

There are two major criticisms that can be made of the functionalist theory of religion.

- It is argued that functionalists neglect the extent to which religion has been **dysfunctional** for society, e.g. in Northern Ireland, religious divisions have caused social disruption and conflict rather than promoted social order.
- Functionalism may exaggerate the importance and influence of religion in modern Christian societies. Evidence suggests that Britain has experienced a decline in Christian religious practices and beliefs, and in the influence of religious institutions. It is difficult to see how religion can be functioning to socialise the majority of society's members into morality and social integration if only a minority of people regularly attend church.

However, **Durkheim** did anticipate the decline of religion because he believed that rational or scientific belief systems would replace irrational religious belief systems. Consequently, he argued that people in modern societies may experience **anomie**, i.e. a moral confusion where they are more likely to be unsure about their religious or supernatural beliefs, and consequently are less likely to be committed to religious belief.

Also, being 'secular' is not the same thing as being 'atheistic'. Atheism means not believing in God whereas secular means non-religious rather than unreligious. Surveys indicate that the majority of people in Britain still see themselves as Christian and British society as a Christian society. Christian values may now be interpreted as social values by members of society. Consequently, belief in God and being British come from the same source. The Durkheimian idea that God = Society, therefore, is still valid.

The neo-functionalist theory of civil religion

AQA **SCLY 3**   OCR **G672**

This links to material in Chapter 2 on national identity.

Bellah argues that **secular belief systems**, such as nationalism, have successfully incorporated elements of religion into their rituals, ceremonies and ideologies, and consequently participation in these movements is similar in character to believing in and belonging to a religious group. Examination of totalitarian systems such as Nazism and Stalinism support this perspective, e.g. mass rallies in Nazi Germany were very similar to evangelical meetings in terms of enthusiasm and commitment. Bellah refers to these pseudo-religions as **civil religion**.

Bellah argues that the American people are also unified by a similar civil religion – a **faith in Americanism**. He notes that God and Americanism are much the same thing because 'God' underpins most aspects of American society. American patriotism and pride often involve the belief that God is on 'our side'. American coins tell the world 'In God We Trust', whilst American Presidents swear an oath of allegiance before God. The phrase 'God Bless America' ends speeches given by dignitaries across the USA and at national events such as the Superbowl.

> **KEY POINT**
>
> Bellah supports Durkheim's thesis about the link between religion and society because the worship of God in the USA is essentially the worship of US society.

The critique of civil religion

The concept of civil religion has been criticised for its **methodological vagueness**. There is little empirical evidence to support the view that national ceremonies are seen by members of a society as sacred or as reinforcing collective moral sentiments. Moreover, there has been little attempt to investigate whether these ceremonies result in social integration. It is merely assumed that they have that effect.

Vicarious religion

Davie argues that in some countries, particularly Norway and Sweden, 'belonging without believing' is the norm. Surveys of people in these countries indicate very little religious belief and yet the churches in these countries are well-maintained because the people are happy to pay a church tax for that very purpose.

Davie argues that a state of **vicarious religion** exists in Sweden which means that the secular proportion of the population is happy to let the religious minority worship on their behalf, i.e. to take on the 'spiritual burden'. Davie argues that vicarious religion means that the system of organised religion is unlikely to experience any further decline in terms of attendance and membership. It also means that the population will always have a religious system to fall back on in times of national tragedy. The churches function as a source of comfort and spiritual healing in the event of a national crisis or disaster that touches the whole society.

> **KEY POINT**
>
> Davie argues, much like Durkheim, that religion reinforces social and national values, and consequently religion and society are one and the same thing.

Marxist accounts of the role of religion in society

> **KEY POINT**
>
> Like Durkheim, **Karl Marx** also argued that religion was a **conservative** force in society. However, Marx did not agree that this force is essentially benevolent and beneficial to society. Rather, Marx argued that religion was part of the **superstructure** of capitalist society and consequently religion was an **ideological apparatus** which functioned to reproduce, maintain and legitimate the class inequalities in income and wealth produced by the infrastructure. In other words, religious ideas and practices exist to serve the interests of the rich and powerful, i.e. the ruling capitalist class.

Marx saw religion as **ideological** in two broad ways.

- It promotes the idea that the existing socio-economic hierarchy is natural and god-given and therefore unchangeable.
- It functioned to cushion the effects of oppression by lulling the working class into a state of **false class consciousness**. The true extent of their exploitation was rendered invisible by religion. In this sense, **religion is the opium of the people**.

Religion is seen as change inhibiting.

Marx suggested that religion is the opium of the people.

- Some religions attract the poor by explaining their subordinate position in society in supernatural terms, e.g. religious theologies might suggest that their poverty is the result of sin and wickedness, or that they have been chosen by God and that their poverty is a test of their commitment to God.
- Religion makes suffering on Earth bearable for the poor by promising them a reward in an after-life. Such promises of salvation may take the form of heaven or redemption through a return to a 'promised land' or the return of a messiah figure, e.g. Rastafarians believe that they will return to Judah once Ras Tafari, their Messiah, is resurrected. Such ideas promote the idea that there is no point in changing the here and now and consequently the poor do little to actively change their situation.

Religion inhibits social change.

- Some religions even present suffering as a virtue in that it is suggested that those who accept their suffering or poverty without question will be rewarded for it. Some religions, in this sense, actively encourage suffering and therefore inequality.

> **KEY POINT**
>
> Marx argued that religion functions to produce passive and fatalistic people who, instead of trying to change the world for the better, merely dream of spiritual alternatives. In this sense, Marx agrees that religion is a conservative social force because it inhibits real social change. As an ideology, it actually maintains and legitimises the status quo of class inequality.

There are a number of examples cited as evidence in favour of Marx's arguments.

- **Halevy** suggests that the **Methodist** religion played an important role in preventing a revolution in Britain in the nineteenth century. He argues that discontented workers in Britain expressed their dissatisfaction with the organisation of capitalist society by deserting the Church of England. They further demonstrated their dissent by joining the Methodist non-conformist movement. However, in other European countries, Halevy points out that workers were engaged in more revolutionary violent protest.

- The Protestant 'moral majority' movement which is very influential in the USA tends to uphold conservative, anti-communist values and has close links with the Republican Party. It is also anti-abortion and anti-homosexual. Fundamentalists suggest that wealth and prosperity are a sign of God's favour, whilst poverty and illness are indicators of sin.
- **Leach** (1988) is critical of the **conservatism** of the Church of England. He analysed the class composition of the General Synod (the ruling body) and noted that 80% of bishops were educated at public school and Oxbridge and most church officers are solidly upper middle class.
- **Hook's** analysis of the **Catholic Church** also argues that the Vatican is essentially a conservative institution as indicated by its traditional stance on contraception, abortion, women priests and homosexuality. He points out that the Vatican's stance on contraception and AIDS in particular is creating hardship in Third World countries especially in Latin America.

In 2010, the Pope announced that the use of condoms might be justified in exceptional circumstances.

Engels: religion as a radical force

> **KEY POINT**
>
> Not all Marxists shared Marx's claim that religion is a conservative force which always supports ruling class interests. **Engels** recognised that religion in some special circumstances could bring about radical social change.

Religion as change promoting.

Engels argued that religion could be a useful tool for bringing about change because:

- few rulers have attempted to prevent mass participation in religion
- religious leaders are more likely to recognise exploitation, oppression and inequality because of their religious education
- religious leaders are not so easily repressed – they may occupy a special or sacred place in their societies which means they are not so easily targeted for assassination and imprisonment.

Engels argued that religion could play a very active role in bringing about revolutionary social change. He focused, as an example, on how the early Christian sects opposed Roman rule. Thus, while Christianity originated as a way of coping with exploitation among oppressed groups, it also became a **source of resistance** to the oppressors and a force for change.

The **neo-Marxist**, **Maduro** suggested that religion could play a progressive role in the political struggles of the oppressed classes. On the one hand, he noted that in many societies the traditional churches, (e.g. the Catholic Church) are conservative institutions and usually supportive of the ruling elite. On the other hand, Maduro argues that in some societies the clergy of such churches can sometimes experience a significant change in attitude as the poor and oppressed bring their discontent to them. The potential for radical positive change is also greatly enhanced if the religion has a **charismatic leader** who can provide a focus for discontent. In this situation, Maduro argues, the suffering and poverty of the oppressed may be voiced by members of the clergy. Furthermore, the clergy may attempt to make the masses more conscious of their exploitation and even suggest ways to help them bring about radical social change.

KEY POINT

From a neo-Marxist perspective, religions can develop into political movements which seek change on Earth rather than salvation in heaven.

There are a number of examples which seem to support Engels and Maduro, e.g. the **Reverend Martin Luther King** and the Southern Baptist Church were at the forefront of the civil rights movement in the USA in the 1960s. The Catholic Church in Poland and the Protestant Church in East Germany played an important role in the collapse of communism in those countries in the early 1990s. In South Africa in the 1980s, **Archbishop Desmond Tutu** was heavily involved in political protests against the apartheid regime.

Weber's explanation of the role of religion in society

AQA **SCLY 3**   OCR **G672**

Max Weber is seen as having been engaged in a debate with the ghost of Karl Marx. They disagreed on many key issues. It is important to appreciate, however, that in some respects their views are similar.

Weber carried out a major comparison of the religious beliefs, practices and economic conditions across China, India and Europe and concluded that Marx was largely correct about the ideological function of religions. Weber agreed that religions were **ideological** in two ways.

- They give assurance to the most fortunate, i.e. the powerful and wealthy, by stressing that their position is natural or god-given.
- They offer religious reasons for poverty and suffering in terms of themes such as wickedness, sins committed in former lives, etc.

KEY POINT

Weber argued, like Marx, that these two roles served to legitimate the status quo, i.e. they aim to preserve the existing set-up of inequality.

Religion as an agency of economic and social change

However, Weber did not accept that religious beliefs were always determined or shaped by the economic infrastructure of a society. Weber believed that religious ideas could be independent of that infrastructure. Moreover, he believed that some religious ideas, specifically Protestant beliefs, had brought about economic and social change in the form of capitalism. Thus, Weber rejected what he saw as the economic determinism of Marx's ideas.

The role of Calvinism

KEY POINT

From his comparative studies, Weber noted that while similar economic conditions prevailed in China, India and Europe, capitalism only developed in Europe. Weber attempted to identify the **independent variable** (major influence) which brought about capitalism in Europe.

Weber noted that capitalism had developed in the late sixteenth and early seventeenth century in those parts of Europe where a particular set of Protestant beliefs known as **Calvinism** were dominant. He concluded that the attitudes and orientations of Calvinism greatly contributed to a **spirit of capitalism** which underpinned the rational pursuit of profit as an end in itself. Calvinism, therefore, provided the cultural conditions for capitalism to develop.

Weber concentrated on two elements of Calvinist beliefs which he claimed brought about the right cultural climate for the development of capitalism.

- **Pre-destination** – Calvinists believed that God had pre-destined the world and that all individuals were assigned either to salvation (the elect) or to damnation. God alone made this decision before an individual was born and, once the decision was made, it could not be changed. However, Calvinists believed that they could at least know the nature of God's decision. God's favour was judged by the degree to which individuals prospered in their work. The accumulation of personal wealth was seen as a sign of God's favour – evidence that the person was one of the elect or the chosen few.
- **The Protestant work ethic** – Calvinism consequently encouraged an approach to industry that emphasised values and actions such as self-discipline, hard work, the rational pursuit of profit, thrift, modesty and the rejection of self-indulgence, gambling, sexual vice, pleasure and lavish spending. Weber called this set of ideas 'the Protestant work ethic' and claimed that it led to the rapid accumulation of profit and **capital** and the emergence of a Calvinist capitalist class, i.e. the industrial bourgeoise.

> So, religion is not necessarily a conservative force in Weber's view.

Weber suggests this protestant ethic led to a 'spirit of capitalism' as non-Calvinists seeing its success adopted this approach. Consequently, Weber claims that Calvinism helped bring about and accelerate the economic change from feudalism to capitalism.

KEY POINT

Weber does not argue that Calvinism caused capitalism. He suggests only that it was the major contributor to a climate of change and noted that for capitalism to emerge many other pre-conditions were important.

For capitalism to develop, Calvinist beliefs would have to be supplemented by:
- a certain level of technology
- a skilled and mobile workforce
- rational modes of law and bureaucracy.

These latter pre-conditions were present in China and India, but the rational spirit in terms of the commitment to **diligence** and **thrift** were only found in Calvinism. Hinduism and Buddhism (India) and Confucianism and Taoism (China) stressed the **spiritual** rather than the **material** which Calvinism emphasised.

Criticisms of Weber

- **Sombart** suggests that Weber was mistaken about the beliefs held by Calvinists. Sombart argues that Calvinism was against greed and the pursuit of money for its own sake. However, Weber notes that hard work and thrift were unintended consequences of the belief in pre-destination.
- Some critics have noted that countries with large Calvinist populations, e.g. Scotland, did not industrialise. However, **Marshall** points out that Scotland lacked Weber's other criteria of capitalist development, such as the skilled technical labour force and the capital needed for investment.
- Some Marxist critics have suggested that slavery, colonialism and piracy generated a super-accumulation of capital for the West which was more influential in the emergence of capitalism than Calvinist beliefs.

- Marxists such as **Kautsky** have suggested that capitalism pre-dated Calvinism. Bourgeoise capitalists were attracted to it because it offered convenient justification for the pursuit of economic interests, i.e. it was an apologia for wealth. Therefore, the Protestant religion was an ideology used to legitimate capitalist interests.

Post-modern theories of religion

AQA **SCLY 3**   OCR **G672**

> **KEY POINT**
>
> The emphasis in post-modern society is on the self, the pursuit of lifestyle choices and the construction of personal identity.

> You can draw on this when discussing debates on the secularisation of society and the strength of religion in society.

Spiritual shopping

Hervieu-Leger (2000) argues that religions are losing their traditional power to impose religious beliefs on people from above. As a result, young people are less likely to inherit a fixed **religious identity** and consequently they are more likely to be ignorant of traditional religion.

However, Hervieu-Leger notes that individual **consumerism** has replaced collective tradition. People today have become **spiritual shoppers** in a religious marketplace characterised by great **diversity** and choice. Religion has become a personal spiritual journey in which people choose the elements of spirituality they want to explore and the groups they wish to join. As a result, Hervieu-Leger argues that two religious groups have emerged in post-modern society.

- **Pilgrims** are in a search for self-discovery and personal development which is achieved by joining New Age spiritual groups or through engaging in individual therapy or meditation.
- **Converts** join religious groups that offer a strong sense of community, usually based on a shared ethnic background or religious doctrine. Examples of such groups would include the evangelical born again churches such as Baptists and Pentecostals.

Globalisation

The world today is more interconnected than ever before – a process known as **globalisation**. However, globalisation is not a recent phenomenon. The major religions have spread across the world for centuries through conquest, colonisation and migration. Globalisation has had two main consequences for religion.

- There is some evidence that globalisation has led to new forms of **religious thinking** that have encouraged economic development in less developed societies, e.g. **Nanda** (2008) found that India's success in the global economy has led to the middle class justifying their wealth by becoming more religious. The professional and managerial middle classes attribute their economic success to Hindu gods and subscribe to a type of Hindu nationalism that sees Indian culture as superior to that of other countries. **Redding** (1990) notes that the economic success of the Asian Tiger countries, such as Singapore, is attributed to a **spirit of capitalism** being encouraged by **Confucianism** – a traditional Chinese belief system which encourages hard work, self-discipline, frugality, education, self-improvement and a commitment to authoritarian leadership.

- **Huntington** claims globalisation has resulted in a **clash** or **conflict** between religious civilisations, particularly Christianity and Islam. Huntington sees the West as under threat from Islam and urges the West to reassert its Christian identity. However, **Jackson** (2006) sees Huntington's work as an example of 'orientalism' – a **Western ideology** that stereotypes Eastern nations, religions and people (especially Muslims) as untrustworthy, inferior, extremist, etc. – and this serves to justify exploitation and human rights abuses by the West.

Fundamentalism

> **KEY POINT**
>
> A consequence of the onset of post-modern society has been the emergence of **fundamentalist** religious factions within all major world religions. Fundamentalism refers to a return to the religious fundamentals or basics of religious roots.

Fundamentalism has a number of characteristics.
- It interprets infallible religious texts and theology literally and selectively.
- It rejects religious pluralism and is intolerant of other religions.
- All areas of social life are defined as sacred – religion shapes all political, economic, social, domestic and individual behaviour.
- The traditional and conservative is favoured at the expense of the modern and liberal which are interpreted as morally corrupt.
- Patriarchal control is regarded as the norm.

> You can draw on this when discussing the secularisation thesis.

Post-modernists have suggested that the rise of fundamentalism may be due to:
- a response to **secularisation**, especially a perceived decline in morality
- a response to **social change**, especially increased social choices with regard to family diversity, sexual permissiveness, gender equality and abortion rights – the aim of Western fundamentalists is to re-assert 'true' religion and restore it to the public role where it can shape the laws and morals of wider society
- a response to **globalisation**, especially the increasing influence of Western consumerism and materialism whose 'decadence' or spiritual emptiness is seen by some members of less developed societies as a threat to their faith and identity. The recent conflicts in Iraq and Afghanistan have been interpreted as part of a Christian crusade against Islam by some Muslim fundamentalists. **Holden** notes that often fundamentalist movements offer hope, direction and certainty in a world which seems increasingly insecure, confusing and morally lost.

Fundamentalists often respond to these 'threats' upon their values by adopting **defensive aggressive strategies** which are based upon the view that their beliefs are more important than the tolerance of those who do not share them. In some cases, fundamentalists argue that their beliefs are so important that they overcome any respect or compassion for others. Such ideas have even extended to the sacrifice of their own lives through suicide attacks.

Post-modernism – an evaluation

Some sociologists believe that post-modernists have taken their analysis too far and are sceptical that we have entered a brand new age of post-modernity.

- Fundamentalism is not as new as post-modernists claim, e.g. there have been many instances of Islamic fundamentalism over the past thousand years.
- **Bruce** argues that consumerist religion is weak religion and that it has little effect on the lives of its believers. He sees it as evidence of increasing secularisation rather than religious revival.

PROGRESS CHECK

1. What does the term 'dysfunctional' mean?
2. According to Marx, is religion a change inhibiting or a change promoting force?
3. According to Engels, is religion a change inhibiting or a change promoting force in society?
4. According to Weber, which Protestant religion contributed to the emergence of capitalism?
5. According to Weber, what is the Protestant Ethic?
6. What does religious 'fundamentalism' involve?

Answers: 1. Damaging or problematic for individuals and / or for society. 2. A change inhibiting force. 3. Religion may be a change inhibiting force. However, under some conditions, religion can promote revolutionary social change. 4. Calvinism. 5. A set of ideas subscribed to by Calvinists which stress hard work, idleness as a sin, thrift, etc. 6. It involves the literal interpretation of sacred texts; the belief that society needs to return to traditional ways of doing things – often those defined by religious principles; and the promotion of conservative views including patriarchal values.

6.3 The significance of religion and religiosity in the contemporary world

LEARNING SUMMARY	**After studying this section, you should be able to understand:**
	- the evidence and arguments in the secularisation debate
	- the concept of secularisation in a global context.

Secularisation

AQA **SCLY 3**   OCR **G672**

Woodhead and Heelas suggest that there are two versions of the secularisation thesis. These are the disappearance thesis and the differentiation thesis.

- The **disappearance thesis** states that modernity is bringing about the death of religion. The significance of religion both for society and for individuals is steadily declining. This process will continue until religion disappears. This thesis tends to use statistical evidence relating to regular church attendance and membership, and other criteria related to Christianity such as the number of baptisms, church weddings and Sunday School attendance in support.

> Think about how reliable and valid such statistical evidence is.

- The **differentiation thesis** states that religion is declining in social significance rather than disappearing. This means that it no longer influences major social institutions like the family, education, the law and the political system as it once did. It has become **disengaged** or differentiated from the wider social system. However, this does not mean we are all becoming atheists. This version of secularisation suggests that religion is separated from society rather than from the individual – it may still have influence or significance in people's private lives.

> **KEY POINT**
>
> What both versions have in common is their emphasis on Western religions, particularly Christianity. Most supporters of the secularisation thesis do not see it as a **global process**, e.g. **Bruce** focuses on what he calls the 'secular West' which he sees as an exception in the broad sweep of human history.

Measuring secularisation: the statistical evidence

- **Crockett** found that just under 40% of the adult population in 1851 attended church. In England and Wales, this figure had dropped to 20% by 1950 and by 2007 only 2% of the British population were attending religious services on most Sundays.
- In 2007, two-thirds of the British population attended a religious service (excluding baptisms, weddings and funerals) no more than once a year or less or never.
- Church membership (i.e. this refers to being born into, baptised, confirmed or married in a particular Christian religion) has significantly declined over the last thirty years, e.g. Anglican membership fell by 179 000 between 1990 and 2005 whilst Catholic membership declined by 574 000 in the same period.
- Attendance at special Christian ceremonies, such as baptism, has also declined. **Bruce** notes that in 1900, 65% of children born alive in England were baptised, but by 2007, fewer than a quarter of all English babies were christened. The number of confirmations has fallen too.
- There has also been a noticeable drop in the number of marriages conducted in church. According to Bruce, nearly 70% of English couples were married in the Church of England at the start of the twentieth century. By 2006, only a third of weddings took place in church.
- Evidence from over 60 years of opinion polls and attitude surveys shows that religious belief is declining in line with the decline in church attendance and membership, e.g. **Robin Gill** reviewed almost 100 national surveys on religious belief from 1939 to 1996. They show a significant decline in belief in a personal God, in Jesus as the son of God, and in traditional teachings about the afterlife and the Bible. In 2005, a Eurobarometer survey found that only 38% of people in Britain believed there was a God compared to 60%–70% in the 1970s.

Evaluation of the statistical evidence

> This links to material in Chapter 5 on the reliability and validity of official statistics.

Official statistics on religious belief and practice have been questioned by sociologists with regard to both their **reliability** and **validity** in the following ways.

- Church membership figures for Britain pose problems of comparability because they are calculated in different ways. Religions do not share any **standardised** ways of counting their memberships.
- **Martin** claims that the relatively high attendance in Victorian Britain may have been influenced by non-religious factors. In the nineteenth century, church going was a sign of middle class respectability. Many Victorians may have attended church to be seen rather than to express religious convictions.

> It is important to question how far the evidence supports a particular view or conclusion.

People may therefore attend church for secular reasons, e.g. in order to feel part of a community or because it is a family tradition.

- **Martin** suggests that those sociologists who argue in favour of secularisation assume there was a 'golden age of religion', but historical documentation on religious belief and practice is poor. Consequently sociologists, such as **Wilson**, have simply assumed the presence of strong religious beliefs in the medieval period.

> Another important link to methodological issues. It is important to consider how sociologists define religious beliefs and how they measure practices.

- Statistics tell us very little about the social meaning of religion, i.e. what religious belief or church-going means to particular individuals. As **Davie** argues, many people believe without belonging. Most people subscribe to religious beliefs although these might be very vague and even contradictory, but they do not see the need to attend church in order to express such belief. **Bellah** notes that religion is now often 'private and individualised' rather than 'public and collectivised'. Such qualitative religious beliefs may be invisible to the sociological eye and consequently difficult to precisely **measure** using quantitative research methods.

> Opinion poll results are a useful source of quantitative data. However, the data has limitations.

- **Opinion poll** evidence is problematic because it tells us very little about these social meanings, e.g. when people say they believe in God in response to a questionnaire survey, this says very little about whether this belief is of major significance in their lives. Similarly, the 2001 Census found that over 37 million people in Britain described themselves as 'Christian'. However, sociologists do not know what meaning that identity has for the 37 million. Interpretivists are interested in the meanings that people attach to their experiences.

> An important methodological point.

- What people say in opinion polls and what they actually do are often not the same thing. Saying that you believe in God has no real consequences for behaviour. It may not have any real meaning for the individual or be held with any conviction. What all opinion polls on religious belief really show is that people have a tendency to say 'yes' to this sort of survey question – it does not necessarily show that people are religious or non-religious.

- Some statistical evidence contradicts the secularisation thesis because there has been a significant increase in the number of people in Britain who identify with religions such as Islam, Hinduism and Sikhism. These religions usually demand a greater commitment than the traditional Christian churches.

> It may be that different things are happening within different religions. In this case, it is difficult to generalise about religion in general.

- There has been a significant increase in numbers involved with new religious movements which include sects and cults, and particularly the evangelical Christian movement. Involvement in the Pentecostal evangelical churches doubled between 1975 and 2003 to approximately 200 000 people.

KEY POINT

Although the statistical evidence in support of the secularisation thesis seems convincing on the surface, it runs into problems in terms of its **reliability**, **validity** and **representativeness**. Other sociologists, therefore, have argued that the role religion plays in political and social life, as well as the meaning it has for individuals, need to be examined.

The disengagement thesis

AQA **SCLY 3**   OCR **G672**

> **KEY POINT**
>
> **Bruce** argues that the church was once at the centre of social and political life, but that during the twentieth century in particular, it has withdrawn almost completely. This process is known as **disengagement** and is seen as an important component of secularisation, e.g. the Church of England exerted considerable influence over affairs of the state from medieval times until the mid twentieth century. However, today, apart from the right of bishops to sit in the British House of Lords, the church is hardly represented in government or political circles.

Bruce also notes that religion exercises a less significant influence over individuals. He suggests that the main reason for this decline is that modern social life has ceased to be community based. People's lives today are dominated by large bureaucracies. Urban lifestyles are generally impersonal and people are generally isolated from their extended kin and neighbours. These processes undermine religion in three ways.

- The lack of a strong sense of local community means that churches can no longer serve as the focal point for communities.
- Modern urban society offers a greater choice of personal services which means that people are less likely to turn to the local priest or church for practical or emotional support.
- The impact of science, media and cultural diversity means that people's religious beliefs are less certain. There are also lots of alternative lifestyle choices available to people such as consumerism and recreation in addition to religion.

Some observers argue that religion only has 'symbolic' value today. **Wilson** argues that the church has been reduced to traditional 'hatching, matching and dispatching' rituals and, consequently, it occupies a marginal status in modern society.

Evaluation of the disengagement thesis

Parsons argues that the church has experienced **structural differentiation** – other social institutions have taken over the political, educational and welfare functions once carried out by the church. However, **Parsons** argues that churches now concentrate purely on the religious, thus making them stronger. Parsons also argues that religious beliefs are still the focus for the ethics and values that underpin most social behaviour.

Casanova (1994) does not believe that religion has withdrawn from public and political life. Instead, he suggests that in the 1980s it was hard to find any serious political conflict anywhere in the world that was not influenced by religion.

Think about how far this applies in the 2010s.

The mass media still defines religious matters as important and newsworthy in that there has been a lot of coverage of the debate about homosexual bishops and women priests. The Church of England still makes a significant contribution to political debate. The Church may have lost political influence, but this may have little to do with disengagement – it may have more to do with supporting causes unpopular with governments in power.

This links to Chapter 3 on education. Many parents choose to send their children to faith schools.

The Church is still involved with secular concerns such as education and welfare, e.g. both the Church of England and the Catholic Church run state comprehensives and sixth form colleges. Both churches are heavily involved with helping the homeless and single parents, whilst church-based pressure groups such as Christian Aid, Save the Children and Cafod work in developing countries to relieve poverty.

The rationalisation or de-sacrilisation argument

AQA **SCLY 3**   OCR **G672**

KEY POINT

Some sociologists have argued that western society has undergone a process of **de-sacrilisation**, meaning that the sacred no longer has a place in contemporary society. Supernatural, or divine, forces are no longer seen as controlling the world, action is no longer directed by religious belief and consequently human consciousness has become secularised.

It is suggested that the modern world has experienced **rationalisation** – scientific thinking based on reason – and that evidence is more important than religious or irrational thinking based on emotion and faith. **Bruce** argues that technological advances reduce the number of things that need to be explained in religious terms. Science and technology have given individuals a greater sense of control over the natural world and less need to resort to supernatural explanations.

Society is now rationally organised into capitalist businesses and legal-rational bureaucracies that impose rational behaviour upon modern populations. Furthermore, rational ideologies and organisations have developed to solve social problems. Ideologies such as communism, and organisations like trade unions and political parties, offer practical solutions to problems rather than religious solutions.

This links to the scientific method discussed in Chapter 5.

Wilson argues that a rational worldview is the enemy of religion. A rational worldview is based on the testing of arguments and beliefs by rational scientific procedures, on assessing truth by means of factors that can be empirically and objectively quantified and measured. On the other hand, religion is based on faith only. Its claim to truth cannot be tested by rational scientific procedures and this undermines its legitimacy.

Arguments against rationalisation

Another important point about the quality of evidence.

The idea that society has become more rational is difficult to operationalise and evaluate. It is largely based on the **impressions** of particular sociologists rather than on hard evidence.

Post-modernists argue that in post-modern society people are experiencing a crisis of meaning – they are dissatisfied with materialism and are seeking to re-discover their spiritual potential. This has resulted in an increased interest in alternative beliefs and practices as symbolised by growing interest in **new age religions**, **sects**, **cults** and **quasi-religions** dealing with fate. Such beliefs are seen as a rejection of science in the post-modern age.

It is argued that most members of society subscribe to a combination of ideas which incorporate both the rational and irrational. These explanations of the world, although seemingly contradictory, exist alongside each other in our minds with no apparent side-effects!

Religious pluralism

Wilson argues that historically, religion was **monolithic** – most societies were dominated by one religious world view or faith which had a monopoly over religious practices and beliefs, e.g. Christianity in the West. Alternative beliefs were either absorbed or suppressed.

> **KEY POINT**
>
> Wilson argues that another major symptom of secularisation has been the fragmentation of monolithic religion into a set of competing beliefs and practices, i.e. **religious pluralism**, e.g. in the nineteenth century, in particular, the Protestant religion split into a number of competing churches, denominations and sects. Consequently the power and influence of religion has grown weaker because religion no longer represents one community. Competition between religions undermines religious credibility and religions can no longer take for granted customer loyalty as they compete for customers in the religious market-place.

Wilson is critical of the emergence of the **ecumenical** movement – this is the trend whereby religions have sought to find common ground and hold joint services. It has resulted in the merger of some religions, e.g. the United Reformed Church is an amalgamation of two or three previously competing religions. Wilson argues that ecumenism is a sign of religion's weakness because it is a response to declining attendance and membership.

Moreover, Wilson is critical of NRMs because he suggests that they trivialise religion. He suggests that NRM members are only temporarily committed to religious beliefs and are more committed to following a charismatic leader or attracted by the lifestyle rather than the belief system. Consequently he argues that many NRMs are short-lived as members drift in and out. They exert no major influence on society. NRMs, Wilson argues, are merely an exotic novelty for a self-selected few, rather than an alternative cultural lifestyle for humankind. **Berger** agrees when he refers to NRMs as the last refuge of the supernatural in a secular society.

The critique of religious pluralism

> **KEY POINT**
>
> Many commentators, especially post-modernists, suggest that religious pluralism indicates that religion is in a state of change rather than decline. It is argued that there is a demand for spiritual diversity in modern societies that cannot be catered for by one religion.

Sociologists, such as **Greeley** and **Nelson**, disagree with Wilson about the role of NRMs. Greeley claims that NRMs are a sign of **religious revival** or **re-sacrilisation**, whilst Nelson believes that only NRMs like the evangelical denominations can help people be spiritually creative. Consequently their beliefs and practices are a more valid indicator of the influence of religion in society because these religious movements are not obsessed with bureaucratic structures. They allow people to express their beliefs and search for spiritual

Another illustration of the problem of measurement.

satisfaction without constraints. They particularly attract young people for this reason. Consequently, attendance at these churches has grown in the last twenty years paralleling the decline of the traditional churches.

Glock and Bellah (1976) agreed with this analysis too. They argue that NRMs are a product of a new religious awareness, an increased sensitivity to what is happening in the world and a search for meaning. Most importantly, Glock and Bellah point out that NRMs make greater demands on their members than conventional churches, e.g. many demand that people give up all their worldly possessions, cut themselves off entirely from their family and friends, devote all of their time to worship or evangelism and give up their name or identity and adopt a new one.

Secularisation in the USA and globally

AQA **SCLY 3**   OCR **G672**

> **KEY POINT**
>
> Many sociologists have suggested that the USA may be the exception to the rule of secularisation in the West because:
> - surveys conducted over the past 50 years indicate a consistently high level of belief in God – between 90–95% of Americans claim to believe in God
> - about 40% of American Protestants and 50% of American Catholics say they attend church on a weekly basis
> - about 5% of the US television audience regularly tune in to religious TV and 20 million watch some religious programming every week.

The secularisation of religious institutions argument

Herberg believes that the religious content of churches, denominations and synagogues in the USA has been watered down. He argues that American religious institutions have compromised their beliefs to fit in with wider US society. They have undergone a process of **internal secularisation**.

> **KEY POINT**
>
> Herberg argues that the high level of attendance at American religious institutions is directed by **secular** rather than religious concerns. He claims that to be an American – to demonstrate an American **identity** – requires a public commitment to American beliefs within a religious organisation. Religion in the USA therefore places little emphasis on theology (belief), but stresses the **American Way of Life** – the core values of American society, such as freedom, democracy and achievement.

This links to material on national identity in Chapter 2.

Scharf suggests that American religion has become a commodity to sell like any other product. The religious marketplace produces greater specialisation and choice as denominations (320 000 in 2007) tailor their product to meet market demand.

However, both Herberg and Berger have been accused of neglecting **American fundamentalist religions** with their commitment to a literal interpretation of the Bible and to strict moral codes based on the 'word of God'.

> **KEY POINT**
>
> Secularisation is generally confined to the organised established churches in European countries. **Globally**, religion is still a potent and dominant force. Religious revival among Christians in the USA, Jews in Israel and Muslims throughout the world has gone unexplained by proponents of the secularisation thesis.

Other views on secularisation

AQA **SCLY 3**   OCR **G672**

The post-modernist perspective on secularisation

Post-modernists argue that secularisation in Britain has occurred because of a general decline in collectivist practices and community. **Individualism** – especially the notion of personal choice – started to dominate society in the latter half of the twentieth century. Consequently, moral judgements and actions were no longer shaped by the wider, generally Christian community. **Hamilton** (2001) suggests that there has been a general decline in the membership of organisations such as trade unions and political parties. Secularisation may be part of this process. Hamilton believes community is being increasingly replaced by **privatisation**. He argues that people may still believe in God, but they are more committed to spending their time with their family or on individual priorities.

Another point related to the problem of measurement in social research.

However, some post-modernists note that the increasing popularity of New Age beliefs suggests the process of secularisation may be exaggerated. **Heelas** (2004) suggests the popularity of New Age beliefs reflects a rejection of science and modernity in the post-modern age. The true extent of New Age beliefs is not known, but the number of internet sites feeding such interests indicates that they are widespread.

The secularisation cycle

According to **Stark and Bainbridge** (1985), secularisation is not an end to religion in itself, but part of a dynamic cycle of secularisation, innovation and religious revival. Stark and Bainbridge argue that religion can never disappear, nor seriously decline, because religion meets the most fundamental needs of individuals for answers to the great questions about the meaning of life and death. Only religion can answer these questions.

> **KEY POINT**
>
> Stark and Bainbridge argue that secularisation is probably a **cyclical process** and we are now passing out of a period of low religious belief into an upswing as we anxiously enter the twenty-first century. In conclusion, then, it may be that religion is merely changing and adapting, rather than being in decline.

PROGRESS CHECK

1. According to writers such as Bruce and Wilson, what has replaced religion in explaining the world?
2. What is meant by 'disengagement'?
3. What is religious pluralism?
4. What does Greeley see NRMs as a sign of?

Answers: 1. Science and rational thought. 2. The withdrawal of the Church from key areas of social life such as politics and education. 3. The fragmentation of monolithic religion into many different religions which compete with each other. 4. A sign of religious revival or resacrilisation.

6.4 Religion and social position

LEARNING SUMMARY

After studying this section, you should be able to understand:

- patterns in religiosity according to gender, ethnicity, social class and age
- sociological explanations for these patterns

Women's participation in religion

AQA **SCLY 3**   OCR **G672**

The evidence suggests that women are more religious than men, irrespective of age. **Miller and Hoffmann** (1995) report that women:

- make up the majority of Christian church-goers and consequently attend church more often than men
- are more likely to express a greater interest and faith in religion and to demonstrate a stronger personal religious commitment than men, e.g. women believe more in God and pray more than men
- believe in a god of love, comfort and forgiveness whereas men prefer a god of power, planning and control.

Sociological explanations for why women are more religious than men

One view is that women feel closer to God because they are involved in the creation of life as mothers and may be more involved with death in their role as carers of the sick, disabled and elderly. **Greeley** (1992) argues that caring and nurturing skills tend to be associated with a more religious outlook.

This links to material on families and gender socialisation in Chapters 1 and 2.

Similarly, some feminist sociologists attribute the more religious nature of women to **gender role socialisation**. **Miller and Hoffman** argue that females are socialised into being submissive, passive, obedient and nurturing – traits compatible with religiosity. Women may also make up the majority of elderly church-goers because they live longer than men.

A link to gender differences in life expectancy.

Woodhead (2005) identifies three female responses to religion.

- **Home-centred women** – tend to be traditionally Christian because Christianity affirms their priorities which are focused on home and children.

This highlights the intersection of gender, social class and religion.

- **Jugglers** – are women who combine home and work. These women are generally educated and middle class. They are interested in New Age movements because these encourage female empowerment and spiritual fulfilment outside the home.

- **Career women** – are more likely to be secularised because religion does not fit in with their demanding work schedules.

Women and new religious movements

The evidence suggests that women are more likely to get involved with sects than men. There are a number of possible reasons for this.

- Women are more likely than men to experience **poverty** and those who experience it are more likely to join sects to compensate for this.
- Women may be more **socially deprived** than men in terms of power, respect, status and job satisfaction. Women in unsatisfying lower/middle class jobs may find satisfaction in the evangelical goals set by conversionist sects, such as Jehovah's Witnesses or Mormons.
- Women tend to be more morally conservative than men and therefore more likely to experience **ethical deprivation**. In the nineteenth century, many sects were initiated by women:
  - Ellen White set up the Seventh Day Adventists
  - Mary Baker Eddy founded Christian Science
  - Ann Lee founded the Shakers
  - The Fox sisters began the Spiritualist movement.

Glock and Stark note that all these types of deprivation can result from patriarchal exploitation. Females may therefore turn to religion as a compensation for their under-privileged position in society.

Women and cults – New Age religions

> **KEY POINT**
>
> Women are more likely than men to get involved in cults and especially those associated with the **New Age movement**, e.g. **Heelas and Woodhead** (2005) found that 80% of the participants in New Age religions and practices in Kendal, Cumbria were female.

Sociologists like **Bruce** note that cult activity tends to be **private** and **individualised**. This may appeal to women who are more likely to be restricted to the private arena of the home especially after childbirth. This also explains their attraction to the more personal style of New Age spiritual practices which allow access via television, DVDs and the internet, and which encourage flexible modes of belief and practice, e.g. hypnotherapy, astrology, pilates, yoga.

Bruce also notes that the emphasis in New Age religions is on the expressive and the natural which may appeal more to feminine values. Women are also more inclined to see themselves as in need of **self-improvement** which is the main service offered by many New Age cults.

Women and fundamentalism

Finally, there is some evidence that some women are attracted to the certainties of fundamentalist religions which define the roles of women in a very traditional way. These women may be rejecting the feminist idea that women can make the most of both career and family. Some women may be attracted to Christian and Islamic fundamentalism because these religions value women's traditional gender roles of mother and home-maker.

Feminist theories of religion

> **KEY POINT**
>
> Feminist sociologists see society as **patriarchal**, i.e. based on male domination and female subordination. Many feminist sociologists regard religion as a patriarchal institution that reflects and perpetuates this inequality between men and women. They see religious beliefs as a patriarchal ideology that legitimises or justifies female subordination.

Evidence of patriarchal influence in religious belief systems are detailed below.

- Religious organisations are mainly **male-dominated** despite the fact that women often participate more than men in religious practices, e.g. Orthodox Judaism and Catholicism forbid women to become priests.
- Places of worship often **segregate** the sexes. In some religions, there are taboos that regard menstruation, pregnancy and childbirth as a problem. They are considered to have a greater capacity to 'pollute' religious rituals and consequently women experiencing these conditions may not be allowed into sacred spaces, e.g. in Islam, menstruating women are not allowed to touch the Qur'an. Some religions regard women's presence as distracting men from worship. Women may not be allowed to preach or lead prayers or read from the sacred texts.
- Sacred texts largely feature the doings of **male gods** or **prophets** and are usually written and interpreted by men. There are many female characters in the biblical texts and some are portrayed as acting charitably or bravely, but the primary roles are reserved for males. All the most significant Old Testament prophets, such as Isaiah and Moses, are male, while in the New Testament, all the apostles are men.
- Religious laws and customs may give women **fewer rights** than men, e.g. in access to divorce, how many spouses they may marry, decision-making and dress codes. Religious influences on cultural norms may lead to unequal treatment, such as genital mutilation or punishments for sexual transgressions. Many religions legitimise and regulate women's traditional domestic and reproductive role, e.g. the Catholic Church bans abortion and artificial contraception.
- Fundamentalist religions stress the importance of women playing a **traditional subordinate role** to men. Consequently, fundamentalist religions are often committed to challenging women's rights to education, careers and decisions about reproduction. They often stress that motherhood should be women's main source of fulfilment.

> **KEY POINT**
>
> Feminist sociologists see religion as an ideological instrument of domination and repression that generally serves the interests of men in preserving, justifying and helping to reproduce, generation by generation, male power in patriarchal societies.

- **Daly** argues that Christianity is a patriarchal religion which eliminated other 'goddess' religions and deliberately played down the role of female figures who played a key role in the growth of Christianity.
- The Muslim feminist, **El Sadaawi** argues that religious belief systems, such as Islam or Christianity, are not in themselves patriarchal or to blame for the oppression of women. Rather, she argues that early societies were patriarchal and therefore men were able to dominate the interpretation of the scriptures and consequently this enabled men to misinterpret religious belief systems to impose their power on women.

It should not be assumed that all religions are equally oppressive to women. There have been some successful challenges to the patriarchal structure of organised religion. Gender neutral language has been introduced in many hymns and prayers, and the requirement in the Christian marriage ceremony for the bride to promise to 'obey' her husband is now also optional. Judaism has allowed women to become rabbis in its non-orthodox denominations since 1972 and some Christian religions, particularly Quakerism, have never been oppressive to women.

> **KEY POINT**
>
> **Watson** notes that the Western **media** has depicted the veil, burkha and hijab as symbols of women's oppression, as constraining and restricting forms of dress, and consequently as a means of male social control over women (alongside forced marriage). However, this is not the viewpoint of many Muslim women and writers. They argue that religious modesty actually has advantages for women which can enable them to cope with male power, especially the power of men to reduce women to sexual objects.

Ethnicity and religion

AQA **SCLY 3**   OCR **G672**

Britain today is a **multi-cultural society** characterised by religious pluralism – a diversity of religious faiths and forms of religious practice. About 72% of people in Britain describe themselves as Christian. Although most Christians in Britain are White, many of them are also of Black African or Caribbean origin.

In addition, in 2006, there were significant numbers of **Muslims** (3.3 million), **Hindus** (1.4 million), **Jews** (500 000), **Sikhs** (200 000) and **Buddhists** (20 000).

> **KEY POINT**
>
> Muslims, Hindus and Black Christians are considerably more likely than White Christians to see religion as important to their **identity**. **O'Beirne** (2004) carried out the first detailed Home Office survey of the nation's beliefs and found that White Christians ranked religion tenth behind family, work, age, interests, education, nationality, gender, income and social class. In contrast, Black people ranked their religious beliefs third, whilst Asians placed it second behind family.

This links to material in Chapter 2 on identity.

African-Caribbean and Black African participation in religion

African-Caribbeans and Black Africans are more religious than White people. According to **Brierley** (2006), in Britain in 2005, 17% of church-goers were Black compared with 12% in 1998. Over half of all churchgoers in London are Black, yet the proportion of Black people in London is less than 20%.

Pentecostalism was the only denomination that grew in the period 1998 to 2005 and it has now replaced Methodism as the third largest Christian denomination. Half of the Pentecostal population is estimated to be either Black African or Caribbean and consequently Pentecostalism is the largest Christian group among British African-Caribbeans today.

There is some evidence that African-Caribbeans are more likely to be involved in sects such as the Seventh Day Adventists, Rastafarianism and the Nation of Islam. Rastafarianism is popular among young African-Caribbean men in inner-city areas like Brixton in London. It gives them a very distinctive **group identity** which is often interpreted by the police and judicial system to be in opposition to establishment values.

Asian participation in religion

Research shows that Muslim men over the age of 35 visit the mosque at least once a week and that this is growing among younger people. It is estimated that practising Muslims will soon outnumber practising Anglicans.

There has also been a growth in the building of mosques and temples, while Christian churches are closing. In 1961, there were just seven mosques, three Sikh temples and one Hindu temple in England and Wales compared with nearly 55 000 churches. By 2005, there were 1700 mosques compared with 47 600 churches.

Explanations for ethnic differences in religious belief and participation

- Ethnic minorities tend to be **economically** and **socially disadvantaged** compared with the majority population, e.g. 63% of Pakistani and Bangladeshi households were living in poverty in 2005 whilst African-Caribbeans experience much higher levels of unemployment compared with the White population. **Weber** (1920) suggested that religions such as Pentecostalism and Rastafarianism may be attractive to some ethnic minority groups because they provide an explanation and justification for their economic deprivation (i.e. a theodicy of disprivilege) and offer hope of salvation, usually in the afterlife.
- Members of ethnic minorities may be more likely to experience **social or status deprivation**, i.e. they may be more likely to feel dissatisfied or marginalised at their lack of status in society because of factors such as racism.
- Religion can be a means of easing the transition into a new culture for recent immigrants. It can provide support and a sense of community for minority groups in their new environment. **Bruce** (2002) argues that religion offers immigrants support and a sense of **cultural identity** in an uncertain or hostile environment. **Bird** (1999) argues that religion functions as a source of

community solidarity for ethnic minorities – it is a means of defending and preserving one's culture and language as well as a way of coping with threats such as racial prejudice and discrimination.

- **Beckford** (2002) suggests that evangelical Christianity gives Black people a sense of purpose, hope and independence.
- Family structures are generally much stronger in Asian communities with strong extended families. This, combined with closer-knit communities, may result in pressure to conform to religious values and behaviour.

This links to material in Chapter 1 on families.

Modood found that religion was important in the lives of minority ethnic communities as an agency of socialisation and as a means of maintaining traditional morality, such as conceptions of mutual responsibility, honour, trust, and the difference between right and wrong. It also helps members of ethnic minority groups to cope with the worries and pressures in life, especially those which arise from racial hostility which might be expressed through prejudice, discrimination and racially motivated attacks.

KEY POINT

This links to material in Chapter 2 on hybrid identities.

Johal notes the emergence of a **hybrid identity** that he calls **Brasian** identity – a blend of British and Asian culture – that is important to young British Asians. He notes that Brasians choose elements of their parents' culture that are important to them and combine them with elements of British culture that they value, e.g. they might expect to marry who they wish rather than have an arranged marriage or a partner from the same ethnic group. However, they might still have a traditional religious wedding. They may not necessarily follow traditional religious customs with regard to diet, alcohol or dress. **Butler** found that Muslim women were committed to Islam, but wanted more choice and independence in their lives.

Class and religion

AQA **SCLY 3**   OCR **G672**

Think about the advantages and disadvantages of using surveys to investigate beliefs.

Research by **Ashworth and Farthing** (2007) demonstrates that church going is mainly associated with the middle classes rather than the working classes. In 2008, a third of owner-occupiers went to church compared with only 19% of council tenants. However, surveys of non-attenders suggest that more members of the middle classes are non-believers or atheists. Surveys indicate that there is a strong belief without belonging among the working classes.

Explanations for class differences in church attendance

- **Aherne and Davie** explain working class non-attendance at church in terms of a general mistrust of institutional life and officialdom. Institutions such as churches are perceived as too closely tied to the ruling establishment and may be interpreted as too official or formal because they issue instructions to people about how they should behave.
- The middle classes tend to be more **geographically mobile** and this can have an impact on churchgoing. **Brierley** (1999) suggests that the church offers people new to an area an opportunity to become part of the community. However, this may have the negative consequence of alienating working class people in poorer areas from churches they perceive to be middle class.

This links to the secularisation debate.

- Church attendance for the middle classes, especially in rural areas, may have become a **secular** or **social activity** – people may go to be seen or because it is the 'thing to do' rather than go to worship God.
- **Economic deprivation** is more likely to be experienced by the working class and the poor – there is some evidence that evangelical Christian sects, the Nation of Islam, Rastafarianism, the Branch Davidians, Jim Jones' People's Temple, etc. appealed mainly to a working class clientele because they offered **divine compensation** for their low economic status.
- **Holden's** work on the Jehovah's Witnesses suggests that the skilled working class and white-collar workers who become members of this sect may do as a result of **social** or **status deprivation**, i.e. they derive little or no satisfaction from their jobs. The evangelical goals of the Witnesses may be an alternative source of status.
- **Wallis** notes that middle class students were attracted to the sects that appeared in the 1960s and 1970s because they were suffering a crisis of meaning in a materialist society. These university educated young people were experiencing **psychic deprivation** and consequently turned to sects that could offer spiritual fulfilment and enlightenment.
- The composition of New Age cults is overwhelmingly middle class. As **Bruce** (1995) argues, spiritual growth appeals mainly to those whose more pressing material needs have been satisfied, but who feel there may be more to life. Interest in the New Age also often depends on having the spare material resources to buy into the services these cults offer, e.g. the cost of investing in the spiritual services offered by religious organisations such as Scientology can be quite high.

Age and religion

AQA **SCLY 3**   OCR **G672**

The general pattern of religious participation is that the older a person is, the more likely they are to attend religious services. According to the 2004 Home Office Citizenship Survey, only 10% of 16 to 24-year olds say they 'belong to a religion'. The equivalent for those aged 25–49 is 43%, and for the over 50s it is 47%.

Davie notes that older people have always been more religious than the young. Attendance amongst young people aged 16–20 in mainstream Christian churches has more or less halved since 1980, e.g. in 2005, two-fifths of churches had no-one under the age of 11 attending services whilst about 30% of church-goers were over 65. The only exception to this rule seems to be the Pentecostal denomination which continues to attract younger members.

Think about how the ageing population might impact on church attendance.

According to **Voas and Crockett** (2005), younger generations of Whites are becoming less and less religious. In surveys of religious belief, young people were most likely to describe themselves as not religious at all. Only 2% of over 65s make this claim.

This has implications for research methods. For example, it is important that questions in surveys and interviews mean the same to all respondents. Think about how the use of triangulation might be advantageous here.

However, research by **Rankin** (2005) seems to suggest that young people are interested in spiritual matters, but that they interpret the term spiritual in a different way to the older generation. Rankin noted the reluctance of young people to identify aspects of their experience as spiritual, but when opportunities were offered for discussion, it became clear that the young people were engaged in the same kinds of soul searching that older people call spiritual.

Age, sects and cults

Young adults are more likely to join **sects**. This is for two main reasons. Firstly, it is because they have more freedom from social ties than older people. They are free to join groups that withdraw from the world, as they do not yet have dependants. Secondly, as traditional religion has less influence in society, the young may experience **anomie** or **ethical deprivation**. Sects offer them moral guidance and a sense of community.

Middle aged, middle class people are more likely to be involved with **cults**. They have too much of a stake in society to join world-rejecting sects. Cults are more appealing because they promise to make their clients more successful in terms of society's goals, as well as making them spiritually fulfilled. Middle aged people also have spare funds to invest in the services that cults offer.

Ethnicity and age

This links to material in Chapter 2 on ethnic identities.

Religion has a profound influence in shaping the **ethnic identity** of young Asians. It seems to have less influence in the shaping of African-Caribbean culture and identity. However, African-Caribbean youth are more likely to be practising Christians, especially born-again Christians than White youth, and are especially likely to be involved in sects and cults such as Rastafarianism, the Seventh Day Adventists, etc.

This highlights the links between ethnicity, age and religion.

Modood et al. (1997) questioned two generations of Asians, African-Caribbeans and Whites regarding the statement 'Religion is very important to how I live my life'. He found that those most in favour of religion were the Pakistani and Bangladeshi samples – 82% of his age 50+ sample and 67% of his 16–34 year age group valued the importance of Islam in their lives. About one third of young Indians saw their religion as important. The lowest figure was for young Whites – only 5% saw religion as important compared with 18% of young African-Caribbeans. In all ethnic groups, the older generation saw religion as more important than the younger generation although the gap was lowest among the Muslim sample.

Sociological explanations for age differences in religious belief and practice

- The **ageing effect** – this is the view that people turn to religion as they get older, e.g. using evidence from the Kendal project (see page 175), **Heelas** (2005) argues that people become more interested in spirituality as they get older. As people approach death, they 'naturally' become more concerned about spiritual matters and the afterlife, repentance of past misdeeds and so on. As a result, they are more likely to go to church, pray, etc.
- **Disengagement** – this is the view that as people get older, they become detached from the integrating mechanisms of society such as work, e.g. they withdraw from public contact as they retire from their work, as their friends die, etc. and are more likely to be socially isolated. Participation in a religion may therefore compensate because religious organisations offer social support and a network of people to relate to.
- The **generational effect** – this is the view that as society becomes more secular, each new generation is less religious than the one before. **Gill** (1998) notes that most children (with the exception of Asian children) are no longer

receiving a religious **socialisation** and those brought up without religious beliefs are less likely to become church-goers later in life. There are therefore more old people than young people in church congregations today because they grew up at a time when religion was more popular.

Explanations for young people's lack of religious belief

- The **declining attraction** of religion – **Brierley** (2002) found that 87% of 10–14 year olds thought church was boring, repetitive, uncool and old-fashioned, as well as being full of old people who were out of touch with the styles and attitudes of young people.
- The **expanded spiritual marketplace** – **Lynch** (2008) suggests that young people are turning away from conventional religion because of the existence of an 'expanded spiritual marketplace' which exposes young people to a wider diversity of religious ideas and practices. Lynch notes these allow young people to express themselves spiritually outside traditional religions.
- The **privatisation of belief** – young people may believe that their religious beliefs are private and consequently 'believe without belonging'. They may prefer not to publicly display their feelings about God.
- **Secular spirituality and the sacred** – Lynch argues that young people may be spiritually inspired by non-religious or secular factors such as drug experiences and music. These may cause them to reflect on the meaning of their lives and the ways they live them. Lynch argues that young people are finding **new forms of spirituality** which may not resemble conventional definitions.
- The **decline of meta-narratives** – post-modernist sociologists argue that young people are more likely than most other social groups to be disenchanted with the world because of their exposure to further and higher education. They may consequently believe that religion has lost the power to explain the world to them.
- **Declining religious education** – religion no longer plays a central role in schools and colleges. Sunday schools are in terminal decline. Most primary and secondary schools resort to a general kind of secular or moral education. This means that the majority of young people don't get any religious education at all, but it also reflects the fact that most of them don't want it.
- **Pragmatic reasons** – young people today (compared with previous generations) have more demands on their time, and they simply have more interesting and enjoyable things to do.

PROGRESS CHECK

1. Which three categories does Woodhead use when analysing women's responses to religion?
2. Identify two minority ethnic groups whose members tend to be more religious than White people.

Answers: 1. Home-centred women, jugglers and career women. 2. People of Asian and African-Caribbean heritage.

6.5 Theories of ideology, science and religion

LEARNING SUMMARY	After studying this section, you should be able to understand:
	• the relationship between religion, science and ideology

Religion and science

AQA **SCLY 3**   OCR **G672**

This links to the scientific approach discussed in Chapter 5.

Religious belief systems dominated thinking about the world up to about 200 years ago. The astronomer **Galileo** was successfully prosecuted for heresy by the Catholic Church in 1632 for suggesting that the Earth was not the centre of the universe. However, scientific belief systems made such tremendous progress in the eighteenth century that this period became known as the **Enlightenment**. This **scientific approach** challenged religious ideas in its insistence that:

- knowledge must be based on **empirical evidence**, i.e. facts that can be observed and measured
- scientists must ignore their personal feelings and remain objective at all times when conducting scientific research
- scientific thinking should be **rational** and **logical**
- scientists' observations and theories must be **testable** by other scientists.

The approach of this scientific belief system causes problems for religious belief systems because:

- the existence of God or gods cannot be tested
- religious belief relies on irrational faith rather than on hard scientific evidence.

See the secularisation debate.

Many commentators believed that the rise of scientific belief systems would result in the decline of religious beliefs and practices. However, although religious beliefs and practices seem to have gone into decline, they have not disappeared because:

- scientists cannot tell people how to live their lives or provide moral codes
- science tells people very little about the things that matter the most to them, i.e. values, hopes, fears, anxieties
- science is not able to make people feel comfortable, especially with regard to the reasons why loved ones fall ill and die, why humans exist, the nature of 'good' and 'evil' and especially what happens after physical death – religion may still have a major role to play in answering such questions.

Religion and science continue to exist side-by-side, but they do so not without tensions. Eminent scientists such as **Dawkins** have been very critical of the problems caused by religion (e.g. war, persecution, suffering, etc.) and in his book *The God Delusion* (2006) he set out to show the irrational nature of religious belief.

You can draw on this when discussing secularisation and rationalisation.

The tension between religion and science is particularly pronounced in the world's most technologically advanced nation – the USA – which paradoxically is the most religious of the advanced industrial democracies of the West. Many Americans actually reject science in favour of the teachings of their faith tradition. While virtually all scientists agree that life on Earth evolved over billions of years, many

Americans (42%) consistently reject the idea of natural evolution because it conflicts with the biblical account of creation. Of those Americans who do support the idea of evolution, a further 21% believe such evolution is guided by a supreme being. As a result of the strength of these beliefs, there has been a reluctance to let teachers teach the theory of evolution in some American States and in many American schools evolution is taught as a competing theory alongside **scientific creationism** – a form of science based on the contents of the Bible which starts with the assumption that biblical content is true and cannot be challenged.

Religion, science and ideology

Generally, then, religious and scientific ideas are in conflict. Sociologists use the term **ideology** to help us understand how conflict between belief systems can occur and how belief systems relate to the distribution of power in society.

KEY POINT

An ideology is a set of shared views or beliefs that help people make sense of the world. Both science and religion are ideologies as well as belief systems. However, sociologists note that ideologies often justify the position of powerful groups in society, e.g. **Marxist sociologists** argue that religion has been used by the rich and powerful as a means of ensuring that their monopoly over wealth and power is not challenged by the poor or the working class.

However, science too has been seen by some sociologists as a type of ideology working in favour of powerful groups. Marxists argue that capitalist use of science and technology results in exploitation of labour in factories in the west and in the developing world, inequalities in income and wealth and environmental destruction and pollution. However, science is often presented in a more benevolent way than this. It is celebrated as providing society with the technology that underpins people's standard of living and materialistic tendencies. This distracts people from the fact that the wealthy may have acquired wealth and power at the expense of workers.

PROGRESS CHECK

1 What is an ideology?
2 How does Dawkins view religious belief?

Answers: 1. A set of ideas that serve to justify inequality. 2. As irrational.

Sample question and model answer

This is a typical OCR question on Religion.

Outline and evaluate the view that religion acts as a conservative influence in society. **(33 marks)**

Many sociologists view religion as having a conservative or change-inhibiting influence in society, e.g. the Roman Catholic Church has a conservative stance on issues such as homosexuality while religious fundamentalism, which has emerged within the major world religions such as Islam, supports conservative values and tradition.

Explicit evaluation.

Functionalist approaches see religion as a conservative force and as fulfilling a positive function in society. Religion provides guidelines for human action (e.g. through its role in socialisation) and contributes to value consensus which is essential for social order and social solidarity. However, the functionalist approach has been criticised for down-playing not only the role of religion in promoting social change, but also its disruptive influence, e.g. in Northern Ireland.

The answer is well structured and the material is presented logically.

Marx also argued that religion acts as a conservative influence in capitalist societies. He described religion as 'the opium of the people' because, like a drug, it cushioned the pain of oppression. Marx argued that religion diverted people's attention away from class inequality and exploitation and served the bourgeoisie by justifying their dominant position as god-given.

Alternative arguments within Marxism explored.

Application of examples.

Not all Marxists, however, see religion as necessarily having a conservative influence on society. Engels recognised that religious leaders could promote radical social change. More recently, Maduro, a Neo-Marxist, argued that religion could play a progressive role in the political struggles of oppressed classes. Religions, particularly those with a charismatic leader, can develop into political movements that seek change on Earth rather than salvation in heaven. Archbishop Desmond Tutu, for example, fought against apartheid in South Africa and Roman Catholic priests who support Liberation Theology challenge poverty and inequality in Latin America.

Alternative arguments explored.

Explicit evaluation.

Weber agreed with Marx that religion could play an ideological role and preserve the status quo. However, Weber also showed how religious ideas in the form of the Calvinist belief in predestination contributed to the development of capitalism in Europe. Weber's critics, however, argue that capitalism developed before Calvinism and that colonialism and slavery were more important than religious beliefs in the emergence of capitalism.

Knowledge and understanding of concepts.

Knowledge of counter arguments.

Supporters of the secularisation thesis suggest that religion no longer has a significant influence or role in society. On the other hand, Islamic fundamentalism is growing and seeks to bring about social change, e.g. by opposing Western culture.

A clear conclusion is reached.

The evidence suggests that the role of religion varies. McGuire argues that the key sociological focus is now on the ways and conditions under which religion promotes, rather than inhibits social change. Religion can be a conservative force if the charismatic leader affirms the status quo, if the beliefs stress that humans are powerless to change the world, if the institution is tied to the established order, if members are drawn from privileged groups and if there are alternative avenues to change. However, it is not necessarily a conservative social influence.

Exam practice questions

Question 1 is a typical AQA question on beliefs in society.

1 Assess the view that religious institutions have become disengaged from society. **(33 marks)**

Question 2 is a typical OCR question on religion.

2 Outline and evaluate the view that religion promotes social solidarity. **(33 marks)**

7 Mass media

The following topics are covered in this chapter:

- Defining and researching the mass media
- Ownership and control of the mass media
- The social construction of news
- Media representations of age, social class, ethnicity, gender, sexuality and disability
- The effect of mass media content on audiences and society
- New media, globalisation and popular culture

7.1 Defining and researching the mass media

LEARNING SUMMARY	After studying this section, you should be able to understand:
	• key media concepts, such as formal content analysis and semiotics
	• the strengths and weaknesses of the key methods of researching the media

Defining the mass media

AQA **SCLY 3**   OCR **G673**

Remember that AQA Unit SCLY 3 and OCR Unit G673 are synoptic units. When revising this topic think about the links with other topics you have studied and with themes and concepts such as power, control and inequality.

> **KEY POINT**
>
> The **mass media** are generally defined by sociologists as those agencies of communication that transmit information, education, news and entertainment to mass audiences.

There are broadly three types of media.

- The **print** media – newspapers, magazines, comics, books and some forms of advertising.
- The **audio-visual** media – terrestrial and satellite television, radio, cinema, DVDs and music. Most companies which produce this type of media are commercially owned, but state-owned public broadcasting such as the BBC also plays a big role in audio-visual production.
- The **cybermedia or digital** media – these are relatively new types of media which are mainly focused on the Internet. Attention has especially been paid to interactive social networking sites such as Facebook, digital media such as mobile phones and MP3 players and the computer games industry.

Researching the mass media

AQA **SCLY 2**   OCR **G671**
    SCLY 3   **G673**
    SCLY 4   **G674**

Quantitative or formal content analysis

> **KEY POINT**
>
> The main method used by sociologists for analysing media reports, whether they are textual or visual, has been **content analysis**. This is essentially a quantitative method which counts the frequency of particular words, images or themes.

This links to material in Chapter 5 on research methods. The media (e.g. the Internet or newspapers) are a source of secondary data. When sociologists use a method such as content analysis to study the media they generate primary data from their own research.

Most researchers use a content analysis schedule, i.e. a list of categories to be observed in the media report, which are ticked off as they are observed. Sampling is an important part of the content analysis method, e.g. if the researcher is interested in how crime is reported in tabloid newspapers, they might sample the coverage of three newspapers on three days of the week over a period of a month. If the researcher is interested in the impact of television advertising on its audience, they may sample television commercials from different parts of the day over several channels over several weeks. Library archives might be sampled to look at media trends over time.

KEY POINT

Feminist sociologists, such as **Lobban**, have undertaken content analyses of children's books, to highlight how boys are usually shown in active, creative, practical roles, whereas girls are shown as passive, domestic, and as followers rather than leaders. This involves creating a list of categories such as 'takes lead' or 'follows', 'gives orders' or 'obeys orders', 'works out of doors' or 'works indoors', 'mends car' or 'does housework', and counting up each occasion on which the characters in the book do these things.

Think about how this linked to gender socialisation.

In some traditional reading books there was a clear assumption that boys were leaders and girls were followers. More recently, however, books have been written which try to avoid these stereotypes.

Formal content analysis has a number of strengths.
- Mass media reports exist in a variety of readily available and accessible forms and consequently it is relatively cheap to construct a sample and content analysis schedule.
- It is regarded as a reasonably **reliable** method, especially if a research team cross-checks its use of the content analysis schedule in order to understand precisely what constitutes a particular category or code.
- It is a non-reactive and unobtrusive method, i.e. the document is not affected by the fact you are using it and no human sample is directly involved in the research.

However formal content analysis does have some limitations.
- The coding results are the end product of personal interpretation which may be unconsciously influenced by the political and ideological values of the researchers, and consequently biased. Other teams of researchers might classify the media content quite differently.
- If researchers look hard enough for something, there is a likelihood that they will find it, especially if what they are looking for is taken out of the context of the overall media report and reduced to a set of statistics.
- Analysing media reports tells us very little about the effect on audiences – we may find evidence of what we are looking for, but that is no guarantee that audiences are taking any notice of it.
- Content analysis ignores questions about why the media report was produced and presented in the way that it was in the first place.

The influence of semiotics

This links to material on research methods in Chapter 5.

> **KEY POINT**
>
> Sociological researchers studying the media have developed more **qualitative** versions of content analysis. These have been influenced by the academic discipline of **semiotics**, i.e. the scientific study of signs or codes. In terms of media texts, semiotics aims to uncover the hidden meanings that lie behind the use of particular words or images. Signs are said to be made up of two parts – the **signifier** (or denotation) and the **signified** (or connotation). The signifier is quite simply what we can see or hear, whereas the signified is its meaning, i.e. what it symbolises.

Cohen looked closely at the language used in the reporting of the conflicts between mods and rockers in the mid 1960s and noted a media propensity to exaggerate the meaning of youth conflict through the use of words such as 'battle', 'riot' and 'crisis'.

However, the **Glasgow University Media Group (GUMG)** were probably the first research group to formally employ semiotics in **textual and visual analysis**. They found that the language and images used by the media are more sympathetic to the interests of the powerful and often devalue the points of view of less powerful groups.

In their study of the way that industrial disputes were reported on television, they observed that journalists often talked about strikers making 'demands' whilst management made 'offers' or 'proposals' which were often 'rejected' by workers. The visual images used by news broadcasts confirmed this 'aggressive greedy worker' versus 'passive, reasonable and generous management' stance constructed by the media by interviewing workers in situations which confirmed the text, e.g. on the picket line with all its associated hustle and bustle and by showing images of the inconvenience 'caused' by the strike. In contrast, management were interviewed in the calm environment of their offices and were very rarely called upon to justify their actions.

Similarly, individuals may also be **labelled** by the media as 'scroungers', 'terrorists' or 'extremists' – these labels serve to undermine the credibility of the powerless. In foreign news reports, the media often make the **ethnocentric** and **ideological** distinction between 'terrorists', who are seen as disrupting friendly regimes, and 'freedom fighters', who are resisting regimes hostile to the West.

The critique of semiotics

Critics of semiotic based research argue that semiotics lack **methodological rigour** because there are few methodological guidelines for practising semiotics. Consequently it has a number of weaknesses.

- It is seen to lack **reliability** because the method is very reliant on the researcher's subjective and often selective interpretation of the text or image which may be at odds with the interpretations of other researchers and the audience. Consequently, it is very doubtful whether such research can be replicated.
- It may lack **validity** because the data collected may merely reflect the sociologist's own biases and prejudices.

● It tells sociologists little about why the text was created in the way it was or about the media's effect on the audience.

The Internet

The Internet provides secondary data. This links to material on secondary sources in Chapter 5.

The Internet is increasingly being used as a source of information about the social world by sociologists. **Lee** argues that the Internet has several advantages for the sociological researcher.

● It is generally an **unobtrusive** method in that sifting through the secondary data does not directly influence or harm human behaviour in any way.

● The **democratic nature** of the Internet has produce fantastic amounts of data for the sociologist to explore – most of it is easily accessible and free of charge. The information available can easily be retrieved even when the data is located at a site thousands of miles away.

● Many **social activities and relationships** which are difficult to study directly are recorded and can be traced on-line, e.g. many illegal and deviant activities are represented on the Internet and in chat rooms. Consequently researchers can study (by examining the websites and/or going into virtual chat-rooms) how people who subscribe to such activities relate to the activity and each other.

This is referred to as the 'digital divide'.

However, **Stein** (2002) urges caution in the use of the Internet as a source of secondary data because its content has not been academically or scientifically verified and checked for **reliability** or accuracy – much of the content of websites is inaccurate and the product of rumour and speculation. Furthermore, Stein argues that access to computers and therefore the Internet, both within western societies in terms of social class and worldwide, is still deeply unequal.

> **PROGRESS CHECK**
>
> **1** What is meant by the term mass media?
> **2** Identify two examples of new media.
>
> Answers: 1. The means of communication that reach large audiences. 2. Possible answers include: the Internet, mobile phones, digital television.

7.2 Ownership and control of the media

LEARNING SUMMARY

After studying this section, you should be able to understand:

● trends and patterns in ownership and control of a range of mass media
● the theoretical perspectives on the relationship between ownership and control of the media

Trends in ownership and control

AQA **SCLY 3**   OCR **G673**

> **KEY POINT**
>
> Recent trends in media ownership and control suggest that the number of companies controlling global mass media has significantly shrunk in recent years. **Bagdikian** (2004) notes that in 1983, 50 corporations controlled the vast majority of all news media in the USA, but by 2004 media ownership was **concentrated** in seven corporations.

Curran (2003) notes that ownership of British newspapers has always been concentrated in the hands of a few powerful 'press barons', e.g. in 1937 four men owned nearly one in every two national and local daily newspapers sold in Britain. Today, seven powerful individuals dominate the ownership of British national daily and Sunday newspapers.

The content of commercial terrestrial television is mainly controlled by one company, ITV plc, whilst access to satellite, cable and digital television in Britain is generally controlled by two companies – News Corp, (owned by Rupert Murdoch) which owns BSkyB, and Virgin Media (owned by Richard Branson).

Global conglomeration

> **KEY POINT**
>
> The major difference in media ownership and control compared with forty years ago is the movement of media corporations into the global marketplace. The major media companies are now **global conglomerations** – transnational corporations (TNCs) with a presence in many countries.

Horizontal and vertical integration

Ownership and control of the mass media is a complex business as the following examples illustrate. Some media companies are characterised by **horizontal integration** or cross media ownership – this refers to the fact that global media corporations often cross media boundaries and invest in a wide range of media products. NewsCorp, for example, owns newspapers, magazines, book publishers, terrestrial and satellite television channels and film studios in several countries.

Some media companies have focused on increasing economic control over all aspects of the production process in order to maximise profits, e.g. film corporations not only make movies, but distribute them to their own cinema chains. This is referred to as **vertical integration**.

Diversification, synergy and technological convergence

Some media corporations are not content to focus on media products, but have **diversified** into other fields. The best example of this is Virgin which began as a music label and record shop chain, but has expanded into a wide range of products and services including cola, vodka, banking, insurance, transport, digital television, cinema and wedding dresses.

Media companies often use their very diverse interests to package or **synergise** their products in several different ways, e.g. a film is often accompanied by a soundtrack album, computer game, ring tone or toy action figures. A company may use its global interests to market one of its own films through its television channels, magazines and newspapers in dozens of countries at the same time.

Technological convergence is a recent trend which involves putting several technologies into one media product. Companies that normally work in quite separate media technology fields are joining up or converging in order to give customers access to a greater range of media services across technologies such as interactive television, lap-tops, MP3 players and mobile phones.

Theories of media ownership and control

> **KEY POINT**
>
> **Doyle** (2002) suggests that examination of ownership and control patterns is important for two reasons.
> - All points of view need to be heard if society is to be truly democratic.
> - Abuses of power and influence by elites need to be monitored by a free media.
>
> Doyle argues that too much concentration of media ownership is dangerous and unhealthy because the media have the power to make or break political careers and have a considerable influence over public opinion.

The pluralist theory of media ownership

> The pluralist approach argues that a wide range of opinions and views exist in society and this range is reflected within the variety of media products available to consumers.

Pluralists argue that media owners are generally responsible in the way that they manage information because media content is mainly shaped by **consumer demand** in the marketplace. They therefore only give the buying public what they want. Moreover, editors, journalists and broadcasters have a strong sense of **professional ethics** which act as a system of checks and controls on potential owner abuse of the media.

Pluralists suggest that the mass media are an essential part of the **democratic process** because the electorate today glean most of their knowledge of the political process from newspapers and television. Pluralists argue that owners, editors and journalists are trustworthy managers and protectors of this process.

Furthermore, pluralists argue that media audiences are the real power holders because they can exercise the right to buy or not to buy. If they did not like the choices that media owners are making available to them, or if they suspected that the media product was biased, such audiences would respond by not buying the product. The media, therefore, supply what the audience wants rather than what the owner decides. If some viewpoints have a greater range of media representing them, this is not necessarily biased. It merely reflects what the audience wants or views as important.

Pluralists also argue that concentration of ownership is a product of **economic rationality** rather than political or sinister motives. It is driven by the need to keep costs low and to maximise profits. Globalisation too results from the need to find new audiences rather than from cultural imperialism.

Pluralists argue that it is practically impossible for owners to interfere with the content of newspapers and television programmes because their businesses are economically far too complex for them to regularly interfere in the day-to-day running or the content.

Public service broadcasting

Pluralists point out that a significant share of the media market in Britain is taken up by **public service broadcasters (PSB)**, i.e. media outlets controlled by the state such as the British Broadcasting Corporation (BBC). The BBC has a legal obligation to inform, to educate and to ensure that all programming is pluralistic and diverse, i.e. that all sections of society are catered for. Pluralists argue that

PSB is impartial and objective, and balances out any potential bias in the private sector.

Pluralists note that the power of media owners is also restricted by **state**, or government, **controls**, e.g. in some societies, owners are not allowed to own too much media or different types of media. Many countries also have cross-ownership rules preventing people from owning more than one type of media. Furthermore, newspapers, television and radio in Britain are subject to legal controls and rules imposed on them by The Press Council and the Office for Communications (Ofcom).

Media professionalism

Pluralists stress that the professionalism of journalists and editors also constrains the power of owners. They argue that journalists are fierce in their pursuit of the truth and consequently they have too much integrity to be biased regularly in favour of one particular perspective. Investigative journalism also has a good reputation in uncovering abuses of power and corruption among the ruling elite.

The Marxist critique of media ownership and control

Marxists argue that the economic system of Britain, i.e. capitalism, is characterised by great inequalities in wealth and income which have been brought about by the exploitation of the labour power of the working classes. Marxists believe that in order to legitimate and reproduce this system of inequality, the capitalist class uses its **cultural power** to dominate institutions like education and the mass media and transmit **ruling class ideology**. The function of these agencies is to socialise the working class into accepting the legitimacy of the capitalist system and capitalist ideas. Consequently, Marxists argue working class people experience **false class-consciousness** – they come to accept that capitalism is a just system that benefits all social groups equally. They fail to see the reality of their situation that they are being exploited by a system that only benefits a powerful minority.

The media and ideology

Marxists believe that media owners (who are members of the capitalist elite) use their media outlets to transmit ruling class ideology. **Miliband** (1973) argued that the role of the media is to shape how we think about the world we live in and suggested that audiences are rarely informed about important issues such as inequalities in wealth or why poverty persists. The capitalist system is rarely criticised or challenged. Instead, Marxists suggest that owners shape media content so that only 'approved' and conformist views are heard.

Tunstall and Palmer (1991) suggest that governments are no longer interested in controlling the activities of media owners because they need their support to either gain power or hang onto it.

Evidence for the ideological nature of ownership and control

Marxists are suggesting that media owners, wealth holders and the political elite are united in some sort of ideological conspiracy to brainwash the general population. However, it is almost impossible to scientifically gather empirical

This links to methodological issues.

evidence that supports this hypothesis. Sociologists generally only have anecdotal evidence to confirm their suspicions that concentration of media ownership is damaging democracy.

However, **Curran's** (2003) detailed systematic examination of the social history of the British press does suggest that the evidence for owner interference in and manipulation of British newspaper content is strong. Curran notes that in the period 1920–50 press barons openly boasted that they ran their newspapers for the express purpose of **propaganda** that reflected their political views. Curran points out that even when engaged in investigative reporting, the majority of newspapers in Britain have supported the Conservative Party.

Curran also notes that the period 1974–92 saw the emergence of Rupert Murdoch. However, Curran rejects the idea that Murdoch is part of a unified capitalist elite but acknowledges that Murdoch's newspapers are conservative in content and strongly supportive of capitalist interests. He argues Murdoch's motives are economic rather than ideological in that Murdoch believes that right wing economic policies are the key to vast profits.

Curran's analysis of British newspapers suggests that both pluralist and Marxist theories may be mistaken in the way they look at media ownership. He argues the pluralist view that media owners do not intervene in media content is evidentially false. Curran argues that since 2000 there has been even greater intervention by owners such as Murdoch. However, Curran disagrees with Marxists about the motive for this. He notes that the actions of media owners are not collectivised, rather they pursue their economic goals in a ruthlessly individualised way in an attempt to obtain a bigger share of the market than their capitalist competitors.

The Glasgow University Media Group

KEY POINT

The **Glasgow University Media Group (GUMG)** suggests that media content does support the interests of those who run the capitalist system. However, this is an unintended by-product of the social backgrounds of journalists and broadcasters rather than a conscious capitalist conspiracy. The GUMG points out that most journalists working for national newspapers, television and radio tend to be overwhelmingly male, White, and middle class, e.g. 54% are privately educated.

The GUMG claims that these journalists and broadcasters tend to believe in middle-of-the-road (consensus) views and ideas because these are generally unthreatening. Journalists believe that these appeal to the majority of their viewers, listeners and readers. Ideas outside this consensus are viewed by journalists as 'extremist'. People who hold these opinions are rarely invited to contribute their views in newspapers or on television, or if they are, they are ridiculed by journalists.

The GUMG argues that these journalists are not motivated by a desire to defend capitalist interests. Media companies are profit-making businesses. Those who commission and plan programmes, or decide newspaper or magazine content, usually play safe by excluding anything that might offend or upset readers or viewers. Losing several thousand readers, or viewers, because they were offended by 'extreme' views and potentially losing millions of pounds in revenue and profit is too much of a risk.

Barnett and Weymour argue that such decisions have had a negative cultural effect in the sense that education, information and news have been increasingly sidelined. They compared television schedules in 1978, 1988 and 1998 and argued that the evidence suggests that television in Britain has been significantly **dumbed down**, e.g. the number of one-off dramas and documentaries has halved, while soap operas and cheap reality shows have increased fivefold. There are also now more repeats and cheap American imports. Time allocated to news programming has fallen dramatically, and more time on serious news programmes is devoted to celebrity news and human interest stories. Barnett and Weymour note that even the BBC is succumbing to these commercial pressures. Furthermore, they conclude that despite having hundreds of television channels, we do not have more choice, just more of the same thing.

Agenda setting

The result of this journalistic consensus, argues the GUMG, is that the media set the agenda and decide what issues are discussed by society and which ones are not. This is known as **agenda setting**. The GUMG argues that the media consequently present society with a fairly narrow agenda for discussion. Agenda setting therefore results in **cultural hegemony**. The basic principles of capitalism – private enterprise, profit, the free market and the rights of property ownership – dominate media content and are presented as 'normal' and 'natural'. There is actually little choice for audiences in that there is no radical alternative to the mainstream newspapers and dissenting views on subjects like the monarchy are rarely presented.

> **PROGRESS CHECK**
>
> 1. Which approach argues that media content reflects consumer demand?
> 2. What does the term 'hegemony' mean?
> 3. Which approach argues that media owners use their media outlets to transmit ruling class ideology?
> 4. What does the term 'agenda setting' refer to?
>
> Answers: 1. The pluralist approach. 2. The dominance of ruling class ideas in society and the acceptance of these ideas by other social groups. 3. The Marxist approach. 4. The power of the media to focus public attention on some issues and, in doing so, to direct public discussion onto these issues.

7.3 The social construction of the news

<table>
<tr><td>LEARNING
SUMMARY</td><td>**After studying this section, you should be able to understand:**

• how news is perceived
• the selection and presentation of news
• sociological theories about news production</td></tr>
</table>

The perception of news

AQA **SCLY 3**   OCR **G673**

News is presented in many different forms in the twenty-first century. However, as recently as in 2005, 72% of people indicated that television was their primary source of news coverage. Only 10% relied upon newspapers to obtain their news, a further 9% relied upon radio and 67% regarded television news as the most trusted news medium and saw it as a 'window on the world' offering the audience fair and unbiased 'evidence' of events as they happened. In contrast, despite sales of about 10 million daily, only 7%, saw newspapers in the same way.

Selection and presentation of news

AQA **SCLY 3**   OCR **G673**

McQuail (1992) argues that 'news' is not objective or impartial. Events happen, but this does not guarantee that they become news – not all events can be reported because of the sheer number of them. McQuail argues that news is a **socially manufactured product** because it is the end result of a **selective process**. **Gatekeepers**, such as editors and journalists, and sometimes proprietors, make choices and judgements about what events are important enough to cover and how to cover them.

Sociologists point out that the process of news selection is biased because it is dependent upon broad influences which include organisational routines and news values.

Organisational or bureaucratic routines

News coverage is shaped by the way television news companies and newspapers are organised. This can be illustrated in a number of ways.

- **Financial constraints** – e.g., sending personnel overseas and booking satellite connections can be very expensive and may result in 'news' reports even if very little is actually happening, in order to justify such heavy costs. There has been a decline in expensive forms of news coverage such as investigative reporting or foreign affairs coverage because news organisations are cutting costs.
- The amount of **time available** for a news bulletin or the **column space** in a newspaper, e.g. events are much more likely to be reported, especially on television, if they can be accompanied by live sound bites of speech and film footage from an actual location.
- **Deadlines** – newspapers by their very nature are dated. All news included usually happened the day before. Television news is more immediate as it is often broadcast as it happens, i.e. rolling news.
- **Audiences** – the content and style of news programmes is often dependent on the type of audience thought to be watching. Newspaper content too is geared to the social characteristics of a newspaper's readers, e.g. *The Sun* is aimed at a working class young readership and so uses simplistic language because it believes that this is what its readership wants.

News values

> **KEY POINT**
>
> **Spencer-Thomas** (2008) notes that editors and journalists use the concept of **news values** to determine the **newsworthiness** of a particular story and to judge whether it will attract a significant readership or audience.

What is regarded as newsworthy varies according to the type of news outlet, i.e. it differs between newspapers, as well as television channels, depending upon the type of person who is thought to be reading or watching. These news values were catalogued by **Galtung and Ruge** (1965) and include:

> Can you think of other examples of extraordinary events or incidents that are seen as newsworthy?

- **Extraordinariness** – unexpected, rare, unpredictable and surprising events have more newsworthiness than routine events because they are out of the ordinary, e.g. the tsunami that hit south-east Asia in 2004 or the unexpected death of Diana, Princess of Wales in 1997.
- **Threshold** – the bigger the size of the event, e.g. war or natural disaster, the more likely it will be reported nationally.
- **Unambiguity** – events that are easy to grasp are more likely to be reported than those which are complex.
- **Reference to elite persons** – the activities of the powerful and more recently, celebrities such as footballers, television personalities and pop stars are perceived as more newsworthy than the exploits of ordinary people.
- **Reference to elite nations** – stories about people who speak English as their first language, look the same and have similar cultures as the audience receive more coverage than those involving people who do not, e.g. the USA is more newsworthy than most other countries. Even disasters are subject to this news value as symbolised by **McLurg's Law** named after a British news editor, who once claimed that 1 dead Briton was worth 5 dead Frenchmen, 20 dead Egyptians, 500 dead Indians and 1000 dead Chinese in terms of news coverage.
- **Personalisation** – complex events and policies are often reduced to conflict between personalities. This is because journalists and editors believe that their audiences will identify with a story if social events are seen as the actions of individuals, e.g. British politics is often presented as a personal showdown between the two party leaders.
- **Frequency** – news events that occur over a short period of time fit in with news schedules better than long-term structural events such as inflation.
- **Narrative** – journalists prefer to present news in the form of a story with heroes and villains, and a beginning, middle and end.
- **Negativity** – bad news is regarded by journalists as more exciting and dramatic than good news and is seen as potentially attracting a bigger audience. Stories about death, tragedy, bankruptcy, violence, damage, natural disasters, political upheaval or extreme weather conditions are therefore always rated above positive stories.

Interesting news stories will, therefore, contain some of these news values, but they are unlikely to contain them all. Research conducted in the USA by **Buckley** gave 12 television editors 64 news stories, which they were asked to classify for newsworthiness. All classified them in a similar manner and those items most likely to be reported were those with the greatest number of news values.

Sociological theories about news production

AQA **SCLY 3**   OCR **G673**

Neo-pluralism

Pluralists argue that journalists are professionals who are disinterested, impartial and objective pursuers of truth. **Neo-pluralists** suggest that, in the modern world of journalism, these goals are increasingly difficult to attain. **Davies** (2008) argues that modern day British journalism is characterised by what he calls churnalism – the uncritical over-reliance by journalists on 'facts' churned out by government spin doctors and public relations experts. He found that 80% of news stories in two national newspapers were sourced in this way over a two week period in 1997. Only 12% of stories were generated by journalists.

The power elite

Bagdikian (2004), in his critique of the American news media, suggests that almost all media owners in the USA are part of a wider **power elite** made up of a powerful industrial, financial and political establishment. Consequently, media owners ensure that the content of news is politically conservative and that their news outlets promote corporate values. Bagdikian notes how such values permeate news, e.g. most newspapers have sections dedicated to business news, but contain little on poverty or the growing gap between the rich and poor in the USA.

The propaganda model of the media

Herman and Chomsky (1988) argue that the media participate in propaganda campaigns helpful to elite interests. They suggest that media performance is largely shaped by market forces and that built into the capitalist system is a range of filters that work ceaselessly to shape media output, e.g. advertisers want their advertising to appear in a supportive selling environment whilst government can pressure the media with threats of withdrawal of TV licences and therefore control the flow of information.

Edwards and Cromwell (2006) argue that particular subjects, e.g. US/British government responsibility for genocide, vast corporate criminality and threats to the very existence of human life, are distorted, suppressed, marginalised and ignored by the British mass media. Leaders of developing countries of whom the West disapprove are uncritically demonised, whilst the USA is presented as the champion of democracy.

Marxist perspectives

The Marxist **Hall** agrees that news is supportive of capitalist interests because those in powerful positions have better access to media institutions than the less powerful. Hall argues that this is a result of the **news values** employed by most journalists. In particular, most journalists rank the views of politicians, police officers, civil servants and business leaders (Hall calls these groups **primary definers**) as more important (or credible) than those of pressure groups, trade unionists or ordinary people. Hall calls this the **hierarchy of credibility**.

However, **Schlesinger** (1990) is critical of theories that focus on the power of elites or owners because the media do not always act in the interests of the powerful. Contemporary politicians are very careful about what they say to the media because they are very aware that the media can shape public perceptions of their policies and practices and perhaps influence voting behaviour, as well as putting them under considerable pressure to resign.

Media owners too are engaged in **competition** with each other, as illustrated by newspaper price wars and the fact that some media owners have engaged in some very public conflicts with each other over matters of media ownership. Schlesinger argues that this does not suggest a unified media.

7.4 Media representations of age, social class, ethnicity, gender, sexuality and disability

LEARNING SUMMARY

After studying this section, you should be able to understand:

- mass media representations of gender
- theoretical perspectives on media representations of gender
- mass media representations of sexuality, disability, social class and age
- mass media representations of ethnic minorities

Media representations of gender

AQA **SCLY 3**   OCR **G673**

The media is an important agency of socialisation.

KEY POINT

Almy et al. (1984) argue that media representations of gender are important because they enter the collective social conscience and reinforce culturally dominant (hegemonic) ideas about gender which represent males as dominant and females as subordinate. Sociologists argue that media representations not only stereotype masculinity and femininity into fairly limited forms of behaviour, but also provide gender role models that males and females are encouraged to aspire to.

In your answers, try to avoid generalising about the media.

However, **Gauntlett** (2008) points out that sociological analysis of media representations needs to be cautious, because of the sheer diversity of media in Britain.

Traditional media representations of femininity

This material is also useful for illustrating the process of gender socialisation.

- Women are generally represented in a narrow range of social roles by various types of media, whilst men are shown performing a full range of social and occupational roles. **Tunstall** (2000) argues that media representations emphasise women's domestic, sexual, consumer and marital activities to the exclusion of all else. The media generally ignore the fact that a majority of British women go out to work. Men, on the other hand, are seldom presented nude or defined by their marital or family status.
- Working women are often portrayed as unfulfilled, unattractive, possibly unstable and unable to sustain relationships. It is often implied that working mothers, rather than working fathers, are guilty of the emotional neglect of their children.
- **Tuchman et al.** (1978) used the term **symbolic annihilation** to describe the way in which women's achievements are often not reported, or are condemned or trivialised by the mass media. Often their achievements are presented as less important than their looks and sex appeal. **Newbold's** research (2002) into television sport presentation shows that what little coverage of women's sport there is tends to sexualise, trivialise and devalue women's sporting accomplishments.
- Research into women's magazines suggests that they strongly encourage women to conform to ideological patriarchal ideals that confirm their

subordinate position compared with men. **Ferguson** (1983) conducted a content analysis of women's magazines from between 1949 and 1974, and 1979 and 1980. She notes that such magazines are organised around **a cult of femininity**, which promotes a traditional ideal where excellence is achieved through caring for others, the family, marriage and appearance. However, Ferguson's ideas were challenged by **Winship** (1987), who argued that women's magazines generally play a supportive and positive role in the lives of women. Winship argues that such magazines present women with a broader range of options than ever before and that they tackle problems that have been largely ignored by the male-dominated media, such as domestic violence and child abuse.

This illustrates how content analysis has been used to analyse gender representations.

- **Wolf** (1990) suggests that the images of women used by the media present women as **sex objects** to be consumed by what **Mulvey** calls the **male gaze**. According to **Kilbourne** (1995), this media representation presents women as mannequins: tall and thin, often US size zero, with very long legs, perfect teeth and hair, and skin without a blemish in sight. Wolf notes that the media encourage women to view their **bodies as a project** in constant need of improvement.

- Content analysis of teenage magazines in Britain indicates that almost 70% of the content and images focus on beauty and fashion, compared with only 12% focused on education or careers. Many encourage the idea that **slimness=happiness** and consequently **Orbach** (1991) suggests that such media imagery creates the potential for eating disorders.

The media as empowering women

> **KEY POINT**
>
> Sociologists have noted the increasing number of positive female roles emerging, especially in television drama and films. It is argued that these reflect the social and cultural changes that females have experienced in the last 25 years, especially the feminisation of the economy, which has meant that women are now more likely to have aspirational attitudes, a positive attitude towards education, careers and an independent income. **Westwood** claims that we are now seeing more **transgressive** (i.e. going beyond gendered expectations) female roles on British television as a result.

Gill (2008) argues that the depiction of women in advertising has changed from women as passive objects of the male gaze, to active, independent and sexually powerful agents. **Gauntlett** (2008) argues that magazines aimed at young women emphasise that women must do their own thing and be themselves, whilst female pop stars, like Lady Gaga, sing about financial and emotional independence. This set of media messages from a range of sources suggest that women can be tough and independent whilst being 'sexy'.

Traditional media representations of masculinity

Easthope (1986) argues that a variety of media, especially Hollywood films and computer games, transmit the view that masculinity based on strength, aggression, competition and violence is biologically determined and, therefore, a natural goal for boys to achieve.

In other words, as linked to 'nature' rather than 'nurture'.

However, the 1980s saw the emergence of a new breed of glossy magazines aimed at middle class young men, such as *GQ*, *Maxim* and *FHM*. The content of such magazines often suggested that:

- men are emotionally vulnerable
- they should be more in touch with their emotions or feminine side
- they should treat women as equals
- they should care more about their appearance
- active fatherhood is an experience worth having.

These magazines were seen by some commentators as evidence of a new type of masculinity – the **new man**. Media representations of this new type of masculinity led to **post-modern sociologists** speculating that masculinity was responding to the growing economic independence and assertiveness of women. The media trumpeted the **metrosexual male**, a type of masculinity that was focused on appearance and fashion and which championed masculine values as caring and generous. The metrosexual male was thought to be in touch with his feminine side, useful around the home and considerate towards his female partner.

However, **Gauntlett** argues that there are still plenty of magazines aimed at men which sexually objectify women and stress images of men as traditionally masculine. **Rutherford** suggests that these magazines are symbolic of what he calls **retributive masculinity** – an attempt to reassert traditional masculine authority by celebrating traditionally male concerns in their content, i.e. 'birds, booze and football'.

Whannel (2002) notes that mass media stories about and images of David Beckham are contradictory, in that they stress Beckham as representative of both metrosexual and retributive versions of masculinity. Whannel notes that media representations of Beckham are fluid – his good looks, his football skills, competitive spirit and his commitment mark him out as a traditional 'real man'. However, this image has been balanced with alternative media representations that stress his metrosexuality, particularly his emotional commitment to his family and the fact that he spends a great deal of time, effort and money on his image.

> Can you think of other examples of people who are represented in contradictory ways?

Theoretical perspectives on media representations of gender

AQA **SCLY 3**   OCR **G673**

Liberal feminism

Liberal feminists believe that media representations lag behind the reality of social and economic conditions. However, they acknowledge that representations of women have changed significantly for the better in the last thirty years.

Some liberal feminists have noted that women's progress as media professionals has slowed down in recent years. The majority of media owners are male and influential positions within the media such as media executives, newspaper editors, senior journalists, producers, television and film directors, and heads of television programming are also dominated by males.

Marxist and socialist feminism

Marxist, or **socialist**, feminists believe that the roots of the stereotypical images of men and women in the media are economic. They are a by-product of the need of media conglomerates in **capitalist societies** to make a profit. The male-dominated media aim to attract the largest audience possible and this leads to an emphasis on the traditional roles of men and women in sitcoms, game shows and soap operas. The alternative images of women encouraged by feminism, e.g. as assertive career women, do not fit easily into this type of media content and consequently such women are ignored, devalued or treated critically.

The media emphasis on women's bodies as projects is the result of the growth of the cosmetic and diet product industries. It is estimated that the diet industry alone is worth $100 billion a year in the USA. Marxists note that the marketing strategies of these industries deliberately manipulate women's anxieties so that they can be exploited as consumers of body-related products.

Radical feminism

Radical feminists argue that traditional hegemonic images of femininity are deliberately transmitted by a male-dominated media to keep women oppressed into a narrow range of roles. This creates a form of **false consciousness** in women and deters them from making the most of the opportunities available to them and consequently men's patriarchal power is rarely challenged. Radical feminists believe that it is no coincidence that, at the same time as women are achieving greater social, political and professional equality, media products symbolically relegate them to subordinate positions as sex objects or mother-housewives.

Post-modernism

Gauntlett (2008) focuses on the relationship between the mass media and **identity** and argues that the mass media today challenge traditional definitions of gender and are actually a force for social change. There has also been a new emphasis in men's media on men's emotions and problems, which has challenged masculine ideals such as toughness and emotional reticence. As a result, the media are now providing alternative gendered images and ideas, which are producing a greater **diversity of choices** for people in constructing their gender identities.

This links to material on identity in Chapter 2.

Representations of sexuality

AQA **SCLY 3**

Homosexuality

> **KEY POINT**
>
> **Batchelor** found that being gay was not generally integrated into mainstream media representations. Rather, when it did appear, e.g. in television drama, it was represented mainly as a source of anxiety or embarrassment, or it was seen as a target for teasing and bullying. The study also found that, in mainstream young people's media, lesbianism was completely invisible.

Media representations of sexuality in Britain are overwhelmingly heterosexual in character. **Gerbner** (2002) argues that the media participate in the **symbolic annihilation** of gays and lesbians by negatively stereotyping them, by rarely portraying them realistically, or by not portraying them at all. **Craig** (1992) suggests that when homosexual characters are portrayed in the media, e.g. in popular drama, they are often stereotyped as having particular amusing or negative psychological and social characteristics.

- **Campness** – this is one of the most widely used gay representations, found mainly in the entertainment media. The camp persona reinforces negative views of gay sexuality by being somewhere in between male and female.
- **Macho** – a look that exaggerates masculinity and which is regarded by heterosexual men as threatening because it subverts traditional ideas of masculinity.
- **Deviant** – gays may be stereotyped as deviants, as evil or as devious in television drama, as sexual predators or as people who feel tremendous guilt about their sexuality. In many cases, gay characters are completely defined by the 'problem' of their sexuality and homosexuality is often constructed to appear morally wrong.
- **Responsible for AIDS** – **Watney** has illustrated how British news coverage of AIDS in the 1980s stereotyped gay people as carriers of a gay plague. He argues that news coverage of AIDS reflected mainstream society's fear and dislike of the gay community and resulted in unsympathetic accounts that strongly implied that homosexual AIDS sufferers only had their own 'immoral and unnatural' behaviour to blame for their condition or death.

Gauntlett argues that lesbian, gay and bisexual people are still under-represented in much of the mainstream media, but things are slowly changing for the better. Gauntlett suggests that tolerance of sexual diversity is slowly growing in society, and images of diverse **sexual identities** with which audiences are unfamiliar may assist in making the population generally more comfortable with these alternative sexual lifestyles.

Representations of disability

AQA **SCLY 3**

Barnes (1992) argues that mass media representations of disability have generally been oppressive and negative. People with disabilities are rarely presented as people with their own identities. Barnes notes several common media representations of people with disabilities.

- **In need of pity and charity** – Barnes claims that this stereotype has grown in popularity in recent years because of television appeals such as *Children in Need*.
- **As victims** – Barnes found that when people with disabilities are featured in television drama, they are three times more likely than able-bodied characters to be killed off.
- **As villains** – people with disabilities are often portrayed as criminals or monsters, e.g. villains in James Bond films often have a physical impairment.
- **As super-cripples** – Barnes notes that people with disabilities are often portrayed as having special powers or as overcoming their impairment and poverty. In Hollywood films, the impaired male body is often visually represented as a perfect physical specimen in a wheelchair. **Ross** notes that disability issues have to be sensational, unexpected or heroic in order to be interpreted by journalists as newsworthy and reported on.
- **As a burden** – television documentaries and news features often focus on carers rather than the people with disabilities.
- **As sexually abnormal** – it is assumed by media representations that people with disabilities do not have sexual feelings or that they are sexually degenerate.
- **As incapable of participating fully in community life** – Barnes calls this the **stereotype of omission** and notes that people with disabilities are rarely

shown as integral and productive members of the community such as students, teachers or parents.

- **As ordinary or normal** – Barnes argues that the media rarely portray people with disabilities as normal people who just happen to have a disability. They consequently fail to reflect the real, everyday experience of disability.

Roper (2003) suggests that mass media representations of disability on telethons can create problems for people with disabilities and suggests that telethons over-rely on 'cute' children who are not that representative of the range of people with disabilities in Britain. Roper argues that telethons are primarily aimed at encouraging the general public to alleviate their guilt and their relief that they are not disabled, by giving money rather than informing the general public of the facts about disability.

Karpf (1988) suggests that there is a need for charities, but that telethons act to keep the audience in the position of givers and to keep recipients in their place as grateful and dependent. Karpf notes that telethons are about entertaining the public, rather than helping us to understand the everyday realities of what it is like to have a disability. Consequently, these media representations merely confirm social prejudices about people with disabilities, e.g. that they are dependent on the help of able-bodied people.

Representations of social class

AQA **SCLY 3**   OCR **G673**

KEY POINT

Mass media representations of social classes rarely focus on the social tensions or class conflict that some critical sociologists see as underpinning society.

Representations of the monarchy

Nairn (1988) notes that contemporary media coverage of the monarchy has focused positively on every trivial detail of their lives, turning the Queen and her family into an on-going **soap opera**, but with a glamour and mystique far greater than any other media personality. Furthermore, mass media representations of the Queen are also aimed at reinforcing a sense of **national identity**, in that she is portrayed as the ultimate symbol of the nation. Consequently, the media regards royal events, such as weddings and funerals, as national events.

This links to material on nationalism in Chapter 2.

Representations of the upper class and wealth

Neo-Marxists argue that mass media representations of social class tend to celebrate **hierarchy** and **wealth**. Those who benefit from these processes, i.e. the monarchy, the upper class and the very wealthy, generally receive a positive press as celebrities who are somehow deserving of their position. The British mass media hardly ever portray the upper classes in a critical light, nor do they often draw any serious attention to inequalities in wealth and pay or the over-representation of public-school products in positions of power.

Newman (2006) argues that the media focus very positively on the concerns of the wealthy and the privileged. He notes that the media over-focuses on consumer items such as luxury cars, costly holiday spots and fashion accessories that only the wealthy can afford. He also notes the enormous amount of print and broadcast media dedicated to daily business news and stock market quotations, despite the fact that few people in Britain own stocks and shares.

Representations of the middle classes

Four broad sociological observations can be made with regard to mass media representations of the **middle classes**.

- The middle class are over-represented on TV dramas and situation comedies.
- Part of the British newspaper market is specifically aimed at the middle classes and their consumption, tastes and interests, e.g. the *Daily Mail*.
- The content of newspapers such as the *Daily Mail* suggests that journalists believe that the middle classes of middle England are generally anxious about the decline of moral standards in society and that they are proud of their British identity and heritage. It is assumed that their readership feels threatened by alien influences such as the Euro, asylum seekers and terrorism. Consequently, newspapers, such as the *Daily Mail*, often crusade on behalf of the middle classes and initiate **moral panics** on issues such as video nasties, paedophilia and asylum seekers.
- Most of the creative personnel in the media are themselves middle class. In news and current affairs, the middle classes dominate positions of authority – the 'expert' is invariably middle class.

Representations of the working class

Newman argues that when news organisations focus on the **working class**, it is generally to **label** them as a problem, e.g. as welfare cheats, drug addicts or criminals. Working class groups, e.g. **youth sub-cultures** such as mods or skinheads, are often the subject of moral panics, whilst reporting of issues such as poverty, unemployment or single-parent families often suggests that personal inadequacy is the main cause of these social problems, rather than government policies or poor business practices. Studies of industrial relations reporting by the Glasgow University Media Group suggest that the media portray 'unreasonable' workers as making trouble for 'reasonable' employers.

Curran and Seaton (2003) note that newspapers aimed at working class audiences assume that they are uninterested in serious analysis of either the political or social organisation of British society. Political debate is often reduced simplistically to conflict between personalities. The content of newspapers such as *The Sun* and the *Daily Star* assumes that such audiences want to read about celebrity gossip and lifestyles, trivial human interest stories and sport.

Representations of poverty

> **KEY POINT**
>
> Newman argues that when the news media turn their attention to the most destitute, the portrayals are often negative or stereotypical. Often, the poor are portrayed in statistical rather than in human terms by news bulletins that focus on the numbers unemployed or on benefits, rather than the individual suffering and personal indignities of poverty.

McKendrick et al. (2008) studied a week's output of mainstream media in 2007 and concluded that coverage of poverty is marginal in British media, in that the causes and consequences of poverty were very rarely explored across the news, documentaries or drama. Dramas such as *Shameless* presented a sanitised picture of poverty, despite featuring characters who were economically deprived, whilst family issue-based programmes such as *The Jeremy Kyle Show* treated poverty as an aspect of entertainment. **Cohen** notes that the media often fails to see the connection between deprivation and wealth.

Representations of age

AQA **SCLY 3**   OCR **G673**

Media representations of different groups of people based on age (i.e. children, adolescents and the elderly), also generalise and categorise people on the basis of **stereotypes**.

Childhood

British children are often depicted in the British media in positive ways. Content analyses of media products suggest that eight stereotypes of children are frequently used by the media.

- As **victims of horrendous crimes** – some critics of the media have suggested that White children who are victims of crime get more media attention than adults or children from ethnic minority backgrounds.
- As **cute** – this is a common stereotype found in television commercials for baby products or toilet rolls.
- As **little devils** – another common stereotype especially found in drama and comedy, e.g. Bart Simpson.
- As **brilliant** – perhaps as child prodigies or as heroes for saving the life of an adult.
- As **brave little angels** – suffering from a long-term terminal disease or disability.
- As **accessories** – stories about celebrities such as Madonna, Angelina Jolie or the Beckhams may focus on how their children humanise them.
- As **modern** – the media may focus on how children 'these days' know so much more 'at their age' than previous generations of children.
- As **active consumers** – television commercials portray children as having a consumer appetite for toys and games. Some family sociologists note that this has led to the emergence of a new family pressure, 'pester power', the power of children to train or manipulate their parents to spend money on consumer goods that will increase the children's status in the eyes of their peers.

> This links to material covered in Chapter 1 on families.

Youth

There are generally two very broad ways in which young people have been targeted and portrayed by the media in Britain.

- There is a whole media industry aimed at **socially constructing youth** in terms of **lifestyle and identity**. Magazines are produced specifically for young people. Record companies, Internet music download sites, mobile telephone companies and radio stations all specifically target and attempt to shape the musical tastes of young people. Networking sites on the Internet, such as Facebook, Bebo and MySpace, allow youth to project their identities around the world.

> This links to material on identities in Chapter 2.

● Youth are often portrayed by news media as a **social problem**, as immoral or anti-authority and consequently constructed as **folk devils** as part of a **moral panic**. The majority of moral panics since the 1950s have been manufactured around concerns about young people's behaviour, such as their membership of specific 'deviant' sub-cultures (e.g., teddy boys, hoodies) or because their behaviour (e.g., drug taking or binge drinking) has attracted the disapproval of those in authority.

Wayne et al. (2008) conducted a content analysis of 2130 news items across all the main television channels during May 2006. They found that young people were mainly represented as a violent threat to society. They found that it was very rare for news items to feature a young person's perspective or opinion. They note that the media only delivers a one-dimensional picture of youth, one that encourages fear and condemnation rather than understanding. Moreover, they argue that it distracts from the real problems that young people face in the modern world such as homelessness, not being able to get onto the housing ladder, unemployment or mental health and that these might be caused by society's, or the government's, failure to take the problems of youth seriously.

The elderly

This shows how age and social class can interact.

Research focusing on media representations of the elderly suggests that age is not the only factor that impacts on the way the media portrays people aged 65 and over. **Newman** (2006) notes that upper class and middle class elderly people are often portrayed in television and film dramas as occupying high-status roles as world leaders, judges, politicians, experts and business executives. Moreover, news programmes seem to work on the assumption that an older male with grey in his hair and lines on his face somehow exudes the necessary authority to impart the news.

This shows how age and gender can interact.

However, female newscasters, such as Anna Ford, have long complained that these older men are often paired with attractive young females, while older women newsreaders are often exiled to radio. Leading female film and television stars are also often relegated to character parts once their looks and bodies are perceived to be on the wane, which seems to be after the age of 40.

Sociological studies show that when the elderly do appear in the media, they tend to be portrayed in the following one-dimensional ways.
● As **grumpy** – conservative, stubborn and resistant to social change.
● As **mentally challenged** – suffering from declining mental functions.
● As **dependent** – helpless and dependent on other younger members of the family or society.
● As **a burden** – as an economic burden on society (in terms of the costs of pensions and health care to the younger generation) and/or as a physical and social burden on younger members of their families (who have to worry about or care for them).
● As **enjoying a second childhood** – as reliving their adolescence and engaging in activities that they have always longed to do before they die.

However, recent research suggests that media producers may be gradually reinventing how they deal with the elderly, especially as they realise that this group may have disposable incomes, i.e. extra money to spend on consumer goods.

Media representations of ethnic minorities

AQA **SCLY 3**   OCR **G673**

> **KEY POINT**
>
> Many sociologists believe that media representations of ethnic minority groups are problematic because they contribute to the reinforcement of negative **racist stereotypes**. Media representations of ethnic minorities may be undermining the concept of a tolerant multicultural society and perpetuating social divisions based on colour, ethnicity and religion.

Evidence suggests that, despite some progress, ethnic minorities are generally under-represented or are represented in stereotyped and negative ways across a range of media content. In particular, newspapers and television news have a tendency to present ethnic minorities as a problem or to associate Black people with physical rather than intellectual activities and to neglect, and even ignore, racism and the inequalities that result from it.

Stereotypical representations

Akinti (2003) argues that television coverage of ethnic minorities over focuses on crime, AIDS in Africa and Black children's under-achievement in schools, whilst ignoring the culture and interests of a huge Black audience and their rich contribution to British society. Akinti claims that news about Black communities always seems to be 'bad news'. **Van Dijk's** (1991) content analysis of tens of thousands of news items across the world over several decades confirms that news representations of Black people can be categorised into several types of stereotypically negative news.

- **Ethnic minorities as criminals** – Black crime is the most frequent issue found in media news coverage of ethnic minorities. Van Dijk found that Black people, particularly African-Caribbeans, tend to be portrayed as criminals, especially in the tabloid press and more recently as members of organised gangs that push drugs and violently defend urban territories.
- **Ethnic minorities and moral panics** – **Watson** (2008) notes that moral panics often result from media stereotyping of Black people as potentially criminal. This effect was first brought to sociological attention by **Hall's** classic study of a 1970s moral panic that was constructed around the folk devil of the 'Black mugger'. Further moral panics have developed around rap music, e.g. in 2003, 'gangsta rap' lyrics came under attack for contributing to an increase in gun crime.
- **Ethnic minorities as a threat** – ethnic minorities are often portrayed as a threat to the majority White culture. It is suggested by some media that immigrants and asylum seekers are only interested in living in Britain because they wish to take fraudulent advantage of Britain's 'generous' welfare state. **Poole** (2000), pre 9/11, argued that Islam has always been demonised and distorted by the Western media. It has traditionally been portrayed as a threat to Western interests. Representations of Islam have been predominantly negative and Muslims have been stereotyped as backward, extremist, fundamentalist and misogynist.
- **Ethnic minorities as dependent** – news stories about less developed countries tend to focus on a 'coup-war-famine-starvation syndrome'. Often such stories imply that the causes of the problems experienced by developing countries are self-inflicted – that they are the result of stupidity, tribal conflict,

too many babies, laziness, corruption and unstable political regimes. External causes such as colonialism, tied aid, transnational exploitation and the unfair terms of world trade are rarely discussed by the British media.

This links to material in Chapter 6 on religion.

- **Ethnic minorities as abnormal** – the cultural practices of ethnic minorities are often called into question and labelled as deviant or abnormal. Many Asian people believe that the media treatment of arranged marriages was often inaccurate and did not reflect the way that the system had changed over time. **Ameli et al.** (2007) note that media discussion around the issue of the wearing of the hijab and the veil is also problematic, often suggesting that it is somehow an inferior form of dress compared with Western female dress codes and that it is unnecessary and problematic. It is often portrayed as a patriarchal and oppressive form of control that exemplifies the misogyny of Islam and symbolises the alleged subordinate position of women in Islam.

- **Ethnic minorities as unimportant** – Van Dijk notes that some sections of the media imply that the lives of White people are somehow more important than the lives of non-White people. News items about disasters in developing countries are often restricted to a few lines or words unless there are also White or British victims. Moreover, Sir Ian Blair, the former Metropolitan police commissioner, claimed that institutionalised racism was present in the British media in the way they reported death from violent crime. He noted that Black and Asian victims of violent death did not get the same attention as White victims. However, the murder of the Black teenager Stephen Lawrence by White racists in 1993 received high-profile coverage, both on television and in the press.

- **Ethnic minorities as invisible** – in 2005, a BBC News Online survey noted that Black and Asian people were represented as newscasters and television journalists, but the range of roles that ethnic minority actors play in television drama is very limited and often reflects low status, e.g. Africans may play cleaners or Asians may play shopkeepers. Ethnic minority audiences were also very hostile towards **tokenism** – the idea that programmes contain characters from ethnic minority groups purely because they 'should'. Ethnic minority audiences complain that Black and Asian people are rarely shown as ordinary citizens who just happen to be Black or Asian.

Media professionals from ethnic minority backgrounds have responded to these inequalities and prejudices by developing media institutions and agencies that specifically target the interests and concerns of ethnic-minority audiences. There is a range of homegrown media agencies that are owned, managed and controlled by ethnic minorities themselves, including newspapers and magazines, e.g. *Eastern Eye*, *Snoop*, *The Voice*, etc, and radio stations such as Sunrise Radio, Asian FX, etc.

PROGRESS CHECK

1. According to Gauntlett, why should sociologists be cautious when discussing media representations of gender or ethnicity?
2. According to Gill, how has the depiction of women in advertising changed?
3. In Nairn's view, how is the Royal Family portrayed in the media?

Answers: 1. There are many different media products (e.g. TV soap operas and the quality press) so it is difficult to generalise about how the media in general represent gender or ethnicity. 2. Women were represented as passive objects of the male gaze but are now represented as active, independent and sexually powerful agents. 3. As an on-going soap opera.

7.5 The effect of media content on audiences and society

LEARNING SUMMARY

After studying this section, you should be able to understand:

- the evidence relating to the relationship between screen violence and violence in real life
- active audience approaches
- the process of moral panics

Mass media effects: the relationship between screen violence and real-life violence

AQA **SCLY 3**   OCR **G673**

Influential psychologists, pressure groups, religious leaders and politicians have suggested that there is a direct causal link between violence in films, television programmes and computer games and violent real-life crime. It is argued that such media content exerts an overwhelmingly **negative effect** on impressionable young audiences. These beliefs have led to increased state control over and censorship of the media in Britain.

> **KEY POINT**
>
> Sociologists have argued that media content can have a direct effect upon their audiences and trigger particular social responses in terms of behaviour and attitudes.

- **Gerbner** (2002) sees a **cause-effect relationship** between screen violence and real-life violence.
- Some feminist sociologists, e.g. **Dworkin** (1988) and **Morgan** (1980) have suggested that there is a strong relationship between the consumption of pornography and sexual crime.
- **Orbach** (1991) and **Wolf** (1990) argue that there is a causal link between representation of (US) size zero models in magazines and eating disorders.
- **Norris** (1996), claims that media coverage of political issues can influence voting behaviour.
- Some early Marxist commentators, particularly those belonging to the Frankfurt School, such as **Marcuse** (1964), believed that the media transmitted a **mass culture** which was directly injected into the hearts and minds of the population making them more vulnerable to ruling class propaganda.

The hypodermic model of media violence

The hypodermic syringe approach to **media effects** believes that a **direct correlation** exists between the violence and anti-social behaviour portrayed in films, on television, in computer games, in rap lyrics, etc. and violence and anti-social behaviour such as drug use and teenage gun/knife crime found in real life. The model suggests that children and teenagers are vulnerable to media content because they are still in the early stages of socialisation and therefore very impressionable.

This debate is on-going and you should illustrate with contemporary examples.

This is relevant to the discussion of experiments in Chapter 5.

Believers in this hypodermic syringe model (also known as the 'magic bullet' theory) point to a number of films which they claim have resulted in young people using extreme violence.

Imitation or copycat violence

Early studies of the relationship between the media and violence focused on conducting experiments in laboratories, e.g. **Bandura et al.** (1963) carried out an experiment on young children which involved exposing them to films and cartoons of a self-righting doll being attacked with a mallet. They concluded on the basis of this experiment that violent media content could lead to imitation or **copycat violence**.

McCabe and Martin (2005) concluded that media violence has a **disinhibition effect** – it convinces children that in some social situations, the 'normal' rules that govern conflict and difference can be suspended, i.e. discussion and negotiation can be replaced with violence with no repercussions.

Desensitisation

Newson argued that sadistic images in films were too easily available and that films encouraged viewers to identify with violent perpetrators rather than victims. Furthermore, Newson noted that children and teenagers are subjected to thousands of killings and acts of violence as they grow up through viewing television and films. Newson suggested that such prolonged exposure to media violence may have a drip-drip effect on young people over the course of their childhood and result in their becoming **desensitised** to violence. Newson argues that they see violence as a normal problem-solving device and concluded that, because of this, the latest generation of young people subscribe to weaker moral codes and are more likely to behave in anti-social ways than previous generations.

Censorship

Newson's report led directly to increased censorship of the film industry with the passing of the Video Recordings (Labelling) Act 1985, which resulted in videos and DVDs being given British Board of Film Classification (BBFC) age certificates. The BBFC also came under increasing pressure to censor films released to British cinemas by insisting on the film makers making cuts relating to bad language, scenes of drug use and violence.

Television too was affected by this climate of censorship. All the television channels agreed on a nine o'clock watershed, i.e. not to show any programmes that used bad language or contained scenes of a sexual or violent nature before this time. Television channels often resorted to issuing warnings before films and even edited out violence themselves or beeped over bad language.

Critique of the hypodermic syringe model

A number of critiques have developed of the imitation-desensitisation model of media effects, e.g. some media sociologists claim that media violence can actually prevent real-life violence.

- **Fesbach and Sanger** (1971) found that screen violence can actually provide a safe outlet for people's aggressive tendencies. This is known as **catharsis**.

They suggest that watching an exciting film releases aggressive energy into safe outlets as the viewers immerse themselves in the action.

- **Young** (1981), argues that seeing the effects of violence and especially the pain and suffering that it causes to the victim and their families, may make us more aware of its consequences and so less inclined to commit violent acts. **Sensitisation** to certain crimes therefore may make people more aware and responsible so that they avoid getting involved in violence.

The methodological critique of the hypodermic syringe model

Gauntlett (2008) argues that people, especially children, do not behave as naturally under laboratory conditions as they would in their everyday environment, e.g. children's media habits are generally influenced and controlled by parents, especially when they are very young.

> Think about how far the laboratory setting might influence behaviour.

The media effects model fails to be precise in how 'violence' should be defined. There are different types of media violence such as in cartoons, images of war and death on news bulletins and sporting violence. It is unclear whether these different types of violence have the same or different effects upon their audiences or whether different audiences react differently to different types and levels of violence. The effects model has been criticised because it tends to be selective in its approach to media violence, i.e. it only really focuses on particular types of fictional violence.

The effects model also fails to put violence into context, e.g. it views all violence as wrong, however trivial, and fails to see that audiences interpret it according to narrative context. Research by **Morrison** suggests that the context in which screen violence occurs affects its impact on the audience.

Some sociologists believe that children are not as vulnerable as the hypodermic syringe model implies, e.g. research indicates that most children can distinguish between fictional/cartoon violence and real violence from a very early age, and generally know that it should not be imitated. Sociologists are generally very critical of the hypodermic syringe model because it fails to recognise that audiences have very different social characteristics in terms of age, maturity, social class, education, family background, parental controls, etc. These characteristics will influence how people respond to and use media content.

Cumberbatch (2004) looked at over 3500 research studies into the effects of screen violence, encompassing film, television, video and more recently, computer and video games. He concluded that there is still no conclusive evidence that violence shown in the media influences or changes people's behaviour.

Active audience approaches

AQA **SCLY 3**   OCR **G673**

> **KEY POINT**
>
> **Active audience approaches** see the media as far less influential. They believe that people have considerable choice in the way they use and interpret the media. There are various versions of this view, outlined on the next page.

The two-step flow model

Katz and Lazarsfeld (1965) suggest that personal relationships and conversations with significant others, such as family members, friends, teachers and work colleagues, result in people modifying or rejecting media messages. They argue that social networks are usually dominated by **opinion leaders**, i.e. people of influence whom others in the network look up to and listen to. These people usually have strong ideas about a range of matters. Moreover, these opinion leaders expose themselves to different types of media and form an opinion on their content. These interpretations are then passed on to other members of their social circle. Katz and Lazarsfeld suggest that media messages have to go through two steps or stages.

- The opinion leader is exposed to the media content.
- Those who respect the opinion leader internalise their interpretation of that content.

> **KEY POINT**
>
> Consequently, media audiences are not directly influenced by the media. Rather, they choose to adopt a particular opinion, attitude and way of behaving after negotiation and discussion with an opinion leader. The audience is, therefore, not passive, but active.

However, critics of this model point out two problems.

- There is no guarantee that the opinion leader has not been subjected to an imitative or desensitising effect, e.g. a leader of a peer group, such as a street gang, might convince other members that violence is acceptable because he has been exposed to computer games that strongly transmit the message that violence is an acceptable problem-solving strategy.
- People who may be most at risk of being influenced by the media may be socially isolated individuals who are not members of any social network and so do not have access to an opinion leader who might help interpret media content in a healthy way.

The selective filter model

In his **selective filter model**, **Klapper** (1960) suggests that, for a media message to have any effect, it must pass through three filters.

- **Selective exposure** – the audience must choose to view, read or listen to the content of specific media. Media messages can have no effect if no one sees or hears them. However, what the audience chooses depends upon their interests, education, work commitments and so on.
- **Selective perception** – the audience may not accept the message; some people may take notice of some media content, but decide to reject or ignore others.
- **Selective retention** – the messages have to 'stick' in the mind of those who have accessed the media content. However, research indicates that most people have a tendency to remember only the things they broadly agree with.

The uses and gratifications model

Blumler and McQuail (1968) and **Lull** (1995) see media audiences as active. Their **uses and gratifications model** suggests that people use the media in order to satisfy particular social needs that they have, e.g. **Wood** (1993) illustrated how teenagers may use horror films to gratify their need for excitement. Blumler and McQuail identify four basic needs which people use the media to satisfy.

- **Diversion** – people may immerse themselves in particular types of media to make up for the lack of satisfaction at work or in their daily lives, e.g. women may compensate for the lack of romance in their marriages by reading Mills and Boon romantic novels. Some people even have alternative lives and identities as avatars on websites such as Second Life.
- **Personal relationships** – media products such as soap operas may compensate for the decline of community in our lives, e.g. socially isolated elderly people may see soap opera characters as companions they can identify with and worry about in the absence of interaction with family members. Cyber-communities on the Internet may also be seen by users as alternative families.
- **Personal identity** – people may use the media to 'make over' or to modify their identity. Social networking websites, such as Facebook, allow people to use the media to present their particular identities to the wider world in a way that they can control.
- **Surveillance** – people use the media to obtain information and news in order to help them make up their minds on particular issues.

Marxists are critical of this model because they suggest that social needs may be socially manufactured by the media and may therefore be 'false needs'.

The reception analysis model

The **reception analysis model** suggests that media content is not passively accepted as truth by audiences. **Morley's** (1980) research into how audiences interpreted the content of a well-known 1970s evening news programme called *Nationwide* examined how the ideological content of the programme (i.e. the messages that were contained in the text and images) were interpreted by 29 groups made up of people from a range of educational and professional backgrounds. Morley found that audiences were very active in their reading of media content and did not automatically accept the media's perspective on a range of issues. Morley concluded that people choose to read or interpret media content in three ways.

- The **preferred (or dominant) reading** accepts the media content as legitimate, e.g. the British people generally approve of the Royal Family, so very few people are likely to interpret stories about them in a critical fashion. This dominant reading is often shared by journalists and editors, and underpins news values.
- The **oppositional reading** opposes the views expressed in media content.
- The **negotiated reading** whereby the audience reinterpret the media content to fit in with their own opinions and values, e.g. they may not have any strong views on the Royal Family, but enjoy reading about celebrity lives.

Morley argues that the average person belongs to several sub-cultural groups and this may complicate a person's reading of media content in the sense that they may not be consistent in their interpretation of it. Reception analysis theory therefore suggests that audiences are not passive, impressionable and **homogeneous**. They act in a variety of subcultural ways and, for this reason, media content is **polysemic**, i.e. it attracts more than one type of reading or interpretation.

The cultural effects model

The Marxist **cultural effects model** sees the media as a very powerful ideological influence that is mainly concerned with transmitting capitalist values and norms. Marxists argue that media content contains strong **ideological** messages that reflect the values of those who own, control and produce the media. They argue that the long-term effect of such media content is that the values of the rich and powerful come to be unconsciously shared by most people – people come to believe in values such as 'happiness is about possessions and money', 'being a celebrity is really important', etc. Marxists believe that television content, in particular, has been deliberately dumbed down and this has resulted in a decline in serious programmes such as news, documentaries and drama that might make audiences think critically about the state of the world. Consequently, there is little serious debate about the organisation of capitalism and the social inequalities and problems that it generates.

> This links to methodological issues.

However, in criticism of the cultural effects model, these 'cause' and 'effects' are very difficult to operationalise and measure. It also implies that Marxists are the only ones who can see the 'true' ideological interpretation of media content, which suggests that most members of society are 'cultural dopes'.

The post-modernist model

Strinati (1995) argues that the media today are the most influential shapers of identity and offer a greater range of consumption choices in terms of **identities and lifestyles**. Moreover, in the post-modern world, the media transmit the idea that the consumption of signs and symbols for their own sake is more important than the goods they represent. In other words, the media encourages the consumption of logos, designer labels and brands, and these become more important to people's sense of identity than the physical clothes and goods themselves.

> This links to material in Chapter 2 on identity and consumption.

Other post-modernists have noted that, since 2000, the globalisation of communication has become more intensive and extensive, and this has had great significance for local cultures, in that all consumers of the global media are both citizens of the world and of their locality. Seeing other global experience allows people to think critically about their own place in the world. However, **Thompson** notes that the interaction between global media and local cultures can also create tensions and hostilities, e.g. the Chinese authorities have attempted to control and limit the contact that the Chinese people have with global media, whilst some Islamic commentators have used global media to convince their local populations of the view that Western culture is decadent and corrupt.

Moral panics

AQA **SCLY 3**   OCR **G673**

Every now and then, the media, particularly the tabloid news media, focus on particular groups and activities and, through the style of their reporting, define these groups and their activities as a problem. This focus creates public anxiety and official censure and control.

What is a moral panic?

The term **moral panic** was popularised by **Cohen** (1972) in his classic work *Folk Devils and Moral Panics*. It refers to media reactions to particular social groups and activities that are defined as threatening social consensus. The reporting creates anxiety or moral panic amongst the general population which puts pressure on the authorities to control the problem and discipline the group responsible. However, the media concern is usually out of proportion to any real threat to society posed by the group or activity.

Both the publicity and social reaction to the panic may create the potential for further crime and deviance in the future. In other words, the social reaction may lead to the **amplification of deviance** by provoking more of the same behaviour.

There have been a number of moral panics in the last 30 years including:

- **Ravers and ecstasy use** – **Redhead** notes that a moral panic in regard to acid house raves in the late 1980s led to the police setting up roadblocks on motorways, turning up at raves in full riot gear and the Criminal Justice Act (1990) which banned illegal parties.
- **Refugees and asylum seekers** – in 2003 there was a moral panic focused on the numbers of refugees and asylum seekers entering Britain and their motives. Elements of the tabloid press, particularly the *Daily Mail* and *The Sun*, focused on the alleged links between asylum seekers and terrorism which created public anxiety.
- **Hoodies** – **Fawbert** (2008) examined newspaper reports and found that 'hoodies' became a commonly used term, especially between 2005 and 2007, to describe young people involved in crime.

Why do moral panics occur?

- **Furedi** argues that moral panics arise when society fails to adapt to dramatic social changes and it is felt that there is a loss of control, especially over powerless groups such as the young. Furedi therefore argues that moral panics are about the wider concerns that the older generation have about the nature of society today – people see themselves (and their families) as at greater risk from a variety of groups. They believe that things are out of control. They perceive, with the media's encouragement, that traditional norms and values no longer have much relevance in their lives. Furedi notes that people feel a very real sense of loss, which makes them extremely susceptible to the anxieties encouraged by media moral panics.
- Some commentators argue that moral panics are simply a product of **news values** and the desire of journalists and editors to sell newspapers – they are a good example of how audiences are manipulated by the media for commercial purposes. However, after a while, news stories exhaust their cycle of newsworthiness and journalists abandon interest in them because they believe their audiences have lost interest too. The social problems, however, do not disappear – they remain dormant until journalists decide at some future date that they can be made newsworthy again and attract a large audience.
- Marxists, such as **Hall**, see moral panics as serving an **ideological function**. His study of the media coverage of Black muggers in the 1970s (**Hall et al.**, 1978) concluded that it had the effect of labelling all young African-Caribbeans as criminals and a potential threat to White people. This served the purpose of diverting attention away from the mismanagement of capitalism by the capitalist class, as well as justifying the introduction and use of more repressive laws and policing.

This links to material on moral panics in Chapter 2.

Always try to illustrate your answers with up-to-date examples

- **Left Realists** argue, however, that moral panics should not be dismissed as a product of ruling class ideology or news values. Moral panics have a very real basis in reality, i.e. the media often identifies groups who are a real threat to those living in inner-city areas. Portraying such crime as a fantasy is naïve because it denies the very real harm that some types of crime have on particular communities or the sense of threat that older people feel.

PROGRESS CHECK

1. What is a homogeneous audience?
2. On what grounds does Gauntlett criticise laboratory-based research?
3. According to Klapper, what three selective filters are at work?
4. According to post-modernism, what is the most important influence on people's identities today?

Answers: 1. An undifferentiated group whose members share the same characteristics. 2. He argues that people's behaviour in artificial laboratory settings is not necessarily the same as their behaviour in natural settings. 3. Selective exposure, perception and retention. 4. The mass media.

7.6 New media, globalisation and popular culture

LEARNING SUMMARY	After studying this section, you should be able to understand:
	• how the term 'new media' is defined
	• debates about the new media

Defining the new media

AQA **SCLY 3**   OCR **G673**

The term **new media** generally refers to two trends that have occurred over the past 30 years.

- The **evolution** of existing media delivery systems. The way media content is delivered has dramatically changed over the last 30 years. As recently as 2000 most people received television pictures through aerials and there were five terrestrial television channels that could be accessed. Digital, high-definition, flat-screen televisions and subscriptions to hundreds of digitalised satellite and cable television channels are now the norm.
- The **emergence** of new delivery technologies – cheap personal computers and mobile-phone technology, and especially texting, are relatively novel forms of communication. However, the most innovative technology that has appeared in the last 20 years is probably the Internet or worldwide web.

There are several characteristics of new media.

- It is based on **digital technology**.
- Different **types of media content**, e.g. music, images and e-mails are often combined or converged into a single delivery system, e.g. television, lap-tops and mobile phones.
- It is **interactive** and lets users select the stories that they want to watch, in the order that they want to watch them. Users can also mix and match the information they want. Users can engage in online discussions or play on-line

live games with each other. They can interact with each other through social networking sites such as Facebook. Users may produce their own films and music and post it on sites such as YouTube and MySpace. User-generated content and information sites, such as Wikipedia and IMDB, are a popular source of knowledge.

- It is **demand led** as consumers are no longer restrained by television schedules. Sky+, Freeview and the BBC IPlayer are good examples of how consumers of new media are encouraged to take an active role in the construction of their own television schedules. Live television can now be paused and watched again later.

Who is using the new media?

Some sociologists have suggested that there now exists a **generational divide** in terms of how people use new media. According to Ofcom, the 16–24-year-old age group spent more time online compared with the 25+ age-group. Up to 70% of this age group use sites such as MySpace and Bebo. It also sent more text messages and watches less television. However, 40% of adults use networking sites such as Facebook, whilst the average age of the on-line gamer is 33 years.

The poor are excluded from the super-information highway because they lack the material resources to plug into this new media revolution, i.e. they are a **digital underclass** who cannot afford to keep up with the middle class technological elite. Some 80% of the richest households in Britain have Internet access, against only 11% of the poorest.

Li and Kirkup (2007) found that men were more likely than women to use e-mail or chat rooms. Men played more computer games than women. Men were more self-confident about their computer skills than women and were more likely to express the opinion that using computers was a male activity and skill.

Debates about new media

AQA **SCLY 3**   OCR **G673**

According to **Curran and Seaton** (2003), two perspectives dominate the debate about the new media in Britain.
- The neophiliac perspective.
- The cultural pessimist perspective.

The neophiliac perspective

Neophiliacs argue that new media is beneficial to society for several reasons.
- **Increased consumer choice** – there are now hundreds of choices available to people in the form of media outlets and delivery systems. It is argued that competition between media institutions results in more quality media output.
- **An e-commerce revolution** – a great deal of retail commerce is conducted on the Internet. Most major commercial companies now have their own websites.
- **Revitalising democracy** – new media technologies may offer opportunities for people to acquire the education and information required to play an active role in democratic societies and to make politicians more accountable to the people. Some media sociologists have suggested that the Internet can revitalise democracy because it gives a voice to those who would otherwise go unheard. It allows like-minded people to join together and take action which may lead to social change. Some neophiliacs who are part of the anti-

global capitalism movement have used the Internet to challenge the power of international capitalism.

The cultural pessimist perspective

Cultural pessimists believe that the revolution in new media technology has been exaggerated by neophiliacs. There are a number of strands to their argument.

- **Cornford and Robins** (1999) argue that new media are not so new and that the media today is an accommodation between old and new because to use a game console, a television is required, while to connect to the Internet, a telephone line is still needed. They suggest, further, that interactivity is not something new because people have written to newspapers and phoned in to radio and television for many years. The only thing that is new about new media is its speed – information, news and entertainment can be accessed in 'real time'.

- Cultural pessimists criticise the idea that new media are increasing the potential for ordinary people to participate more fully in the democratic process and cultural life. The Internet is actually dominated by a small number of media corporations. Over three-quarters of the 31 most visited news and entertainment websites are affiliated with the largest media corporations, according to **Curran**.

- There are some negative effects associated with the commercialisation of the Internet, e.g. many companies that sell products and services on the Internet engage in consumer surveillance. New technologies, e.g. in the form of cookies, can monitor and process the data generated by interactive media usage so they can segment and target potential future audiences and thus enhance profits.

- **Hill and Hughes** (1997) challenge the view that cyberspace is more likely to contain web content that supports alternative minority political issues or views – 78% of political opinions expressed on the American websites were mainstream.

- Cultural pessimists argue that increased choice of media delivery systems and particularly the digitalisation of television, has led to a decline in the quality of **popular culture**. **Harvey** suggests that digital television may have dramatically increased the number of channels for viewers to choose from, but this has led to a dumbing down of popular culture as television companies fill these channels with cheap imported material, films, repeats, sport, reality television shows and gambling. Harvey argues that, increasingly, television culture transmits a **candy floss culture** that speaks to everyone in general and no one in particular.

- Some sociologists, politicians and cultural commentators argue that new media, particularly the Internet, is in need of state regulation. All points of view are represented on the Internet, but it is argued that easy access to pornography, and homophobic, racist and terrorism-inciting sites is taking free speech too far.

Post-modernism and the media

> **KEY POINT**
>
> Post-modernists argue that the media, and the popular culture that it generates, shape our identities and lifestyles today much more than traditional influences such as family, community, social class, gender, nation or ethnicity.

Post-modernists also argue that the media has also changed and shaped our consumption patterns by making us more aware of the diversity of choices that exist in the post-modern world, e.g. many people now feel that they no longer belong to real communities. The proto-communities of Internet chat-rooms, blogging and on-line fantasy gaming, such as **Second Life**, and the imagined communities of television soap operas, are increasingly replacing the role of neighbours and extended kin in our lives.

The globalisation of media too means that we now have more **globalised cultural influences** available to us in terms of lifestyle choices and consumption. This globalisation takes several forms.
- Ownership of mass media is no longer restricted by **national boundaries**. Moguls, such as **Rupert Murdoch**, and media conglomerates, such as Time Warner, own hundreds of media companies spread throughout the world.
- **Satellite television** has opened up the world to the television viewer.
- **Access** to the worldwide web via the Internet, global webservers (such as AOL or Google) and new technology (such as wireless broadband) mean that we can access information and entertainment in all parts of the world.
- **Advertising** occurs on a global scale and particular brands and logos have become globalised as a result.

Post-modernists see the global media as beneficial because it is primarily responsible for diffusing different cultural styles around the world and creating new **global hybrid styles** in fashion, music, consumption and lifestyle. It is argued that, in the post-modern global world, this cultural diversity and pluralism will become the global norm.

However, Marxists argue that globalisation restricts choice because transnational media companies and their owners have too much **power**. Marxists are particularly concerned that local media and cultures may be replaced by a **global culture**. **Kellner** (1999) suggests that this global media culture is about sameness and that it erases individuality, specificity and difference. However, **Cohen and Kennedy** (2000) suggest that cultural pessimists under-estimate the strength of local cultures – they note that people do not generally abandon their cultural traditions, family duties, religious beliefs and national identities because they listen to Madonna or watch a Disney film. Rather, they appropriate elements of global culture, and mix and match with elements of local culture, in much the same way as the citizens of the USA and Britain.

The critique of post-modernism

Post-modernists have been criticised for exaggerating the extent of social change. Evidence from attitude surveys indicates that many people see social class, ethnicity, family, nation and religion as still having a profound influence over their lives and identities. Media influence is undoubtedly important, but it is not the determining factor in most people's lifestyle choices.

There is also a rather naïve element to post-modernist analyses, in that they tend to ignore the fact that a substantial number of people are unable to make consumption choices because of **inequalities** brought about by traditional influences such as unemployment, poverty, racial discrimination and patriarchy. Traditional forms of inequality remain a crucial influence, as access to the Internet, digital television and so on is denied to many people in Britain.

Exam practice questions

Question 1 is a typical OCR question on mass media.

1 Outline and assess the view that control of the mass media is concentrated in the hands of owners. **(50 marks)**

2 Read Item A below and answer the questions that follow.

Item A
Gauntlett (2008) highlights several key themes of masculinity that are presented in men's magazines. Such themes include the idea that men like to look at women and men like cars, gadgets and sport. Gauntlett argues that 'lads' mags' all project the same images of women, men and men's interests which include semi-naked females, sport and alcohol.

Critics of the media argue that they present narrow stereotypical images of ethnicity and gender. Some sociologists, however, regard the concept of a stereotype as useless for investigating media texts' representations of gender. Barker argues that stereotypes are condemned not only for misrepresenting the real world (e.g. by reinforcing the false stereotype that women are always available for sex), but also for being too close to the real world (e.g. by showing women mainly in the home and servicing men, which many women actually do).

Question 2 resembles the sort of question that you could be asked on the AQA examination.

(a) Identify and briefly explain three ways in which the media 'present narrow stereotypical images of ethnicity'. (Item A). **(9 marks)**

(b) Using material from Item A and elsewhere assess the view that media representations of women and men challenge gender stereotypes. **(18 marks)**

Crime and deviance

The following topics are covered in this chapter:

- Measuring trends and patterns in crime and victimisation
- Sociological explanations of crime
- Theories of social order and social control
- Suicide

8.1 Measuring trends and patterns in crime and victimisation

LEARNING SUMMARY

After studying this section, you should be able to understand:

- the different methods that the state and sociologists use to measure crime
- patterns and trends in crime over the past forty years
- the role of agents of social control in the construction of the official statistics of crime
- patterns and explanations of victimisation

Measuring crime: official statistics

AQA **SCLY 2**   OCR **G671**
    SCLY 4   **G673**

Remember that OCR Unit G673 and AQA Unit 4 SCLY 4 are synoptic. When revising crime and deviance think about the links with themes such as socialisation, identity, power and control and concepts such as social class and peer groups. Also think about how material in this topic relates to topics such as education and media.

You could refer to the official statistics of police-recorded crime as an example when answering relevant questions on secondary data.

KEY POINT

The **official statistics** of crime are collected by the police and the courts and collated and published by the Home Office. They are used to establish trends and patterns in criminal activity, especially in regard to the volume of crime and the social characteristics of criminality.

The volume of crime

Between 1971 and 1993 there was a dramatic rise in the volume of police-recorded crime in Britain. All major categories of crime experienced substantial increases, e.g. violent crime increased four-fold in this period, although the proportion of crimes that was recorded as violent never exceeded 12% of all crime. Most crime was, and indeed still remains, property crime.

Since 1993, the crime rate has significantly fallen, despite the fact that the general public, encouraged by the media, believe it to be rising. The period from 2003 has seen a sharp fall in property crime, especially burglary. Since 2007, violent crime has also shown signs of decline.

The social distribution of crime by age

The peak age for known offenders for both males and females was 14 in 1958 and 18 in 2010. The official statistics show that juvenile crime has declined in recent years after having reached a peak in 1984–5. In 1958, 56% of all offenders found guilty were aged 20 years or under compared with about 33% in 2007. However, the official statistics of crime recorded by the police do indicate that burglary, robbery, violence and criminal damage are most likely to be juvenile rather than adult offences.

The distribution of crime by social class

Examination of the employment status of convicted offenders suggests that over 80% are from the manual working classes. **Hagell and Newburn's** study of persistent young offenders found that only 8% came from middle class backgrounds. Offences are also distinguishable by social class. Middle class offenders tend to be associated with **white-collar crime**, fraud and tax evasion, whilst working class offenders are mainly found guilty of burglary and street crime.

The social distribution of crime by ethnicity

The statistics show an over-representation of ethnic minority men and women, and particularly African-Caribbeans, in prison. One-tenth of male prisoners and one-fifth of female prisoners are African-Caribbean, yet this ethnic minority group only makes up 2.3% of the population. **Smith** (1997) notes that Black youth are more likely to be cautioned than any other ethnic minority group.

The social distribution of crime by gender

The number of female offenders has risen faster than the number of male offenders since 1958, but approximately 85–90% of offenders found guilty or cautioned for serious offences are male. Male crime generally outnumbers female crime by a ratio of 5 to 1. Men and women are generally convicted for different types of offences, e.g. men dominate all offences and when females are convicted it is likely to be for theft (shoplifting).

The social distribution of crime by region

Urban areas, especially inner-city council estates, have higher rates of crime than the suburbs or rural areas. Official surveys on crime risks indicate that members of young households living in inner-cities, e.g. students, are ten times more likely to be burgled than older people living in rural areas.

The official crime statistics, reliability and validity

> **KEY POINT**
>
> Sociologists point out that the official statistics of crimes recorded by the police do not comprise the total volume of crime. There is a 'dark figure' of unrecorded crime, a phenomenon which is now more widely acknowledged.

Pilkington (1995) notes the following.
- The official statistics do not comprise a complete record of criminal offences known to the authorities, e.g. they don't cover offences dealt with by the Revenue and Customs.
- The number of recorded offences depends on **official counting procedures** which frequently change.

Unreported crime is part of the hidden figure of unrecorded crime.

In your answers, always illustrate with relevant examples if possible.

KEY POINT

Over 80% of all recorded crimes result from reports by the public, but crime may not be **reported** to the police because:
- victims may not be aware a crime has taken place, e.g. fraud
- victims may not be believed, e.g. child abuse
- the victim might feel the offence is too trivial, e.g. vandalism
- the victim may feel that the offence won't be taken seriously or may fear embarrassment or humiliation at the hands of the police and/or courts, e.g. rape
- the victim or community may distrust the police.

Around 40% of crimes reported to the police are not recorded by them and therefore do not end up in the official statistics.

KEY POINT

Barclay (1995) argues that the net sum of all these processes is that only 2% of offences committed actually lead to a conviction in the criminal courts.

The Home Office interpretation of the official crime statistics

Home Office research suggests that the rise in crime is an **artificial** phenomenon – a rise in **reporting** rather than a real increase.
- Living standards have risen rapidly since the 1950s and modern society is more materialistic. This has resulted in more consumer items (e.g. cars and DVDs) to steal and a greater public intolerance of property crime. People are therefore more likely to report it. The popularity of insurance has given people more incentive to report theft, whilst increased ownership of mobile phones may have made it easier to report crime.
- Public attitudes towards violence have changed, e.g. the greater stress on women's rights has produced a less tolerant attitude towards domestic violence.
- The official statistics on victimless crimes such as soft drug use and prostitution cannot be regarded as **reliable** because the 39 police forces in England and Wales exercise varying amounts of discretion in dealing with these offences. Some forces elect to regularly crack down on these whilst others may ignore or neglect them.
- The increase in the number of police officers (by 2010 there was 15 000 more than in 1979) and the use of modern technology (especially computers and surveillance cameras in city centres and football stadiums) has led to more efficient monitoring and recording of crime.
- The Labour government of 1997–2010 introduced hundreds of new laws especially pertaining to violence, e.g. racial attacks became a serious offence thus creating the potential for thousands of new crimes.

1. Which agency is responsible for the collection of official statistics on crime?
2. What is the peak age for committing a criminal act?
3. What is the 'dark figure of crime'?
4. What is the ratio of male crime to female crime?
5. Why is Home Office research sceptical that there has been a rise in crime?

Answers: 1. The Home Office. 2. 18 years. 3. Unreported and unrecorded crime. 4, 5 to 1, 5. They suggest it is a rise in reporting rather than in actual crime.

The social construction of official crime statistics

AQA **SCLY 2**   OCR **G671**
      SCLY 4   **G673**

KEY POINT

Interpretivist sociologists argue that we need to understand that the official crime statistics are a **social construction** in that they originate in interaction between police officers, victims, witnesses and suspects. They point out that such interaction is not equally balanced because police officers have the power to choose to ignore an incident, to give a warning or to arrest.

Studies of police officers on patrol indicate that they, like most members of society, are likely to operate using **stereotypical** assumptions, or **labels**, about what constitutes 'suspicious' or 'criminal' in terms of social types and behaviour, e.g. the decision to stop or arrest someone may be based on whether they correspond to a particular stereotype.

There is strong evidence to suggest that **racial profiling**, or stereotyping, by some police officers may be a crucial element governing their interaction with Black people, especially African-Caribbeans, i.e. some officers see all Black people as potentially criminal.

Holdaway (2002) argues that there is still substantial evidence of police stereotyping of ethnic minorities in the form of derogatory language, jokes and banter and this **racist culture** often underpins the decision to stop Black people. In other words, Black people may be over-represented in the official crime statistics, not because they are more criminal, but because they are targeted by some police officers.

However, it is not just Black people who are stereotyped by the police. It may also be the case that young people in general, males and working class people fit a stereotype of a criminal and may be more likely to be the subject of police attention than older people, females and the middle class respectively. For instance, feminist criminologists argue that male officers tend to adopt paternalistic attitudes towards female offenders who are less likely to be stopped, arrested and charged. Females are less likely to be stereotyped as 'suspicious' or criminal and, when found committing criminal offences, are more likely to be cautioned rather than arrested and charged.

The courts

KEY POINT

Research into the social background of magistrates and judges has also raised the question of whether there is class, gender and racial bias in the judicial system which may partly be responsible for the over proportionate number of young people, Black people and working class people in the official crime statistics and the prison population.

Research by **Hood** has shown that almost 80% of magistrates are from the professional classes I and II, whilst there is a marked absence of unskilled working class, Black and Asian magistrates. **Griffiths'** research into the social and educational backgrounds of the judiciary indicates that the vast majority of judges originate in upper class backgrounds as seen in the fact that up to 70% of them attended the top public schools and Oxbridge. Griffiths also found that judges tend to be disproportionately male and White and rather old.

Griffiths argues that these very narrow social backgrounds make it difficult for magistrates and judges to understand the situations and experiences of the working class and Black people who appear in front of them, e.g. **Box's** research found that magistrates and judges are more likely to see middle class criminality as an 'accident' or as 'out of character', and consequently, to treat such offenders more leniently than working class or Black offenders.

Hood's study of 3300 cases heard in the West Midlands Crown Courts in 1989 found that Black males have a 17% greater chance of receiving a custodial sentence than Whites for the same offence and that the average length of prison sentence was longer for both Blacks and Asians when they pleaded not guilty.

The radical critique of the official crime statistics

KEY POINT

According to traditional **Marxists**, working class crime may dominate the official statistics, but it is a minor problem when compared with crimes committed by the powerful such as **white-collar crime, corporate crime** and **state crime**.

White-collar, corporate and state crime do not generally appear in the official statistics because:
- they are undiscovered
- if they are discovered, they are not defined as 'serious crimes'
- if they are defined as crimes, they tend to be unreported, or they are not pursued as relentlessly as working class crime by the police
- if they are detected, they are 'under-punished'.

Box argued that the law and the official statistics are used to criminalise the activities of the powerless and give society the impression that the 'problem population' is the working class and ethnic minority groups. However, the official statistics render the crimes of the powerful invisible. From Box's perspective, the official statistics are **ideological** – they support the interests of the powerful and justify the continuation of class inequality. They tell sociologists very little about the real level of crime in society and do little to improve sociological understanding of criminality.

The Left Realist view

The **Left Realists Young and Lea** agree that the official crime statistics may be unreliable because of the over-policing of certain social groups and the neglect of white-collar crime. However, using data from **victim surveys** of inner-city areas they conclude that **interpretivists** are wrong to suggest that the statistics are mainly a product of police and judicial processes. They suggest that crime is mainly committed by working class and Black people and it causes real fear and pain for working class and Black people living in inner-city areas who are its main victims. They therefore conclude that the statistics are a useful tool used alongside victim surveys and self-report studies for uncovering the reality of crime.

Researching victims: the British Crime Survey

AQA **SCLY 2**   OCR **G671**
   SCLY 4   **G673**

This links to material in Chapter 5 on methods of research. The BCS is an example of a social survey. It is a secondary source of quantitative data.

KEY POINT

The British Crime Survey (BCS) conducted by the Home Office is a major **victim survey** which started in 1983 and is now conducted annually. The 2008 survey conducted 46 983 face-to-face structured interviews with a sample of people aged 16 and over living in private households in England and Wales. Trained interviewers use lap-top computers to record the responses. The sample is randomly selected from the Postcode Address File (a sampling frame). It is designed to be as nationally representative a **sample** as possible in order to **generalise** the results to the country as a whole. The overall response rate in 2007 was 76%, although this is lower in inner-city areas.

Those who take part are asked about their experiences of being a victim of crime in the past year. The interviews mainly focus on people's personal experience of property crimes such as vehicle related thefts and burglary and violent crimes such as assaults. It also includes questions on people's attitudes towards the police.

The findings of the BCS

- Throughout the 1990s, the BCS showed that only a minority of crimes (1 in 4) were reported to the police. This suggested that police-recorded crime statistics were the tip of a much larger crime iceberg. However, the latest BCS statistics indicate that the gap between crime reported to the BCS and crimes reported to and recorded by the police is at its most narrow since 1983. This confirms that crime is now falling.
- The majority of crimes are property-related, e.g. criminal damage accounts for one in five (21%) crimes recorded by the police.
- Violent crime represents around 21% of BCS crime compared with the 19% shown in police statistics. Since 2007 BCS violent crime has fallen by 12%.
- Men were almost twice as likely as women to have been victims of violence, with young men aged 16 to 24 having the highest risk (13%).
- However, women still worry more than men about all crimes except vehicle crime – nearly one-third worried about the possibility of being raped and a third of elderly women say that they feel very unsafe out alone after dark. The surveys also show that those who fear violent crime the most (the elderly, women) are least likely to be victims of it. Conversely, those who have least fear of crime (young men) are most likely to be victims.

You could use the BCS as an example when answering relevant questions on social surveys, official statistics or secondary data.

The strengths of the BCS

Supporters of the BCS claim that the survey is more **valid** than the official crime statistics because they uncover the dark figure of crime, i.e. crimes not reported to the police and therefore not recorded by them.

It is also thought to provide the most **reliable** measure of national trends in crime over time when used alongside statistics relating to reported and recorded crime. This is because BCS data is unaffected by whether the public report crime or by changes to the way in which the police record crime. Moreover, the methodology of the BCS has remained much the same since the survey began in 1981. Therefore it is the best guide to long-term trends.

The use of structured interviews offers greater opportunity for reliable data. The BCS's use of standardised questions and responses, piloting in advance and training of interviewers all contribute to its **reliability**.

The limitations of BCS methodology

- The survey does not cover commercial victimisation, e.g. thefts from businesses and shops, and fraud.
- It excludes most victimless crimes.
- It does not currently cover crimes against children, i.e. 16 and under.
- The samples used by the BCS are not representative of the national population because owner-occupiers and 16–24 year olds are generally over-represented, whilst the unemployed are under-represented.
- It is not really 'British' as Scotland and Northern Ireland are not covered by the BCS.
- It relies on victims having objective knowledge of the crimes committed against them. However, people's memories with regard to traumatic events are often **unreliable** – there is a danger of exaggeration and telescoping incidents, i.e. moving them forwards and backwards in time.
- People may not be aware that they have been victims – especially if they are elderly.
- Marxists point out that the general public are usually unaware that they may have been victims of crimes committed by the economically powerful, e.g. corporate crime.
- **Pilkington** notes that the BCS distorts the meaning of the numbers – violent and sexual offences against the person may constitute a relatively small proportion of recorded offences, but they often have a much more traumatic effect upon victims compared with property crime. Their seriousness is evident by the number and length of prison sentences they warrant, i.e. over 40% of prisoners are serving time for violent or sexual crime.
- Left Realist sociologists, such as **Young and Lea**, argue that the BCS tells sociologists little about the day-to-day experience of living in high crime areas such as the inner-city or problem council estates, e.g. living in these areas may mean that residents have an above average chance of being victims of both property and violent crime.
- Left Realists and feminists argue that structured interviews with their pre-coded closed questions and responses end up imposing the definitions and priorities of government sociologists on respondents in the interview.

Left Realist and feminist victim surveys

AQA **SCLY 2** OCR **G671**
    SCLY 4   **G673**

An alternative approach to the BCS has been developed by **Left Realist** sociologists who suggest that the BCS has tended to neglect the concentration of crime in the inner city and on deprived council estates.

> Think about how the interviewer's social characteristics could affect the nature and quality of the data.

The **Islington Crime Survey** carried out by the left realist sociologists **Lea and Young** used sympathetic unstructured interviewing techniques. They asked people living in inner London about serious crime such as sexual assault, domestic violence and racial attacks and found that a full third of all households had been touched by serious crime in the previous twelve months.

The Islington Crime Survey found that crime shaped people's lives to a considerable degree – a quarter of all people always avoided going out after dark because of **fear of crime** and 28% felt unsafe in their own homes. Women in the Islington Crime Survey experienced what was a curfew on their activities – over half the women never went out after dark because of their fear of crime. **Zedner** noted that this fear was realistic in the context of this urban area and rational when the extent of unreported rape is taken into account.

Left Realist surveys have found that fear of crime is highest among the poor which reflects the fact that they are most at risk from crime, e.g. the Merseyside Crime Survey carried out by **Kinsey** in 1984 found that in terms of quantity and impact of crime, the poor suffer more than the wealthy from the effects of crime.

Feminist approaches to victim surveys

Feminist victim surveys have tended to produce **qualitative data** on female victims of male crimes, most notably domestic violence and sexual attacks in which the main perpetrators are male.

> Think about why the research team decided to use unstructured interviews rather than other methods such as structured interviews. Why do you think the interviewers were both female?

The first victim survey carried out into domestic violence was conducted by the husband and wife team of **Dobash and Dobash** in Glasgow and Edinburgh (Scotland) in 1980. Their two female researchers carried out 109 unstructured interviews with women who had experience of such violence – 42 of the women were living or had been living in a women's refuge.

Walklate's victim surveys, based on unstructured interviews, found that many female victims of domestic violence are unable to leave their partners because of the **gendered power relationships** that shape and govern women's lives, e.g. they are less likely to have economic resources and therefore potential independence, they have nowhere else to go (the number of refuges in Britain is in decline), they often blame themselves and threats of further violence, and losing their children undermine their confidence. **Kelly's** research into 'survivors' of domestic violence found that many women were undermined by verbal abuse, as well as physical violence.

The feminist researchers **Hanmer and Saunders** carried out a series of unstructured interviews with women living in one randomly selected street in Leeds during the 1980s using sympathetic and trained female interviewers. They found that 20% of these women had been sexually assaulted, but had not reported the crime against them.

Self-report studies

AQA **SCLY 2** OCR **G671**
SCLY 4 **G673**

Some criminologists have used a type of questionnaire called a **self-report** in an attempt to uncover the true amount of crime in society. These self-completion questionnaires which attempt to improve validity by stressing **confidentiality** and **anonymity** involve asking people to disclose their own dishonest and violent behaviour which may have gone undetected by the police and therefore unrecorded.

Studies based on self-reports, e.g. **Belson** on adolescent boys in London and **Campbell** on girls, indicate that the majority of respondents admit to some kind of illegal activity which suggests that the volume of crime in the official crime statistics should be greater. They also challenge the picture of the typical criminal as male and working class. Self-reports indicate that females and middle class males are just as likely to commit crime. In particular, self-report studies have challenged the idea that females commit significantly less crime than males. Campbell found that the ratio of male crime to female crime is 1.5 to 1 rather than 7 to 1.

The 2003 Offending, Crime and Justice self-report survey found that 40% of Whites admitted offences compared with 28% of Blacks and 21% of Asians. A self-report survey conducted by **Sharp and Budd** (2005) found that people from mixed-race backgrounds were most likely to admit soft drug use, whilst 6% of Whites admitted using heroin and cocaine compared with only 2% of Black people and 1% of Asians.

Evaluating self-report studies

Marsh notes that self-report studies may be **unreliable** because, despite guarantees of confidentiality and anonymity, some respondents may still not admit committing criminal offences. Although a self-report study is replicable because it is a standardised questionnaire, disagreements between sociologists about what crimes should be included in the list, their order and so on, mean that different surveys are not always directly comparable.

Validity is also undermined by both **under-reporting** and **over-reporting**. People may under-report, because self-report studies are retrospective and depend on respondents being able to remember what crimes they have committed in the previous 12 months. They may also conceal their crimes because they fear the police might be informed. Others may exaggerate their offences to create an impression of 'being tough'. People are especially unlikely to co-operate with questionnaires which ask them to admit to sensitive and loaded issues such as domestic violence or racist attacks. Attempts to check the honesty of respondents have indicated that about a quarter of respondents are liable to conceal wrong-doings.

The **representativeness** of self-report questionnaires has also been questioned.
- It is impossible to include all criminal acts in a questionnaire or interview which means that the researcher has to be **selective**, which raises problems as to which offences should be included and which should not.
- Most self-report questionnaires are limited in their representation of crime because they are concerned with petty offences rather than serious crimes. However, the inclusion of large numbers of trivial offences can distort the results.

- Overlap between the types of crime listed in self-report studies can lead to respondents reporting the same crime twice.

The representativeness of such questionnaires is limited in that they are largely distributed to young people. It would be difficult to get businessmen or women to co-operate with such a method in regard to admitting various types of white-collar or corporate crime. The samples of young people used in self-report studies are often **unrepresentative** because such questionnaires are often distributed in schools and colleges and tend to miss out school drop-outs and truants. There is some criminological evidence that young people who truant regularly or drop-out of school are more likely to become delinquent.

Low or varying response rates can also be a problem. **Junger-Tas** (1989) reports a sliding scale of responses to self-report questionnaires depending on how much contact respondents have had with the police. Response rates from individuals with a criminal record were lower than from those without.

PROGRESS CHECK

1. What are victim studies?
2. In what way does the British Crime Survey support the idea that there is a dark figure of crime?
3. Who are the main victims of crime according to the BCS?
4. In what way does the Islington survey contradict the BCS in regard to likely victims of crime?

Answers: 1. Questionnaire surveys which aim to uncover from victims themselves the extent and nature of crime in Britain. 2. Only one in four crimes is reported to the police. 3. Young men. 4. It concludes that people living in the inner-city, females and the elderly are more likely than young men to be the victims of crime.

8.2 Sociological explanations of crime

LEARNING SUMMARY

After studying this section, you should be able to understand:

- a range of sociological theories which explain the social distribution of crime by age, ethnicity, gender, locality and social class
- recent trends in regard to green crime, human rights abuses and state crime
- the relationship between globalisation and crime

Social class and crime

AQA **SCLY 4**   OCR **G673**

KEY POINT

Until the late 1960s, theories of deviance tended to blame the deviant or deviant's home **background and culture**. Such theories saw definitions of deviance as fixed and universal. Usually these theories accepted the picture of crime portrayed by the official statistics, i.e. as a working class problem.

Inadequate socialisation

West was typical of the inadequate socialisation approach and argued that working class criminality was due to inadequate **socialisation** or poor **parenting**. In his study of 411 working class boys monitored from age 8–19, 20% became delinquent – these mainly came from broken homes (single-parent families) or from families in which fathers were unemployed or on low incomes.

This links to material on socialisation in Chapters 1 and 2.

Functionalism

The **functionalist Merton** argues that society encourages its members to subscribe to the **goal** of material success. However, society is unable to provide the **legitimate means** for everyone to achieve that success because not everyone can gain qualifications and not everyone can get access to jobs. Working class people are more likely than any other group to be denied these means. Their opportunities are blocked and consequently they experience feelings of **anomie** – they feel alienated by their failure to achieve their aspirations and as a result become frustrated with society. Merton argued that individuals could respond to this **strain** between goals and means in a number of ways.

This is sometimes referred to as 'strain theory'.

- They could **conform** – most working class people cope with their disappointment by accepting their lot. They continue to do their best and make the most of what society offers them.
- They could **innovate** – some people continue to conform to the cultural goals, i.e. they strongly wish for material success, but they adopt non-conventional and illegal means of achieving that success in that they engage in criminal actions.
- They could become **ritualists** – some people lose sight of their goals, but plod on in meaningless jobs, working hard but never really thinking about what they are trying to achieve.
- They could become **retreatists** – a small number of people simply drop out of conventional society and therefore reject both the goals and the means. They are the deviants such as drug addicts, vagrants, suicides and so on.
- They could become **rebels** – a few may rebel and seek to replace the shared goals with alternative, often opposing goals and values, e.g. they set about achieving them by revolutionary means via terrorism.

Merton explains crime committed by the poor and working class as a reaction to the social organisation of society, i.e. the social structure. Paradoxically crime, a deviant and non-conformist activity, is caused by conformity to the dominant value system. The criminal therefore is not that dissimilar to the law abiding citizen. Both are shaped by the same desires and goals, i.e. to achieve material success.

Evaluation of Merton

A number of concerns have been raised about Merton's theory of why poorer people are likely to turn to crime.

- Merton does not explain why an individual chooses one particular form of deviant adaptation rather than another, e.g. why do some react by committing crime, but others conform?
- There are some doubts that all members of society aspire to material success. There are people whose first goal is altruism rather than material success. Their primary goal is to help others less fortunate than themselves, e.g. nurses, teachers and social workers are typical of workers who are not aiming for material success.

- Merton's theory explains utilitarian crime, i.e. crimes which result in a material or financial benefit, but it does not explain crimes of violence such as rape, child abuse and domestic violence.
- It fails to explain collective forms of crime, especially the sorts of crimes committed by young people in gangs, e.g. vandalism, territorial gun and knife crime, tagging and joy-riding. These types of crime do not seem on the surface to be motivated by material goals.
- Merton fails to explain why some members of the middle class who have access to the means, (i.e. they are educationally successful and have access to professional and managerial careers) commit white-collar and corporate crime. These types of crime arise out of access to opportunities rather than lack of access to them.
- Some Marxist sociologists claim that Merton does not deal with the issue of **power** adequately. He fails to ask who benefits from the capitalist system and especially the laws that underpin it. Marxists, such as **Taylor** and **Box**, suggest that the ruling capitalist class benefits the most from the way laws are currently organised.

American sub-cultural theory – youth crime

Cohen adapts **Merton's** theory to explain the **collectivist** or gang crime committed by juvenile delinquents. He argues that working class boys commit juvenile delinquency for two reasons.

- Their parents fail to equip them with the right skills required for success in education and consequently they under-achieve at school.
- Society encourages young people to acquire status through educational success. However, working class boys' under-achievement means that they are allocated to bottom streams or sets. Schools and teachers therefore deny them **status**.

This links to material in Chapter 3 on education.

In frustration, working class boys form **anti-school sub-cultures (counter-cultures)** which turn the value system of the school upside down and award status for deviant activities. Cohen therefore blames a combination of inadequate socialisation and society's stress on acquiring status.

However, some sociologists have questioned the view that working class boys are interested in achieving status from teachers. **Willis** argues that the boys in his study who rejected school wanted factory jobs and therefore did not see the point of qualifications. **Cohen** also fails to acknowledge that most working class boys generally **conform** at school and in society even when they leave education with no qualifications. Marxist critics of Cohen suggest that he should be asking why conformity rather than delinquency is the norm. Feminists note that he ignores working class girls and assumes that delinquency is mainly a male problem.

Sub-cultures and focal concerns

Miller rejects Cohen's arguments. Instead, he argues that working class juvenile delinquents are merely acting out and exaggerating the mainstream values of **working class sub-culture**.

Miller argues that working class values are the product of the type of work performed by manual workers which is routine, boring and lacking in power and autonomy. Miller suggests that working class male culture has developed a series of **focal concerns** which give meaning to their lives outside work. Living out these focal concerns compensates for the boredom of their jobs.

- An **acceptance** that violence is a part of life and you need to be able to look after yourself.
- A heightened sense of **masculinity** or manliness, e.g. being tough, being able to 'hold your drink', 'getting loaded' and womanising.
- **Smartness**, e.g. looking good and feeling 'sharp', being 'streetwise'.
- **Excitement**, e.g. looking for 'kicks' or a desire for fun.
- **Fatalism**, i.e. an acceptance of fate and that nothing much can be done with their lives.
- **Autonomy**, i.e. an attitude that says 'nobody will push us around' especially people in authority, e.g., the police and schoolteachers.

In conclusion Miller blames crime committed by the working class, especially young working class males, on what he sees as the inherently **deviant nature** of working class culture.

Sub-cultures and illegitimate opportunity structures

Like Cohen and Merton, **Cloward and Ohlin** also explain deviance in terms of the **social structure** of society. They argue that because of their lower position in the class structure of society, working class people face greater pressures to deviate in order to achieve economic success.

Cloward and Ohlin argue that in addition to the legitimate opportunity structure of education and work, there also exists **an illegitimate opportunity structure**. How well a criminal gets on in the criminal world depends on the type of criminal opportunities that are available to them in their area. Cloward and Ohlin identify three types of illegitimate opportunities which produce three different types of sub-cultures.

- **Criminal sub-cultures** emerge in areas where people are exposed to an established pattern of illegitimate opportunity. Organised crime is a good example of this type of pattern. These types of crime organisation are often organised hierarchically and bureaucratically, i.e. people have specific roles and tasks and can be promoted in much the same way as someone working for a legitimate organisation. Those at the bottom may have role models at the top that they want to emulate. A good example of this type of opportunity structure in action is **Venkatesh's** research *Gang Leader For A Day*.
- In areas which lack access to organised crime hierarchies some young people may turn to gangs, or **conflict sub-cultures**, which engage in highly masculinised territorial or respect-driven violence.
- If young people fail to gain access to either the criminal or conflict sub-cultures, they may form **retreatist sub-cultures** in which drug use and property crime (to finance it) are the major activities.

Criticisms of sub-cultural theory

Matza, an interpretivist sociologist, argues that sub-cultural theories overpredict delinquency. In other words, most working class young people experience status frustration, anomie and subscribe to working class values, but do not become delinquents. Matza argues that all young people are potentially deviant, but only a minority of youth actually become delinquent. Furthermore, some young people drift in and out of delinquency before they eventually grow out of it when they reach adulthood.

Matza notes that many delinquent youths use **techniques of neutralisation** to justify their actions. They explain their actions with reference to individual justifications, e.g. 'I didn't mean any harm'. They very rarely make any reference to a sub-cultural or gang cause.

Finally, Matza argues that sub-cultural theories neglect the **distribution of power**. He argues that most people subscribe to deviant or subterranean values in that humans crave excitement, want to be outrageous, etc. However, some powerless groups, such as young working class and Black people, are more likely to come to the attention of the authorities and be **labelled** as deviant compared with more powerful groups, e.g. middle class rugby union players often act in outrageous ways, yet they are very rarely labelled as deviant or delinquent.

Ecological theory

Shaw and McKay examined the organisation of cities and observed that most were organised into distinct **neighbourhoods**, or **zones**, with their own set of values and lifestyles. They paid particular attention to 'zone two', i.e. the **inner-city** which they called the 'zone of transition' which was characterised by cheap rented housing, poverty, high numbers of immigrants and high crime rates.

Shaw and McKay concluded that the constant movement of people in and out of the area (population turnover) prevented the formation of stable communities and a sense of social control. Instead it produced a state of **social disorganisation**, i.e. there was little sense of community. Consequently, people were unlikely to feel a sense of duty and obligation to each other and therefore people felt little guilt about committing crime against their neighbours.

They also observed that in areas of social disorganisation, different **delinquent values** develop – a **sub-culture of delinquency** – in which young males learn criminal skills and traditions from older ones. Criminal behaviour such as territorial gang violence, theft from cars, drug dealing and joy-riding become a normal part of everyday life and these delinquent values are **culturally transmitted** from one generation to the next.

However, Shaw and McKay's analysis of crime has been criticised as **tautological**, i.e. it is unclear whether high crime rates are a consequence of social disorganisation or are a factor contributing to it. The ecological theory fails to explain why the majority of people living in urban areas choose not to commit crime. It suggests that people are easily influenced by those around them and cannot exercise free will. The disproportionate amount of urban crime in the crime statistics may actually be due to over-policing of these areas.

Traditional Marxism

Gordon argues that working class crime is an inevitable product of **capitalism** and the **inequality** that it generates. He argues that inequalities in wealth and income create poverty and homelessness for the working class and crime is a rational response to these problems. This idea is supported by research which shows property crime rising during recession.

Gordon suggests that capitalism encourages **crimogenic** values, such as greed and materialism, which are conducive to all classes committing crime. Such values also promote non-economic crimes such as violence, rape, child abuse, vandalism and hooliganism. This is because inequalities in wealth and power lead to frustration, hostility, envy and alienation for some members of the working class who may commit crime in an attempt to achieve power and status. This theory argues that it is surprising that there is not more working class crime.

White-collar and corporate crime

Marxist sociologists argue that more attention needs to be paid by law enforcement agencies to **white-collar** and **corporate crime**. **Sutherland** defined white-collar crime as a crime committed by a person of 'respectability and high social status' in the course of their job, whilst **Croall** defines it as crime committed in the course of legitimate employment which involves the abuse of an occupational role. Croall suggests fraud, accounting offences, tax evasion, insider dealing and computer crime are typical white-collar crimes committed by those at the top of the **occupational hierarchy**.

Croall (2001) notes that the powerful and wealthy, i.e. those who either own the means of production or who manage them, have greater opportunities than most to make large sums of money from crime and that companies themselves commit crimes (i.e. corporate crime) by failing to comply with standards of health, safety or quality laid down by the law. There are many types of corporate crime including crimes against consumers, crimes against employees and financial frauds (e.g. Enron).

Croall (2001) argues that a number of factors combine to reduce the extent and seriousness of white-collar and corporate crime in the eyes of the general public.

- Such crimes are often **invisible** (there is no 'blood on the streets').
- They are **complex** (usually they involve the abuse of technical, financial and scientific knowledge).
- Victimisation tends to be **indirect** (offenders and victims rarely come face-to-face). Consequently we fear white-collar crime less than conventional crime.
- Such crimes also tend to be **morally ambiguous**, e.g. many people do not see crimes such as tax evasion as wrong in the same way that mugging is seen as wrong.
- Both the police (who only deal with a small amount of white-collar crime) and civil agencies may lack the resources to detect and prosecute such crime. They may prefer to deal with the offence 'off the record'.
- Most white-collar and corporate crime, if detected, is rarely prosecuted.

> Think about whether this is still the case during a recession when the government is making spending cuts. The UK Uncut group, for example, protests against tax avoidance practised by big businesses.

KEY POINT

White-collar crime therefore is not socially constructed as crime and not seen by the general public as a problem despite the fact that its financial costs to society far exceed that of conventional working class crime.

The New Criminology – Neo-Marxism

Taylor, Walton and Young argue that capitalist society is characterised by **class inequality**. This theory suggests that working class people choose to commit crime because of their experience of the injustices of capitalism. Therefore working class crime is political – it is a deliberate and conscious reaction to working class people interpreting their position at the bottom of the socio-economic hierarchy as unfair and exploitative. Working class crime therefore is an attempt to alter capitalism, e.g. crimes against property, such as theft and burglary, are aimed at the redistribution of wealth, whilst vandalism is a symbolic attack on capitalism's obsession with property. However, these ideas have been accused of being overly romantic. They fail to explain why most victims of crime are working class or in what way violent crimes are political.

Left Realism

This is an influential and important theory of crime.

Young and Lea agree that working class crime committed by young people is a very real problem in the inner-cities which is 'wearing down' whole working class communities, as indicated by victim surveys. This theory argues that working class and Black youth turn to street crime because of **relative deprivation**. In comparison with their peers (i.e. middle class and White youth), they feel deprived in terms of education, jobs, income, standard of living, etc. Moreover, they feel they have little power to change their situation. They may feel that nobody listens to them or that they are picked on, e.g. police harassment. In reaction to these interpretations of relative deprivation and feelings of being **marginalised**, some young people may turn to sub-cultures. These may be positive and offer status through legitimate and conventional means (e.g. a church group) or negative in that status is awarded for deviant behaviour which may involve crime.

PROGRESS CHECK

1. What three types of deviance are identified by Robert Merton?
2. What causes working-class juvenile delinquency according to Cohen?
3. What do Taylor, Walton and Young mean when they say crime is political?
4. What types of crime are neglected by the agents of social control in a capitalist system?
5. What two factors do Left Realists blame for crime?

Answers: 1. Innovation (crime), retreatism and rebellion. 2. Status frustration. 3. It is a conscious reaction to the inequalities, exploitation and oppression of capitalism. 4. Those carried out by members of the economically dominant classes such as white-collar and corporate crimes. 5. Relative deprivation and lack of power (marginalisation).

Gender and crime

AQA **SCLY 4**   OCR **G673**

Patterns of crime by gender

KEY POINT

The official crime statistics tend to show that women commit less crime than men. Approximately 80% of those convicted of serious crimes are men. By the age of 40, 9% of females had criminal records compared with 32% of men. Consequently, in 2008, there were 4474 women in prison out of a total prison population of 83 000.

The majority of women in prison have been convicted of non-violent crimes, especially property crime. Males are more likely to be repeat offenders, to have longer criminal careers and to commit more serious crime, e.g. males are 15 times more likely to be murderers.

Is female crime under-estimated by the official crime statistics?

Some sociologists argue that the amount of female crime is under-estimated by the official crime statistics. Two arguments support this view.

- Female crimes, such as shoplifting and prostitution, are less likely to be reported compared with the types of violent or sexual crimes committed by men.
- When women do commit crimes, they are less likely to be arrested, prosecuted or convicted than men. It is suggested that **police culture** (which is overwhelmingly male) is 'paternalistic' and sexist. Females do not fit police stereotypes about 'suspicious' or 'criminal' behaviour and consequently females are less likely to be stopped, arrested or charged. **Pollack** and others have suggested that the police and the courts treat female offenders more leniently.

This **chivalry factor**, as it has become known, has been lent support by the fact that the police are more likely to caution females than males. According to Ministry of Justice statistics, 49% of females recorded as offending received a caution in 2007, whereas only 30% of male offenders received the same.

Self-report surveys too, most notably by **Graham and Bowling** (1995) and **Flood-Page** (2000), are often cited as evidence that females are committing more crime than is recorded. However, such reports tend to focus on fairly trivial crimes.

Steffensmeier argues that women are treated more leniently by the courts because judges are reluctant to separate women from children and regard women as less dangerous than men. **Hood** (1992) studied over 3000 court cases in which males and females were found guilty of similar crimes and found that women were one-third less likely to be sent to prison.

Evaluating the chivalry factor

There is lots of evidence against the chivalry factor.

- Women may appear to be treated more leniently simply because the offences they commit are less serious than those committed by men.
- Feminists, such as **Heidensohn**, argue that women are actually treated more harshly than men especially if they don't fit the **feminine stereotype** of how a woman should behave or look. Studies indicate that women who are not seen as good mothers, or who are interpreted as sexually promiscuous, are more likely to be given prison terms. Women who are regarded as unfeminine because they are openly lesbian or feminist, or who belong to deviant youth sub-cultures are also more likely to be sent to prison if found guilty.
- The chivalry factor does not take account of factors such as social class, ethnicity and age, i.e. certain groups of women, e.g. working class, African-Caribbean women, are more likely to be treated harshly by the police and judiciary.

Explanations for why women commit less crime than men

This links to material in Chapters 1 and 2 on socialisation.

- **Differential socialisation** – both **Smart** and **Oakley** have suggested that males are socialised into being tough, aggressive and risk-taking. This may mean that they are more inclined to commit criminal acts of violence. Females, on the other hand, are socialised into accepting passive caring roles.

- **Differential controls – Heidensohn** argues that females are generally more conformist than males and this is because patriarchal society imposes greater control over their behaviour. Smart notes that girls are more strictly supervised by their parents, especially in terms of activities outside the home and have less opportunity to engage in juvenile delinquency. In contrast, males are more likely to spend their spare time with their peers in public spaces where opportunities for delinquency might arise, e.g. hanging around the street corner in town at night.
- **McRobbie and Garber's** work concluded that the **stresses of adolescence** were different for girls and their lives revolved around a **bedroom culture**. They are more likely than boys to socialise with their friends in the home rather than in the street or other public places and consequently less likely to engage in disorder and come into contact with the police.
- **Heidensohn** notes that women are more likely to be **controlled by** their family roles as wives and mothers – the latter role, in particular, means they have little time or opportunity for illegal activity.

> This links to material in Chapter 1 on families.

- **Rational choices – Carlen** found that the working class women in prison who she interviewed committed crime for rational reasons because the benefits of crime outweighed the costs. This was because they had failed to gain qualifications and consequently they were unemployed and on benefits. Furthermore, the women had not benefitted from family life either – many had been abused, half had spent time in care and many were homeless and poor because they had run away from either home or care. Many of the women consequently made the rational decision that crime was their only route to a decent standard of living. However, critics suggest that Carlen under-plays the role of free will and choice in offending. Many women in poverty do not choose to commit crime. Furthermore, her very small sample may not be representative of female criminals in general.

> It is important to consider how sample size can affect representativeness and generalisability.

- **Drugs and excitement – Croall** suggests teenage girls are motivated to commit crime by three inter-related factors.
    - By a drug habit (which often leads to prostitution and shoplifting).
    - By the excitement that often accompanies the risk of committing crime.
    - By the image and identity which fuels conspicuous consumption of goods such as designer label clothing (which are often the main target of their crimes).
- The **feminisation of poverty – Walklate** suggests that because of factors such as low pay, low benefits and the increasing number of single-mothers, female economic crimes such as shoplifting and social security fraud, may have increased in reaction to the increasing poverty experienced by some vulnerable groups of women.
- **Liberation theory – Adler** argues that as society becomes less patriarchal and as women's economic opportunities become similar to men's, so women's crime rates will rise. There is some evidence to support these observations. The overall rate of female offending has risen sharply in the past 20 years. Between 1981 and 1997, the number of girls under 18 convicted of violent offences in England and Wales doubled (from 65 per 100 000 to 135 per 100 000). Women now account for about 20% of violent crime. However, critics of this explanation point out that most female offenders are working class and that they are probably motivated by many of the same factors that motivate working class men, i.e. poverty and the feelings of humiliation, powerlessness, envy, hostility etc that accompany their marginalised position in society.

Masculinity and crime

Messerschmidt (1993) suggests that traditionally males were brought up to subscribe to a **hegemonic masculine value system** organised around values and norms, such as power and authority, being in control of others, sexual reputation, toughness (usually expressed through aggression, confrontation or force), risk-taking, living on the edge and thrill-seeking, pleasure and excitement. Conformity to these values meant that such men often crossed the line between conformist and criminal behaviour in order to gain reputations and the respect of other men.

However, Messerschmidt has been criticised because it is unclear whether masculinity is the cause of crime or whether it is just one way in which criminality is expressed.

Post-modern studies of masculinity and crime

Katz (1988) argues that in order to understand the motives for crime, we need to look at the pleasure or thrill that is derived from it which he calls **transgression**. Different crimes provide different thrills. Katz argues that violence may seem irrational, but the pleasure derived from the thrill and power exercised over others is actually quite rational in the context of masculinity.

Lyng (2002) argues that young men search for pleasure through risk-taking. Crime is **edgework** – it is located on the edge between security and danger. The thrill or excitement is focused on the uncertainty of whether the crime being committed will result in capture and punishment. In this sense, crime is a form of gambling and consequently both thrilling and pleasurable.

Ethnicity and crime

AQA **SCLY 4**   OCR **G673**

African-Caribbean people and, to a lesser extent, Asian people are over-represented in the official crime statistics and in the prison population. Black people make up about 11% of the prison population. In female prisons, they make up 1 in 5 of female prisoners. Yet Black people make up only 2.8% of the population of Britain. Asians make up 6% of the prison population, but only 5% of the general population.

Sociological explanations of ethnic minority crime

Morris argues that most crime is committed by the young and ethnic minority groups have a higher proportion of young people than the White population. However, if this was the cause of crime, young Asians would show up in the statistics more than they do, because the majority of Asians in Britain are aged under 30.

Phillips and Bowling (2007) argue that since the 1970s the Black community has been subjected to oppressive **military-style policing** which has resulted in Black people's over-representation in the criminal statistics. Home Office statistics on police **stop and search**, released in March 2010, support the idea that racial stereotyping underpins policing because they reveal that the police stop and search Black people and Asians six times and two times respectively more than White people.

Interpretivist studies of policing confirm that the decisions of police officers to stop, search and arrest young African-Caribbean males are based on negative racial profiling or stereotyping. Phillips and Bowling found that a substantial minority of White police officers hold negative stereotypes about ethnic minorities and this leads to officers deliberately targeting African-Caribbeans in particular. **Holdaway** found that such stereotypes are endorsed and upheld by the **canteen culture** of rank and file officers. Research by **Hood** also indicates the possibility of some bias in the judicial process. He concluded that young African-Caribbean males were more likely to receive custodial sentences than young White males for the same type of offences.

Cashmore, using the ideas of **Merton**, argues that young African-Caribbeans in Britain are encouraged like everybody else to pursue material success, but their opportunities are blocked by factors such as racism, failing inner-city schools and unemployment. Young Blacks experience anomie and **alienation** – they are aware that their situation arises from being Black in a predominantly White society. They consequently turn to street crime (i.e. innovation) to earn money and gain respect and status from their peers.

However, Left Realists point out that these blocked opportunities are experienced by the majority of African-Caribbeans, but Cashmore fails to explain why only a small proportion of young Blacks actually turn to crime.

The neo-Marxist **Gilroy** argues that crime committed by young African-Caribbeans is political because it is frequently motivated by their interpretation of their position in British society. He argues that a lot of Black street crime is a conscious and deliberate reaction to the way white society has historically treated Black people via slavery and colonialism and the institutional racism they experience on a daily basis.

However, the fact that most African-Caribbeans are law abiding citizens challenges the view that crime is part of an anti-colonial or anti-racist struggle. The first generation of immigrants had first-hand experience of colonialism and racism, but did not turn to crime to make their protest. Moreover, Left Realists point out that if African-Caribbean crime is a political protest against White racism, why are a great number of victims of crime Black? There is also no empirical evidence that Black youth have the political motives that Gilroy identifies.

The theories of **Sewell** (2003) have become increasingly influential in recent years. He identifies a number of risk factors, which he argues are responsible for the relatively high levels of crime amongst African-Caribbean boys.

Sewell's most controversial risk factors relate to the quality of African-Caribbean family life. He notes that many African-Caribbean boys come from families in which the father is absent. The absence of an alpha male in their lives means that boundaries are not set for disciplined behaviour. He acknowledges that mothers cope well in a difficult situation, but argues that such boys often go through a period of crisis in their teens as a direct result of their father's absence or lack of contact. Sewell argues that Black youth experience a **triple quandary** as a result of this crisis.

> This links to material in Chapter 1 on families.

- They feel that they do not fit into the dominant mainstream culture. They feel rejected by it because they perceive the education system, teachers, police-officers, employers, etc. to be racist and working against their interests.
- They become anxious about how they are perceived by society and especially by their Black peers. They therefore seek to position themselves in a positive way by constructing a **deviant** and **highly masculine identity**. Sewell argues that **peer group pressure** is extremely influential because for many Black males in an urban context, how they are constructed as a hyper-male and gangsta in

> This links to material in Chapter 2 on the agencies of socialisation and identity.

the eyes of their peers is central to their identity. It is a comfort zone, i.e. their peer group's acceptance of this identity compensates for rejection by their fathers, the education system, White society and so on. This **street culture** becomes the arena in which young Black males gain respect or 'front' by engaging in deviant and criminal activities in order to prove their manhood. This type of behaviour is likely to lead to confrontation with authority.

- Many aspects of this ultra-masculine identity are shaped by **media culture**, such as MTV, rap music and advertising. This encourages a stress on status being achieved through a consumer culture which views material things such as designer labels, trainers and jewellery (i.e. 'bling') as more important than education. Moreover the street culture takes its lead from deviant or questionable role models, such as 50 Cent, who boast about their sexual conquests and gun-centred lifestyles.

> This links to material in Chapter 7 on the influence of the mass media.

The **Left Realists**, **Lea and Young**, suggest that:

- Young Black people experience **relative deprivation** in that they compare their economic position, especially access to consumer goods, with that of their White peers. However, their opportunities are likely to be blocked because of institutional racism in employment, education, housing and day-to-day dealings with the police.
- Consequently, they feel **marginalised**, i.e. they feel that they lack any power to change their world and are consequently frustrated and alienated.
- Lea and Young suggest that some young Black people may respond to this situation in a deviant **sub-cultural** fashion, i.e. they turn to drug dealing, mugging and territorial sub-cultures or gangs.

However, they stress that crime is only one sub-cultural response, e.g. some may turn to religious sub-cultures or other more conformist responses.

> This approach to crime is linked to the right-wing theories of Wilson who advocates zero tolerance of crime.

From a **Right Realist** perspective, it is argued that crime among Asian youth may be low because Asian families exercise stricter controls over young people which may limit their opportunity for crime. They are also more likely to be economically involved in some way in their community and are therefore less likely to be economically marginalised or frustrated by racism. Asian culture may provide a safety net if members 'fail' in mainstream society, which also minimises these risk factors.

However, there is evidence that the crime rate among Asian people is rising. Since 9/11, the number of young Muslims who are stopped and arrested has risen leading to accusations that the authorities are Islamophobic.

State crime

AQA **SCLY 4**

> **KEY POINT**
>
> **Green and Ward** (2005) define state crime as acts which break international law or deviant activities carried out either by or with the cooperation of state agencies. State crime is usually carried out to further state policies and can include genocide, war crimes, torture, selling weapons to repressive regimes, invading less powerful states, supporting terrorism, abusing people's human rights and assassination.

However, state crime is difficult to construct as crime because powerful groups such as governments are able to dominate discussion as to what constitutes legitimate violence. Consequently, definitions of what constitutes a terrorist or freedom fighter are influenced by the causes that the British state supports. Similarly, Nazi and Japanese actions during the Second World War are defined as 'war crimes' whilst Allied excessive military actions are defined as necessary actions because the victors write the history books. The State may also argue that illegal actions like torture or assassination were carried out in the public interest, for example, torture might lead to British lives being saved.

Finally, measuring the extent of state crimes is difficult because these tend to be carried out by the state's most secretive agencies, i.e. the security services whose actions are largely hidden by the Official Secrets Act. Disclosure of such activities is defined as not being in the public interest. **Cohen** points out that the State and its agents would probably use techniques of neutralisation to deny such crimes anyway such as 'it didn't happen' or 'I was merely following orders'.

Globalisation and crime

AQA **SCLY 4**

> **KEY POINT**
>
> **Globalisation** refers to the increasing inter-connectedness of societies, so that what happens in one locality is shaped by distant events in another, and vice versa. **Held *et al.*** suggest that there has been a globalisation of crime. The same processes that have brought about the globalisation of legitimate business activities have also brought about the spread of **transnational organised crime**.

Castells (1998) argues that there is now a global criminal economy worth over £1 trillion per year, e.g. global criminals traffic in drugs, weapons, illegal immigrants especially sex workers, tobacco, alcohol, cars, counterfeit goods, body parts, cultural artefacts, endangered species and nuclear materials. Furthermore, money laundering is estimated as involving $1.5 trillion a year and global cyber-crimes are increasing at a dramatic rate. Finally, international terrorism is a fact of the modern world.

This global criminal economy has both a **demand** side and a **supply** side. The rich West demands drugs, sex workers, etc. while global criminal gangs source these in Eastern Europe and the developing world and supply them to the West.

Green crime

Green crime is crime against the environment. Much of it can be linked to globalisation and the increasing inter-connectedness of societies, e.g. atmospheric pollution from industry in one country can have a significant negative effect on the eco-system of neighbouring countries.

> **KEY POINT**
>
> Some criminologists have noted that many global environmental problems, such as greenhouse gas emissions created by the toxic pollution produced by big business, are often not covered by existing international or local laws because such laws have often been shaped by powerful capitalist and industrial interests. Moreover, such interests have taken an active part in undermining the scientific status of research which suggests that there is a relationship between global warming and industrial output.

Criminologists, such as **White** (2008), argue that sociologists need to abandon the idea that green crime involves breaking the law because the laws are generally weakly enforced and because laws regarding the environment are inconsistent across the world.

> **KEY POINT**
>
> White argues that green crime should be re-defined as meaning any action that harms the physical environment and/or the humans and animals that live in it.

South (2008) classifies such harm into two general types.

- **Primary crimes** – these relate to the destruction and degradation of the earth's resources and include air pollution, deforestation, species decline, animal rights and water pollution.
- **Secondary crimes** – these relate to the breaking or manipulation of existing laws or regulations relating to the environment and include state violence against groups attempting to protect the environment and the illegal dumping of hazardous waste.

However, critics of green criminology suggest that it is too dependent on dubious value judgements about 'wrong' behaviour and consequently is not an objective assessment of 'real' crime.

8.3 Theories of social order and social control

> **LEARNING SUMMARY**
>
> **After studying this section, you should be able to understand:**
> - different theoretical explanations of social order and control
> - crime prevention and issues relating to control
> - the relationship between the media and crime

Functionalist theories of social order and control

AQA **SCLY 4**   OCR **G673**

> **KEY POINT**
>
> **Functionalists** argue that social order depends upon shared norms and values, i.e. value consensus, that are acquired through **socialisation**. Deviance is behaviour that challenges the consensus.

Durkheim believed that deviance is present in all societies and consequently it has a positive **function** to play. He concluded that a certain amount of deviance was functional or beneficial to society because:

- acts of deviance can bring about necessary social change
- deviance can act as an early warning system that part of society is malfunctioning and is in need of social engineering
- deviance provokes collective outrage and therefore social integration and solidarity against outsiders such as criminals
- punishment of criminals is applied on behalf of the collective and reinforces value consensus

- deviance and its punishments are part of the **secondary socialisation process** in that they reinforce what counts as acceptable and unacceptable behaviour.

Other functionalists such as **Davis and Polsky** argue that deviance can be a **safety valve** for problems within important institutions such as the family. They argue that prostitution and pornography respectively may be lesser evils than the breakdown of the family or sexual crime.

This functionalist theory of deviance has some fundamental weaknesses. Firstly, it does not explain why some groups are more prone to deviance than others. Secondly, some types of deviance are neither functional nor beneficial (e.g., child abuse). Thirdly, they under-estimate the degree of conflict in society and exaggerate the extent of consensus in society.

Labelling theory

AQA **SCLY 4**   OCR **G673**

> **KEY POINT**
>
> Deviance has been defined by sociologists in different ways. One way of defining deviance is in terms of **norm-breaking behaviour**. In this view, deviance refers to non-conformist behaviour which attracts moral disapproval from members of society. A deviant person is simply someone who acts in a deviant manner by failing to comply with society's norms and values.

Deviant behaviour is controlled by the use of **informal sanctions** within social groups such as families, friends and peers. These sanctions may be positive or negative. Within a family, for example, **positive sanctions** may take the form of praise, love and material rewards, whilst **negative sanctions** may include smacking, scolding, 'grounding' and disowning.

> Such groups as families and peers operate as agencies of informal social control and also as agencies of socialisation.

A **crime** is an illegal act which fails to comply with the criminal law. Such behaviour is controlled via sanctions which are enforced by **agencies of formal social control** such as the police, magistrates and the judiciary. Deviant activity is not necessarily illegal, e.g. 'breaking wind' in public is regarded by many as deviant, but it is not against the law!

The social construction of crime and deviance

> **KEY POINT**
>
> **Labelling theory** notes that what is defined as deviant is not absolute, fixed or universal – rather it is relative to specific cultures, times and places. In this way, labelling theory defines deviance in **relative** rather than in **absolute terms**. According to labelling theory, deviancy can be understood not in terms of a person's actions or behaviour, but in terms of the **social reaction** to that behaviour. In this view, deviant behaviour is behaviour that others **label** as such.

What is constructed as crime or deviance depends on a number of factors.
- The **historical period**, e.g. abortion, homosexuality and blasphemy have all been defined as crimes in the past in Britain.
- The culture, e.g. selling marijuana is legal in Holland, but illegal in Britain.

- Particular **social situations** or places, e.g. nudity is acceptable in your bathroom, but not in the street or on football pitches.
- The **interpretations** of those who enforce the law, e.g. the police use their discretion to stop, search and arrest particular individuals, as well as to record, or not record, crime reported to them by victims and the general public.
- **Interests of powerful groups**, e.g. the failure to see business crime as 'real' crime may reflect the ability of business groups to influence the law and its interpretation.
- The **powerlessness of groups** such as the working class, young people, women and ethnic minority groups, e.g. the existence of a number of laws controlling young people, the neglect of domestic violence and of racially motivated crimes may reflect the lack of influence that these groups have.

KEY POINT

Labelling theory argues that crime and deviance are a matter of **interpretation** because recognition of deviance require two activities: a group or individual must act in a particular fashion and another group with more power must label the initial activity as deviant. There is therefore no such thing as a deviant act in itself – an act only becomes deviant when there is **societal reaction** to it.

Becker argues that powerful groups, such as the middle class, shape societal reaction by making rules or laws. Those who break laws are labelled via policing or media-fuelled moral panics. **Lemert** suggests that the deviant label becomes a master status which may have negative consequences in terms of prejudice and discrimination and self-fulfilling prophecies (once labelled, people may then see themselves as deviant). Labelling theory notes that sub-cultures may be the consequence of negative labelling. Sub-cultures are viewed positively by labelling theory because they confer normality and status on those negatively labelled by society – which may compensate for the societal reaction, e.g. gay culture.

In criticism of labelling theory, it is argued that the act of deviance is always more important than the reaction. People who commit deviant acts know full well what they are doing – self-awareness of their deviant activity does not suddenly result from having a label slapped on them. Labelling theory also fails to explain why people commit deviance in the first place. Finally, its view that further deviance is the consequence of being labelled underestimates the **degree of choice** that deviants have.

Traditional Marxism, crime and social control

AQA **SCLY 4**   OCR **G673**

Traditional Marxism argues that the law and agents of social control, such as the police and courts, exist to **reproduce**, **maintain** and **legitimate class inequality** on behalf of the ruling class. In other words, the official crime statistics and law are **ideological**. Their function is to protect the interests of the ruling class, i.e. wealth, private property and profit and to divert attention away from white-collar, and corporate crime committed by the ruling capitalist class.

The legal system as an ideological state apparatus.

The capitalist class also has the power to prevent laws being passed that are not in its interest or to make sure that such laws are weak, e.g. breaking health and safety laws and endangering the lives of workers is not punishable by prison. Many infractions are dealt with by the Health and Safety Executive (HSE) informally and involve minimal punishment.

Finally, enforcement of the law is also **selective** and **partial** in that working class crimes are more severely punished than middle class crimes which are either poorly policed and/or weakly punished.

In criticism of Marxism, it is argued that they over-emphasise social class and neglect how the law and criminal justice system may reflect **patriarchal** inequalities and **institutional racism**. They have been accused of being over-simplistic in their view that power is concentrated in the hands of a ruling capitalist class. There may be a plurality of interest groups who benefit from the law.

New Right theories

AQA **SCLY 4**   OCR **G673**

An influential theory, particularly in the USA.

Hirschi's control theory has strongly influenced New Right theories of crime. He argues that much criminality is **opportunistic** – people choose to commit crime by **rationally** weighing up the **benefits** against the **risks** and **costs** (getting caught and being punished).

Most people do not commit crime because they have **controls** in their lives which mean that the costs of crime far outweigh the benefits of crime. Such controls include **attachment** to family (e.g. marriage and children), **commitment** to a career, active **involvement** in a community and reputation, and **belief** in rules and discipline. Certain groups, e.g. the young, the working class and the underclass, are less likely to have such controls in their lives and the benefits of crime clearly outweigh the risks of being caught and punished.

Crime prevention and control

AQA **SCLY 4**   OCR **G673**

> **KEY POINT**
>
> There are four broad strategies that can be used to prevent crime and to encourage people to conform. These are:
> - situational crime prevention (SCP)
> - environmental crime prevention (ECP)
> - social and community crime prevention
> - punishment.

Situational crime prevention (SCP)

Situational crime prevention (SCP) refers to measures aimed at **reducing opportunities** for crime. These measures are based on the **Right Realist** ideas that crime is the result of criminals making rational choices to commit crime because the benefits of crime outweigh the costs, e.g. the chances of being caught are low and/or punishments are weak. Right realists argue that most crime is opportunistic, so opportunities for crime in particular situations need to be reduced. They therefore recommend:
- **target hardening** – locking doors and windows and installing alarms increases the effort a burglar needs to make in order to break into a property
- **increased surveillance** in shops via CCTV, security guards or store detectives increases the likelihood of shoplifters being caught.

Critique of situational crime prevention

Some criminologists argue that SCP strategies **displace crime** rather than reduce it. Criminals simply move to where targets are softer. Such displacement can take several forms.

- **Spatial** – moving somewhere else to commit crime.
- **Temporal** – committing it at a different time.
- **Target** – choosing a different victim.
- **Tactical** – using a different method.
- **Functional** – committing a different type of crime.

Criminologists are also critical of SCP.

- These strategies over-focus on opportunistic petty street crime and burglary, and ignore white-collar, corporate and state crimes which are more costly and harmful.
- Violent crimes are probably motivated by alcohol and drugs rather than rational thinking about the costs and benefits of crime.
- Marxists claim that SCP approaches ignore the root causes of crime such as poverty and inequality.

Environmental crime prevention (ECP)

> **KEY POINT**
>
> The Right Realist **Wilson** argues that crime is caused by neighbourhood disorder. Wilson's **theory of broken windows** argues that if signs of urban disorder and lack of respect for others are allowed to develop and persist, this encourages further problems. He argues that areas will deteriorate if anti-social behaviour, aggressive begging, drug dealing, public drug use, drunkenness, graffiti, dog fouling, littering, vandalism and leaving broken windows unrepaired are not tackled by the authorities or community. Failure to deal with these problems sends out a clear signal to criminals and deviants that no one cares which encourages criminals to step up their deviant activities.

Wilson argues that in such neighbourhoods, both **formal** and **informal social controls** are often weak. The police are often over-stretched and consequently are only concerned with serious crimes. They do not have the time or resources to tackle petty crime. Respected members of the neighbourhood feel intimidated and powerless, and eventually move away which encourages more deviants to move into the area.

Wilson's solution to such problems of disorder is a three-fold strategy.

- **Environment improvement** – any signs of urban disorder must be dealt with immediately, e.g. broken windows repaired, graffiti cleaned up.
- All new council buildings should not exceed three floors and all residents should be encouraged to take **responsibility** for communal space in order to protect it from outsiders.
- The police should adopt a **zero tolerance policing strategy** – instead of merely reacting to crime, they must aggressively tackle even the slightest signs of disorder and deviance. Zero tolerance policing was famously adopted in New York to tackle graffiti on the subway, fare dodging, drug dealing, begging, etc. Between 1993 and 1996, there was a significant drop in crime, including a 50% fall in the homicide rate.

Social and community crime prevention

Left Realists, and other critical criminologists such as **Marxists**, argue that both SCP and ECP are doomed to failure because they are treating the symptoms rather than the cause of the social disease of crime, i.e. poverty and deprivation. They argue that politicians need to improve social conditions so that people are no longer motivated to look for opportunities for crime.

> **KEY POINT**
>
> Left Realists argue that government needs to tackle educational under-achievement, unemployment, low pay, discrimination and poverty. Marxists argue that inequalities in wealth and income need to be reduced and more investment in creating jobs in poor communities is required. There needs to be a concerted attempt to improve people's economic and social opportunities so that those in poverty and on welfare benefits do not feel massive humiliation and resentment.

Punishment

The one measure that most people believe to be effective in preventing and reducing crime is **punishment**, especially prison. There are essentially two broad justifications for punishment, **reduction** and **retribution**.

Reduction
One justification for punishing offenders is that it prevents future crime in three ways.
- **Deterrence** – the Right Realist position suggests that 'prison works' because severe prison sentences deter many potential offenders away from crime.
- **Rehabilitation** – this is the idea that punishment can be used to reform or change offenders so that they do not return to their criminal careers. Education and training in vocational skills are encouraged so that prisoners can earn a honest living on release.
- **Incapacitation** – prison is important because it takes known criminals off the street so they cannot offend again. In the USA, it has involved the 'three strikes and you're out' policy – committing even a minor third offence can lead to lengthy prison time.

Retribution
Retribution is based on the belief that society should take its revenge on offenders for breaching its moral code. It expresses society's outrage and stresses that punishments should be severe so that they fit the crime. There is some concern that punishments in Britain are too weak and that consequently prison does not work.

Does prison work?

Britain has invested heavily in prisons and, as a result, the prison population rose from approximately 60 000 in 1997 to 77 000 in 2006 and 83 000 in 2007. It is projected to rise further during the 2010s on current rates. Britain has more life sentenced prisoners than the whole of Western Europe combined.

Matthews (1997) argues that the scale of imprisonment has little effect on the crime rate. He notes that rather than reducing crime, prisons act as 'universities of crime' and that they are an 'expensive way of making bad people worse'. At best, prisons are simply **warehouses** in which the reasons for offending are very rarely addressed and little attempt is made to reform or rehabilitate the offender. Matthews also points out that a substantial section of the prison population should not be in prison because they are either drug addicts or they are mentally ill. These people need treatment rather than punishment.

Solomon (2006) suggests that many people are being imprisoned for relatively minor offences for which community punishments may be more suitable. Many people whose offences would not have attracted a custodial sentence in the past are now being sent to prison.

Finally, the high rates of **recidivism** (repeat offenders) suggest that prison does not deter. Two-thirds of released prisoners re-offend as do 71% of juvenile offenders within two years of release.

Moral panic theory and deviancy amplification

AQA **SCLY 3** OCR **G673**
  SCLY 4

This links to material in Chapter 7 on the mass media.

Moral panic theory, an off-shoot of **labelling theory**, examines the role of the mass media in the societal reaction to crime and deviance. **Cohen** argues that a moral panic is an exaggerated over-reaction by society to a perceived problem – usually driven or inspired by the media – where the reaction ends up amplifying the problem out of all proportion to its real seriousness. According to Cohen, moral panics have a number of stages.

- A moral panic begins when the media identify a group as a **folk devil**, or as a threat to societal values.
- The media present the group in a negative and stereotypical fashion using sensationalist and exaggerated headlines and emotive language which **demonises** the group as a social problem.
- **Moral entrepreneurs** such as politicians, editors and religious leaders, condemn the group and its behaviour.
- The media engages in **symbolisation**, i.e. it focuses on the symbols of the group in terms of its dress, hairstyles or music which it associates with trouble, violence, etc. so that the group becomes visible to the general public.
- The media **predicts** further trouble from the group.
- This creates **public anxiety** and puts a great deal of pressure on the authorities – politicians, police and courts – to stamp down hard on the problem group and its activity and therefore control it. New laws, increased policing and severe punishments often result at this stage. However, a **self-fulfilling prophecy** may develop as the group resists the attempts to control it which leads to more arrests, more reporting and a confirmation that there was a problem. A **deviancy amplification spiral** therefore results, i.e. deviance increases as a result of the moral panic.

The causes of moral panics

Stan Cohen's *Folk Devils and Moral Panics* is a key study. It focused on the mods and rockers phenomenon of the mid 1960s.

Moral panics seem to arise most often when society is undergoing a change or modernisation, e.g. the first moral panics about youth in the 1950s and 1960s coincided with youth becoming a distinctive consumer group with values, norms of behaviour, consumption patterns and tastes very different from adults. Studies of moral panics from this period suggest that the older generation was concerned that such social and economic developments were under-mining both the moral order and their traditional authority.

Some commentators claim that moral panics do not reflect social or moral anxieties held by a majority of society's members. Rather, they are quite simply the product of the desire of journalists and editors to sell newspapers. They are a good example of how audiences are manipulated by the media for commercial purposes.

Left Realists argue that moral panics are often based in reality or fact, i.e. the groups identified are often a very real threat to those living in inner-city areas. Left Realists, however, note that moral panic theorists often deny the reality of the subject matter of moral panics and portray them as fantasies made up by journalists. **Young and Lea** note that portraying such crime as a fantasy product of the mass media is naïve because such crime has real negative outcomes for people living in inner-city areas.

Marxists argue that the **interactionist** explanation for moral panics is too vague especially in terms of who benefits from such panics. They also suggest moral panics are an ideological tool of the capitalist class aimed not only at diverting attention away from the crises which often beset capitalism, but also at dividing and ruling sections of the working class. **Hall** claims that a moral panic was created around mugging in the 1970s which had the effect of **labelling** all young African-Caribbeans as criminals and as a potential threat to White people. Hall claims this served the ideological purpose of turning the White working class against the Black working class. It also justified increasing the powers of the police.

> **KEY POINT**
>
> Marxists argue that the function of moral panics is to identify the 'enemy within' – those groups who have been identified by the ruling class as 'troublesome' or rebellious. The moral panic aims to justify tighter control of these groups in order to get them back into line.

Crime and the mass media

AQA **SCLY 3**   OCR **G673**
         SCLY 4

There is a strong relationship between mass media (e.g. newspapers, magazines, television) and crime. About 30% of newspaper content is devoted to crime on average. Moreover, the media over-represent murder and sexual crime despite these crimes only accounting for about 3% of all recorded crime. According to **Felson**, the media also reinforce the following myths or fallacies about crime.

- The **age fallacy** – the media portray both criminals and their victims as mainly adult, despite the fact that most criminals and their victims are relatively young.
- The **class fallacy** – victims of crime are mainly portrayed as middle class, despite the fact that most victims of crime come from working class poorer backgrounds.
- The **dramatic fallacy** – the media over-report violence and under-report everyday crimes. They selectively report the official crime statistics, i.e. by focusing on crimes which have increased whilst neglecting falls.
- The **police fallacy** – media coverage exaggerates police success in clearing up crime.
- The **victim fallacy** – the media highlight crime risks to women and the elderly and neglect the fact that young males, ethnic minorities and poorer people living in the inner-city are most at risk.
- The **ingenuity fallacy** – media images lead people to believe that to commit crime and to solve it, both criminals and detectives need to be clever.

Soothill and Walby's (1991) research into British newspapers found evidence of a media pre-occupation with **sex crimes**. They found that newspaper reporting of rape cases increased from under a quarter of all cases in 1951 to over a third in 1985. They also note that such coverage misrepresents the reality of rape, e.g. newspapers over focus on rape by strangers despite the fact that these are the exception rather than the rule – most rapists are actually known to their victims.

News values and crime coverage

This links to material in Chapter 7 on news values.

> **KEY POINT**
>
> Most media sociologists agree that news does not just happen; rather it is a **social construction**. This means that it is the outcome of a social process in which some potential stories are selected while others are rejected. A central part of the **manufacture of the news** is the concept of **news values** – criteria used by reporters and editors to decide whether a story is **newsworthy** or not, i.e. whether it will appeal to an audience and sell newspapers or attract viewers.

Key news values are noted below.
- **Dramatisation** – the reporting of crimes can easily be under-pinned by a narrative or story, action and excitement.
- **Personalisation** – crimes are human interest stories – journalists can easily focus on the personal elements, e.g. tragedy and motives.
- **Higher status** – crimes involving celebrities are very newsworthy, e.g. George Michael going to prison.
- **Novelty or unexpectedness** – some crimes might be unexpected, e.g. an assassination.
- **Risk** – victim-centred stories about vulnerability and fear are popular.
- **Violence** – audiences are fascinated by visible and spectacular acts.
- **Bad news** – crime is generally bad news which tends to sell more newspapers than good news.

The media as a possible cause of crime

This links to material in Chapter 7 on the hypodermic syringe model of media effects.

> **KEY POINT**
>
> It is suggested that some audiences may **imitate** violent, immoral or anti-social behaviour, particularly violence seen in films, on television and in computer games. The media is seen by some as a **powerful secondary agent of socialisation** which shapes the behaviour of young people and produces a **copycat effect**.

In addition to imitation, the content of the mass media has been accused of causing crime and deviance by:
- arousal – through viewing violent or sexual imagery
- encouraging deviant role models whose behaviour influences children
- desensitisation – through repeated viewings of violence
- the transmission of knowledge of criminal techniques
- the glamorisation of crime.

Literally thousands of studies into the link between the media and crime have been undertaken. However, many media sociologists such as **Gauntlett** note that the idea of a straightforward link between the media and crime is simplistic because it fails to recognise that audiences differ in terms of age, social class, intelligence or level of education and consequently do not react in the same way to media content. The copycat argument also fails to appreciate the **nature of violence** – most experts argue that it is caused by a complex range and combination of possible factors, e.g. poor socialisation, bad parenting, peer group influences, mental illness, drugs and alcohol.

Sparks notes that a lot of media effects studies ignore the meanings that viewers give to media violence. There is evidence that audiences interpret violence in cartoons, horror films and news quite differently, e.g. **Buckingham's** research into how children use the media suggests that even very young children are more media-literate than we credit them and use the media in a responsible way.

Cumberbatch reviewed over 3500 studies on the relationship between the media and violence and failed to find one that proved the connection. None disproved it either. As he concludes: 'the jury is still out on this issue'.

The media, relative deprivation and crime

Some sociologists suggest that the media is responsible for crime by stimulating desire for money or unaffordable consumer goods through advertising. **Reiner** and other Mertonian sociologists argue that the mass media help to increase people's sense of **relative deprivation** and anomie – the feeling of being deprived compared with others and frustration that they are not sharing in the material success enjoyed by those on their television screens, in their newspapers and celebrity magazines. This may fuel resentment and violent crime.

Fear of crime

Some sociologists argue that the distorted and exaggerated media representation of crime is creating unnecessary and unrealistic **fear of crime** among women and the elderly. Research evidence supports the view that there is a link between media representations of violence and fear of crime. **Schlesinger and Tumber** found a correlation between media consumption and fear of crime, with tabloid readers and heavy users of television expressing a greater fear of becoming a victim, especially of violence.

8.4 Suicide

LEARNING SUMMARY	**After studying this section, you should be able to understand:** • theoretical approaches to the study of suicide • the methodological implications of studying and researching suicide

Durkheim's study of suicide

AQA **SCLY 4**   OCR **G673**

The classic sociological study of suicide was carried out by **Emile Durkheim** in 1897 and is based upon two central ideas.
- Durkheim was a **positivist** and consequently he believed that **individual action** was shaped by the **social structure**. He therefore aimed to show that the 'supreme' individual act, i.e. suicide, was the product of social influences beyond the control of the individual.

This links to material in Chapter 5 on positivism. You can draw on this material when answering relevant questions on theories and methods.

- Durkheim believed that by studying patterns in suicide objectively and rigorously, sociology could prove itself to be a **scientific discipline**.

Durkheim examined official statistics in regard to suicide and observed three trends in suicide rates.

- Within single societies, the rate of suicide remains fairly constant over time.
- Suicide rates varied consistently between different societies.
- The suicide rate varied between different groups within the same society.

Durkheim therefore suggested that suicide rates were **social facts**, i.e. they were socially determined by the organisation of societies (i.e. their social structures).

Durkheim drew on suicide statistics as a secondary source of quantitative data.

Using the **comparative method** of research, Durkheim manipulated non-social and social variables by examining groups of statistics in order to discover the cause of suicide. He eliminated non-social variables such as climate, heredity, alcoholism and the seasons. He also examined psychological variables, e.g. he discovered a high rate of insanity amongst Jews, but a low level of suicide. Consequently, he dismissed mental illness as a 'cause' of suicide.

After examining a number of social variables, Durkheim concluded that suicide varies inversely with the extent of integration of the social group that the individual is part of. He identified four types of suicide – egoistic, altruistic, anomic and fatalistic suicide.

All of these types of suicide are influenced by the organisation of society, i.e. by the social structure.

Types of suicide

Durkheim claimed that **egoistic suicide** was the most common type of suicide found in western societies. He suggested that it is the product of **excessive individualism** or egoism. This means that the social ties which bind the individual into society or social groups like the family are weak and so they experience a **lack of integration** into social life. Durkheim claimed that three social factors are responsible for the strength or weakness of an individual's ties to a social group: religious social controls, family life and political environment.

Under integration.

- Durkheim noted that people who belong to the Catholic religion are less likely to commit suicide than Protestants. He argued that Catholics are **more integrated** into their communities because of the ritualistic character of their beliefs and practices whereas Protestants experience weaker levels of integration because their religion stresses **free enquiry** and therefore less social control.
- Durkheim also suggested that marriage and family life have an integrating effect upon individuals. Being happily married with lots of children and extended family results in high levels of integration, whereas being single or divorced means that some people are more prone to 'egoism'.
- Furthermore, Durkheim argued that strong sentiments in terms of nationalism or patriotism that are present in the political environment can affect suicide rates too. He noted that political upheaval and war promote strong feelings of integration as people pull together in a common cause against an enemy. In this case there is less suicide.

Over-integration.

Altruistic suicide is the product of **too much integration** – the individual is too weak to resist the demands of the group, e.g. mass suicides by religious sects are a good example of this type.

Under-regulation.

Anomic suicide is the product of the **lack of regulation** of the individual by society. In periods of economic depression or prosperity, people may be confused about goals and values as their circumstances radically change and they become more likely to attempt suicide, e.g. a sudden loss of wealth is anomic and may tip some people over into suicidal behaviour.

Fatalistic suicide is caused by the **over-regulation** of the individual by society, e.g. prison suicides may be the result of people believing that their lives are no longer their own.

Over-regulation.

Other functionalist theories of suicide

Halbwachs (1930) continued Durkheim's theme and suggested that **urbanisation** was the key variable in determining social integration because city life was characterised by isolation, impersonal relationships and lack of community and integration.

Criticisms of Durkheim

Think about why it is important to be able to operationalise concepts when carrying out research.

- It has been suggested that suicide statistics collected between 1840 and 1870 are not accurate. Durkheim assumes that these are reliable. However, there was no systematic medical examination of the dead in many parts of Europe until the late nineteenth century and even then examinations in rural areas were less frequent and thorough than those in urban areas. In other words, these official statistics may not be **reliable** or **valid indicators** of the real level of suicide in this period.
- Durkheim failed to explain why suicide is the most likely result of under or over-integration. He does not show why some other course of action, e.g. crime is less likely.
- Durkheim's concepts particularly 'social integration', 'egoism', 'excessive individualism' and 'anomie' are a bit vague and consequently very difficult to operationalise, test and measure.

Remember that interpretivists are anti-positivist. See Chapter 5.

- Durkheim did not offer any guidance on how to recognise different types of suicide. Without knowing the intention of the deceased, it is difficult to use Durkheim's classification. This critique comes from an interpretivist perspective.

Interpretivist theories of suicide

AQA **SCLY 4**   OCR **G673**

The cultural meaning of suicide

You can draw on this material when answering relevant questions on sociological methods.

Douglas (1967) contends that Durkheim failed to acknowledge that suicide rates reflect the cultural meanings attached to suicidal action in a particular society. Cultural interpretations of suicide can influence the statistics in a variety of ways.

- Societies do not share the same meaning of suicide, e.g., in some societies (such as Japan), suicidal action is regarded as positive or honourable, whilst in others (such as European societies) it is regarded as negative, deviant or morally wrong. Therefore, people's potential for suicide will, to some extent, depend upon the societal interpretation of suicide.
- Durkheim himself was guilty of imposing his own interpretations of suicide on his study because (a) he believed suicide to be morally wrong and consequently he did not consider that in some societies suicide might be a normal response to circumstances other than social integration or regulation, and (b) he believed that women were less likely to commit suicide because he believed them to be less mentally active than males. Consequently he did not consider gender as a serious influence on the suicide rate.

- Douglas suggests that the more integrated a community is, the more likely it will be that a higher proportion of suicide will be **covered up** rather than prevented. These types of society tend to interpret suicide as very wrong and shameful, therefore, relatives and friends may make a greater effort to hide evidence of suicide. If the individual died in an integrated community, officials such as doctors, police and coroners may be less willing to believe that the death was due to suicide. Douglas is therefore arguing that social integration influences the **recording** of the death as a suicide not the decision to kill oneself.
- **McCarthy and Walsh** (1975) studied the suicide rate in Dublin between 1964 and 1968 and estimated that the suicide rate should have been four times greater than that estimated by official records. They argue that officials such as police officers, doctors and court officials were happy to confirm the desire of relatives to bring in accident verdicts rather than suicide verdicts even when the evidence overwhelmingly suggested suicide. This was because of the negative interpretations or social meanings attached to suicide in that society, i.e. it was a mortal sin that reflected very badly on the surviving family members.

The social construction of suicide statistics

Atkinson (1978) also suggests that suicide rates are **socially constructed**. He argues that suicide statistics are the end product of a complex set of interactions and interpretations involving victims, doctors, friends and relatives of the deceased and, most importantly, coroners.

In the same way official crime statistics can be seen as socially constructed and as the end product of interactions involving witnesses, victims, suspects, offenders and police officers.

Atkinson's research focused on coroners – legal officers who investigate suspicious deaths. He notes that a death is not a suicide until it is **labelled** as such by a coroner's court.

The role of coroners

Coroners have to follow certain formal rules when investigating how a person died, e.g. a **post-mortem** must be carried out and the coroner's officers will investigate the circumstances of the death – they will collect evidence. Coroners weigh up that evidence and must reach one of a number of legal verdicts available: natural causes, open verdict, accident, suicide or homicide. For a death to be recorded as a suicide, it must be proved that the victim **intended** to die.

Atkinson shows that suicidal cues (evidence) are selected and interpreted by coroners as indicators of intent. **Primary cues**, e.g. suicide notes and the mode of death, come from the scene of death, whereas **secondary cues** are uncovered in the life history of the deceased.

Primary cues in themselves are insufficient to prove intent, e.g. suicide notes may not be left or may be destroyed whilst modes of death, such as overdoses, could be accidents. Therefore secondary cues are more important – the coroner will focus on the **biography** of the individual, seeking events, e.g. divorce, redundancy and mental illness, which they regard as causing great unhappiness and despair.

However, Atkinson points out that coroners subscribe to different interpretations as to what constitutes a life threatening situation in a person's life. Most will be influenced by the **dominant cultural meanings** about suicide, i.e. that it is caused by great unhappiness or despair, but their **individual interpretation** of what counts as great unhappiness or despair is likely to differ.

Think about why Taylor chose these methods.

Research by **Taylor** (1982) based on interviews with coroners and their officers and observation of inquests confirmed Atkinson's findings. Taylor's study discovered that the most common interpretations held by coroners in regard to suicidal intent were breakdown in personal relationship, unemployment, redundancy, history of mental, physical illness and/or treatment and broken home in childhood. Taylor concludes that where coroners discover these secondary cues, they are more likely to bring in a suicide verdict.

Atkinson also argues that the life history or biography of the deceased is to some extent negotiated with relatives. The coroner receives much of the information relating to the deceased's state of mind and behaviour from significant witnesses such as family and friends and distant witnesses such as neighbours, colleagues, doctors during the inquest. Such witnesses will also subscribe to cultural meanings about suicide and may attempt to persuade the coroner to see the deceased in a certain way, e.g. those witnesses who believe that it is acceptable to commit suicide if one is terminally ill may stress the pain and suffering of the deceased whilst those who subscribe to the view that suicide is morally wrong or a sign of weakness may stress that the deceased was 'looking forward to the future'.

Taylor claims that social integration in the form of family and friends has an important effect or bias on the recognition and recording of suicide. Taylor investigated 32 deaths on the London Underground in 1982 in which the mode and scene of death were identical and no suicide notes were left. Only 17 of these were eventually labelled as suicides. On observation of the inquests, Taylor concluded that suicide verdicts were not returned on the other 15 because of significant witnesses influencing the coroner's interpretation of secondary cues.

The open verdict

This links to material on experiments in Chapter 5.

Atkinson has drawn attention to the **unreliability** and **invalidity** of suicide statistics by examining the use of the open verdict in the Britain. He argues that the open verdict probably results in the suicide rate being an underestimate of the true amount of suicide in Britain. Atkinson carried out a **social experiment** in which he gave the same information about sudden deaths to a group of English and Danish coroners and asked them to decide upon a verdict. The English coroners were much more cautious than their Danish counterparts in terms of final verdicts. The Danish coroners tended to be more rigorous in their scrutiny of the evidence because the open verdict does not exist in the Danish judicial system. English coroners were much more likely to say that they could not reach a verdict.

The work of Steve Taylor

Taylor (1988) attempts to combine Durkheimian and interpretivist approaches. Like Durkheim, Taylor suggests that the social structure of Britain is important because it brings about levels of **certainty** and **uncertainty** in people's lives, e.g. working class people may experience more uncertainty than certainty because of the potential of unemployment, etc. In a patriarchal society, a career woman may face particular conflicts that do not exist for men, which may increase her sense of uncertainty. Stable lives, argues Taylor, arise from people's interpretations that they are experiencing a balance between certainty and uncertainty.

Taylor advances the view that suicide is more likely in situations where the individual interprets their social situation as one of either complete certainty or complete uncertainty. In the former, people may feel that they know everything worth knowing or experiencing, e.g. they may be certain that they are going to prison because they have committed a crime. This certainty may produce a **purposive suicide**.

Alternatively, some people may feel very uncertain about their futures and attempt what Taylor calls **ordeal suicides** – these people don't know whether they want to live or die. The suicidal action is a type of test.

Both sets of suicidal interpretations may be the product of their experience of the way society is organised. However, Taylor does stress that the suicidal response is only one possible way of reacting to this experience. Certainty and uncertainty can lead to other non-suicidal options.

> **KEY POINT**
>
> In conclusion, then, both Atkinson and Taylor suggest that we cannot take the suicide statistics at face value in the way that Durkheim did. We must look at the ways such statistics are socially constructed. It may be that the official suicide statistics tell us more about the ways in which they are collected and interpreted by coroners than about the causes of suicide.

Exam practice questions

This is an example of a synoptic question that reflects the type of question that you could be asked in the AQA examination. You will be rewarded for applying your knowledge and understanding of sociological research methods to the study of this issue in crime and deviance.

This is an example of a synoptic question that reflects the type of question that you could be asked in the OCR examination.

1. Read Item A and then answer the question that follows.

   Item A
   There are several ways of measuring the extent of crime in Britain including surveys of the public and official statistics of crimes recorded by the police. Victim surveys such as the British Crime Survey (BCS) question respondents about their experiences of crime. The BCS is carried out annually and the results are published by the Home Office together with the official statistics of police-recorded crime. The BCS measures crime via household surveys in England and Wales and has a response rate of around 75%. It questions respondents about whether they have been victims of particular offences (e.g. assault and car theft) during the last twelve months and, if so, whether they reported the crimes to the police.

   However, the BCS does not cover 'victimless' crimes (such as drug use) or crimes such as murder and fraud.

   Using material from Item A and elsewhere, assess the strengths and limitations of using victim surveys as a way of 'measuring the extent of crime in Britain' (Line 1, Item A). **(15 marks)**

2. Outline and assess sociological explanations for the relatively low recorded rates of white-collar crime. **(50 marks)**

Sample question and model answer

This is an example of a synoptic question that reflects the type of question that you could be asked in the OCR examination. When answering synoptic questions on crime and deviance, try to draw on relevant themes and concepts from across the specification such as socialisation, identity, social class, power and peer groups. Also try to link this topic to other relevant topics that you have studied such as education and mass media.

Useful illustrations.

The theory is outlined.

An alternative example which would have been truly synoptic could have focussed on how some teachers label students which contributes to the development of deviant subcultures in schools. It is important to draw on topics across the specification.

It is important to apply relevant contemporary examples such as these.

Explicit assessment – weaknesses.

Explicit assessment – weaknesses.

Explicit assessment – strengths.

Outline and assess labelling theory as an explanation of deviant behaviour.

(50 marks)

Labelling theorists such as Becker and Lemert argue that `deviance' is relative rather than absolute. What is regarded as deviant by one person or group (e.g. smoking cannabis in a cafe or assisted suicide) may be perfectly acceptable to another. Deviance, therefore, is a matter of interpretation and an act only becomes deviant as a result of societal reaction. Becker argues that social groups create deviance by making the rules whose infraction constitutes deviance and applying those rules to particular people, thus labelling them as outsiders. In other words, the powerful, by making and applying social rules, define what counts as deviance, e.g. the middle class make rules for the working class and men make rules for women.

Labelling theory explores the role of agencies of social control, e.g. the police and the media, in the labelling process. Several studies of the police from a labelling perspective (e.g. Cicourel, Holdaway) indicate that labelling or stereotyping by some police officers may result in particular groups (e.g. young Black men, working class males) being disproportionally represented in crime statistics and in prisons. Studies of the media, e.g. by Cohen, indicate that sensationalist coverage may lead to groups such as mods and rockers (or, more recently, `hoodies' and asylum seekers) being labelled as folk devils which fuels a moral panic around them.

For those labelled as deviant, the label may become a master status and may lead to a self-fulfilling prophecy, e.g. the `ex-con' label may lead to prejudice and discrimination in employment and may result in the labelled person drifting back into a life of crime within a criminal sub-culture of similarly labelled people.

Labelling theory has been extensively criticised. First, Ackers argues that it places too much emphasis on societal reaction. Some actions, e.g. murder and child abuse, are inherently deviant and therefore the societal reaction is less significant than the act. Second, labelling theory is too deterministic and it underestimates the degree of choice and consciousness that individuals have. Third, it fails to explain the origins of deviance and why some people commit deviant acts in the first place. Marxists, in particular, argue that labelling theory neglects structural factors such as social class. Marxists emphasise the ideological nature of labelling processes - labelling mainly serves to safeguard the major priorities of capitalism, namely wealth, profit and private property.

Left Realists, such as Young and Lea, criticise labelling theory and argue that some powerless groups such as young Black men do commit more street crime than other social groups. They argue that we need to understand how certain groups interpret their position in the structure of society, e.g. how young Black men interpret institutional racism and labelling by the agencies of social control. Young and Lea suggest that young Black men may respond to feelings of relative deprivation and marginalisation by turning to either legitimate or illegitimate sub-cultures. Young and Lea therefore acknowledge some strengths of labelling theory and adapt these to account for the reality of inner-city crime.

Despite the limitations, labelling theory has made a significant contribution to the sociological understanding of deviance. It has shown that defining deviance is not a straightforward process. It has also highlighted the consequences of the labelling process and shown that definitions of deviance originate in power differences. Consequently, we now understand that deviance is not absolute, unchanging or universal.

9 Stratification, differentiation and social inequality

The following topics are covered in this chapter:

- **Theories of stratification**
- **Changes in the class structure**
- **Social mobility**
- **Dimensions of inequality**

9.1 Theories of stratification

LEARNING SUMMARY

After studying this section, you should be able to understand:

- different types of social stratification
- different theories of stratification
- the problems of defining and measuring social class
- patterns and trends in life chances by social class

Types of social stratification

AQA **SCLY 4**   OCR **G674**

Social inequality is a key theme of sociology.

Remember that AQA unit 4 SCLY 4 and OCR unit G674 are synoptic. When revising stratification, differentiation and social inequality think about the links with themes and concepts such as socialisation, culture and identity, peer group, social inequality and power. Also think about how material in this topic relates to topics across the specification such as education and family.

> **KEY POINT**
>
> **Social stratification** refers to the division of society into a pattern of layers, or strata, made up of a **hierarchy** of unequal social groups. In other words, a society characterised by stratification will contain **inequalities** based upon factors such as wealth and income, occupation and status, social class, political power, religion, ethnicity, gender and age. One or two groups will dominate others.

Sociologists have identified four types of stratification system some of which are still in existence today:

- the caste system
- the feudal system
- apartheid
- social class.

The caste system

Although officially banned in India today, this Hindu system of stratification is still enormously influential. People in caste societies occupy **ascribed roles** based upon religious purity. The caste system is a **closed society** – people are born into **castes** and cannot move out of them during the course of their lives.

The feudal system

The **feudal system** was founded in medieval Europe and was a hierarchical system based on ownership of land, with the King at the top and peasants at the bottom. Feudal societies, too, were mainly **closed societies** – people's positions were largely **ascribed** and it was rare for people to be upwardly mobile.

Apartheid

Apartheid was a system that existed from the late 1940s to the mid 1990s in South Africa. It categorised people into layers on the basis of ethnicity and skin colour.

Social class

> The main type of stratification in Britain.

Social class is mainly found in modern industrial societies such as Britain. Social classes are groups of people who share a similar **economic position**, e.g. occupation, income and ownership of wealth. They also have similar levels of education, status and lifestyle (i.e. living standards) and power.

Class systems are different to the previous systems in the following respects.
- They are not based on religion, law or race, but on **economic factors**, e.g. job or money.
- There is no clear distinction between classes – it is difficult to say where the working class finishes and the middle class begins.
- All members of society whether working or middle or upper classes have **equal rights**.
- There are no legal restrictions on marriage between the classes.
- Social class societies are **open societies** – people can experience downward or upward **social mobility**, i.e. you can move up or down the class structure through jobs, the acquisition of wealth or marriage.

> This links to material in Chapter 3 on education.

- Such systems are usually **meritocratic** – that is people are not born into ascribed roles. We are encouraged to better ourselves through achievement at school, e.g. via qualifications and at work by working hard, and gaining promotion.

Theories of stratification

AQA **SCLY 4** OCR **G674**

Functionalism

> Functionalism views stratification positively.

KEY POINT

Davis and Moore argue that stratification makes a contribution to **social order** – consequently they argue that class inequality is beneficial, positive and necessary. This is because all societies have to ensure that their most functionally important positions are filled with people who are highly talented and skilled. Talent and skill, however, are in short supply and top jobs require an intensive amount of training and time to acquire the necessary expertise. Educational qualifications and the **stratification system** function to allocate all individuals to an occupational role that suits their abilities.

Stratification encourages all members of society to work to the best of their ability because class societies are **meritocracies** – high rewards in the form of income and status are guaranteed in order to motivate gifted people to make the necessary sacrifices in terms of years spent in education and training. Inequality also motivates – those at the top will wish to retain their advantages, whilst those placed elsewhere will wish to improve on their position.

Evaluation of functionalism

Davis and Moore suggest that **unequal rewards** e.g. in salary and status are the product of consensus. However:

- There exists a substantial level of social resentment about the unequal distribution of income and wealth as illustrated by on-going controversies over 'fat cat' levels of pay and bonuses.
- Unequal rewards may be the product of **inequalities in power**. Some groups may be able to use their economic and political power to increase their rewards against the will of the people.
- High rewards also go to people, e.g. celebrities who play no functionally important roles.
- Lots of occupations can be seen to be functionally essential to the smooth running of society, but they are not highly rewarded, e.g. nurses. Although Davis and Moore would argue that the type of people who qualify to become nurses are not in short supply.
- The **dysfunctions of stratification** are neglected by Davis and Moore, e.g. **poverty** is a major problem for people and negatively impacts on mortality, health, education and family life.

> Poverty is a good example of a social problem that links to topics across the specification.

Marxism

> Marxism views stratification negatively.

Marx argued that history is the **history of class struggle**. Apart from primitive communism which existed in early hunting and gathering society, all stages of history, i.e. ancient slavery, feudalism and capitalism, have been characterised by the existence of class societies. One class, usually a minority which has military or economic power (or both), dominates a larger subordinate class, e.g. slaveholders-slaves, king/barons and peasants.

Social class is essentially the product of the mode of production of a society. The mode of production of modern western societies, such as in Britain is **industrial-capitalist**. In feudal societies, it was agricultural. The mode of production is made up of the relationship between the means of production and the social relations of production. In a capitalist society:

- The **means of production** refers to resources such as land, factories, machinery and raw materials which are owned by the **capitalist class** or **bourgeoisie**. This group is in an extremely powerful and privileged position. The workers, or **proletariat**, do not own productive property. Their only asset is their **labour power**.
- The **social relations of production** refers to the economic relationship between the bourgeoisie and proletariat as the latter hires out its labour power to the former. Inequality, exploitation and conflict result from the fact that it is in the interests of the capitalist class to keep wages low in order to increase profits. Moreover, the value of the worker's labour power is worth a good deal more than the wage paid by the employer for it. Marxists therefore see the relationship between the bourgeoisie and proletariat as deeply unequal, exploitative and the cause of **class conflict**.

Marx argued that capitalism's pursuit of profit means that workers lose control over the work process as new technology is introduced. However, workers very rarely see themselves as exploited because they are suffering from **false class consciousness**. They have been socialised by **ideological apparatuses** such as education and the media into believing that their position at the lower end of the socio-economic hierarchy is deserved and therefore natural.

> This links to material in the chapters on education and the mass media.

Evaluation of Marxism

Marx was an **economic determinist**, or **reductionist**, in that he saw all major ideas as the product of the economic relationship between the bourgeoisie and proletariat. However, conflicts resulting from **nationalism**, **ethnicity** and **gender** cannot be explained adequately in economic terms.

Marx also made certain predictions, e.g. that the working class would experience so much poverty and misery that they would eventually overthrow the capitalist class, that the middle class would disappear and that communism would replace capitalism, but these have not come true. The living standards of the working class have actually risen, the middle classes have grown in numbers and communism was rejected in Eastern Europe. Western class-based societies may have problems such as poverty and homelessness, but they have a reasonably good record in terms of democracy and trade union rights.

Max Weber

Weber recognised that social class had a profound effect on people's **life chances** (i.e. their chances of getting on in terms of jobs, health, etc.) but argued that **status** was also an important source of power. Marx defined social class in terms of productive property. However, Weber defined it differently in terms of **market position**, which is made up of income, skills and qualifications. On this basis, he argued that within social classes, there exists a range of life chances.

Weber also argued that **status inequality** derives from **class inequality**, i.e. people who occupy high occupational roles generally have high social status. However, status can also derive from other sources of **power** such as gender, ethnicity and religion. Weber noted that status was also linked to **consumption styles** (i.e. how people spend their money), e.g. some people derive status from **conspicuous consumption** (i.e. being seen to buy expensive designer products). This idea has led to the **post-modernist** idea that in the twenty-first century consumption style rather than social class will structure people's identity.

> This links to material in Chapter 2 on the sources of identity.

Evaluation of Weber

Marxists argue that Weber was too concerned with identifying trivial market details and neglected the basic split between capitalists and workers. Marxists argue that class and status are strongly linked, e.g. the capitalist class not only has wealth, but also high status and political power. Weber recognises that these overlap, but suggests that a person can have wealth, but little status, e.g. a lottery millionaire.

Measuring social class

AQA **SCLY 4**   OCR **G674**

> **KEY POINT**
>
> **Occupation** is the most common indicator of social class used by governments, by advertising agencies when they are doing market research and by sociologists when they are doing social surveys. Information on occupation is easy to obtain and it is generally a good guide to people's skills and qualifications, their income, their future and their present standard of living. Occupation also leads to **status** in modern society – most people judge people's social standing by the jobs they do.

This is referred to in Chapter 3 on education.

There are a number of ways of categorising people into social classes in Britain. The best known, and most widely used way until 2000, was the **Registrar General's (RG) scale**. This divided the population into the following five social classes.

- Class I: Professional, e.g. accountants, doctors and solicitors.
- Class II: Intermediate, e.g. teachers, managers, pilots and farmers.
- Class IIIN: Skilled non manual, e.g. office workers and shop assistants.

KEY POINT

All of the above are **middle class** occupations; those who work in these categories are often called white-collar workers.

- Class IIIM: Skilled manual, e.g. electricians, plumbers and factory foremen.
- Class IV: Semi-skilled manual, e.g. agricultural workers and postal workers.
- Class V: unskilled manual, e.g. road-sweepers, labourers and refuse collectors.

KEY POINT

The last three categories are generally regarded as the **working classes** and are often called **blue-collar** workers.

Defining and operationalising concepts such as social class is a key part of the research process in sociology.

There are problems in using occupation to determine social class as illustrated by the following.

- If we use occupation we exclude the wealthy upper class who own property and have a great deal of power, but who often don't have jobs because they live off rents, stocks and shares.
- Groups outside paid employment are excluded, such as housewives and the never employed.
- Classifying unemployed people on the basis of their last job assumes that they continue to enjoy the same income, status, lifestyle, etc. as they had before they became unemployed. This is unlikely to be the case.
- The RG scale was based on the job of the head of the household, generally assumed to be the man. Married women therefore were classified on the basis of their husbands occupation rather than their own. This is obviously sexist and dated considering the number of women who now work and who hold professional positions.
- The focus on the head of the household neglected those families in which both partners are important in bringing home a wage (**dual-career families**), e.g. their joint incomes could give them the lifestyle of a higher social class.
- In some families, both parents may be breadwinners. However, when the female had a higher status and a higher paid job than the male, she would be classed in the husband's lower occupational class. Some sociologists therefore suggested that the RG scale was dated because it did not consider these **cross-class families**.
- There are major differences between occupations within the social classes, e.g. in terms of income. Social Class I includes doctors, but this group includes surgeons who are paid vast sums and junior doctors who are relatively poorly paid. Teachers are in Social Class II, but this class also includes Members of Parliament!

The National Statistics Socio-economic Classification (NS-SEC)

In the year 2000, the RG scale was replaced by the **National Statistics Socio-economic Classification (NS-SEC)** devised by John Goldthorpe. The RG's scale has been abandoned because it failed to reflect the massive decline in manufacturing, the huge increase in service industries (finance and retail) and the huge shift in the proportion of women in the workforce.

The NS-SEC is based on data from the Labour Force Survey on the employment conditions of over 65 000 individuals across 371 occupations. It differs from the RG scale in the following respects.

- It is no longer based purely on skill like the RG's scale. Rather it is based on **employment relations**, i.e. whether people are employers, self-employed or employees, whether they exercise authority, etc. and **market conditions**, i.e. salary scales, promotion prospects, sick pay, how much control people have over hours worked or how work is done, etc.
- It recognises eight social classes rather than five, including the long-term unemployed and the never worked.
- This classification system no longer divides workers along manual and non-manual lines. Each category contains both manual and non-manual workers.
- Class 8 (i.e. the never worked) might be termed the **underclass**. The RG's scale suffered from the weakness of not having a category that effectively accounted for this group.
- Occupations, such as check-out assistants and sales assistants, who used to be in Class IIIN have been dropped to Class 6 because of their relatively poor conditions of employment, i.e. their market situation has deteriorated in terms of pay, job security, autonomy, etc.
- The self-employed are recognised as a separate category.
- Women are recognised as a distinct group of wage earners and are no longer categorised according to the occupation of their husbands or fathers.

The main categories of the NS-SEC are:

1.1 Employers in large organisations
1.2 Higher professional occupations
2 Lower professional and higher technical occupations
3 Intermediate occupations
4 Employers in small organisations
5 Lower supervisory occupations
6 Semi-routine occupations
7 Routine occupations
8 Never worked and long-term unemployed

However, a number of potential weaknesses have been identified with regard to the NS-SEC.

- It is still based primarily on **occupation**. This may differ from what people understand by the term 'social class' and especially people's subjective interpretation of their own class position.
- The NS-SEC has taken into consideration **changing class boundaries**, e.g. the fact that the social position of clerical workers has declined. However, there are still significant differences between occupations, within one category. Furthermore, this classification tells us little about the huge differences within occupations – compare a GP's or junior doctor's salary with that of a consultant, or a solicitor with that of a judge.
- It still fails to account for those who are wealthy enough not to have to work.

Patterns and trends in life chances by social class

AQA **SCLY 4**   OCR **G674**

Trends in income, wealth and poverty

Between 1979 and 1997, the gap between the rich and poor in Britain in terms of income widened until it was at its most unequal since records began. Income rose on average by 36% in this period, but whilst the poorest 10% of people experienced a 17% decline, the top 10% of earners saw their wages rise by 62%.

In 2003, the richest 10% of the population received nearly one-third of total disposable income compared with only 3% received by the poorest 10%. However, despite a commitment to eradicate poverty, income inequality worsened further under Labour – in 2007, the top 0.1% received 4.3% of all income whilst the poorest 10% received only 3%.

Roberts argues that these **income inequalities** are the direct result of class inequalities in that upper-middle class company executives and senior managers are able fix their own salaries, unlike people in working class occupations who are told how much they will earn. The former can also supplement their salaries with financially lucrative stock options, bonuses and profit-sharing deals because they have day-to-day operational control over corporations and, in some cases, actually own the majority of shares in the company. One example is Philip Green who, in October 2005, was the chief executive of Arcadia, and was criticised for paying himself £1.4 billion in salary. Moreover, the reduction in tax rates for top earners from 83% to 40% in 1979 enormously benefited this group.

Poverty

In 2000, the Low Pay Unit estimated that 45% of British semi-skilled and unskilled workers were earning less than two-thirds of the average wage. Furthermore, many of them were caught in the **poverty trap**, i.e. they earn above the minimum level required to claim benefits, but the deduction of tax, etc. takes them below it. Similarly, many on benefits actually end up worse off if they take low-paid work because they are no longer eligible for state support.

The number of people experiencing **relative poverty** in Britain has continued to rise steeply since 1997, e.g. **Savage** estimates that in 1997 there were three times as many people in relative poverty than there were in the 1970s. Child poverty has particularly increased – 40% of children are born into families in the bottom 30% of income distribution and the government has estimated that up to 25% of children will be in poverty as adults. **Feinstein** (2007), in a survey of 17 000 children born in 1970, found that a child born to a labourer was six times more likely to suffer extreme poverty by the age of 30 than one born to a lawyer.

Wealth

The twentieth century saw some redistribution of **wealth** in Britain. In 1911, the most wealthy 1% of the population held 69% of all wealth, yet by 1993 this had declined to 17%. However, this redistribution did not benefit the mass of the population. Rather, the very wealthy 1% passed its wealth to its children in order to avoid paying taxes in the form of death duties. In 2003, the top 1% and top 10% owned 18% and 50% of the nation's wealth respectively.

Roberts observed that the least wealthy half of the population owned just 7% of all wealth and that about 30% of adults do not own the home in which they live. About one half of all employees do not have an occupational pension to see them through old age. At least one half of the population has near-zero assets and when bank overdrafts, mortgages and credit cards are taken into consideration, most are in debt. Roberts notes that it is only the extremely wealthy who can expect to die with most of their wealth intact and observes that the proportion of the population with enough wealth to ensure that they do not have to work for others is still less than 1%.

Health

This links to material in Chapter 4 on health.

The evidence suggests that the working class experience poorer **mortality rates** and **morbidity rates** than the middle classes, e.g. 3500 more working class babies would survive per year if the working class infant mortality rate was reduced to middle class levels. Babies born to professional fathers have levels of infant mortality half that of babies born to unskilled manual fathers.

Death rates for Britain fell steadily between 1972 and 1997, but death rates for professionals fell by 44% and for the unskilled by only 10%. **Bartley *et al.*** (1996) note that men in social class I had only two-thirds the chance of dying between 1986 and 1989 compared with the male population as a whole. However, unskilled manual workers were one-third more likely to die compared with the male population as a whole. Despite the national health Service (NHS) providing free universal health care to all, men in social class V were twice as likely to die before men in social class I.

Education

> **KEY POINT**
>
> Only about 7% of all children are educated at private schools, but these pupils take up 45% of Oxbridge places. Some commentators have observed that public schools (the costs of which average £25 000 per annum) are the cement in the class walls that divide British society.

Research by the Sutton Trust research charity suggests that the 70th brightest sixth-former at Westminster or Eton is as likely to get a place at Oxbridge as the very brightest sixth-formers at a large comprehensive school. Other Sutton Trust studies show quite clearly that those in high status jobs, such as senior politicians, top business leaders, judges or journalists are often privately and Oxbridge educated. Moreover, the 'old school tie' network ensures important and valuable social contacts for years to come, particularly in the finance sector of the economy.

This is sometimes referred to as 'social capital'.

On the other hand, many working class children perform relatively poorly in the educational system, e.g. more working class children leave school at the age of 16 with no qualifications than middle class 16-year-olds and, while the number of working class 18-year-olds entering university has increased, the number of middle class undergraduates still far exceeds them.

> **PROGRESS CHECK**
>
> 1. How did the Registrar-General's scale classify the occupations of teacher and refuse collector?
> 2. Why do you think feminists were very critical of the RG scale?
> 3. Why do you think Marxists were very critical of the RG scale?
> 4. What is a cross-class family?
> 5. What is the NS-SEC classification based on?
>
> Answers: 1. As Social Class II and V respectively. 2. Because it was based on head of household and assumed that this was the male. Women were therefore classified according to their husband's or father's jobs. 3. It doesn't include the upper class who live off their wealth. 4. A family in which there are two breadwinners who have jobs that are classified in different classes. 5. The employment relations and market conditions of jobs.

9.2 Changes in the class structure

LEARNING SUMMARY	After studying this section, you should be able to understand: • changes in structures of inequality and their implications for particular social groups • sociological explanations of changes in class structure

Changes in structures of inequality

AQA **SCLY 4**   OCR **G674**

The upper class

It has been argued that the upper class, especially the landed gentry have declined in wealth, power and influence over the course of the twentieth century. In particular:

- many upper class families have had to sell their country houses
- some have been forced to take on paid work and consequently experienced downward mobility
- some sociologists suggest that the upper class is in danger of being assimilated into the upper-middle class.

A number of observations about the contemporary nature of the upper class can be made on the basis of the evidence available.

Inherited wealth

The upper class is still very wealthy. The top 10% of the population still own about one half of the country's wealth, whilst the top 1% own about one-third of it. Furthermore, the evidence suggests that **inheritance** is very important. In general, individuals or families are wealthy because their fathers are also rich. Inheritance is responsible for most of the inequality in the distribution of wealth, i.e. the richest 1% of the population is redistributing its wealth to the richest 10% via trust funds in order to avoid families paying inheritance tax.

Scott argues that the upper class is a **unified property class** which owns and controls major sections of the manufacturing, financial (e.g. banks) and retail (e.g. supermarkets) sectors. Moreover, a significant proportion of this group is made up of the traditional 'landed gentry' and aristocracy who have 'merged' with the industrial rich via investment and marriage.

The evidence also suggests that the upper class practises **self-recruitment** and **social closure** (i.e. wealth and power is kept within the class) via:

- marriage between wealthy families
- an old-boy network based upon public school and Oxbridge links
- inter-locking directorships (i.e. upper class individuals will sit on the boards of several companies)
- membership of exclusive gentlemen's clubs.

A major means of ensuring social closure is the emphasis on **public school education**. Generation after generation of upper class children have been educated at fee paying public schools, such as Eton, Harrow, Winchester, Westminster, Charterhouse and Rugby. The large movement of such pupils into the elite universities of Oxford and Cambridge reinforces such students' belief in their 'difference' from the rest of society and their sense of entitlement.

> **KEY POINT**
>
> A good example of the power of social closure can be seen if we examine the political establishment following the General Election in May 2010. Despite the fact that only 7.3% of the British population attend private fee paying schools, 56% of the coalition cabinet in 2010 went to private schools as did 35% of MPs. Furthermore, 20 MPs were educated at one school alone (Eton), including David Cameron, the Prime Minister. The majority of the Coalition cabinet also attended Oxbridge.

Scott argues that the upper class's influence is not confined to business. There is overwhelming evidence that those in top positions in politics, the civil service, the church, the armed services and the professions come disproportionately from upper class families. Scott refers to this group as the '**establishment**' – a coherent and self-recruiting body of men with a similarity of outlook who are able to wield immense **power**. However, exactly how this group interacts and whether they do so for their own benefit is extremely difficult to prove.

The super class

Adonis and Pollard (1998) suggest that the upper class is in the process of assimilating a new group which they call the **super class**. This group is based on people in the old professions (especially law) who have made their fortunes in the City, accountants and managers of investment funds and directors of the former public utilities (e.g. water, gas, electricity, British Rail, etc.) who earn astronomical salaries. Members of this super class tend to **inter-marry** and therefore earn combined super salaries. They can be distinguished from the rest of society by their **consumption patterns**, which revolve around nannies and servants, second homes, exotic holidays, private health and pension schemes and private education for their children. Most of this super class live in London and the south-east.

The middle classes

The process of globalisation has implications across various topics, including crime, religion and the mass media.

In 1911, 80% of workers were in manual occupations (i.e. working class jobs). However, this number fell to 52% in 1981 and to 32.7% in 1991 as both the **primary** and **secondary sectors** of the economy went into decline because of new technologies, the oil crisis and **globalisation** (i.e. the same raw materials and goods can be produced more cheaply in developing countries).

Since 2000, non-manual workers (i.e. traditionally seen as the middle class) have become the largest occupational group in the workforce. This was because the tertiary or service sector of the economy that is organised around education, welfare, retail and finance have expanded hugely since the 1980s. Mass secondary education and the expansion of both further and higher education have ensured the existence of a well educated and qualified workforce. The service sector is made up of a mainly male professional workforce at its top end but, as a result of changes in women's social position, the bulk of workers in this sector are female.

Savage (1995) notes that in 1991, 29.4% of the workforce worked in the professions and management, 10.7% were self-employed and 27.2% were routine white-collar workers. In other words, 67.3% of the working population could be considered as middle class. As Savage notes, there are now more university lecturers than coal miners.

The boundary problem

Sociologists tend not to agree on which occupational groups should be classified as middle class. This is the so-called **boundary problem**. Traditionally, differentiating between the middle class and working class was a simple task. It involved distinguishing between white-collar or non-manual workers on the one hand and blue-collar or manual workers on the other. Generally, the former enjoyed better working conditions in terms of pay, holidays, promotion possibilities, etc. Today this distinction is not so clear-cut.

> **KEY POINT**
>
> **Savage** (1992) argues that the middle class is now **fragmented** and can be seen in terms of **class fractions**. Savage identifies six class fractions – higher and lower professionals, higher and middle managers, the self-employed or 'petit-bourgeoisie' and routine white-collar workers.

Higher and lower professionals

Savage et al. argue that the **professional sector** mainly recruits internally, i.e. the sons and daughters of professionals, such as doctors, solicitors and teachers, are likely to end up as professionals themselves. The position of professional workers is based on the possession of **educational qualifications**. Savage argues that professionals possess **economic capital** (i.e. a very good standard of living, savings, etc.) and **cultural capital** (e.g. they see the worth of education and other cultural assets such as taste in high culture) which they pass on to their children. Moreover, professionals have strong **occupational associations** that protect and actively pursue their interests (e.g. the Law Society, the British Medical Association) although the lower down the professional ladder, the weaker these associations/unions become (e.g. those of teachers).

The concept of class identity is also relevant to material in Chapter 2.

The result of such associations actively pursuing the interests of professionals is high rewards, status and job security. Savage concludes that professionals are aware of their common interests and are quite willing to take **collectivistic** action to protect those interests. In this sense, then, professionals have a greater sense of **class identity** than any other middle class group.

However, there is a danger that as the state sector becomes increasingly privatised, and/or subjected to financial cuts, many professionals will face an increased threat of redundancy and reduced promotional opportunities as a result of (for example) de-layering (a reduction in the number of 'tiers' of management in an organisation).

Higher and middle managers

Savage suggests that many managers have been upwardly mobile from the routine white-collar sector or from the skilled working class and consequently they often lack qualifications such as degrees. Many will have worked their way up through an organisation. Their social position, therefore, is likely to be the result of **experience** and **reputation** rather than qualifications.

Savage argues that **job security** differentiates professionals from managers – managers are less likely to have job security and are constantly under threat from recession, mergers or downsizing. Middle managers, e.g. bank managers, may find themselves unemployed, downwardly mobile into the routine white-collar sector or they might become self-employed.

The self-employed

An example of a middle class fraction.

Between 1981 and 1991, the number of **self-employed** or **petit-bourgeoisie** rose from 6.7% of the workforce to over 10%. Research by **Fielding** (1995) examined what the self-employed in 1981 were doing in 1991. Fielding showed that two-thirds of his sample were a relatively stable and secure part of the workforce in that they remained self-employed over this ten-year period. The character of the self-employed has changed in some respects too. The number of managers who prefer to work for themselves, i.e. as consultants, rose considerably in the 1980s especially in the finance and computer industries.

Routine white-collar workers

Marxists such as **Harry Braverman** argue that routine white-collar workers are no longer middle class. Braverman argues that they have been subjected to a process of **proletarianisation**. This means that they have lost the social and economic advantages such as superior pay and working conditions that they enjoyed over manual workers. Braverman argues that, since the 1990s, employers have used technology, especially computers, to break down complex white-collar skills such as book-keeping into simplistic routine tasks. This process, known as **de-skilling**, is an attempt to increase output, maximise efficiency and reduce costs. Control over the work process has therefore been removed from many non-manual workers.

These developments have been accompanied by the parallel development of **feminising** the routine white-collar workforce especially in the financial sector, because female workers are generally cheap to employ and are seen by employers as more adaptable and amenable to this type of work.

> **KEY POINT**
>
> Braverman therefore concludes that de-skilling means that occupations that were once middle class are today in all respects indistinguishable from those of manual workers.

This links to discussions of class identity in Chapter 2.

However, **Marshall et al.** (1988) have challenged the idea of proletarianisation. In a national random sample of female workers, they found that it was mainly manual workers who claimed that their work had been de-skilled. Over 90% of non-manual workers felt that little had changed, and most identified with the middle class rather than the working class. They were also more likely to vote Conservative than Labour. Marshall et al. concluded that proletarianisation among routine white-collar workers was not taking place.

The working class

Lockwood's (1966) research in the 1960s found that many workers, especially in industrial areas, subscribed to a value system that he called **proletarian traditionalist**. Workers felt a strong sense of loyalty to each other because of shared work experience. They had a keen sense of class solidarity and consciousness and tended to see society in terms of **them versus us**, i.e. employers versus employees.

The embourgeoisement thesis

However, it was argued in the 1960s by **Zweig** that a section of the working class – skilled manual workers – had adopted the economic and cultural lifestyle of the middle class. This argument was known as the **embourgeoisement thesis** because it insisted that skilled workers had developed bourgeois values and were supportive of the Conservative Party.

This idea was investigated by **Goldthorpe and Lockwood** in their *Affluent Worker* study of car assembly workers at the Vauxhall factory in Luton in the late 1960s. They found little evidence to support Zweig's assertion because 77% of their sample voted Labour. However, they did argue that there were signs of **convergence** between working class and middle class lifestyles. Goldthorpe and Lockwood suggested that the economic basis for **class identity** and solidarity was weakening and identified the emergence of the 'privatised instrumentalist' worker who saw work as a means to an end rather than as a source of identity. These affluent workers were more **home-centred** than traditional working class groups and were less likely to subscribe to the notion of working class community and 'them versus us' attitudes. If they took any form of collectivistic action, it was in pursuit of higher pay or to protect living standards relative to other groups of workers who they perceived as 'better-off'.

> This links to discussions of class identity in Chapter 2.

However, **Devine** (1992) undertook a second study of the Vauxhall plant at Luton in the late 1980s and she argued that Goldthorpe and Lockwood's study may have exaggerated the degree of working class privatisation. She found that workers retained strong kinship and friendship links and had a reasonably developed working class identity in that they were critically aware of class inequalities such as the unequal distribution of wealth and income.

Although the concept of embourgeoisement is now rarely used, it is frequently argued that the working class have fragmented into at least two different layers.

- The **traditional** working class, in decline and typically situated in the north of England.
- A **new** working class found in the newer manufacturing industries, mainly situated in the south, who enjoy a relatively affluent lifestyle, but still see themselves as working class.

The underclass

There are two versions of the **underclass** theory – one which blames the victim and one which blames society. The **victim-blaming** version is associated with the **New Right** and sociologists such as **Murray** and **Saunders**. It is suggested that the underclass is a distinct group that exists in the inner-city and on council estates which subscribes to a 'way of life' or culture made up of deviant values and norms. It is argued that such values include being work-shy, being welfare-dependent, lacking commitment to family life and engaging in criminality. New Right sociologists argue that this value system differs sufficiently significantly from the mainstream working class for this group to constitute a separate and distinct social grouping. Moreover, this underclass is reproduced generation by generation as parents **socialise** their children into this **culture**. The Welfare State is seen as perpetuating such a system because knowledge that benefits are available demotivates people in their search for work.

> This version draws on several themes and concepts across the specification including culture, norms and values, crime and socialisation.

In contrast, the **structural view** of the underclass focuses on structural features of society and stresses that structural obstacles, beyond the control of individuals, are responsible for their poverty and encourage fatalism and dependency, e.g. many people are long-term unemployed because of recession or the fact that goods can be produced more cheaply in the Third World. Groups such as ethnic minorities may be denied access to jobs and decent housing because of racism. Single mothers may find it impossible to return to work because of a lack of free child-care.

> **KEY POINT**
>
> This approach to the underclass therefore argues that poverty needs to be seriously tackled if the underclass is not to be scapegoated for its position at the bottom of the socio-economic hierarchy.

This links to material in Chapter 4.

Charlesworth's study of working class people in Rotherham in Yorkshire is typical of an approach to the working class which suggests they are victims of economic forces beyond their control. Charlesworth found class seeping into all aspects of life in Rotherham. Generally, he found that people's lives were characterised by suffering and depression, especially if they were unemployed. Charlesworth found that miserable economic conditions have a profound negative effect on people's physical and mental health. Many of the unemployed workers experienced a lack of identity and a strong sense of being devalued. Furthermore, working class boys saw no point in working at school or in achieving qualifications if they were not able to obtain decent work.

This links to material in Chapter 3.

Post-modernism and the death of social class

In the 1990s, post-modernist sociologists argued that class had ceased to be the prime determinant of identity. It is suggested that societies were now organised around **consumption** rather than production. Consequently, people identified themselves in terms of what they consume rather than in terms of social class position. Class identity therefore fragmented into numerous separate and individualised identities.

Look back at the chapter on education to illustrate the view that social class is still very important.

These ideas have been echoed by politicians who, in recent years, have been fond of suggesting that social class is dead or in decline, for example, in 1999 Tony Blair claimed that 'we are all middle class now'.

This links to discussions of social class and identity in Chapter 2.

However, the evidence does not support these post-modernist or political claims. **Marshall's** research suggests that post-modernist ideas may be exaggerated. Surveys indicate that social class is still a significant source of identity for many. Members of a range of classes are aware of class differences and are happy to identify themselves using class categories. Finally, post-modernists conveniently ignore the view that consumption depends on having a job and adequate levels of income, e.g. poverty is going to inhibit any desire to pursue a post-modern lifestyle. In other words, consumption and social class are closely related.

9.3 Social mobility

LEARNING SUMMARY	After studying this section, you should be able to understand:
	• the definition of social mobility
	• the nature and extent of social mobility in Britain

Defining social mobility

AQA **SCLY 4**

Social mobility studies provide evidence for sociologists to assess whether Britain is a meritocratic society.

KEY POINT

Social mobility refers to the movement of individuals between social classes. Such movement can be either upward or downward. Sociologists distinguish between **inter-generational mobility** (movement between generations, e.g. father and son) and **intra-generational mobility** (movement between jobs within the lifetime of an individual, e.g. starting on the shop-floor and working up to company director).

- Functionalist and New Right thinkers believe that social mobility studies are important because they support their belief that Britain is an open society or a meritocracy offering equal opportunities.
- Weberians argue that social mobility studies are important in order to test theories such as embourgeoisement and proletarianisation.
- Marxists argue that social mobility studies are useful in exposing the 'myth of meritocracy'.

Studies of social mobility

AQA **SCLY 4**

The Oxford (Nuffield) Mobility Study (OMS)

Think about how feminist approaches would criticise this study.

The Oxford (Nuffield) Mobility Study (OMS), conducted in 1972 and associated with the sociologists **Goldthorpe and Heath**, carried out 10 000 interviews with men aged between 20 and 64 years of age. Goldthorpe allocated these men to three broad classes (the **service class**, the **intermediate class** and the **working class**) on the basis of market situation (e.g. salary, fringe benefits, promotion prospects, job security) and work situation (e.g. power, control, autonomy). The research uncovered three major findings.

- The OMS found that only a small minority of the service class in 1972 had been born into that class. Most of the service class in 1972 was recruited from either the intermediate or working class.
- The OMS found high rates of **absolute mobility**. This refers to the total mobility that takes place within a society. Comparing sons with fathers in their sample, the OMS discovered much greater opportunities of being upwardly mobile into the service class in the 1950s and 1960s. However, as Goldthorpe pointed out, this was not necessarily the product of meritocracy. Rather Goldthorpe identified three alternative reasons for this profound change.
  - The service class had almost doubled in numbers because of changes in the job market created by post-war economic expansion in areas such as the Welfare State. This led to a greater demand for professionals and bureaucrats in the fields of education, welfare and health. Moreover, the

nature of the economy changed and the financial sector, in particular, had expanded in the 1950s at the expense of heavy industry.

– The fertility rates of the service class were too low to cope with the growth of service sector jobs. This sector therefore had no choice but to recruit from other social classes.

– The introduction of free secondary education in 1944 made this recruitment easier because for the first time people from other social classes, especially the working class, had access to educational qualifications.

● However, the OMS also challenged the view that this evidence indicates meritocracy by examining rates of **relative mobility**. This refers to comparisons of mobility between different social groups. The OMS data indicated that some social groups were more likely than others to fill the top service jobs. Analysis of the OMS data revealed the 1:2:4 **Rule of Relative Hope** which suggests that for every one working class male who reaches the service class, two males from the intermediate class achieve the same goal, whilst four sons of the service class would remain in the class of their fathers.

> The OMS does not support the view that Britain is a meritocracy.

Other studies of social mobility

Social mobility studies in the 1980s confirm the pessimistic conclusions of the OMS. **The Scottish Mobility Study (SMS)**, conducted by **Payne** (1987), noted that the potential for social mobility was dependent upon age and region, e.g. working class young people working in urban areas in the south of England were more likely to experience upward mobility compared with those in the north and Scotland. Moreover, living and working in urban areas generally led to more opportunities than living and working in rural areas.

> The SMS and the EUMS do not support the view that Britain is a meritocracy.

The Essex University Mobility Study (EUMS) led by **Marshall** (1984) found that someone starting in the service class, rather than the working class, had a seven times greater chance of ending up in the service class. The figure increased to thirteen for women. One explanation for these continuing disparities is that the expansion of service class jobs has slowed down and even ended. This is supported by recent upward trends in middle class unemployment levels.

The Saunders critique

The **New Right** sociologist **Saunders** (1995) argues that all mobility studies acknowledge improvements in absolute levels of mobility and that this is convincing evidence that capitalism has opened up new opportunities for advancement and brought benefits to the working class.

> The NCDS is an example of a longitudinal study. It is a secondary source of quantitative data.

Saunders, using data from the **National Child Development Study (NCDS)**, argues that there is a **genetic** base to social mobility and suggests that people with middle class jobs are generally brighter than those with working class jobs. Saunders claims that, like height and weight, there is a genetic base to most of the abilities and intelligence that people develop. Bright parents, therefore, have bright children. Saunders argues that the best predictor of where we end up in terms of occupations and social class is innate ability or merit, which he claims is twice as important as social class background. He also suggests that middle class parents are better at motivating their children. He further concludes that private schooling, cultural capital, material conditions in the home and parental contact with schools are only a minor influence on a child's future destination.

> Think about how Saunders would position himself in the Nature vs. Nurture debate.

> This links to material in Chapter 3 on education.

Criticising Saunders

Saunders' methodology has come under sustained attack. **Roberts** (2001) is critical of Saunders' use of intelligence tests and argues that it is impossible to measure raw innate ability. He argues that performance in intelligence tests, the construction of such tests, and definitions of ability and intelligence are socially constructed, i.e. they reflect middle class and academic definitions which bear little resemblance to the complex abilities and types of intelligence found in working class environments.

Best (2005) argues that Saunders' sample was biased towards the middle class because he excluded part-time workers, housewives and the unemployed. Moreover, other research has clearly shown that some teachers often **label** working class pupils negatively, thereby affecting their motivation. These classroom practices may lead to a **self-fulfilling prophecy** of low achievement. Apparent low ability and motivation may, therefore, be the product of social class in the sense that working class children may not receive the same degree of positive attention from teachers as do middle class children.

> This links to the discussion in Chapter 3 of working class under-achievement in education.

Savage and Egerton (1997), using the same NCDS data as Saunders, argue that people from working class backgrounds need to have more intelligence and more qualifications to reach the same positions as their middle class peers. They note that both the ruling class and the service class are able to find ways of preventing even their less 'able' sons from moving down the social ladder. They found that low-ability children with service class fathers had much more chance of staying in the service class than ending up in other classes. Furthermore, 75% of high-ability sons of service class fathers ended up in the service class compared to only 45% of the high ability sons of working class fathers. This disparity was even greater for working class, high-ability girls who, it seems, had less than half the chance of their service class counterparts of ending up in that class.

> This illustrates one way in which gender and social class interact.

KEY POINT

Savage and Egerton concluded that working class girls need to have higher levels of ability than working class males if they are to progress into the service class. They argue that Saunders' focus on innate ability serves to justify inequality because the idea that some people are 'naturally' less intelligent hides the real cause of their inequality: their social class position.

Twenty-first century mobility studies

The social mobility study of **Blanden et al.** (2005) looked at children born in 1970 and classified them into four income **quartiles** on the basis of family income at the time they were born and what they were earning as adults. They discovered that 37% of children in Britain born into the lowest income group remained there and would probably do so for the rest of their lives. Only an extremely small number of children from the bottom quartiles were able to use educational qualifications in order to make it into the top quartiles. In contrast, children from the highest income group were most likely to be earning high incomes as adults regardless of educational qualifications.

However, **Gorard** (2008) points out that Blanden only used families that had both a father and a son with a known earned income. They ignored all women, most single-parent families and the unemployed. Moreover, Gorard suggests that they focused only on the bad news and ignored the good news that 63% of children born into the bottom quartile moved out of it in terms of income earned as adults.

However, **Goldthorpe and Jackson's** (2007) study of mobility patterns is just as pessimistic as that of Blanden and colleagues. They suggest that there is unlikely to be a return to the generally rising rates of upward mobility that characterised the middle decades of the twentieth century. They argue that the growth of the service sector has peaked and that opportunities for short range upward mobility within the working class have been restricted by a sharp decline in skilled manual jobs.

Social mobility studies of women

The evidence suggests women experience less upward mobility than men. The EUMS found that even when their male and female samples had the same qualifications, women were not as upwardly mobile as men. The **Open University People in Society Survey (OUPSS)** conducted in 1987 concluded that women were more likely to be downwardly mobile compared with men because of career interruptions, e.g. pregnancy, child-care, being the secondary breadwinner. Other social factors such as divorce and the likelihood of being head of a single-parent family also impede upward mobility. When women did experience upward mobility, it was limited to travelling from skilled manual to skilled non-manual.

A study funded by the Economic and Social Research Council, *Twenty-Something in the 90s* (1997), looked at a group of 26-year olds who were born in 1970. It confirmed that class of origin was still a major factor affecting mobility for both men and women. The study noted, however, that middle class women were just as likely as middle class men to go to university and from there into well paid jobs. Unskilled women were 30 times less likely to work full-time compared with professional women. In spite of this, the study found that women's career development opportunities are still influenced by discrimination from male employers and by the fact that society expects women's primary responsibility to be domestic work and childcare, which forces them to downplay their careers.

Ethnic-minority social mobility patterns

Roberts argues that all non-White minorities experience an **ethnic penalty** with regard to social mobility, in that educational and occupational outcomes are lower and the risks of unemployment are higher compared with White people with similar qualifications. People of Indian heritage are the only ethnic group that does not experience this ethnic penalty.

The ethnic group which seems to experience the greatest inequality in terms of social mobility are African-Caribbeans. This group is most likely to under-perform in education and is most likely to be unemployed.

Platt (2005) notes that many immigrants to Britain in the 1950s experienced **downward mobility**, in that well qualified Asians were forced to take jobs in manual work. Platt conducted a study of second and third generation Asians and African-Caribbeans and compared job destinations with parents, who were often immigrants. She found that 35% of her Indian sample and 22% of her African-Caribbean sample had service class jobs, compared with 38% of her White control sample. However, like the OMS before her, she concludes that this is due to the expansion of the service class and contraction of the working class rather than to any significant change in equal opportunities. She also noted that the children of African-Caribbeans employed in the service class were less likely than Indians to stay in that class. They were more likely than any other group to experience downward social mobility to the working class.

> **KEY POINT**
>
> Platt concludes that, in the face of **institutional racism** and **economic deprivation**, social class may be weak in protecting ethnic minority groups against the possibility of downward social mobility.

PROGRESS CHECK

1. Define inter-generational and intra-generational mobility.
2. What is meant by absolute mobility?
3. Identify three reasons why absolute mobility increased up to the 1980s.
4. What is relative mobility?
5. What is the 1.2.4 Rule of Relative Hope?
6. How does the EUMS confirm the findings of the OMS?
7. What two factors does Saunders use to explain middle-class advantages in mobility?

Answers: 1. Inter-generational mobility means movement between generations whilst intra-generational mobility means movement within one's lifetime. 2. The total mobility that takes place within a society. 3. The increase in the size of the service class, the failure of the service class fertility rate to cope with this increase and a more qualified population. 4. Mobility as compared between different social classes. 5. Data that reveals that the children of professionals have more opportunity of becoming professionals themselves than working class children. 6. The chances of working class children getting top jobs has narrowed even further. 7. Genetic advantages and superior child-rearing practices.

9.4 Dimensions of inequality

LEARNING SUMMARY

After studying this section, you should be able to understand:
- patterns and trends in life chances by ethnicity, gender, disability and age
- the different dimensions of inequality in terms of class, status and power

Ethnicity and inequality

AQA **SCLY 4**   OCR **G674**

The term **race** refers to the classification of human beings into different biological groups on the basis of physical characteristics such as skin colour. **Ethnicity** refers to the cultural and social characteristics of particular groups such as language, shared history, religion and cultural traditions. Usually the term ethnicity is used in relation to comparatively small and powerless minorities who subscribe to significantly different customs and beliefs from a majority culture, which they live alongside.

This links to material in Chapter 8.

> **KEY POINT**
>
> There is a good deal of evidence that **ethnic minority** groups in Britain are subjected to **racism**. Racism refers to a combination of discriminatory practices, unequal relations and power and prejudice. **Institutional racism** is the idea that racist assumptions are built into the rules and routines of Britain's social institutions, thus neglecting the specific needs of ethnic minorities. Recently both the Home Office and the London Metropolitan Police have separately admitted that their organisations are institutionally racist. This type of racism is taken for granted and habitual. In other words, it has become so institutionalised, it is not recognised as racism, e.g. in the police force, the practice of automatically assuming that Black youth are suspicious or criminal.

Prejudice refers to a type of negative thinking that relies heavily on stereotypes which are usually factually incorrect, exaggerated and distorted. **Discrimination** is prejudice put into practice. There are several different types.

This is relevant to material in Chapter 3.

- **Name-calling and bullying** – in 2002, the Department for Education and Skills found that 25% of pupils from ethnic minority backgrounds in mainly White schools had experienced racist name calling within the previous seven days, whilst a third of the pupils of ethnic minority backgrounds reported experiences of hurtful name calling and verbal abuse either at school or during the school journey.

This is relevant to material in Chapter 8.

- **Racial attacks** – according to the Institute of Race Relations, between 1991 and 1997 there were over 65 murders in Britain with a suspected or known racial motive. More than 61 000 complaints of racially motivated crime were made in 2006–07, a rise of 28% in just five years.
- **Employer racism** – in 2004, a BBC survey showed ethnic minority applicants still face major discrimination in the job market. CVs from six fictitious candidates – who were given traditionally White English, Black African-Caribbean or Muslim names – were sent by BBC Radio Five Live to 50 well known firms covering a representative sample of jobs. All the applicants were given the same standard of qualifications and experience, but their CVs were presented differently. White 'candidates' were far more likely to be offered an interview than similarly qualified Black or Asian 'candidates'. Almost a quarter of applications by two White candidates resulted in interview offers compared with only 9% of the Muslim applications and 13% by the African-Caribbean candidates. In 2007, the Commission for Racial Equality reported that they had received 5000 complaints from ethnic minority workers during the first half of 2007.

Ethnicity, workplace inequality and discrimination

Ethnic minorities are disadvantaged compared with the ethnic majority population. In 2007, the **unemployment rate** for ethnic minorities was over 11% – twice the national average. In 2004, White people had the lowest unemployment rates at 5%. The highest unemployment rates were among Black African-Caribbean men (14%). Indian men (7%) had the lowest unemployment rates among the ethnic minority groups. In 2004, 37% of Bangladeshis aged 16–24 and 35% of Pakistanis were unemployed compared with 11% of White young people. Furthermore, an African-Caribbean graduate is more than twice as likely to be unemployed as a White graduate, while an African graduate is seven times as likely.

Ethnic minority men were less likely than White men in 2004 to be employed in skilled trades (12% compared with 20%) and more likely than White men to be employed in unskilled jobs (16% compared with 12%).

The manual jobs that are available to ethnic minorities are often dirty, poorly paid and involve unsociable hours, e.g. shift-work. Ethnic minority men are over-represented in the service sector, especially in restaurant businesses.

Ethnic minorities also generally earn **low incomes** because of their likelihood of occupying semi-skilled and unskilled manual work, e.g. in 2004 White men were paid an average of £1.80 per hour more than ethnic minority men. Research by The Joseph Rowntree Foundation in 2007 found that men from ethnic minorities in managerial and professional jobs earn up to 25% less than their White colleagues. African-Caribbean and Bangladeshi men were most likely to face the greatest pay discrimination. Indian men were the least likely to be discriminated against, but they were still earning less than White men doing the same job.

> **KEY POINT**
>
> However, a degree of upward social mobility exists within British Asian communities, e.g. 47% of Indian men were professional, managerial and technical workers in 2000, compared with 41% of White men.

Sociological explanations for ethnic inequalities

AQA **SCLY 4**   OCR **G674**

The host-immigrant model or assimilation theory

Patterson's (1965) **host-immigrant** model depicts Britain in the 1950s as a basically stable, homogeneous and orderly society with a high degree of consensus over values and norms. However, Patterson claims that this equilibrium was disturbed by the arrival of immigrant 'strangers' who subscribed to different cultural values. Patterson suggested that there were three causes of racial tension and prejudice.

- White people's (i.e. the host culture) fear of strangers, cultural difference and social change.
- The White working class's resentment at having to compete with ethnic minorities for scarce resources such as jobs and housing.
- The failure of ethnic minorities to assimilate, i.e. to become totally British and integrate – they tended to live in segregated communities rather than socially mixing.

This model has influenced political responses to racial tensions, e.g. the Labour government of 1997–2010 introduced 45-minute multiple-choice nationality or **citizenship tests**. In order to get British citizenship, immigrants must successfully answer questions on aspects of British culture and swear an oath of allegiance to the Queen. Some commentators have suggested that this Britishness test should have a language component to ensure all potential citizens can speak and write English.

Critics of this assimilationist host-immigrant approach point out that African-Caribbeans are the most assimilated of all ethnic minority groups. They speak English as a first language at home, they inter-marry into the White population, their children mix freely and easily with White children and they are usually Christian. There are no cultural barriers preventing them from assimilating into

British cultural life. However, the economic, social and educational position of African-Caribbean people is no better than it was 50 years ago. They are still more likely to be unemployed and in poverty than White people and their children are still most likely to fail academically or be excluded from school.

> **KEY POINT**
>
> Patterson can also be criticised because she failed to acknowledge that Britain is a **multicultural society** and that the concept of assimilation is **ethnocentric** – it fails to recognise that no one culture is superior and that all cultures, British and ethnic minority, have similar value. The host-immigrant model focuses so much on culture that it tends to end up 'blaming the victim' or scapegoating them, by attributing racism and racial inequality to their 'strange' cultures.

Weberian explanations

Parkin argues that ethnic inequalities stem from **status inequality** which Weberian sociologists see as being just as influential as social class. Status and power are in the hands of the majority ethnic group, making it difficult for ethnic minority groups to compete equally, e.g. for jobs and housing.

The **dual labour market theory** of **Barron and Norris** suggests that there are two labour markets – the **primary sector** characterised by secure, well paid jobs with long-term promotion prospects dominated by white men, and the **secondary sector**, characterised by low-paid, unskilled and insecure jobs. Barron and Norris point out that Black people are more likely to be found in the secondary sector. They are less likely to gain primary sector employment because employers may subscribe to racist beliefs about the unsuitability of Black people and practise discrimination against them when applying for jobs or deny them responsibility and promotion.

The focus here is on racism.

> **KEY POINT**
>
> Some Weberians, especially **Rex and Tomlinson**, argue that ethnic minority experience of both class and status inequality can lead to **poverty** – which is made more severe by racism. Consequently, a **Black underclass** may exist which lacks any power to change its situation and which feels alienated and frustrated. This sometimes results in inner-city riots.

In criticism, there is considerable overlap between the White and Black population in terms of poverty and unemployment. However, some members of the White working class do not recognise the common economic situation they share with Black and Asian workers.

Marxist explanations

The concept of 'ideology' can be applied within topics across the specification.

Marxists are adamant that Black people are part of the exploited working class and they generally see status inequality as less important than **class inequality**. They argue that racism is a **capitalist ideology** aimed at encouraging White workers to perceive Black workers as a threat to their jobs. Marxists therefore see racism as a **divide and rule** tactic. Black people can also be scapegoated for unemployment (e.g. beliefs like 'they've come over here to take our jobs') or for inner-city decline (e.g. 'this was a nice neighbourhood before they moved in').

The focus here is on how racism benefits capitalism.

Criticisms of Marxism

It is difficult to prove that racism is a capitalist ideology. If racism is of benefit to capitalism, this is probably an accidental by-product rather than a deliberately constructed ideology.

Robert Miles

Miles argues that we should see ethnic minorities as members of **racialised class fractions**, meaning that there are significant cultural differences between them and the White working class. Miles argues that the class position of ethnic minorities is complicated by the fact that they are treated by White society as socially and culturally different, and consequently they have become the victims of **racist ideologies** that prevent their full inclusion into British society.

At the same time, ethnic minorities too may set themselves apart from the White majority by stressing and celebrating their unique cultural Identity, e.g. young African-Caribbeans may stress black power through membership of the Rastafarian sect or by stressing elements of black history. Asians may stress family ties and community. The result of this may be little contact between Black, Asian and White working class communities which may encourage greater suspicion and mutual hostility.

> This relates to material in Chapter 6 on sects.

Miles also notes that some ethnic minorities who are members of the middle class may see their interests as lying with capitalism. Their ethnic culture, e.g. the Asian emphasis on entrepreneurship, enterprise and mutual support, may be advantageous in achieving business success. Recent statistics suggest that there are currently over 5000 Muslim millionaires in Britain. However, Miles points out that racism probably means that the white middle class do not accept that Asian professionals have the same status as them. They are, therefore, a racialised class fraction within the middle class.

PROGRESS CHECK

1. What is the difference between race and ethnicity?
2. What is meant by institutional racism?
3. Which two ethnic-minority groups are relatively successful in gaining access to professional and managerial jobs?
4. What do Weberians see as the main cause of ethnic inequalities generally?
5. Why do Marxists see racism as an ideology that benefits capitalism?
6. What does Miles mean when he says Black people exist as a racialised class fraction within the working class?

Answers: 1. Race refers to physical differences whilst ethnicity refers to cultural differences. 2. Racist assumptions that are built into the rules and routines of institutions in such a way that racist practices go unrecognised as such. 3. Indians and Chinese. 4. Status inequality in the form of racism. 5. It divides and rules the working class and diverts White working class grievances away from employers to Black people. 6. They are objectively part of the working class but will never be accepted as such by the White working class. They therefore develop alternative ethnic identities.

Gender and inequality

AQA **SCLY 4**   OCR **G674**

Since the 1950s there has been a trend towards the **feminisation** of the labour force, e.g. between 1969 and 1989 the number of female workers in Britain rose by 2.25 million (whereas males rose by only 0.5 million). In 2008, there were 13.6 million of each sex in the British workforce.

Labour market segmentation

Sociologists have noted that the labour market is both **horizontally** and **vertically** segregated in terms of gender.

Horizontal and vertical segregation are also discussed in Chapter 3 on education (3.3).

- **Horizontal segregation** refers to the sectors in which people work. A survey by the Equal Opportunities Commission (EOC) in 1996 concluded that women in the public sector were mainly employed in health and education, especially teaching, e.g. nursing and primary school teaching is almost exclusively female. In the private sector women are over concentrated in clerical, administrative, retail and personal services such as catering, whereas men are mainly found in the skilled manual and upper professional sectors, e.g. a fifth of women in employment, 20% do administrative or secretarial work, compared with 4% of men. There is some evidence that horizontal segregation may be in decline because there has been a decline in areas traditionally dominated by men such as factory work and heavy industry. Increasing female educational success, especially in higher education, has resulted in more women entering areas of work currently dominated by men, such as the medical, legal and financial sectors of the economy, e.g. in 2005, according to the Women and Work Commission, 75% of pharmacists, nearly 40% of accountants and about 50% of solicitors were women.

- **Vertical segregation** refers to levels of jobs and pay. Women tend to be concentrated at the lower levels of employment in terms of skill and consequently status, e.g. 66% of full-time secondary school teachers in 2007 in England were female, but only 30% of secondary school heads were. In 2007, male primary school teachers were three times more likely than female primary teachers to become head teachers.

- Even when women gain access to the upper professional or management sector, they are likely to encounter a **glass ceiling** or an invisible barrier to promotion. In 2008, women made up only 11% of directors of the top 100 British companies, a quarter of NHS consultants, 10% of high court judges and just two out of 17 national newspaper editors. The Equality and Human Rights Commission estimated in 2008 that it will take another 73 years for women to achieve equality in top management jobs in Britain's top 100 companies. Women are also more likely than men to be employed in part-time work and in temporary or casual work.

- There exists a **gender pay gap**. In 1998, the EOC noted that the average gross weekly pay of all women was only 72.5% of men's earnings. The EOC estimates that the average pay gap between men and women is 17%. However, it rises to 22.3% in the private sector, although it is only 13.4% in the state sector, e.g. the difference in earnings in 2006 between men and women in health and social work jobs was 32%, and in banking and insurance it was 41%.

Sociological explanations of gender inequality

AQA **SCLY 4**   OCR **G674**

Functionalism and human capital theory

Functionalist sociologists suggest that the pay gap between men and women is justified because men have more **human capital** than women. Functionalists claim that women are less committed to paid work and are more likely to take career breaks or to opt for part-time work in order to continue to care for their families. Men, on the other hand, build up their skills, qualifications and experience because they are in receipt of more education and training and their employment is not interrupted by family commitments.

However, human capital theory has been criticised by **Olsen and Walby** (2004). They used data from the British Household Panel Survey to investigate the causes of pay differences between men and women. Olsen and Walby argue that the main cause of women's low pay is 'systematic disadvantage in acquiring human capital', e.g. pay is lower in occupations where there are high concentrations of women. This is because these jobs provide less training and promotion prospects than those jobs in which men are in the majority. Furthermore, human capital theory assumes that experience of employment increases wages, yet experience of part-time work which is female dominated is actually associated with a slight reduction in wages.

This is an example of a secondary source of quantitative data.

The dual labour market theory

The **dual labour market theory** of **Barron and Norris** suggests that women are more likely than men to be found in the **secondary labour market** because employers subscribe to stereotypical beliefs about the unsuitability of women. Promotion streams are organised in ways that match the life experiences of men better than those of women because employers demand continuous service. Barron and Norris argue that women are more likely to be found in the disadvantaged secondary sector for three reasons.

This theory has also been applied to explain the experiences of minority ethnic groups.

Focuses on male domination of the primary labour market.

- There is some evidence that employers may hold stereotypical beliefs about the 'unsuitability' of women for primary sector roles. **West and Zimmerman** (1991) noted that employers in the 1990s subscribed to myths and negative stereotypes about women workers such as:
  - male workers do not like working for a female manager – employers are therefore reluctant to promote females to management positions
  - women are less dependable because they often take time off work to deal with family commitments
  - women will stop work when they marry and have children, so there is little point investing in their long-term training.
- **Caplow** (1954) argues that women's continuous employment is undermined by motherhood and the fact that the husband's career and pay is often regarded as more important. Therefore, if his job requires a move to another part of the country, wives are often forced to interrupt their careers and give up their jobs.
- The Equal Pay and Sex Discrimination Acts are ineffective because they fail to protect women's employment rights. **Coussins** (1976) noted that the government has done little to promote free or cheap nursery care or to encourage employers to provide crèche facilities for their workers who are mothers.

This links to material in Chapter 1 on families.

Neo-Weberian sociologists, such as **Barron** and **Norris**, are therefore arguing that women experience **status inequality** because of **patriarchy**. The patriarchal nature of society makes discrimination against women at work both 'natural' and possible. Better qualifications and increased ambition for women may not therefore automatically dismantle gender divisions in employment. Women with the same qualifications as men will continue to be disadvantaged as long as these two labour markets continue to exist and are underpinned with patriarchal assumptions about the role of women.

However, in criticism, **Bradley** points out that Barron and Norris fail to explain gender inequalities within one sector, e.g. teaching is not a secondary labour market job yet women are less likely than men to gain high status jobs in this profession.

Liberal feminism

Think about other areas in which the idea of 'social construction' is applied.

Liberal feminists argue that gender roles are largely **socially constructed** through the **socialisation process**, primarily in the family, but also through such secondary agencies as the education system and the mass media. In other words, **gender role socialisation** is responsible for reproducing a sexual division of labour in which masculinity is largely seen as dominant and femininity as subordinate. Liberal feminist research in the 1970s, in particular, focused on how the dominant images of females disseminated by such agencies as the family and education. Mass media stressed marriage as a priority and education and careers as secondary.

This illustrates the relevance of gender inequalities to topics across the specification.

Liberal feminists have suggested that these processes are now coming to an end. **Sharpe's** work on the attitudes of teenage girls suggests that education and careers are now a priority for young women, whilst females have also enjoyed great educational success in recent years. Another liberal feminist, **Oakley**, argues that the main reason for the subordination of women in the labour market is the dominance of the mother–housewife role for women. She argues that patriarchal ideology stresses the view that a woman's major function is to raise children and that family rather than career should be the main focus of their lives. The fact that female professional workers are three times more likely not to be married than their male counterparts also supports this view, as does the fact that being childless increases a woman's chances of becoming a director of a major company.

In your answers, it is important to show an awareness of social changes.

In criticism, **Walby** (1990) suggests that although there is evidence that masculinity and femininity are socially constructed, liberal feminism does not explain why this leads to men dominating and women being oppressed. Second, it implies that people passively accept their gender identities and underestimates the **degree of resistance** of women. Third, it fails to acknowledge that women's experiences differ according to social class and ethnicity.

When revising this and other topics, think about how gender, social class and ethnicity interact.

Marxist-feminism

Marxist-feminists suggest that **capitalist ideologies** locate women in the home. The idea that married women have less right to a job than men is common among management, unions and women themselves. Women make up a **reserve army of labour** which is hired when the economy is booming. Therefore when women are made unemployed, such ideology operates to suggest that 'women have gone back to their proper jobs'.

This approach focuses on capitalism.

According to **Benston** (1972), women benefit capitalism in two important ways.
- Women provide free domestic labour, which functions to make male workers more effective. The housewife, by providing a comfortable home, meals, etc. provides emotional and domestic support for her husband so that he can return to work as a healthy and efficient worker. Women have returned to the labour market in large numbers since the 1980s, but surveys indicate that women in relationships with men still take most of the responsibility for housework and child-care.

This links to material in Chapter 1 on families.

- Women are also responsible for raising the **future labour force** at no extra cost to the capitalist class.

The reserve army of labour theory has its criticisms.
- It does not explain why male and female labour is put to different uses. In other words, it fails to explain why there are men's jobs and women's jobs.
- If women are cheaper to employ than men, surely capitalists would get rid of the more expensive men. In other words, men's jobs would be more insecure.

- **Walby** (1986) points out that when women stay at home this is damaging to capitalism because women competing with men for jobs would probably lower wages and increase profits. Women who earn also have superior spending power, which boosts capitalism.
- Some feminists have suggested that if patriarchy is universal, i.e. found in all societies, then its origin may be biological. It has been suggested that whilst women are in the stages of advanced pregnancy, childbirth and childrearing, they are more likely to be dependent on men. Patriarchy may therefore be the product of women's reproductive role rather than capitalism.

Triple-systems theory

> When revising, think about how the concept of patriarchy can be applied within different topics across the specification.

> **KEY POINT**
>
> **Sylvia Walby's triple-systems theory** develops the concept of patriarchy to explain gender stratification and suggests that patriarchy has three elements to it.
> - **Subordination** – patriarchal institutions like the family, media and education inevitably produce unequal relations between men and women.
> - **Oppression** – women experience sexism because men discriminate against them on the basis of unfounded stereotypes or ideology.
> - **Exploitation** – men exploit women's skills and labour without rewarding them sufficiently, e.g. in the home.

Walby argues that **patriarchy interacts with capitalism and racism to produce gender stratification**. This results in the subordination, exploitation and oppression of women in the family, at work, in sexual relations (e.g. the sexual double standard) and in culture systems (e.g. the mass media represents women either as sex objects, as appendages of men or as mothers). The State, too, acts in the interests of men rather than women, e.g. in terms of taxation and welfare rules, and the weakness of laws protecting women at work. However, Walby does acknowledge that inequalities between men and women vary over time and in intensity, e.g. young women are now achieving better educational qualifications than young men.

Criticisms of feminist approaches

Feminist theory has not gone uncriticised. A huge amount of debate has been generated by all the approaches explored above.

> When revising bear in mind that women are not necessarily a homogeneous group. It is important to consider how women may be divided by social class or ethnicity.

- There does not seem to be much agreement between feminists about how patriarchy should be defined, what its causes are and the forms that it takes in modern societies.
- **Delamont** (2001) has pointed out that feminist writers seem to assume that women share a common position of exploitation and she suggests that there are many **divisions** between women on grounds of income and social class, ethnicity and religion.
- Feminists often fail to take into account the changing nature of modern societies, which has resulted in women rapidly acquiring social, legal, educational and economic benefits. It is argued that if modern societies were truly patriarchal, women would remain fixed into a subordinate position. This is obviously not the case in Britain today.

Rational choice theory

Hakim is extremely critical of all the previous feminist positions. She argues that feminist theories of patriarchy are both inaccurate and misleading and that women are not victims of unfair employment practices or patriarchy. Rather they make **rational choices** in terms of the type of work they do, e.g. they choose part-time work in order to manage child-care and housework because they choose to put child-care first. She argues that a lack of available and affordable child-care is not a major barrier to women getting jobs because mothers prioritise child-rearing over employment. In other words, women are not as committed to careers as men.

This sort of data on British social attitudes is usually collected by using social surveys. Think about the strengths and limitations of using surveys to measure social attitudes towards family life.

Scott (2008) found that support for gender equality appears to be declining across Britain because of concerns that women who play a full role in the workforce do so at the expense of family life. She found that women and men are becoming more likely to believe that both the mother and the family will suffer if a woman works full-time. In 1994, 51% of women and 52% of men in Britain said they believed family life would not suffer if a woman went to work. By 2002, those proportions had fallen to 46% of women and 42% of men. There was also a decline in the number of people thinking that the best way for a woman to be independent is to have a job.

Hakim's work has also provoked criticism, e.g. **Ginn and Arber** point out that all too often it is employers' attitudes rather than women's attitudes that confine women to the secondary labour market.

Disability

AQA **SCLY 4**

Defining disability

> **KEY POINT**
>
> A great deal of the literature on disability tends to use the two related concepts of **impairment** and **disability** interchangeably. Impairment refers to any psychological, physical or anatomical loss or abnormality that affects how a person functions on an everyday basis. Disability refers to the resulting **disadvantages** experienced by people with impairments that make it difficult for them to perform their 'normal' roles and which may result in **inequality** compared with non-disabled people.

According to the Department of Work and Pensions (DWP), in 2006 there were 10.1 million people living in Britain who were classed as 'disabled'. Of this group, 9.5 million are adults, with 4.6 million being over retirement age, whilst 700 000 are children.

The medical model

This links to material in Chapter 4.

The medical model explains the economic disadvantages experienced by people with disabilities in terms of individual impairment. **Hyde** (2001) notes that health, housing, employment, educational and welfare policies aimed at providing services for people with disabilities overwhelmingly focus on individual limitations. However, critics such as **Davies** note that this model ignores the wider social influences that impact on the individual over which they have no control, e.g. the medical model fails to recognise social barriers that prevent people with disabilities from fully participating in society.

The social model

Shearer (1981) argues that 'disability' is something imposed on disabled people by the patterns and social expectations of a society organised by and for the non-disabled. The social model, therefore, argues that 'disabled people' are actually disabled and stratified by society rather than by their impairment. In particular, the social model highlights two major social barriers that prevent people with disabilities from participating fully in society.

- Social institutions act in a **discriminatory** fashion that undermines disabled people's potential for independence.
- The **attitudes** and **beliefs** (i.e. prejudices and stereotypes) that non-disabled people hold portray people with disabilities in a negative light and consequently oppress them.

Thompson (1993) argues that there exists a combination of social forces, cultural values and personal prejudices that marginalise people with disabilities and produce a type of inequality which he calls **disableism**.

Marxist theory of disability

This view is also discussed in Chapter 4 on health.

Oliver argues that industrialisation and the factory system introduced intense labour processes such as assembly line production and, as a result, the worth of individuals came to be assessed according to their economic value – efficient, quick work was seen as immensely profitable.

Paid employment, especially in factories, became the main source of **identity** and **status**. Those among the working class who were not employed, e.g. the chronically sick and disabled, were seen to have an inferior social status compared with waged workers. Oliver argues that this social exclusion of disabled people from economic life was reinforced by state policy in the nineteenth century in two ways.

- The state transferred the responsibility for the assessment, treatment and care of people with disabilities to medical professionals. This resulted in the ideological dominance of the medical model of disability.
- Disabled people were increasingly committed to long-stay hospitals – their treatment often resulted in institutionalisation.

Disability, inequality and stratification

AQA **SCLY 4**

Bear in mind that people with disabilities are not a homogeneous group. They also belong to a social class, ethnic and age group.

This links to discussions of media representations in Chapter 7.

Hyde argues that disableism, and the inequality that results, can clearly be seen in the prejudice that underpins everyday beliefs, language and mass media representations of disabled people. Moreover, Hyde argues that disableism takes institutional forms too and can be clearly seen in the following routine practices.

- **Morris** (1992) argues that prejudicial attitudes towards people with disabilities revolve around the view that they should be segregated from non-disabled society. **Davies** notes that people with disabilities are often seen as possessing **discrediting** characteristics, e.g. wheelchair users are often stereotyped as ugly, **asexual**, intellectually impaired, unable to speak for themselves, bitter and dependent. Furthermore, they are most often portrayed as deserving of our pity.

- **Media representations**, too, reinforce prejudicial attitudes towards people with disabilities in two ways. **Barnes** (1992) notes the existence of negative stereotypes on television and in the print media and suggests that people with disabilities are often portrayed as pitiable, pathetic and evil. He also argues that even what most people might regard as positive images are actually stereotypical assumptions, e.g. stories about the 'extraordinary heroism' or 'remarkable courage' of people with disabilities present them as 'super-cripples', whilst television appeals such as 'Children in Need' reinforce the notion that people with disabilities should be the recipients of our pity and charity. Barnes notes that we rarely see media images of disability that reflect the real-life experience of people with disabilities.

> This links to discussions of labelling theory and labelling processes within education, the media and the criminal justice system.

Davies argues that such stereotyping is immensely powerful because it results in **social segregation**. Non-disabled people have very little contact with people with disabilities. It also acts as a **master status**, in that people with disabilities are often seen exclusively in terms of their impairment. This creates the potential for a **self-fulfilling prophecy** as people with disabilities learn that dependency and helplessness are expected of them. Hyde notes that disabled people may develop a negative self-identity. They may lack self confidence and self-esteem and passively accept discrimination, exclusion and disadvantage.

Institutional forms of discrimination

Hyde (2001) argues that institutional discriminatory practices against people with disabilities are common, e.g. although access to services like shops, public transport or leisure facilities is steadily improving, there is still widespread inaccessibility, which can actively restrict people's opportunities. Hyde suggests that people with disabilities are still often **excluded** from mainstream social activities by the leisure and retail industries, as well as from transport systems.

> This links to material in Chapter 3 on different types of school. Can you think of an argument for and against special schools?

Hyde notes that large numbers of children and young people with impairments continue to be educated in **special schools**. He argues that this segregation from mainstream education reinforces cultural prejudice and discrimination.

Disability and employment

In 2005, only 50% of people with disabilities were in employment compared with 81% of the non-disabled. Furthermore, people with disabilities were nearly four times more likely than non-disabled workers to be unemployed, i.e. 47% of disabled workers were unemployed in 2005, though they were also more likely to be in part-time work and manual jobs compared with non-disabled workers.

Low pay is another aspect of the **institutional discrimination** experienced by people with disabilities in employment. In 2005, disabled workers received average gross hourly pay that was 10% less than that received by non-disabled workers. Research also suggests that disabled applicants for jobs are six times more likely to be refused an interview than non-disabled applicants, even when they have suitable skills and qualifications. Furthermore, employers are often reluctant to adapt their working environments to the needs of disabled workers.

Disability and poverty

A report by Leonard Cheshire Disability estimated that up to 3 million people with disabilities were **trapped in poverty** in 2007. The report notes that people with disabilities are twice as likely to live in poverty as non-disabled people, i.e. 16% of non-disabled people live in relative poverty compared with 30% of people with disabilities. This is because, compared with the able-bodied, people with disabilities face extra costs related to managing their impairment, such as paying for adaptations to the home, social care support, mobility aids or communication aids. When these extra costs of disability are taken into account, the report estimates that about 50% of people with disabilities are living below or around the official **poverty line**, set at 60% of average national income.

Disability and politics

Oliver (1990) notes that people with disabilities are excluded from the formal political process and that they are often not invited to take part in official discussions about their rights and needs. Legislation on disability is often made by able-bodied politicians and civil servants, who have a poor understanding of what people with disabilities need. Inappropriate services are often the result. Even the charities and pressure groups that represent the interests of people with disabilities often fail to provide them with a voice in their management.

Many people with disabilities have responded to this lack of political representation by embarking on what has been described as the '**last great civil rights battle**'. Hyde notes that these disabled activists have challenged negative stereotypes by becoming self-organised. The movement is aimed at transforming official responses to the needs of people with disabilities and developing a positive disabled identity.

Age stratification

AQA **SCLY 4**   OCR **G674**

> **KEY POINT**
>
> In most societies, age is divided up into significant periods – childhood, youth or adolescence, young adulthood, middle age and old age. These periods have different social meanings attached to them with regard to social expectations about behaviour and lifestyle, responsibilities to others, independence and dependence, and so on. These age categories, or **age strata**, are not 'natural', but created by society. They are **social constructions**.

The elderly – the demographic picture

This links to material in Chapter 1.

The decline in the death rate, especially the infant mortality rate and the increase in life expectancy, has led to an **ageing of the population**. There are increasing numbers of people aged 65 and over and decreasing numbers of children under 16. Between 1971 and 2004, the number of people aged under the age of 16 declined by 18% while the number of people aged over 65 increased by 29%. Consequently, in 2008, about 18% of the population, i.e. approximately 11 million people were over retirement age.

Age and inequality

The annual *Spotlight* report by **Help the Aged** (2008) suggests that in 2005–06, 11% of British pensioners, i.e. 1.2 million people, were living in **severe poverty** on less than half of average earnings. Nearly double that number – 21%, or 2.2 million people – were classified as living in poverty, with incomes less than 60% of average earnings. These figures suggest that nearly a third of the elderly are in poverty. The *Spotlight* report claims that such poverty is having a negative effect on the **health** of the elderly – one in four of the elderly poor suffered illness as a direct result of poverty.

There is some evidence that in 2007 an additional 200 000 pensioners were experiencing 'fuel poverty', meaning that they were spending at least 10% of their income on electricity, gas and coal just to stay warm.

Age, gender, ethnicity and social class

> When revising it is important to consider other ways in which age, gender, ethnicity and social class interact to bring about inequality.

KEY POINT

Age interacts with social class and gender to bring about inequality. People who are poor in old age are most likely to be those who have earned least in their working lives, i.e. women and those employed in manual jobs.

Davidson notes that the majority of those people who are not eligible for – or who cannot afford the contributions required for – participation in private occupational pension schemes are female. This is because they are more likely to have their careers interrupted by pregnancy and child-care, and are more likely to be employed in low-paid, part-time work for a significant period of their lives. **Mordaunt et al.** (2003) report that as a result, twice as many elderly women compared with men rely on benefits and one in four single (never married, widowed or divorced) women pensioners in Britain live in poverty.

> It is important not to view 'the elderly' as a homogeneous group. They also, for example, have a social class and ethnic identity.

Scase and Scales (2000) argue that 'the elderly' are likely to be split between **affluent early retirees** and those who are on or close to the **breadline**. This latter group may have to continue working beyond retirement age in order to avoid severe poverty, especially as the value of state pensions relative to earnings has been declining since the early 1990s. **Ray et al.** (2006) also note that the retirement age often differs according to **social class** and **status**, e.g. senior business executives and political leaders have the power to resist the official legal retirement requirement and consequently they may avoid the potential poverty, and negative connotations associated with being elderly or retired.

The effects of ageism

> Can you think of examples of ways in which young people might experience ageism?

Butler (1969) defined **ageism** as a process of **negative stereotyping** and **discrimination** against people purely on the grounds of their chronological age. The elderly have mainly been the victims of this discrimination. Butler suggested that discrimination against older people was composed of three connected elements.

- Prejudicial attitudes towards older persons, old age and the ageing process.
- Discriminatory practices against older people.
- Institutional practices and policies that perpetuate stereotypes about older people.

Institutional ageism

> This links to material in Chapter 4 on health.

Greengross argues that the NHS is guilty of **institutional ageism** because older patients in the NHS are treated differently from the young. Older people are subjected to discrimination in that they are often omitted from clinical trials or are denied particular treatment or operations on the basis of their chronological age. Greengross notes that these decisions are usually based on prejudiced views of what a 'good innings' is, or on the view that the interventions are not worth pursuing because a person is 'too old'.

Greengross also notes that the elderly experience ageism with regard to services that other members of society take for granted, e.g. ageism practised by financial services may mean that older people have difficulty in hiring a car, getting insurance, getting a credit card or negotiating a loan.

Ageist attitudes

It can be argued that all these ageist practices result in negative stereotypes under-pinning social attitudes about the elderly in modern Britain, so dehumanising members of this group. The elderly have already lost a major source of status, respect, identity and economic security (work) when they have been forced to retire. However, ageist practices and stereotypes result in their association, particularly by the young, with dependence, vulnerability and disability. The elderly are generally seen as making little or no contribution to society and/or as a burden on society.

The young

Like the elderly, the young also make up a large subgroup of the poor. A quarter of children live in households receiving less than 60% of the average median income. In addition, many young people of working age face social deprivation caused by low pay, student loans, ineligibility for benefits and unemployment. In 2005, the unemployment rate for those under 25 was over 18%.

Young people at work

Most young workers earn relatively little and are given less responsibility and status in almost every occupational sector. In 2010, some 227 000 18 to 20-year-old workers earn the **minimum wage**. Young workers are central to many industries, but are generally subjected to the worst pay and conditions and required to be the most 'flexible'. This is particularly evident in retail and catering. More than two-thirds of McDonalds' staff are aged under 20, while the Restaurateurs' Association says that in the commercial sector of the hospitality industry, 31% of staff are aged 16 to 24. Of the nearly two million young people aged between 16 and 24 in full-time education, 40% are also in paid employment.

Theoretical explanations of age inequality

AQA **SCLY 4**   OCR **G674**

Functionalism

Functionalists such as **Parsons** (1977) considered age to be of increasing importance in modern societies. In pre-industrial society, Parsons argued, age did not really matter because **family** determined one's place in society. However, since industrialisation, people have been more socially and geographically mobile, and age groups have become more important. Parsons argued that they provide **role sets** that create a link between the kinship group and the wider society.

Pilcher (1995) suggests that youth is a **stage of transition** that connects childhood (which is mainly experienced as dependency upon adults in families and schools) to adulthood (which is mainly experienced as independence at work and in relationships that might lead to the setting-up of families). In this sense, age is important as a mechanism of **social integration** – it allows people to move from one social institution to another without too much social disturbance or conflict. However, critics note that there is a strong possibility that such social order might be undermined by unemployment, low pay, the expensive housing market, the lengthening of education and higher education costs. All these trends are likely to lead to more dependence on the family.

This links to material in Chapter 1 on families.

Functionalists, such as **Cummings and Henry** (1961), suggest that the way society treats older members has positive benefits for society. The ageing process and the social reaction to it is part of a mutual process in which the elderly, either by voluntary choice or legal compulsion, are encouraged to abandon their occupational roles within the specialised division of labour. The implication here is that the ageing process inevitably leads to social incompetence.

This process of **social disengagement** functions to allow younger members of society to take the place of older members in the specialised division of labour with minimum disruption to either social order or economic efficiency. However, critics of **disengagement theory** point out that retirement from work and society is often not voluntary. Moreover, this disengagement also has negative consequences for the self-esteem of the elderly in terms of ageism. Critics of functionalism point out that disengagement often leads to the neglect of the experience, skills and talents of older members of society which could still be of great benefit to society. Furthermore, disengagement theory ignores the fact that many old people continue to be active participants in society.

Marxism

According to Marxists, the young provide a cheap **pool of flexible labour** that can be hired and fired as necessary. They tend not to have dependants and so are willing to work for low wages. In terms of full-time employment, their lack of experience legitimates low pay and competition for jobs keeps wages low.

Marxists, such as **Phillipson** (1982), suggest that the logic of capitalism is incompatible with the needs of the elderly. Consequently, they are neglected by the capitalist system because they no longer have the disposable income or spending power which is so attractive to capitalists. Moreover, as **Kidd** (2001) notes, because their labour power is no longer of any use to capitalism, the elderly are seen as a drain on its resources through their use of welfare and health provision. Consequently, in capitalist societies such as Britain, early retirement and increasing life expectancy mean that the elderly have little or no **status** because they are likely to possess little **economic power**. As a result, the elderly are more likely to be in poverty and to experience ill-health as an aspect of that poverty.

Post-modernist theory

Post-modernists, such as **Blaikie** (1999), argue that chronological age, ageism and age determined inequality are less likely to shape people's life experience in the twenty-first century. Such approaches suggest that British society has undergone a social transformation from social experiences based on **collective identities** originating in social class and generation to an increasingly **individualised** and **consumerist culture** in which old age can be avoided by

This links to material in Chapter 2 on identities.

investing in a diverse choice of youth preserving techniques and lifestyles. However, critics argue that not everyone can afford to purchase the techniques and lifestyles, even if they aspire to them.

PROGRESS CHECK

1. According to the social model, what are the two major barriers that may prevent people with disabilities from participating fully in society?
2. What is meant by the term 'ageism'?
3. According to post-modernist approaches, is chronological age likely to have more or less influence in shaping people's lives in the future?

Answers: 1. Institutional ageism/social institutions that act in discriminatory ways; the prejudices against people with disabilities. 2. A process of negative stereotyping and discrimination on the basis of age. 3. Less influence.

Exam practice questions

Question 1 is an example of a synoptic question that reflects the type of question that you could be asked in the AQA examination. You will be rewarded for applying your knowledge and understanding of sociological research methods to the study of this issue in stratification and differentiation.

Question 2 is an example of a synoptic question that reflects the type of question that you could be asked in the OCR examination. In answering such questions, you should draw on your knowledge of the relevant material in Chapter 9. However, to maximise your marks, you should also draw on your wider sociological knowledge of social inequality and difference from relevant topics across the specification.

1. Read Item A and then answer the question that follows.

Item A
The British Social Attitudes Survey is an annual household survey. It generates data on the public's changing attitudes towards social, economic, political and moral issues. It involves interviews with around 3350 adults who are selected on the basis of random probability sampling. The response rate is around 52–53%.

Data from the British Social Attitudes Survey (2008) can be used to highlight changing social attitudes to gender, e.g. in 1989, 32% of male respondents and 26% of female respondents agreed with the statement that a man's job is to earn money and a woman's job is to look after the home and family. In 2006, only 17% of men and 15% of women agreed with this statement.

However, while attitudes to gender roles may have changed a lot since the late 1980s, men's participation in household tasks has not changed significantly, e.g. the British Social Attitudes Survey (2008) found that in most cases, women 'always' or 'usually' do the laundry.

Using material from Item A and elsewhere, assess the strengths and limitations of social surveys as a means of investigating people's views on gender issues. **(15 marks)**

2. Outline and assess Marxist explanations of social class inequality. **(40 marks)**

10 Theory and method

The following topics are covered in this chapter:

- Is sociology a science?
- Subjectivity, objectivity and value-freedom
- Sociological theories of society
- Sociology and social policy

10.1 Is sociology a science?

LEARNING SUMMARY

After studying this section, you should be able to understand:

- the nature of science
- the strengths and weaknesses of arguments that suggest sociology is scientific
- the relationship between positivism, interpretivism and sociological methods

The nature of science

AQA **SCLY 2**
   SCLY 4

Remember that AQA Unit 4 SCLY 4 and OCR Unit G674 are synoptic.

This links to material in Chapter 6 on different belief systems.

KEY POINT

Lawson argues that science differs from other **belief systems** because it provides objective evidence for its propositions using logical and systematic means of collecting data. In other words, it is **empirical**. Science is an attempt to create knowledge that is 'true' and certain. Other belief systems such as common sense and religion are based upon individual perceptions and beliefs. They are partial and subjective. They depend upon faith or experience rather than fact.

Positivism

Positivism was also discussed in Chapter 5.

Positivists are thinkers who believe that science – and science alone – can provide unbiased knowledge which is generalisable (i.e. it is true in many situations, not just one specific case) and which can solve social and sociological problems.

Auguste Comte

Positivist sociology originated with the work of **Auguste Comte** (1798–1857). He believed that the social world closely resembled the natural physical world and argued that both were made up of **objective facts**, which were independent of individuals and waiting to be discovered. Comte believed that behaviour in both the natural and social world was governed by **external laws**. He argued that sociology could be a **science of society** engaged in discovering the social laws governing human behaviour.

Comte believed that society should be studied using **scientific methods** of analysis to produce accurate, quantified data. The term **positivism** derives from this emphasis upon the positive sciences, on tested and systematic experience.

> **KEY POINT**
>
> Positivism is closely identified with and its methodology closely modelled on the traditional scientific world.

The aim of positivists – whether they are natural or social scientists – is to produce **scientific laws** about any phenomena: laws that accurately describe the causes, functioning and consequences of phenomena. Positivists have developed a 'model' scientific approach to research which is known as the **hypothetico-deductive approach**. This involves a number of logical steps in carrying out research.

- **Observation** – a phenomenon or problem is observed to exist and needs explanation.
- **Hypothesis** – a possible explanation is put forward.
- **Experiment** – the hypothesis is subjected to rigorous testing to see if it holds up.
- **Theorising** – if confirmed by the experiment, a law is created which explains all identical phenomena or problems.

See also the discussion of these steps in Chapter 5.

In the testing of hypotheses, the **laboratory experiment** is the preferred technique of the positivist natural scientist.

> **KEY POINT**
>
> The sociological positivist insists in the testing of hypotheses, the **laboratory experiment** is the preferred technique of the positivist natural scientist.
>
> The sociological positivist insists that the methods and techniques applied in research should display certain essential features.
>
> - They must be **objective**, possibly **quantitative** (involving numbers or statistics) and under the control of the researcher.
> - They should satisfy the criteria of **reliability**, that is, if repeated, the same findings would always emerge.
> - The method of collection should be **systematic** and **standardised**.
> - The findings should be **generalisable** so that social laws (even if only partial laws) can be established.
>
> Positivists argue that **official statistics** meet these scientific criteria. There is little opportunity for error or subjectivity to affect the 'truth' of hard data such as birth or death statistics. The **social survey** incorporating the use of questionnaires and structured interviews is popular with positivist sociologists because it gathers quantifiable data. It is regarded as objective and reliable.

As part of your revision think about how positivist sociologists would view methods such as unstructured interviews or participant observation.

Karl Popper

Karl Popper argued that the most important characteristic of scientific knowledge was that it should be capable of being **proved false**. Popper claimed that there is no such thing as 'objective truth'. He claimed that at the very best only partial truth can be achieved because all knowledge is **provisional** or temporary. Popper proposed a scientific method which he called the **conjecture and refutation** model of science which is based on the following logic.

- Scientists make **observations**, although these are limited by the fact that the scientists are **socialised** into particular scientific communities which structure the observation.
- **Hypotheses** or **conjectures** are generated by such observations.
- Experimentation should apply the **principle of falsification**, i.e. the scientist should look for evidence that proves the hypothesis wrong because no amount of evidence in support of a hypothesis can ever prove that hypothesis. On the other hand, a single item of evidence which contradicts the hypothesis will prove it wrong.

> **KEY POINT**
>
> Popper argued that we can never be conclusively right, we can only be conclusively wrong.
>
> Popper therefore concluded that scientists should engage in **industrious scepticism**. Popper was sceptical about the scientific status of sociology because he argued that it deals in **theoretical concepts** that are not open to **empirical falsification**.

Popper was particularly critical of Marxism.

Feyerabend and Kaplan

Paul Feyerabend argues that science is not as logical or as rational as the previous two models of science claim. Feyerabend suggests that what scientists say they do is quite different from what they *actually* do. He claims that there is no such thing as a special scientific method good for all times and places – rather, the rule in science is that 'anything goes'.

A good example of this is Fleming's discovery of penicillin.

Kaplan agrees with Feyerabend and notes that when scientists come to write up their findings in scientific journals, they fail to account for all the blind alleys, false starts, strokes of luck and inspired guesses which are part of their everyday science.

The realist position

Realists, too, believe that positivists and Popper are mistaken about the nature of science. **Sayer** suggests that many sciences are engaged in the study of **unobservable phenomena** such as evolution, sub-atomic particles, magnetic fields, continental drift and black holes. Therefore a number of disciplines which are readily accepted as sciences such as seismology, meteorology, astronomy, and even physics, are based on unobservable structures and processes rather than on hard empirical data.

Keat notes that many sciences cannot make precise **predictions**, e.g. the science of medicine cannot predict with any certainty who will become ill, seismologists cannot predict exactly when an earthquake will occur and meteorologists did not predict the 1987 hurricane in the south-east of England. Sayer and Keat call these types of science **open sciences**. Sociology may be classed as an open science because it, too, is concerned with explaining underlying structures.

Thomas Kuhn

Another example of the way in which the concept of socialisation has been applied.

Kuhn also challenged the positivist and Popperian notion that science is a **method** of collecting data about the world. Kuhn claimed that scientific enquiry is characterised by **conservatism** because scientists are **socialised** into basic assumptions called **paradigms** that they take for granted and rarely question. A paradigm is a particular way of looking at the natural world. It affects the way a scientist sees the world and his or her choice of research method. All evidence gathered is guided by the paradigm. The method of collecting data is therefore dependent upon the dominant paradigm and its dominance blocks the ability of scientists to see contradictory evidence.

In physics, a Newtonian paradigm was overthrown by one based on Einstein's work.

Scientific progress only occurs when pieces of evidence (**anomalies**) build up which cannot be ignored. The established paradigm then loses its credibility and is overthrown in a period of **scientific revolution**. Scientists produce a new paradigm that explains what the old paradigm could not and **normal science** resumes. Kuhn therefore challenged the view that science is a method. Rather he saw science as a **body of knowledge**, i.e. a paradigm. Scientific method depends upon the dominant paradigm of the time. Scientific method is therefore not free to wander in any direction it wishes. It is constrained by 'taken for granted' assumptions about how the world is. Scientific knowledge is therefore **socially produced** rather than discovered.

An example of the way in which the idea of 'social construction' can be applied.

If we accept Kuhn's definition of science as a body of knowledge, then sociology is probably not scientific. It is doubtful whether there has been one sociological paradigm dominant at any one time. However, an alternative argument might be that sociology until the 1960s was dominated by a functionalist or positivist paradigm until it was overthrown by a conflict (or interpretivist) paradigm in the 1970s. Sociologists also point out that the natural sciences are characterised by competing paradigms rather than any paradigmatic unity.

Interpretivist sociology

Also known as anti-positivism.

Interpretivist sociologists are very sceptical about sociology's claim to scientific status. They argue that the logic and methods of the natural sciences are inappropriate for sociological enquiry because the **subject matter** of sociology and the subject matter of the natural sciences are very different. Human beings are active, conscious beings, who are aware of what is going on in a social situation and are capable of making choices about how to act. Natural phenomena lack this **consciousness**.

> **KEY POINT**
>
> Interpretivists believe that social reality is not the product of external social laws. Instead, they suggest that society is **socially constructed**. It is the product of **interaction** and the **interpretations or meanings** that we bring to interaction. People interpret the actions of others and react accordingly. Therefore in order to explain social action, we need to see it from the point of view of the participants. The researchers' task is to investigate how the people under scrutiny view the world around them and how they make sense of it in *their terms*. Interpretivist sociology has therefore developed research methods which aim to do this.
>
> Interpretivist methods aim to be **qualitative** in that they seek to reveal the meanings behind social action. Therefore **ethnographic methods**, i.e. those that focus on the everyday life of 'social factors', such as observation and unstructured interviews are preferred. Emphasis is placed upon *verstehen* (a type of social empathy) and **validity**, and research findings aim to reflect the reality of those being studied.

Think about how interpretivist sociologists would view methods such as questionnaires or structured interviews.

Post-modernism

Post-modernists point out that science dominated the modern world as a '**big theory**' **meta-narrative**. However, it is argued that in the post-modern world science no longer has the monopoly on truth because knowledge is characterised by **diversity**, e.g. a range of ideas have appeared that are challenging science's view of the world – including New Age movements, environmental and green movements, alternative medicines and fundamentalist 'back to tradition' beliefs. Moreover, the status of science is in decline as people increasingly distrust it in the light of environmental damage, pollution and anxieties about nuclear power.

This links to material in Chapters 4 and 6.

PROGRESS CHECK

1. What, according to positivists, is the only belief system capable of producing unbiased knowledge?
2. Which research method is the preferred technique of the positivist natural scientist?
3. Why did Popper believe Sociology to be unscientific?
4. What is a paradigm?
5. How is society socially constructed according to interpretivist sociologists?

Answers: 1. Science. 2. The laboratory experiment. 3. Because it dealt with concepts and theories which were impossible to falsify. 4. A dominant way of looking at the world and approaching problems which scientists are socialised into. 5. Through interaction and the interpretations we bring to it.

10.2 Subjectivity, objectivity and value-freedom

LEARNING SUMMARY	After studying this section, you should be able to understand: • value-freedom, objectivity and subjectivity • the debate about whether sociology can or should be value-free

Objectivity through neutrality

AQA **SCLY 4**   OCR **G671** **G674**

Functionalism

Functionalist sociologists argue that sociological research should avoid **subjectivity**, i.e. being influenced by the personal views and political prejudices of the researcher. They argue that social scientists should not aim to change society. Rather, they should subscribe to **objectivity through neutrality** or **value-freedom**. In this sense, objective social scientists are presented by functionalists as disinterested and trustworthy pursuers of truth. Moral problems therefore are not the scientist's concern because objectivity excludes moral issues. Functionalists argue that science should not concern itself with value judgements.

In functionalist theory, therefore, value-freedom has three dimensions.

- The sociologist should not allow their **prejudices or beliefs** to influence the **research design or process**. It is important that the research tool, e.g. the questionnaire or interview, does not in any way lead the respondents towards the researcher's own beliefs about an issue.
- It is also important that research **data** is **interpreted objectively** by the researcher. **Selectivity** on the basis of prejudice and belief would invalidate the research findings. Sociologists should aim only to see facts as they *are*, not as they may wish to see them.
- It is believed that the job of the sociologist is to objectively carry out research and how the research data is used by **social policy makers** is not the business of the sociologist. It is the functionalist view that it is not the job of the sociologist to solve problems or change society.

The critique of value-freedom

It is argued by some sociologists that the influence of values cannot be avoided in the research process. At the very beginning of research, at the proposal and funding stage, the choice of research topic depends upon those with power making value judgements about what is interesting and worthwhile. These might be university heads of department, funding bodies, government ministers or businesses.

> Research which is critical of government or big business is less likely to be funded.

Gomm argues that when academic resources are low (especially when governments are cutting back on university spending), sociological research may be monopolised by the state and big business. This may mean that it only focuses on issues that these groups see as important, e.g. corporate business has funded an enormous amount of research in the USA aimed at improving worker productivity (e.g. the Hawthorne experiment conducted by **Mayo**).

The research process

> For example, interview bias.

Some sociologists, notably **Derek Phillips**, have argued that data collection is itself a **social process** so we can expect bias and invalidity to arise out of the effects of **interaction**. Some members of society, when faced with a questionnaire or interview, may seek social approval and may therefore act in ways they feel the sociologist will expect or agree with.

The nature of sociology

> This shows how the concepts of socialisation and culture can be applied.

It is argued that the very nature of sociology means that it is **value-laden**. **Alvin Gouldner** argues that value-free sociology is a myth because it is impossible to separate sociologists from what they observe – knowledge does not exist outside of people. It is a **social product**, the result of human actions and values. According to Gouldner, all researchers possess **domain assumptions** – a world-view that is the result of **socialisation** into a particular **culture**. As a result, most sociology reflects Western, capitalist and patriarchal values, e.g. the work of Rostow and modernisation theory stresses the superiority of US democracy and capitalism. Rostow goes as far as calling communism 'a disease'.

Similarly, **Gomm** argues that sociology is a **social activity** carried out by real people in a world characterised by conflicts of interest between different social groups. Any research, therefore, must inevitably take one side or the other, whether the researcher admits this or not. Sociological research, according to Gomm, reflects **ideological** beliefs, e.g. some sociologists – functionalists, sub-culturalists and cultural deprivationists – believe that society is characterised by a consensus on values. These sociologists tend not to engage in social dissent or criticism. Rather, they support the status quo and thus, unconsciously, the values of the establishment. Examples of such sociological ideas would include:

- 'Poverty is the fault of the individual or the culture.'
- 'Crime is a working-class phenomenon.'
- 'Working class culture is inferior to middle class culture.'

This links to material in Chapter 3 on educational under-achievement.

Gomm suggests that by presenting facts as 'truth', such sociologists are able to deny responsibility for the way in which their research is used by policy-makers, e.g. compensatory education (EPAs) introduced in the 1960s was based on the idea that working class culture was somehow inferior. Such policy distracted from other possible causes, e.g. the role of the school and the 'cultural capital' held by the middle class. Gomm suggests that the most important aspect of sociological research therefore is what is not investigated. Such sociology is therefore **ideological** because it helps maintain social inequality.

Marxism

Marxists argue that the major function of scientific knowledge is the maintenance and legitimisation of **inequality**. In this sense, then, science is not objective or value-free. Instead, it supports powerful capitalist interests such as big business or the military.

Prescriptive research

KEY POINT

Some sociologists have rejected the concept of value-freedom because they suggest that it is undesirable to pretend to be value-free. This theme has been taken up by critical sociologists who feel that they must take sides. Many Marxists, such as **Corrigan** and **Willis**, feel they should take the side of the working class. Feminists obviously take the side of women, whilst many involved in labelling studies such as **Becker** take the side of the deviant or the 'underdog'.

Such perspectives acknowledge that values do and should enter sociological research. They argue that sociology should not and cannot be morally neutral or indifferent. Rather, sociology is value-laden. Moreover sociology *should be* **prescriptive** – it should suggest ways forward in order to create a better society.

PROGRESS CHECK

1. What did both Comte and Durkheim believe should be the main purpose of sociology?
2. What is objectivity through neutrality?

Answers: 1. To change society for the better. 2. The idea that sociologists should not take sides and instead be the disinterested pursuers of truth.

10.3 Sociological theories of society

LEARNING SUMMARY

After studying this section, you should be able to understand:

- structuralist theories including consensus and conflict theories
- social action theories
- structuration theory
- the concepts of modernity and post-modernity

Structuralist theories of society

AQA **SCLY 4**

Structural theories are macro-theories in that they study the effects of social structure on social life.

Structuralist theories see human behaviour as constrained, and even determined by, the social organisation of society, i.e. the **social structure** that is made up of inter-related institutions such as families, schools, religion, the economy and the political system. These theories see society as something that **exists externally** to individuals. We are born into a society that already exists and when we die, society continues on regardless. We cannot see or touch society, but we feel its influence on a daily basis because it shapes what we think, feel and do. Structural theories, therefore, argue that we are pushed into courses of action by social structures over which we normally have little or no control. In this sense these theories suggest that people are the product or puppets of society.

When revising think about how structural theories would view methods such as social surveys. How would they view methods such as unstructured interviews?

> **KEY POINT**
>
> Structural theorists take a **positivist** approach in terms of research techniques. They generally use **scientific methods** because their focus on social forces bringing about patterns in human behaviour requires **reliable** techniques of **measurement**.

Consensus theory – functionalism

Functionalism is a structural theory because it sees society as a social system made up of inter-related and inter-dependent institutions such as education, work, religion, law and the family. The main function of these institutions is to maintain **social equilibrium** or **order**. An organic analogy is often employed to illustrate this idea. This suggests society is similar to the human body because our internal organs work together to bring about our physical health – or equilibrium.

Functionalists see individual action as the product of social institutions such as the family and education **socialising** the young into cultural values and norms. The result of this is **value consensus** – people believe in much the same thing and consequently their **actions are patterned and predictable**. Individuals behave similarly in the same social context because they have been socialised into the same cultural rules and goals. Functionalists also see social institutions such as education and work organisations as allocating people to roles in which they will make an effective contribution to the day-to-day running of society.

Functionalists, such as Durkheim, see suicide as influenced by social structure. This is discussed in Chapter 8.

Functionalists, therefore, believe that human action is controlled and shaped by **social forces** (i.e. value consensus and the need to maintain social order) beyond the individual's control. The result of this conformity is **social stability** and the **reproduction of society**, generation by generation. These controls do not exclude the possibility of social change. Functionalists argue that occasionally consensus may break down or be challenged on some issues. However, the likely result of this is gradual change as social institutions adapt to solve the problem and re-establish social order.

Criticism of functionalism

It is argued that functionalists over-emphasise **consensus** and order and play down conflict. They tend to focus on the functions or benefits of social institutions and consequently neglect the **dysfunctions** or harm that institutions can cause individuals, e.g. the family is nearly always seen as a harmonious institution by functionalists and consequently social problems such as domestic violence are rarely acknowledged. Finally, functionalist theory has been accused of **ethnocentrism**, meaning that its view of society and its institutions is an attempt to impose a middle class (and American) view of the world on the rest of us.

Conflict theory – Marxism

Marxism is a **structuralist theory** because it sees society as being made up of two interlocking parts. The most important part – the **infrastructure** – is the economic system, i.e. the way society produces goods. In capitalist societies, goods are mainly manufactured in factories. This production involves a relationship between two economic groups or **classes**. The **bourgeoisie** or capitalist class (also known as the 'ruling class') owns the **means of production** (i.e. land, factories and machines). The **proletariat** (or working class) hires out its labour power (i.e. its skills and strength) to the capitalist class for a wage.

> This links to material in Chapter 9 on social inequality.

The relationship between these two classes is unequal and based on **conflict** because the bourgeoisie aim to extract the maximum labour from workers at the lowest possible cost. The result is that the bourgeoisie exploit the labour of the working class especially because the value of labour when, e.g. sold as a product is worth more than the wage paid. This **surplus value** is pocketed by the capitalist class and is the basis of the vast profits made by many employers. These profits are responsible for the great **inequalities** in wealth and income between the ruling class and the working class.

> The superstructure is a product of the infrastructure. Its role is to help reproduce and legitimise social class inequalities.

The second part of the capitalist social system – the **superstructure** – is made up of social institutions such as the family, education and mass media. Marxists argue that capitalist societies are inherently unstable because of class conflict. However, the function of the superstructure is to reproduce the values and ideas of the ruling class (i.e. **ideology**) so that the working class are unaware of the conflicts of interest that divide them from the capitalist class. The true nature of their exploitation therefore goes unrecognised by the working class or is accepted as natural and inevitable. This **false class-consciousness** ensures that working class conformity and class inequalities in areas such as income, education and health are reproduced generation by generation. Marxists are therefore suggesting that working class behaviour is constrained and shaped by ideology and ultimately by the class inequality that characterises the infrastructure. Free will and social change can only come about once workers become politically conscious and collectively take action.

Criticisms of Marxism

Marxism may put too much emphasis on conflict. Capitalism has considerably improved the standard of living of the working class. It may be that the working class are aware of inequality and exploitation, but they feel that their standard of living compensates for this. They may therefore actively choose to go to work despite this knowledge. Marxism has also been criticised for **economic reductionism**, i.e. reducing all behaviour to class relationships. They may neglect the fact that social behaviour can also be influenced by religious, patriarchal, nationalistic and ethnic structures.

Conflict theory – Feminism

Feminist theory has been very critical of much sociological theory and argues that prior to the 1960s, sociology was 'malestream' in that it largely excluded women and was rarely interested in their behaviour. In the 1970s, feminists set themselves the task of demonstrating how the **patriarchal** (male dominated) structure and organisation of society kept women as a disadvantaged, subordinate and dominated group in most areas of life. On the whole, feminist theories have subscribed to a **conflict perspective** in that they generally see men exploiting women and consequently benefiting in various ways from gender inequality. However, feminism has split into various types that analyse gender relationships in different ways.

Liberal feminism

Liberal feminists tend to be optimistic about social change.

Liberal feminists see society as patriarchal, but suggest that women's opportunities are improving because of the feminisation of the economy, improved educational achievement and a radical change in attitudes that **Wilkinson** terms a **genderquake**. They also note that marriage has become egalitarian because women now have reproductive rights, divorce and economic power derived from better wages.

Socialisation and culture are key concepts that apply to topics across the specifications.

Liberal feminist research generally focuses on how social institutions such as the family, education and mass media encourage male exploitation of women. They argue that these institutions function to ensure that **gender role socialisation** shapes men and women's behaviour according to patriarchal **culture**. However, they argue that gender role socialisation in families is slowly changing in favour of females in that girls are no longer viewed as second class citizens or encouraged to see themselves as subordinate to males. Liberal feminists are therefore very optimistic about the future of females in modern societies.

Marxist-feminism

Marxist feminists generally see women's oppression as a product of the economic position of women. It is argued that women occupy a more subordinate position than men in terms of the class relationships that characterise the infrastructure. Women are semi-proletarianised workers because they are economically below the working class in that they earn less than men and are mainly responsible for domestic labour in the home – which they perform free of charge.

Marxists-feminists such as **Benston** argue that the bourgeoisie uses gender to divide and rule the male and female working class. Patriarchal ideology transmits the idea that women are inferior and subordinate to men in order for capitalism to control and exploit men and women.

Benston argues that capitalism transmits the idea that women's family role as mothers, nurturers and housewives is their most important function because women's domestic labour is crucial to capitalism in two important respects.

- Capitalism requires a **future workforce** – it is the role of the mother-housewife to reproduce and to bring up the future workforce free of charge to the capitalist class.
- The present workforce requires **maintenance** – it needs to be fed and its batteries recharged to be efficient. The housewife role maintains the health and efficiency of the male workforce at no extra cost to the capitalist class.

Radical feminism

Radical feminists suggest that **patriarchy** is far more important than other forms of inequality. They explain women's oppression by arguing that societies are characterised by patriarchal structures. **Delphy**, for example, argues that men and women constitute separate classes and quite simply, men exploit and oppress women. They do this through the use of **ideology** (e.g., through ideas such as a woman's place is in the home or a real woman has children) and the use of physical power or violence, e.g. domestic violence or the threat of rape.

Many radical feminists suggest that patriarchal attitudes and practices are embedded in social institutions that **socialise** both men and women into male-centred ideas and culture. Some argue that the family is the main source of patriarchy. This has led to radical feminists believing that patriarchy permeates the relationship between men and women at two levels. Firstly, it is found in the **structural and ideological features** of social institutions and, secondly, it exists at the **private** level of intimate relations between men and women, i.e. the 'sexual politics' level.

> **KEY POINT**
>
> **Dual-systems theory** combines Marxist and radical feminist ideas and acknowledges that both capitalism and patriarchy are the cause and means of women's oppression and subordination.

Social action or interpretivist theories

AQA **SCLY 2**   OCR **G671**
     SCLY 4   **G674**

Social action theory, also known as **phenomenology** or **interpretivism**, takes a **micro** approach to explaining and understanding human behaviour. It stresses the ability of individuals to exert control over their own actions. The individual is not seen as a passive recipient of society's directions, but as an **active creator** of social behaviour. In this sense, society does not have an independent existence or objective reality. Social situations are not the product of structural factors. Rather, they are the outcome of human beings making choices to engage in **interaction** with each other and the **shared interpretations or meanings** we bring to those interactions. The social world is a world of meaning. In this sense society is the sum of interaction and interpretation and people shape society rather than society shaping people.

When revising consider how interpretivists would view methods such as unstructured interviews. How would they view methods such as social surveys?

KEY POINT

The research methods of interpretivists are devised to make it possible to get at the individual's consciousness and to spell out the shared world-view. Interpretive researchers exploit to the full the fact that their sociological skills make it possible for them to get inside the heads of others and see the world as others see it.

Structuration theory

In recent years, sociologists such as **Giddens**, **Willis** and **Taylor** have argued that the structural and social action approaches need to be combined. **Structuration theory**, which originated with Giddens, stresses that individual action is to some extent shaped by social factors beyond our control, for example social class, race and gender. However, Giddens points out that individuals react to these forces in a variety of ways, e.g. some will negotiate a path through these external pressures whilst others may attempt to resist them altogether. Similarly, people might choose to behave in a certain way, but their choices are limited or shaped by the structure of their society.

Modernity and post-modernity

AQA **SCLY 4**   OCR **G674**

Modernity refers to the modern world which is generally seen as beginning with industrial production and associated with:
- urbanisation (i.e. the growth of cities)
- the growth of the bureaucratic state
- the rise in status of scientific thinking.

Many of the classic sociological theories aimed to explain why modern societies had come about (i.e. social change) and/or to describe and explain why they were organised the way they were. This led to the development of 'big stories' or **meta-narratives**, such as functionalism and Marxism, which claimed a monopoly of truth in regard to explaining the way society worked and had come about.

Post-modernist thinkers argue that in the late twentieth century, society has progressed into a post-modern age. This is characterised by:
- changes in the nature of work, e.g. more flexible working practices
- the **globalisation** of both production and consumption
- the shrinking of space and time because of developments in communication networks like the Internet, e-mail and satellite television
- the loss of faith in science as seen in the rise of environmental politics
- the emphasis on consumption of information
- the emphasis on style and **conspicuous consumption**
- **cultural diversity and pluralism** in a range of social contexts, e.g. the family, media or youth culture.

These changes mean that how we think and how we use knowledge have also changed. Society has become disillusioned with 'big ideas' that claimed to have all the answers because these in reality only created more problems. In a rapidly changing and fragmented world, no theory can lay claim to the truth because of the sheer diversity of experience, institutions and contexts that exist in the world today. Post-modern theories, on the other hand, point out that there are competing theories, many of which will have something valid to offer about the nature of post-modern society.

PROGRESS CHECK

1. What is a structural theory?
2. What do functionalists probably overemphasise?
3. What is the infrastructure?
4. What is *verstehen*?
5. What is the post-modern claim in regard to 'big stories' such as Marxism and functionalism?

Answers: 1. One which believes that human behaviour is determined by the organisation of society, i.e. its social structure. 2. Consensus and social order. 3. It is a Marxist concept meaning the economic systems and the unequal class relationships that underpin it. 4. Empathetic understanding. 5. People have lost faith in them as truth.

10.4 Sociology and social policy

LEARNING SUMMARY

After studying this section, you should be able to understand:
- social and sociological problems
- perspectives on social policy and sociology

Social and sociological problems

AQA **SCLY 4**

In order to understand the relationship between sociology and **social policy**, it is useful to distinguish between **social problems** and **sociological problems**.

Social problems

According to **Worsley** (1977), a social problem is social behaviour that causes 'public friction and/or private misery' which results in calls for government and/or community intervention to solve it, e.g. poverty, educational under-achievement, crime, anti-social behaviour and juvenile delinquency are all seen as social problems by members of society, and governments have produced social policies to tackle them.

Sociological problems

Worsley states that a sociological problem is any pattern of relationships that need an explanation. In other words, a sociological problem is any piece of social behaviour, individual or collective, that we wish to make sense of. This might be something that society regards as a social problem, e.g. why some people are poor, commit crime, or fail in school. But it can also include behaviour that society does not define as a problem, e.g. why most people are law-abiding or why people want to get married.

'Normal' behaviour is just as interesting to sociologists as behaviour that people define as a social problem. **Simmel** (1950), for example, was interested in uncovering the common characteristics present in all social interactions whether these took place in families or queues.

However, some sociologists are focused on solving social problems such as crime, e.g. sociologists who feel strongly about the relationship between poverty and crime have conducted research aimed at discovering solutions to this social problem. Similarly, many sociologists are employed directly by government departments such as the Home Office. These sociologists often have a direct input into making policies and evaluating their effectiveness, e.g. in reducing crime.

The influence of sociology on social policy

However, there is no guarantee that policy-makers will use the findings of sociological research because there are many factors that affect whether sociological research influences policy.

- **Electoral popularity** – research findings may result in a sociologist recommending a policy that might be unpopular with voters, e.g. drugs are a very emotive issue – the recommendation that heroin and cocaine should be de-criminalised in order to cut crime rates is likely to be rejected by most governments.
- **Ideology** – if the researcher's perspective is similar to the political ideology of the government, they are likely to influence social policy, e.g. New Right criminologists and social policies such as zero tolerance, target hardening and targeting the urban underclass have been very influential on both Conservative and Labour crime policies in recent decades.
- **Interest groups** – pressure groups seek to influence government policies, e.g. business interests have persuaded governments to build more privately run prisons in recent years.
- **Globalisation** – what happens elsewhere in the world because of the inter-connectedness of global markets, especially financial markets, has an impact on domestic policy.
- **Critical sociology** – Marxist or feminist sociologists who are critical of the government or the traditional ways in which social institutions, such as the police or judiciary, are run may not be listened to by politicians and civil servants because they are regarded as extremist.
- **Cost** – the government may be sympathetic to a sociologist's ideas, but they may lack funds or have other spending priorities.

This links to material in Chapter 7 on the mass media.

However, social scientists' ideas sometimes become part of mainstream culture and influence the way people see social problems. This in turn can affect the policies that governments produce, e.g. **Newson** argued in the 1980s that there was a direct link between violence being committed by children and young people and violence in films and videos. This led to a climate of opinion orchestrated by the tabloid newspapers that led to the government tightening up the censorship and certification of both television content and films.

Perspectives on social policy and sociology

AQA **SCLY 4**

Different sociological perspectives have different ideas about the relationship between sociology and social policy.

Positivism and functionalism

Early classical positivists such as **Comte** and **Durkheim** stressed that sociology was a **science of society** and consequently believed that it was the job of the sociologist to discover the causes of social problems and recommend **social policy solutions** to them. They saw sociologists as **social engineers** whose job was to fix society when it malfunctioned.

Functionalists see society as characterised by **social order** because it is underpinned by **value consensus** rather than conflict. They see governments and social policy as serving the interests of all the social groups that make up society, e.g. the law and policing serve all members of the community.

Modern day functionalists believe that the role of the sociologist is to provide politicians and civil servants with objective, scientific evidence. They might also provide the State with recommendations for action. However, it is the job of the government to assess the validity of these findings and whether they should act upon them. Functionalists generally favour cautious and gradualist social policies, i.e. 'piecemeal social engineering'. In other words, they favour tackling one specific issue at a time.

Criticisms of the functionalist approach to social policy

This links to material in Chapter 8 on crime and deviance.

However, Marxists argue that functionalists ignore the fact that social order is an illusion and that the organisation of capitalism is actually underpinned by class inequality and exploitation rather than by social order and consensus, e.g. Marxists argue that the law does not treat all social groups equally – rather some groups benefit from the law at the expense of others. The piecemeal approach of functionalism is therefore criticised because it fails to address the fundamental problem which from a Marxist perspective is the way the basic economic and social structure of society is organised.

The New Right

New Right sociologists such as **Murray**, **Marsland** and **Saunders** believe that governments should not interfere with society. Social policy therefore should be kept to a minimum.

However, Marsland argues that social problems such as poverty and crime have been caused by too much social policy, especially in the field of welfare provision. Marsland argues that the Welfare State has created a feckless and welfare-dependent criminal **underclass**. Murray (1984) argues that generous welfare benefits and council housing for lone parents act as **perverse incentives** that weaken the self-reliance of families. The New Right believe that social policy should aim to re-establish individual responsibility in people so that they become more independent and responsible for both themselves and their families. The role of social policy therefore should be to enable people to stand on their own two feet and not to be over-dependent on the state and social policy.

New Right sociologists and criminologists, such as **Wilson** and **Kelling**, have influenced both Conservative and Labour crime policies in recent years. However, critical criminologists have questioned the validity of their research findings particularly with regard to the existence of an underclass in Britain.

The social democratic perspective

An ideological opponent of the New Right is the **social democratic perspective** which favours increased social policy, particularly a major redistribution of wealth and income from the rich to the poor and increased welfare spending. Social democratic sociologists and criminologists such as **Young and Lea** suggest that social problems such as crime cannot be addressed properly whilst problems such as poverty, inequality and racism persist. Such sociologists argue that they should be involved in researching social problems like crime and making policy recommendations to rid society of them.

Criticisms of the social democratic perspective

However, Marxists criticise the social democratic perspective for not going far enough. Marxists claim that the deeply unequal and divisive organisation of capitalism is ultimately responsible for these inequalities. Capitalism therefore needs to be abolished and replaced with a more humanitarian system.

Marxism

This links to material in Chapter 8 on crime and deviance.

Marxists see modern capitalist societies as underpinned by **class inequality** and exploitation. The ruling capitalist class exploit the labour of the working class and accumulate massive wealth as a result. Consequently, the state and social policy do not benefit all members of society. Rather, from a Marxist perspective, the state and social policy serve the interests of the capitalist ruling class. In particular, the state and social policy serve to reproduce and justify class inequalities, e.g. Marxists argue that the law and crime statistics are used by the ruling class to justify the over-policing and social control of the poor.

Marxists recognise that some social policies benefit the working class. However, Marxists point out that such policies are often under-resourced and policed very weakly, e.g. health and safety legislation has benefitted workers, but employers who breach these laws are very rarely charged with serious crimes or labelled as criminals. Marxists also note that cuts in welfare disproportionately affect the working class. Finally, Marxists note that social policy fails to challenge the fundamental inequalities in income and wealth that underpin capitalism.

Marxists therefore argue that social problems are mainly the product of the way capitalism is organised and consequently only a revolution to overthrow capitalism and create a **classless society** will rid society of these problems. The role of the Marxist sociologist is therefore to criticise capitalist society, to reveal the true extent of class inequality and exploitation and to encourage the working class to resist and even overthrow the capitalist system.

Criticisms of Marxism

However, critics argue that Marxist views on social policy and the role of sociologists are both impractical and unrealistic. Social democrats argue that capitalism is unlikely to be dismantled and that critical sociologists need to focus on collecting scientific evidence that convinces policy-makers that structural changes are necessary.

Feminism

Liberal feminist sociologists also see modern societies such as Britain as underpinned by conflict. However, they suggest that this is **gender conflict**. Britain is seen as a patriarchal (male-dominated) society and consequently feminists argue that both social policy and sociological research has resulted in male dominance and female subordination, e.g. they note that New Right sociological thinking has encouraged social policy-makers to favour the traditional model of the family in which it is pre-supposed that women will take most responsibility for housework and childcare.

This links to material in Chapter 1 on families.

> **KEY POINT**
>
> Liberal feminist sociological research has been very influential over the past thirty years and has been responsible for much anti-discrimination and equal opportunities social policy such as the Equal Pay Act. Educational social policy has gradually led to females raising their educational achievements in British schools.

Radical feminists see men and women as constituting separate classes and argue that men generally oppress women through the use or threat of physical and sexual violence. They argue that women need to separate themselves from men to be free from patriarchy. However, their influence on social policy has been mixed because they are viewed by social policy-makers as hostile to any decision-making process which involves men making decisions about women's lives.

However, **Marxist feminists** reject the view that social policy can bring about gender equality. Marxist-feminists suggest that patriarchy is an ideology used by the capitalist class to divide and rule working class men and women. They therefore call for the dismantling of the capitalist system.

Post-modernism

Post-modernists criticise attempts by sociologists to influence policy. This is because post-modernists believe that it is impossible to discover objective truth. They argue that all knowledge produced by research is **relative** rather than absolute. Sociological evidence is merely one version of reality and consequently, it is not a satisfactory basis for policy-making.

Exam practice question

This is an example of a synoptic question that reflects the type of question that you could be asked in the AQA examination. In your response, you should discuss both sociological theory and research studies. You should also draw on material from topics across the specification.

1 'Marxists see social class as central to the sociological analysis of society. It influences identity, social relationships, and political orientations. However, Marxism is not a unified body of thought. For example, there are now Neo-Marxists and Marxist feminists.'

Assess the contribution of Marxist theories and research to the understanding of contemporary society. **(33 marks)**

Exam practice answers

1 The family

1 **(a)** Note the focus on *identify* (you must briefly state each feature) and *explain* (you must develop your response by discussing each feature in more depth). So you must illustrate whatever features of the reconstituted family (or step/blended family) you decide to focus on which could be any two of:
- origins or causes, e.g. a previously divorced woman with children might marry a single childless man
- most comprise a stepfather, biological mother and her child/ren who live together
- children may be half siblings or step siblings
- relationships with other types of family
- potential tensions between family members, e.g. children having to adjust to different expectations of behaviour.

1 **(b)** Note the focus on *outline* (you must describe the view) and *evaluate* (you must criticise/assess it). This question is worth 33 marks. Therefore it is worth writing at least two sides of A4.

In your introduction, you could explain the term New Right (e.g. as a more recent reworking of the functionalist perspective) and explain, with examples, what is meant by family diversity.

You could develop your answer by discussing the New Right criticisms of/concerns with diversity, e.g. their view that the increase in family diversity is linked to a decline of the traditional nuclear family unit and family values, and the emergence of an underclass containing, e.g. young men, who have not been adequately socialised to accept their familial responsibilities.

You could show how the New Right approach links the decline of the nuclear family to government policies (on issues such as divorce, abortion, homosexuality and discrimination/equal opportunities). You could also show how the New Right approach links the decline of the nuclear family to the rise of feminism.

Your evaluation might include a discussion of alternative interpretations of recent social trends in families and households, e.g. the view that marriage remains popular, that the majority of births outside marriage are jointly registered and that cohabitation is often a phase before marriage rather than an alternative to it.

In your evaluation, you might also explore the feminist view that the New Right approach embodies a patriarchal ideology which serves to justify female oppression. You could discuss Barrett and McIntosh's view that the New Right's familial ideology is anti-social because it dismisses alternative family types such as lone-parent families as deviant and as linked to social problems. You might also examine the post-modern view that family diversity reflects the increased choices available to people in terms of families, lifestyles and living arrangements.

Your conclusion should follow on from the arguments made in the main body of your answer and should link directly to the set question. You might conclude that:
- New Right views have made a valuable contribution to the sociological understanding of family diversity in contemporary Britain.
- New Right views have added some valuable insights to the sociological understanding of family diversity in contemporary Britain.
- Compared with other approaches (e.g. feminism and/or post-modernism), New Right views have added little to the sociological understanding of family diversity in contemporary Britain.

2 **(a)** Note the focus on *identify* (you must briefly state each reason) and *explain* (you must develop your response by discussing each reason in more depth). Possible reasons include:
- The proportion of the population over retirement age is gradually increasing, as a result of longer life expectancy linked to factors such as Welfare State provisions, improvements in diet and nutrition, improvements in public health services and advances in medicine and surgery.
- Changing patterns of fertility, including the trend towards a smaller family size, women are having fewer children and they are having them later in life. This is linked to the availability of effective birth control methods.
- The impact of feminism – many women now choose to combine motherhood with a career and, as a result, they have fewer children than was the case a generation ago.

2 **(b)** Note the focus on *outline* (you must describe the view) and *evaluate* (you must criticise/assess it). This question is worth 33 marks. Therefore it is worth writing at least two sides of A4.

In your introduction, you could explain what is meant by 'dysfunctional' and give an indication of the extent of one-parent families. In the main body, you could:
- Outline the functionalist view that the nuclear family is functional for individuals and for society whilst other family types are less functional.
- Outline the New Right view on the shortcomings of lone-parent families. Other aspects worth mentioning include the economic costs of one-parent families, welfare dependency and the social problems associated with children raised in one-parent families.

Evaluation could focus on the following ideas:
- How the ideology of familism which stresses the nuclear family ideal has led to the negative labelling of one-parent families (see Chester, Popay, etc.). Illustrate with examples.
- How single-parent families have been scapegoated for social problems cause by structural factors such as unemployment.
- Poverty: illustrate the financial problems faced by many one-parents. Stress that such problems are hardly an incentive to choose this option.
- Nuclear families may also be dysfunctional (e.g. domestic violence). It is often preferable for a child to live with one caring parent than with two parents who are in conflict with each other and who may scapegoat the child. You could refer to the feminist and Marxist approaches and to the work of critics such as Phoenix and Cashmore.
- However, add a word of caution – children from one-parent families tend to do less well in education than children from two-parent families, although we do not know what causes these differences in achievement. For example, it could be the lack of a father or poverty.

Your conclusion should follow on from the arguments made in the main body of your answer and should link directly to the set question. You might conclude by:
- Agreeing with the functionalist and New Right view that one-parent families are dysfunctional.
- Arguing that the situation of one-parent families varies according to factors such as income, social class and whether contact is maintained with the non-resident parent so it is difficult to generalise.
- Disagreeing with the functionalist and New Right view that one-parent families are dysfunctional.

Exam practice answers

2 Socialisation, culture and identity

1 (a) Norms refer to guidelines on how we are expected to behave in specific contexts, e.g. we are expected to turn off our mobile phone during the screening of a film at the cinema.

1 (b) Sex refers to biological differences between males and females, e.g. differences in hormones, chromosomes and genitalia. Gender refers to socially constructed differences that are associated with masculinity and femininity, e.g. traditionally men had the role of breadwinner, while women had the role of homemaker; baby girls are often dressed in pink while baby boys are often dressed in blue.

1 (c) It is important to provide three different ways. Possible ways include:
- In schools with an academic culture, students may be encouraged by their peers to work hard, compete and strive for exam success and academic achievement.
- Some students may be encouraged by their peers to join an anti-school culture that challenges the school rules and resists teachers.
- In some localities, young people may experience peer pressure to join gangs.
- Some young people may conform to deviant group norms/behaviour in order to gain acceptance within the group and to avoid being excluded.
- The peer group may use negative sanctions such as bullying, ridicule and gossip to influence other young people, e.g. ridiculing someone's style of dress.
- The peer group may encourage its members to engage in forms of political action.

1 (d) In your introduction, you could explain what is meant by 'functionalism' and 'primary socialisation'. In the main body, you could:
- Outline the functionalist view of the primary socialisation process within families, e.g. drawing on the work of Murdock and Parsons.
- Outline the view that primary socialisation is seen as providing children with a sense of identity.

Evaluation could focus on the following ideas:
- The view of Marxists such as Zaretsky that primary socialisation involves the transmission of ruling class ideology rather than shared values.
- The view of feminists that primary socialisation involves the construction of gender and the transmission of patriarchal ideology.
- The view of interpretivists that children should not be seen simply as 'empty vessels' and that socialisation should be seen as a two-way process.
- Functionalism presents the socialisation process too positively, ignores social change and tends to underplay the role and power of agencies such as the mass media in the socialisation process.

Your conclusion should follow on from the arguments made in the main body of your answer and should link directly to the set question. You might conclude by:
- Arguing that functionalism has made a valuable contribution to the sociological understanding of the process of primary socialisation.
- Arguing that functionalism has provided some (albeit limited) insights into the process of primary socialisation.
- Arguing that other approaches (e.g. feminism, interactionism) have made more valuable contributions.

1 (e) In your introduction, you could explain what is meant by 'social class' and 'identity'. In the main body, you could:
- Draw on the material in Item B and post-modernist ideas (e.g. those of Pakulski and Waters) to argue in favour of the view that social class is no longer

relevant as a source of identity, e.g. compared to the 1950s. Link this to social changes such as the apparent disappearance of traditional working class communities (Item B) and to changes associated with the increase in individualisation and choice (Item B) in post-modern societies.
- Discuss the idea that societies are now organised around consumption rather than production. As a result, people's identities are linked to what they consume rather than to their social class positions.
- Discuss the idea that identities based on factors such as age, gender and ethnicity are now more significant than those based on class.

Evaluation could focus on the following ideas:
- Post-modernists tend to ignore social divisions based on wealth and income. They also ignore the fact that consumption is linked to income and paid employment and therefore to social class.
- Marshall argues that people recognise class differences and continue to identify themselves in class terms.
- Among the upper class, social class identity remains significant.

Your conclusion should follow on from the arguments made in the main body of your answer and should link directly to the set question. You might conclude by arguing that social class:
- is no longer significant as a source of identity in contemporary society
- is becoming less significant than other factors
- remains a key social division and thus a major source of identity.

2 You should provide a clear definition of ethnicity. For example:
Ethnicity refers to a set of cultural norms and values that distinguish one ethnic group from another. The members of an ethnic group share an identity based on their cultural traditions or characteristics including their religion or language. Britain is a culturally diverse society with a range of minority ethnic groups including people of African-Caribbean, Indian, Irish and Polish heritage. Features of ethnic minority identity may include, e.g. physical characteristics such as skin colour, a shared language other than English, religious beliefs and the experience of racism. You could illustrate with examples of studies of ethnicity such as the work of Singh Ghumann, Modood, Sewell or Johal.

3 Agencies of socialisation include families, the education system, peer groups, religions, the mass media and workplaces. You could focus on any two of these. For example:
- Families transmit values and norms through the primary socialisation process. As an agency of socialisation, the family teaches norms such as table manners and values such as respect for life. The family also operates as an informal mechanism of social control by rewarding appropriate behaviour/conformity to norms and values and punishing inappropriate behaviour. However, feminists take a different view and argue that families engage in gender socialisation (e.g. through the processes of manipulation and canalisation) and transmit values and norms that reproduce patriarchy.
- Functionalists believe that the education system socialises children into universal and agreed values such as achievement, individualism and respect for authority which are essential to the maintenance of social order, e.g. via the exam system, students come to appreciate that individual achievement is based on ability and effort. Students are expected to conform to school rules, e.g. regarding punctuality and may be punished if they fail to comply with these. By contrast,

Marxists argue that the hidden curriculum transmits values (such as competition and consumerism) that serve to reproduce capitalism.

- Peer groups operate through the peer group pressure that they exert on members to conform to group norms and values. Members may face negative sanctions (such as rejection or ridicule) if they deviate from group norms and positive sanctions (e.g. acceptance) if they conform to group norms. In the workplace, for instance, occupational peer groups teach new workers the informal/unwritten rules that underpin work.

3 Education

1 The term *meritocracy* refers to a system in which social position is earned on the basis of individual merit, talents, effort and abilities rather than based on factors such as social class, gender or ethnicity.

2 Possible reasons include:
- The impact of the introduction of equal opportunities policies and changing practices in education, e.g. checking teaching and learning resources for sexist stereotypes.
- The introduction of assessment based on coursework (e.g. at GCSE and A Level) may have suited the learning styles of girls more than boys, e.g. girls are often more conscientious and more motivated than boys and this will impact on their achievements in coursework.
- With the introduction of the National Curriculum in the late 1980s, pupils were no longer able to opt out of science at 14. This helped to raise girls' achievements in science subjects and opened up career opportunities (e.g. in medicine) for them.
- The impact of feminism in securing equal rights for females in education and employment, backed up by anti-discrimination legislation.
- As a result of changing social attitudes, many females now see education and careers as having a greater priority than marriages and families

3 It is important to focus explicitly on school processes and to discuss (i.e. analyse and evaluate) how these may be linked to the underachievement of some minority ethnic pupils. Possible ways include:
- The workings of the hidden curriculum such as stereotyping in teaching and learning resources, the near invisibility of black role models in the curriculum (e.g. Tikly's work) and ethnocentricity within the curriculum.
- Teacher stereotyping of minority ethnic pupils, e.g. studies by Brittan, Brah and Minhas.
- Teacher expectations, labelling and the self-fulfilling prophecy, e.g. studies by Connolly, Gillborn and Mirza.
- Pupil resistance and the emergence of anti-school cultures within schools, e.g. the work of Troyna and/or Sewell.
- Racism within schools, e.g. studies have linked the relatively high rates of exclusion among African-Caribbean heritage students to institutional racism.

4 In your introduction, you could explain what is meant by 'reproduce' and 'class inequalities in wealth and power'. You could also indicate that this view is linked to the Marxist approach. In the main body, you could:
- Draw on the material in Item A and the work of Marxist writers (e.g. Althusser on the hidden curriculum, Bowles and Gintis on the correspondence between school and work) to argue in favour of the view that the education system reproduces social class inequalities in capitalist societies over time.
- Discuss the role of the independent sector (and particularly public schools) in reproducing the class system.
- Discuss the limited impact of government policies in reducing class-based inequalities, e.g. widening participation policies.

Evaluation could focus on the following ideas:
- Criticisms of the Marxist approach, e.g. it is over-deterministic, drawing on Willis's ideas in Item A.
- The functionalist view that the education system functions to reproduce value consensus and social solidarity (e.g. Durkheim) and is based on meritocratic principles (e.g. Davis and Moore).
- The feminist view that education reproduces gender and patriarchal ideology.
- The view that the education system reproduces inequalities based on ethnicity.
- The post-modernist view that social class is no longer so significant in post-modern societies that are characterised by individualisation.
- The positive impact of government policies in reducing class based inequalities, e.g. widening participation policies, the EMA.

Your conclusion should follow on from the arguments made in the main body of your answer and should link directly to the set question. You might conclude by arguing that:
- The education system continues to reproduce class based inequalities in wealth and power from one generation to the next.
- The education system has changed and has become more meritocratic.
- It is important to explore how class, gender and ethnicity intersect or interrelate when explaining inequalities in wealth and power.

5 In your introduction, you could explain briefly what is meant by 'educational policies' and 'equality of opportunity'. You could also indicate that 1988 is significant because major changes were introduced as a result of the 1988 Education Reform Act. In the main body, you could discuss the different policies and assess how far they were successful in increasing equality of opportunity. Such policies include:
- The introduction of the National Curriculum. Pupils were no longer able to opt out of science at 14. This helped to increase equality of opportunity by raising girls' achievements in science subjects and has opened up career opportunities (e.g. in medicine) for them.
- Marketisation of education. This aimed to raise standards for all pupils by encouraging schools to compete to attract pupils (and parents) by publishing exam results and OFSTED inspection reports. However, critics argue that marketisation has had unintended consequences that impact negatively on equal opportunities, e.g. Whitty sees marketisation as contributing to the increase in social class differences in education.
- Under the Labour government (1997–2010), some schools were 'named and shamed' as under-achieving in order to raise standards. However, such a policy could have the unintended consequence of leading to a self-fulfilling prophecy.
- Widening participation, e.g. via the New Deal, increasing participation in HE, Aim Higher, the EMA and Excellence in Cities. However, more recent changes to the funding of HE and the withdrawal of the EMA may impact most on students from disadvantaged backgrounds.
- Raising awareness of institutional racism (based on unintentional prejudice and discrimination) within schools and colleges.

As part of your evaluation, you could also:
- Argue that educational policies have not gone far enough in addressing inequality, e.g. having an independent sector alongside a state sector means that parents with financial and cultural capital can exercise greatest choice.
- Draw on Marxist ideas to argue that educational policies alone cannot address the inequalities inherent in capitalism.

Exam practice answers

- Draw on feminist ideas to argue that educational policies alone cannot address the inequalities inherent in patriarchy.

Your conclusion should follow on from the arguments made in the main body of your answer and should link directly to the set question. You might conclude by arguing that:
- These policies have helped significantly to provide equal opportunities in education and to address inequalities based on social class, ethnicity and gender, e.g. the educational achievements of girls have risen markedly.
- These policies have not addressed inequalities in outcome, e.g. the achievements of working class boys.

6   In your introduction, you could explain what is meant by 'school-based factors' (e.g. school processes, relationships and classroom interaction) and give an indication of the pattern of under-achievement among working class boys. In the main body, you could discuss the interactionist approach which links school processes to educational outcomes. You could also examine the different school-based factors and assess their significance in explaining working class boys' educational underachievement. Such factors include:
- The workings of the hidden curriculum, e.g. the curriculum focuses on middle class culture.
- Teacher stereotyping of working class boys.
- Teacher expectations, labelling and the self-fulfilling prophecy, e.g. studies by Browne and Mitsos.
- Pupil resistance and the emergence of anti-school cultures within schools, e.g. the work of Paul Willis highlighted working class boys' resistance to teachers and the authority structure.

Evaluation could focus on the following ideas:
- The Marxist critique of the interactionist approach, e.g. the focus on classroom interaction underplays social class inequalities in capitalist society.
- Other factors outside the school are also important. It is necessary to take account of the impact of educational policies and funding on achievement.
- Structural factors such as changes to the labour market are also significant. Economic changes have led to a 'crisis in masculinity' (Mac An Ghaill). As a result, working class males may see education and qualifications as irrelevant.
- Home factors such as the role of cultural and financial capital in educational outcomes are also important.

Your conclusion should follow on from the arguments made in the main body of your answer and should link directly to the set question. You might conclude by arguing that:
- In-school factors are the most significant.
- It is important to consider a range of factors including home-based factors, structural factors and social policies.

4 Health

1   Infant mortality refers to the death of infants before they reach the age of one. It is usually expressed as a rate per 1000 live births in a given year.

2   Possible answers include:
- People might go to the gym regularly, carry out weight training exercises and build up body muscle to change the shape of their body.
- They might have cosmetic surgery, e.g. breast implants to change their physical appearance.
- They might have procedures such as a face lift or Botox in order to attempt to reduce the visible signs of ageing.
- They might undergo gender reassignment surgery.

3   In your introduction, you could briefly summarise the patterns between ethnicity, health and illness. In the main body, you could examine possible reasons such as:
- Poverty and racism which act as a double disadvantage and may lead to stress among minority ethnic groups (e.g. Virdee's work).

- Cultural practices, e.g. linked to diet. However, critics argue that the problem lies not with minority ethnic cultures, but with the NHS and medical professionals' ethnocentric response to different cultures.
- Linked to this is the operation of institutional racism, e.g. when a hospital fails to provide an appropriate service to people because of their ethnic origin or culture.
- Materialist explanations – health inequalities experienced by minority ethnic groups reflect social and economic inequalities, e.g. in access to housing. This highlights the way in which social class and ethnicity can intersect in creating health inequalities.
- The implications of the 'inverse care law' for minority ethnic communities.

In your conclusion, you could argue that:
- one of these reasons explains ethnic inequalities in health most adequately
- a combination of factors is responsible
- ethnic inequalities in health cannot be understood in isolation and are closely linked to social class inequalities.

4   In your introduction, you could explain what is meant by the 'biomedical model of health and illness'. In your main body, you could argue in favour of the biomedical model. You could refer to:
- Item A – the biomedical model would see the eradication of infectious diseases such as TB and smallpox and the increase in life expectancy as linked closely to biomedical advances.
- Other strengths of this approach, e.g. science has successfully addressed many health problems, cured diseases, reduced death rates and increased life expectancy.

Your evaluation could:
- Draw on McKeown's ideas in Item A that medical treatments such as vaccinations came about after the decline in diseases rather than causing it. People became more resistant to disease because of social changes and public health measures.
- Discuss the social model of health and illness and its criticism of the biomedical model, e.g. in the social model, the process of becoming ill is seen as socially constructed; there are historical and cross-cultural differences in how health and illness are defined.
- Discuss iatrogenesis (illness may be caused by medical examination or treatment) and the bio-medicalisation of childbirth.

In your conclusion, you could argue that:
- the biomedical model has made a significant contribution to the understanding and treatment of health and illness.
- sociological approaches have successfully challenged the biomedical approach by highlighting the socio-economic contexts of health and illness.

5   (a)   You could focus on two of the following possible causes:
- Differences in access to private health care, private health insurance and private health schemes (e.g. as a 'perk' at work) which are linked to social class and income.
- Cultural differences, e.g. working class people tend to lead less healthy lifestyles and are more likely to smoke. However, cultural explanations neglect economic circumstances, e.g. poverty may be the cause of inadequate diets.
- Inequalities in the distribution of NHS resources (the social administration view). Tudor Hart identifies an 'inverse care law'. However, critics of this view suggest that reorganisation within the NHS has tackled the inequalities associated with the inverse care law.

- Marxist views, e.g. Doyal and Pennell argue that ill health is linked to capitalism's pursuit of profit. In this view, ill health has material causes, e.g. it results from poverty and inadequate housing. Critics, however, argue that capitalism has dramatically improved people's living conditions, life styles and life expectancy. On the other hand, life expectancy and infant mortality are still linked to social class in the twenty-first century.

5 (b) In your introduction, you could explain what is meant by 'mental illness' (e.g. behaviour that prevents individuals from functioning adequately in their society) and 'socially defined' (e.g. it is socially constructed and linked to labelling processes and interaction between individuals). In the main body, you could point out that what is considered as 'functioning adequately' may depend on the interpretations of powerful groups i.e. it is socially defined. You could include the following points:
- Both Scheff and Szasz have claimed that what is 'normal' or 'mad' behaviour is a matter of interpretation.
- Definitions and interpretations of behaviour are relative rather than fixed and absolute – they vary historically and cross-culturally. Szasz argues that definitions of mental illness are simply means of controlling behaviour that is seen by powerful groups as objectionable.
- Busfield argues that the diagnosis of mental illness in women may reflect negative stereotypes held by doctors about female behaviour.
- Similarly, Rastafarians may end up as patients within the mental health system as a result of labelling processes operating within the criminal justice system.
- Rosenhan's study of pseudo-patients suggests that medical professionals may not diagnose schizophrenia accurately and that once labelled as schizophrenic, the label will stick. Similarly, Katz's work illustrates international differences in the diagnosis of schizophrenia.

Evaluation could focus on the following ideas:
- Structuralist approaches focus on examining how the structure of society (rather than interaction or labelling processes) causes mental illness.
- Biomedical approaches see mental illness as a biological or physical phenomenon.
- Gove rejects the idea that mental illness involves a labelling process because the vast majority of people who are treated for mental illness have serious problems. Labelling theory fails to explain why some people become mentally ill in the first place.

Your conclusion should follow on from the arguments made in the main body of your answer and should link directly to the set question. You might conclude by arguing that:
- Mental illness is socially defined/socially constructed.
- The incidence of mental illness varies between social groups and structuralist approaches provide a more adequate explanation of mental illness than interactionists/labelling theorists.

6 (a) You could focus on two of the following possible ways:
- The housewife role involves repetitive tasks, has low status and may lead to feelings of social isolation. The feminist approach argues that being married has a negative impact on women's mental health.
- The triple shift involves combining paid work, housework and emotional work thus many women lead more stressful lives than men. This may affect their mental health. However, it may be that women are more likely than men to be labelled or diagnosed as mentally ill within a male-dominated psychiatric profession.
- As housewives and mothers, women are less likely to experience work-related stress and industrial accidents. However, employment patterns and gender roles have changed so this may no longer apply in the twenty-first century.
- As mothers and carers, many women are engaged in emotion work. They may be more aware of health issues and thus more likely to visit the doctor than men.

6 (b) In your introduction, you could explain what is meant by 'life expectancy' and 'medical advances'. In the main body, you could discuss:
- the biomedical model of health which supports the view that the increase in life expectancy is linked primarily to medical advances, e.g. developments in surgery, treatment and medication.

In your evaluation, you could criticise the biomedical model by referring, for example, to:
- iatrogenesis (illness may be caused by medical examination or treatment)
- the bio-medicalisation of childbirth.

You could also contrast the biomedical view with the social view. You could discuss the following ideas:
- McKeown's social model of health and illness – public health measures and improvements in diet are also key factors.
- Life expectancy varies between social groups, e.g. between social classes and ethnic groups. It is therefore linked to factors such as inequalities in access to NHS resources (the inverse care law) and to private health care. The 'inverse prevention law' (e.g. Gordon et al.) is also relevant.
- Life expectancy can be seen as a social product, e.g. the rates are linked to poverty and vary between regions and between nations.
- Mortality rates are linked to position at work, e.g. Davey Smith's writing.
- Feminist explanations of women's longer life expectancy, (e.g. linked to gender role socialisation processes).

Your conclusion should follow on from the arguments made in the main body of your answer and should link directly to the set question. You might conclude by:
- Agreeing that increases in life expectancy are mainly linked to medical advances.
- Arguing that life expectancy can also be seen as a social product arising from the way society is structured and from social inequalities.

5 Research methods

1 This term refers to the study of people in their everyday settings (e.g. people interacting in classrooms or in gangs) rather than in an artificial setting such as a laboratory in a university.

2 Possible advantages include:
- Closed questions can be answered relatively quickly, e.g. by ticking boxes.
- The results of closed questions are relatively quick and easy to analyse and quantify.

Possible disadvantages include:
- Closed questions limit the respondent to the pre-set answers provided.
- The researcher might not anticipate all possible answers and some answers may not be included.
- Researcher imposition – the researcher has already mapped out respondents' experiences, etc. in advance of carrying out the research.

Exam practice answers

- Closed questions are not appropriate for uncovering meanings and exploring how people experience situations.

3   Possible issues include:
- Informed consent – the researcher must ensure that potential research participants understand fully what the research is about and what taking part will involve otherwise potential participants will not be in a position to make an informed decision when giving or withholding their consent.
- Whether the use of covert research is justified. On the one hand, covert research gets round the observer effect and may be the only possible way of getting essential data. On the other hand, it violates the principle of informed consent and may invade people's privacy.
- When publishing reports or books about the research, the researcher must ensure that the anonymity and privacy of research participants is respected and that individuals or institutions cannot be identified. Otherwise, there is the risk that participants may face ridicule or reprisal as a result of taking part.
- Researchers sometimes face the ethical dilemma of deciding whether to participate in illegal or immoral activities, e.g. covert participant observers who study deviant groups may risk 'blowing their cover' if they refuse to participate in some activities.

4   In your introduction, you could explain briefly what is meant by 'theoretical considerations' and refer to positivism and interpretivism. In the main body, you could discuss the link between theoretical position and choice of methods. In doing so, you could discuss:
- The link between positivism, the scientific method, the concern with issues such as objectivity, reliability, replicability, representativeness and generalisability. Such concerns lead positivists to choose quantitative methods such as social surveys, postal questionnaires and structured interviews.
- The interpretivist concern with issues such as validity, empathy, meaning, interaction and exploring how people make sense of their experiences and the meaning they attach to them. Such concerns lead interpretivists to choose qualitative methods such as unstructured interviews and participant observation.

As part of your evaluation, you could discuss:
- The view that, in practice, sociologists do not see quantitative and qualitative methods as mutually exclusive. They will often use whatever methods fit the purpose. Some use a mixture of quantitative and qualitative methods in one study as a way of checking the reliability and validity of their findings. Others use various methods (both quantitative and qualitative) in one study in order to build up a more complete account of the topic being investigated.
- The significance of other influences on choice of research methods such as:
  - practical issues, e.g. how much time is available, the size of the research budget, the size of the research team.
  - the topic itself, e.g. self-completion questionnaires would be inappropriate in a study of how people experience living with literacy problems.
  - ethical issues, e.g. what methods are feasible in moral terms.

Your conclusion should follow on from the arguments made in the main body of your answer and should link directly to the set question. You might conclude by arguing that:
- Theoretical considerations are the most important issue influencing choice of research methods.
- Theoretical considerations are an important issue influencing choice of research methods.

- Other issues (e.g. the research topic and research questions or funding) are more important in practice.

6 Religion

1   In your introduction, you could explain what is meant by 'religious institutions' (e.g. churches, denominations) and 'disengaged from society' (e.g. that religious institutions such as churches have become less engaged in the activities of the wider society) and link this to the concept of secularisation. In the main body, you could discuss the supporting evidence and arguments:
- the view that religious institutions have withdrawn from many areas of life, e.g. the Church of England has now withdrawn almost entirely from political life and, as a result, has lost influence and power; religious education is not taught in many schools; the Welfare State now provides health and welfare services.
- Wilson's view that the Church occupies a marginal role limited to providing services around births, marriages and deaths.
- Bruce's argument that modern social life is no longer community based which undermines religion.

In your evaluation, you could discuss the following evidence and arguments:
- Parsons' argument on structural differentiation which allows churches to focus purely on religious matters and thereby strengthens them.
- Parsons' view that religious beliefs inform the ethics and values that underpin most social behaviour.
- The continuing role of religion in state education (e.g. faith schools) and welfare (e.g. Cafod).
- Continuing media interest in religious and moral matters e.g. the ordination of women priests.
- The power of the churches remains strong, e.g. the monarch in Britain is crowned by the Archbishop of Canterbury.
- Religious pluralism, e.g. Greeley argues that NRMs are a sign of religious revival.
- Casanova's view that political conflict around the world is influenced by religion. Illustrate with contemporary examples of conflicts linked to religion.
- Globally, religion is a powerful force, e.g. the RC church has influence over states in Europe and in Latin America; the rise of religious fundamentalism.

Your conclusion should follow on from the arguments made in the main body of your answer and should link directly to the set question. You might conclude by:
- Arguing that religious institutions have not become disengaged from the wider society particularly from a global perspective.
- Agreeing that religious institutions have become disengaged from society and therefore lost influence.

2   In your introduction, you could explain what is meant by 'social solidarity' and link this to the functionalist approach. In the main body, you could discuss the supporting evidence and arguments:
- Durkheim's view that the function of religion is to promote social order and that the role of collective worship is to promote social solidarity.
- Malinowski's view that religion promotes social order and reduces the potential for disruption.
- Parsons' view that religious beliefs form the basis of social control.
- The functionalist view that religion acts as an agency of socialisation and promotes social solidarity and preserves the status quo.
- The neo-functionalist view that in the USA, faith in Americanism operates as a civil religion and promotes social solidarity.
- Davie's view that religion reinforces social and national values.

In your evaluation, you could:

- Argue that functionalists neglect the dysfunctional aspects of religion and its role in creating conflict. Illustrate with examples, e.g. Northern Ireland.
- Argue that functionalists neglect the evidence for secularisation. If religion is losing social significance then it becomes more difficult to argue that it promotes social solidarity.
- Argue that in societies based on religious pluralism, it becomes more difficult to argue that one religion promotes social solidarity.
- Discuss the Marxist view that religion functions to reproduce social class inequalities within capitalist societies.
- Discuss the view that religion can promote radical social change. Illustrate with examples.

Your conclusion should follow on from the arguments made in the main body of your answer and should link directly to the set question. You might conclude by:

- Agreeing that the main role of religion is to promote social solidarity.
- Arguing that the main role of religion is to legitimise inequality.
- Arguing that the role of religion varies.

7 Mass media

1 In your introduction, you could define the 'mass media', explain the term 'control' (e.g. over content or political slant) and outline the patterns of ownership (e.g. trends towards concentration, conglomeration, and globalisation). In the main body, you could begin by presenting the evidence and arguments in favour of the view that control lies with owners:

- The different Marxist perspectives including the view that media owners, who are members of the capitalist class, use their media outlets to transmit ruling class ideology. You could draw on Curran's research findings to support the idea that owners run newspapers for propaganda purposes. However, Curran argues that owners have economic motives for intervening in content and they are in fierce competition with each other rather than operating in a collective or united way.
- The GUMG argues that media content supports the interests of the capitalist owners. However, this is an unintended outcome of the social background of media personnel rather than reflecting their desire to defend capitalist interests.

As part of your assessment, you could contrast these different Marxist views with pluralist views. You could include the following points:

- In the pluralist view, media content reflects consumer demand in the competitive marketplace. Control rests in the hands of consumers through their market power rather than in owners' hands.
- Concentration of ownership is a product of economic rationality.
- Owners could not conceivably interfere in the day-to-day running or content of their media given the size of media enterprises today.

You could also examine other influences on/arguments about content and control:

- The BBC does not have owners and is controlled by the State.
- The State regulates the media and its content, e.g. through government legislation.
- The impact of gate keepers and news values as controls over content.
- The media generate revenue from advertisers who can exert control.
- The new media empower everyone to produce media content so the power and influence of owners will diminish.

Your conclusion should follow on from the arguments made in the main body of your answer and should link directly to the set question. You might conclude by:

- Agreeing that power and control are concentrated in the owners' hands.
- Arguing that the consumers are in control through their purchasing power.
- Arguing that media professionals are in control.

2 **(a)** Possible ways include:

- By focussing on numbers, e.g. in relation to immigration.
- By associating some minority ethnic groups with criminal activity, e.g. Stuart Hall's writing on 'mugging' and links to moral panics.
- Islamophobia – by focusing narrowly on issues such as forced marriage, the hijab, fundamentalism and terrorism when discussing Muslim communities in Britain.
- By focusing narrowly on the involvement of minority ethnic groups and black role models in sport and music but neglecting their contributions/achievements in other areas of life.

2 **(b)** Note that the question asks you to use material from the Item and elsewhere and that it asks for an assessment. Note also that it is asking about representations of both women and men. In your introduction, you could define 'gender stereotypes'. You could begin the main body of your answer by supporting the view that media representations of women and men challenge traditional gender stereotypes. For example:

- As a result of social and cultural changes over the past 25 years, the media now present increasing numbers of positive female roles. Westwood argues that there are now more transgressive female roles on British television.
- In advertising, women are no longer presented as passive objects of the male gaze. Instead, they are presented as active, independent and sexually powerful agents, e.g. Gill, 2008.
- Gauntlett (2008) argues that young women's magazines emphasise self-determination. Pop lyrics focus on women's financial and emotional independence.
- Men's magazines challenge traditional gender stereotypes by suggesting, for example, that men are emotionally vulnerable. They also present alternative or new masculinities such as the metrosexual.
- By challenging traditional definitions of gender, the media are a force for social change and provide a diversity of choices for people in constructing their gender identities.

You could then criticise the view by arguing that media representations inform and reinforce gender stereotypes. You could:

- Draw on Item A and Gauntlett's view that 'lads' mags' all project the same images of women, men and men's interests, e.g. semi-naked females, sport and alcohol. This reinforces rather than challenges stereotypes.
- Discuss Rutherford's view of men's magazines and retributive masculinity.
- Draw on Item A to argue that women are predominantly portrayed either as mothers and housewives or as available for sex at any time.
- Discuss the Marxist feminist view that the roots of the traditional gender stereotypes in the media are economic – linked to capitalist media conglomerates' search for increased profits.
- Discuss the radical feminist view that the traditional gender stereotypes in the media are rooted in patriarchy.

In your conclusion, you could argue that:
- It is impossible to generalise because the media are so diverse.
- There is evidence of change – traditional gender representations are now being challenged.
- Very little has changed – the media continue to reinforce gender stereotypes.

8 Crime and deviance

1 Possible strengths include:
- The BCS has a large sample size. It is carried out annually (Item A) and allows researchers to identify patterns and trends over time in the crime rate.
- The BCS uses standardised questions, pilots in advance and uses trained interviewers which all contribute to its reliability in measuring the extent of crime in Britain.
- It includes unreported and unrecorded crime – so is a more valid measure of the extent of crime than the official statistics of crimes recorded by the police.
- The Islington Crime Survey (ICS) undertaken by Left Realist sociologists Lea and Young was based on unstructured interviews and covered crimes such as sexual assault, domestic violence and racist attacks. It found that serious crime was extensive and one third of households had been affected by it.
- Victim surveys are useful when used alongside other sources.

Possible limitations include:
- The BCS is based on social surveys which have methodological problems, e.g. researcher imposition. It is based on surveys of households (Item A) and therefore excludes people who do not live in households. The BCS has a non-response rate of 25% (Item A) thus the findings may not be representative or generalisable.
- It focuses on specific offences (e.g. assault and car theft – Item A) and excludes some crimes including victimless crimes (Item A), fraud and sexual crimes. Thus it tells us nothing about the extent of these in Britain.
- BCS respondents have to rely on memory, may exaggerate or telescope incidents.
- Respondents may not be aware that they have been a victim of crime.
- The ICS was carried out in London and did not attempt to measure the extent of crime in Britain. The BCS only covers England and Wales (Item A).
- Victim surveys carried out by feminist researchers have tended to focus on the lived experiences of being a victim of crime rather than on quantifying the extent of crime in Britain.

2 In your introduction, you could briefly define the term 'white-collar crime' with examples and state that 'recorded' refers to crimes that appear in the official statistics of crimes recorded by the police. In the main body, you could outline the main sociological explanations:
- Taken at face value, the relatively low recorded rates of white-collar crime suggest that this type of crime is less widespread than other types, e.g. burglary or assault. The recorded rates simply reflect the reality in terms of which social groups commit crime.
- White-collar crimes (e.g. fraud) are less likely to be witnessed so victims may be unaware that a crime has taken place. They are also less likely to be reported to the police than street crimes or burglaries.
- The social construction of official crime statistics – these statistics are the end product of policing (e.g. interactions between police, witnesses, victims and suspects, racial profiling and other stereotyping) and judicial practices which are systematically biased against working class people.
- The radical critique of crime statistics – white-collar crimes are not defined as 'serious crimes' by the law and its

agents, are selectively policed and under-punished. Outline the reasons for this by referring to the Marxist theory of crime and social control – the law and the official crime statistics have an ideological role in rendering the crimes of the powerful invisible and criminalising the working class in order to distract attention from class inequality in capitalist society. However, there are now public protests against alleged tax avoidance practised by big business, e.g. organised by UK Uncut.

As part of your assessment, you could:
- Evaluate the Marxist approach by discussing the work of Croall on white-collar and corporate crime and the practical reasons why such crimes go unreported, undetected and under-punished.
- Indicate that Left Realists acknowledge white-collar crime, but they point out that it is working-class crime, street crime and burglary that cause real fear in communities.

Your conclusion should follow on from the arguments made in the main body of your answer and should link directly to the set question. You might conclude by:
- Arguing that white-collar crime is not as extensive as other types of crime and thus there are less counts of it in the official statistics.
- Arguing that the statistics are socially constructed and biased.
- Arguing that the statistics contribute little to the sociological understanding of white-collar crime because they simply reflect patterns of power and class inequality in capitalist society.

9 Stratification, differentiation and social inequality

1 Possible strengths include:
- The sample is selected randomly (Item A) which ensures that everyone has a chance of taking part in the survey. The results are seen as representative of the population and generalisations can be drawn about people's views on gender.
- In the survey, the questions about gender attitudes are standardised. All respondents answer exactly the same questions in the same order so it is possible to replicate the study in order to check the reliability of the data on gender attitudes. Positivist sociologists in particular would support the use of social surveys on attitudes for these reasons.
- The survey is carried out annually so it is possible to identify how far attitudes have changed over time, e.g. attitudes towards gender roles in 1989 compared with 2006 (Item A). It is also possible to compare responses to the same question to highlight similarities and differences (e.g. between men and women or older and younger respondents).

Possible limitations include:
- The British Social Attitudes Survey is a household survey (Item A). It does not question people who do not live in households so it is not entirely representative of attitudes to gender.
- The response rate is low (Item A). It is possible that the people who agree to take part are those who have particularly strong ideas on gender: This raises questions about how far the results are representative and generalisable.
- When discussing issues such as gender, the social characteristics of the interviewer (e.g. their gender, age, ethnicity or social class) may influence the interviewee.
- The interviewee may provide answers that they consider to be socially acceptable or try to shock the interviewer. In this case, the results will be invalid.
- Whilst the British Social Attitudes Survey might provide abundant quantitative data on attitudes, the survey method is less appropriate for exploring the meaning behind people's answers and how they experience

gender roles in their daily lives. It does not allow probing of answers or empathetic understanding. Interpretivist sociologists would criticise the use of social surveys for these reasons and would prefer to use more qualitative methods in order to uncover the meanings behind the statistics shown in Item A.

2 In outlining the Marxist explanations of social class inequality, you could present and describe Marx's use of the following concepts:
- Capitalist mode of production.
- Private property.
- Social relations of production (i.e. the relationship between the bourgeoisie and the proletariat, labour power and surplus value, exploitation).
- The means of production.
- The role of ideology.
- False class consciousness.
- Class conflict.

You could also describe the ways neo-Marxists and Marxist-feminists have drawn on these concepts and applied them to societies in the twentieth and twenty-first centuries. You could, for example, refer to studies of social class and educational inequality that draw on the concept of cultural capital. You could also refer to studies of crime and deviance or the mass media (e.g. Stuart Hall), or to debates on domestic labour and the reserve army of labour (e.g. Benston). Your assessment of Marxist explanations of social class inequality could focus on the following strengths:
- This approach has provided sociology with an effective and convincing analysis of how economic relationships can lead to social and economic inequalities.
- It has highlighted and analysed changes to the class structure, e.g. proletarianisation.

Your assessment could focus on the following limitations:
- Economic determinism.
- Marx's views on revolutionary change in advanced capitalist societies such as Britain (e.g. that the middle class would disappear and the proletariat would eventually recognise their exploitation and overthrow the ruling class) are open to criticism.

Your assessment of Marxist explanations could also focus on alternative theoretical approaches to social class inequality:
- Weberian accounts of class, status and power which focus on economic relationships but also differences in status and power.
- Functionalist accounts of social stratification, meritocracy and role allocation – social class and unequal rewards are necessary to ensure that the most talented people are attracted to the most demanding and functionally important jobs.
- Radical feminists focus on gender inequalities within patriarchy.
- In post-modern societies, the focus is on constructing identities through consumption. Social class is no longer an important part of people's identities.
- Contemporary studies of inequality now focus on the intersection of social class, gender, ethnicity and age.

In your conclusion, you could highlight the unique contribution of the Marxist approach to the sociological understanding of social class inequality. Alternatively, you could argue that a contrasting approach (e.g. Weberian or post-modernist) provides a more adequate explanation of social class inequality or that studies of inequality should focus more fully on the ways in which class is related to gender, ethnicity and age.

10 Theory and method

1 In discussing Marxist theories, you could refer to the use of concepts such as:
- Capitalist mode of production.
- Social class in capitalist society (i.e. the relationship between the bourgeoisie and the proletariat, labour power and surplus value, exploitation).
- The means of production, e.g. land, factories and technology.
- The role of ideology in capitalist societies.

You could also discuss the theories and research undertaken by neo-Marxists and Marxist-feminists within areas such as education, families, health, the mass media and religion. You could, for example, refer to:
- studies of working class resistance in education (e.g. Paul Willis's *Learning to Labour*)
- studies of social class and educational inequality that draw on Bourdieu's concept of cultural capital
- studies of crime and deviance or the mass media (e.g. Stuart Hall on 'mugging' and moral panics, the work of the GUMG)
- debates on domestic labour and the reserve army of labour (e.g. Benston).

In assessing their contribution, you could highlight the following strengths:
- These theories and research studies highlight social class inequalities and challenge the idea of meritocracy (e.g. in education). Neo-marxist studies and theories illuminate the process of working class resistance in education.
- They ask questions about what is going on beneath the surface and, e.g. show how moral panics serve the interests of capitalism.
- Marxist-feminists highlight the ways in which capitalism and patriarchy can interact in oppressing women.

You could also highlight the following weaknesses:
- Marxist approaches tend to under-play inequalities based on ethnicity, gender and age and overplay conflict.
- As structuralist theories, they tend to focus on how the social structure of capitalism affects the superstructure and individuals, but under-play interaction at the micro-level.
- Post-modernist approaches question the significance of meta-narratives such as Marxism in the post-modern world.

In your conclusion, you could argue that:
- Marxist inspired theories and research make a significant contribution to the sociological understanding of contemporary society particularly in fields such as education, the mass media and crime.
- Other sociological theories and research studies (e.g. feminist) make a more significant contribution.

Index